John T. Edge directs the Southern Foodways Alliance at the University of Mississippi. He is a contributing editor at *Garden & Gun* and a columnist for the *Oxford American*. In 2012, he won the James Beard Foundation's M. F. K. Fisher Distinguished Writing Award. Edge has written or edited more than a dozen books. He has served as the culinary curator for the weekend edition of NPR's *All Things Considered* and written the "United Tastes" column for *The New York Times*. Edge lives in Oxford, Mississippi, with his son, Jess, and his wife, Blair Hobbs. Follow him on Twitter @johntedge, on Instagram @johntedge, or on the web at potlikkerpapers.com.

★ ★ ★

Praise for *The Potlikker Papers*

A *Publishers Weekly* Best Book of the Year
A *San Francisco Chronicle* Food Book of the Year
A *Smithsonian* Food Book of the Year
An NPR Book of the Year
A *Wine Enthusiast* Book of the Year
A *Paste* Book of the Year

"Long one of the key voices in the discussion of Southern cuisine, Edge challenges the accepted narrative . . . [and] watch[es] the momentum build until the South comes into its own."
—*The New York Times Book Review*

"[A] wonderful surveyor of the last fifty years of Southern history. . . . Edge shows that we aren't just what we eat; we are where that food was grown, how it was cooked, who cooked it, and who all gets to eat it with us."
—*The New Republic*

"A panoramic mural of the South's culinary heritage, illuminating the region's troubled place at the American table and the unsung role of cooks in the quest for social justice."
—*O, The Oprah Magazine*

"To read *The Potlikker Papers* is to understand modern Southern history at a deeper level than you're used to. Not just a history of Southern food; it also stands as a singularly important history of the South itself."
—*The Bitter Southerner*

"Is *The Potlikker Papers* a history of the South by way of food stories, or a story about Southern food by way of our history? By the time you come to the end of this rigorous volume, you'll know that the two are indivisible."
—*The Atlanta Journal Constitution*

"This fascinating book . . . pulls no punches in [its] exploration of the legacy of racial strife in the South and the central role played by cooks, waiters, and restaurants during the civil rights movement. . . . You'll be hard-pressed to find a more complete take on the South's complicated culinary legacy and its impact on the nation." —*Wine Enthusiast*

"Edge, director of the Southern Foodways Alliance at the University of Mississippi, uses food as a lens to explore Southern identity, seeking to reconcile a legacy of slavery and Jim Crow with who claims the Southern table today." —NPR

"A legitimate coup. The book traces the culinary and social history of food in the American South—and doesn't pull any punches about our country's past or present." —*Paste*

"An insightful, refreshing, and at times revealingly ugly examination of food and its place in the South . . . is a must-read force for good." —*Charleston City Paper*

"Edge uncovers the rich narratives that lie beneath Southern food, illustrating the tangled and compelling webs of politics and social history that are often served up alongside our biscuits and gravy. . . . A satisfying repast of tales that illustrate that the food history of the modern South reveals the dynamic character of Southern history itself." —*BookPage*

"[Edge] has created a canon of Southern food writing that follows in the tradition of legends like John Egerton and Vertamae Grosvenor. . . . Edge asks us to consider how we, as Americans, active and passive Southerners, journalists, and eaters, can begin to set the record straight in this very moment—to tell the histories of those living and working in the South with truth and humanity." —*Saveur*

"Masterful . . . illuminates these hidden corners of the region's cuisine like no other. . . . Edge expertly sieves through decades of cultural influences to explore how today's rich culinary tradition emerged." —*Garden & Gun*

"The one food book you must read this year . . . No matter the subject, there is always something to learn from Edge's work. . . . *The Potlikker Papers* is a reminder of where we've been, how far we've come, and how far we still have to go."   —*Southern Living*

"Edge's research and command of prose make this a necessary history."
                                                          —*Booklist* (starred review)

"In the South, Edge notes, food and eating intertwine inextricably with politics and social history, and he deftly traces these connections from the civil rights movement to today's Southern eclectic cultural cuisine. . . . "[An] excellent culinary history."   —*Publishers Weekly* (starred review)

"Mixing deep scholarship, charming anecdotes, and his own extensive culinary explorations . . . this is a book for foodies, but it is also for readers who . . . care deeply about regionalism, individual health, and race relations."   —*Kirkus Reviews* (starred review)

"John T. Edge wonderfully tells the story, through grits, pone, and pig meat, of the ever-morphing American South—fleshing out the caricatures of Harland Sanders and Paul Prudhomme, traveling history's through lines from the lunch-counter protests of the Civil Rights era to the latter-day flowering of pitmaster chic. So good, so fun, so thorough, so important."   —David Kamp, author of *The United States of Arugula*

"There are certain writers who you just know have found the perfect form for their creative expression, and so it is with John T. Edge, our preeminent chronicler of Southern food and culture. In this rich, compact history of the South through its food and cooks . . . Edge has produced a wonderful narrative of the region's evolution on race, gender, and justice, with a light-handed knowingness at once sympathetic and critical."
   —Diane McWhorter, Pulitzer Prize–winning author of *Carry Me Home*

"If I know anything about Southern cuisine it's because of John T. Edge. Somehow he's weaved together a story of how Southern food shaped not only what was on the table, but American history."
                                            —David Chang, CEO/founder, Momofuku

"Edge's book means to be about food, but quickly veers into a close examination of the Deep South, before revealing itself as the smartest history of race in America in a generation." —Jack Hitt, author of *Bunch of Amateurs*

"*The Potlikker Papers* takes readers on an exceptional journey through the modern American South . . . John T. Edge's profound analysis of the region's vibrant—but always contested—food cultures skillfully navigates the rough road from the civil rights movement's bus boycotts to the vibrant culinary diversity of the contemporary South. This work is essential reading in the American canon of foodways scholarship." —Marcie Cohen Ferris, author of *The Edible South*

"With his trademark style of compelling storytelling, Edge sets a table where everyone is welcome and every story matters. . . . *The Potlikker Papers* inspirited me with renewed hope for unity not just in Edge's beloved South but anywhere there is food to eat and people to eat it." —Toni Tipton-Martin, author of *The Jemima Code*

"John T. Edge has unearthed an extraordinary people's history of the South, brilliantly told 'through its most influential export: food.' Like its namesake broth, *The Potlikker Papers* is a concentrated, complicated account of the little-known cooks and humble community-builders who fed each other and fueled a movement for inclusion." —Beth Macy, author of *Truevine* and *Factory Man*

"Confidence is a funny thing. Without it, you may cling to poles, draw boundaries, and take aim at the *other*. The South never had much confidence in me, a foul-mouthed, shants-wearing, first-generation Taiwanese-Chinese-American conceived in Maryland and raised in Orlando. I left as soon as I could swearing I'd never open my heart again. I hadn't thought about it for quite some time, but then John T. boiled off the greens, discarded the nasty bits, and served me potlikker. . . . It gives me confidence that one day I can love the South all over again." —Eddie Huang, author of *Fresh Off the Boat*

The
Potlikker Papers

A Food History of the Modern South

JOHN T. EDGE

PENGUIN BOOKS

For Jessica B. Harris, who schooled me

PENGUIN BOOKS

An imprint of Penguin Random House LLC
375 Hudson Street
New York, New York 10014
penguin.com

First published in the United States of America by Penguin Press,
an imprint of Penguin Random House LLC, 2017
Published in Penguin Books 2018

Photograph credits appear on pages 367–368.

ISBN 9780143111016 (paperback)

THE LIBRARY OF CONGRESS HAS CATALOGED THE
HARDCOVER EDITION AS FOLLOWS:
Names: Edge, John T., author.
Title: The potlikker papers : a food history of the modern South / John T. Edge.
Description: New York City : Penguin Press, 2017. | Includes bibliographical
references and index.
Identifiers: LCCN 2016029615 (print) | LCCN 2016031102 (ebook) | ISBN
9781594206559 (hardcover) | ISBN 9780698195875 (ebook)
Subjects: LCSH: Cooking, American--Southern style. | Food—Southern States—History.
Classification: LCC TX715.2.S68 E328 2017 (print) | LCC TX715.2.S68 (ebook) |
DDC 641.5975—dc23
LC record available at https://lccn.loc.gov/2016029615

Printed in the United States of America
1   3   5   7   9   10   8   6   4   2

DESIGNED BY AMANDA DEWEY

AUTHOR'S NOTE

I learned much of what I know while studying at the Center for the Study of Southern Culture at the University of Mississippi, and, later, directing the Southern Foodways Alliance at that same university. Research and writing for magazines and newspapers including *Oxford American, Garden & Gun, The New York Times, Departures, Parade,* and *Gourmet* informed the work that follows. I wrote most of *The Potlikker Papers* at Rivendell Writers' Colony, high on the mountain in Sewanee, Tennessee, and in my backyard toolshed in Oxford, Mississippi.

Foreword (to)
John Egerton

I learned to explore my native region while borrowing from John Egerton, the Nashville journalist and social historian. Over a half-century career, Egerton sketched a democratic portrait of the American South and its peoples. His books were laments on race and class. They were catalogues of regional distinctiveness and documents of its presumed demise. They were rousts of the demons that lurked in this briar patch. They were jousts plotted to dislodge the wealthy and powerful from their perches.

Reading his words, I learned that writing about food didn't have to be an exercise in indulgence. Following his lead, I took tentative steps toward paying down the debts of pleasure and sustenance owed to our forebears. I had company. Borrowing from Egerton, two generations of thinkers and writers and cooks gained moral clarity and recognized common purpose. Buoyed by his leadership, the South rose to prominence as a culinary citadel.

A love of the region and a belief in the possibilities of the common table drove his queries. Time and again, Egerton asked how Southerners could reconcile a history of gross injustice with a deserved reputation for great food and warm hospitality. Egerton wondered how a culture rife with bigotry could produce hickory-smoked whole hog barbecue, parchment-crust fried okra, and downy spoonbread soufflés. He begged answers to why blacks and women, long subjects of grievous mistreatment, had done most of the heavy lifting but received niggling credit.

Egerton offered no palliative answers. Instead, he adopted what he called "the unwritten law of compensation, simplistically overstated," in which bad places make good books, good music, good art, and good food. "The more messed-up a place is, the more inventive and freewheeling its creative voices," he said. "Richly varied forms of artistic expression seem to burst forth from violent or repressive or otherwise dysfunctional societies."

As his career progressed, Egerton recognized that the South might realize its potential on farms and in kitchens. He believed that time at table offered reconciling possibilities. But before all could claim seats and revel in country ham and buttermilk biscuits and hope, he said more work needed to be done.

"Not infrequently, Southern food now unlocks the rusty gates of race and class, age and sex," Egerton wrote in his 1987 book, *Southern Food: At Home, on the Road, in History*. "On such occasions, a place at the table is like a ringside seat at the historical and ongoing drama of life in the region."

I conceived this book as a sequel to that one. And I imagined that John Egerton would write this foreword. When he died unexpectedly in the fall of 2013, I lost more than a friend and mentor. I lost my foreword writer. Thanks, John, for the place at the table. I've tried hard not to squander your generous gifts.

Contents

Gentrification (1980s & 1990s)

New Respect (1990s–2010s)

Future Tenses (2010s Forward)

The
Potlikker Papers

In the 1970s, black Southerners on a path to economic independence developed fast-food businesses. Here, Mahalia Jackson and Russell Sugarmon reviewed plans for the Memphis opening of Mahalia Jackson's Fried Chicken.

Potlikker:
An Introduction

The collards at Bertha's Kitchen in North Charleston, South Carolina, are back-of-the-stove paragons. Simmered in a pigtail- and neckbone-perfumed potlikker, those greens showcase the talents of the black women who stir Bertha's pots and the vitality of the crops that thrive in the Lowcountry loam. At the time of my visit in 2012, Joseph Fields, whose family has farmed nearby Johns Island for three generations, grew the greens for Bertha's and a dozen other Charleston area restaurants. After a lunch of fried pork chops, red rice, and collards, I walked the crop rows with Fields, regarding his harvest to come.

We spoke of how global warming has transformed harvest patterns. We talked of the declining ranks of black farmers and the increasing number of white consumers who valorize their labor. We puzzled through why crackling cornbread, buckshot with pork skin shards, disappeared from cafés at about the time fried pig ears became salad garnishes in fine dining restaurants. As Fields rounded a turnrow, I asked how his family came to farm this land.

Gesturing toward an unseen house in the distance, Fields told me that his grandmother, Molly Johnson, earned the dollars to buy the family farm by wet-nursing the white baby of a nearby plantation owner. By bringing a white mouth to her black breast, Fields told me that his forebear nourished two families, one white and one black. He told me this without malice. His eyes didn't blink. His voice didn't climb a register. He simply shared a truth about his family and the South. In the telling, Joseph Fields made explicit the kind of complicated narratives that are deeply embedded in our food culture.

"Eating is an agricultural act," Kentucky native Wendell Berry once wrote. In the South, that equation has been fraught, for in addition to being virtuous work in which writers like Berry take justifiable pride, agriculture begat the region's original sin: slavery. During the antebellum era, demand for enslaved labor to plant and harvest the fecund South drove a national dependence on cheap farmworkers. After the Civil War, white efforts to retain and later disinherit that labor have limited the horizons of black and white Southerners alike.

The journey from that original sin to this multicultural present shows how and why food culture matters and means. Over a long and strange and perilous evolution, out of a crucible of love and hate, in fields, before stoves, and at tables, this book illuminates the South and its people, revealing where we have been, who we are now, and what we may become.

For the last sixty years, the span of this book, the dishes we have cooked and the meals we have staged have served the region and the nation as emblems of Southern struggles. Conversations about food have offered paths to grasp bigger truths about race and identity, gender and ethnicity, subjugation and creativity. Today, Southern food serves as an American lingua franca. Like the Black Power fist and the magnolia blossom, fried chicken discloses, cornbread suggests, potlikker tells.

Definitions of the South typically depend on geography or secession. The former defines a broad swath of land, comparable in size and sweep to Western Europe, south of the Ohio River and beneath the line mapped in the 1760s by Charles Mason and Jeremiah Dixon. The latter relies on a rejected political gambit, defined by brutality, economics, and global trade. Neither suits.

The adjective *Southern* and the noun *Southerner* have, since the nineteenth century, referenced the white South and the Confederate South. Those limited categories failed the people of the region. The South was never monochromatic. Over three centuries, Southerners of many hues have shared histories and shouldered burdens. Novelist Ralph Ellison, a grandson of slaves, sketched the interdependence when he said, "You can't be Southern without being black, and you can't be a black Southerner without being white."

Instead of a myth-veiled cultural monolith, I see the South as an album of snapshots. I hear the region like it's a jukebox of 45s. The South I sample is a menu of dishes. Shaped by a four-century-long call-and-response between masters and enslaved peoples, a back-and-forth between Native Americans and immigrants, the region I know, the place that comes to life in *The Potlikker Papers*, rejects easy encapsulation.

Southern history encompasses migrations from Africa to the Americas, from farms to factories, from the rural South to the urban North and back again. On this land, we have waged wars and lost and won battles. Southerners have endured horrors and celebrated beauty. We have made the long trek from abject poverty to fitful prosperity.

Parsed into five sections that track the region's evolution chronologically and thematically, this book begins in 1955 as black cooks and maids in Alabama challenged Jim Crow and his henchmen and concludes in 2015 as a newer South came into focus, enriched by the arrival of immigrants and emboldened by the truth telling of men like Joseph Fields. Along the way, *The Potlikker Papers* marks the rise of the folk that began in the Tennessee hills in the 1970s, the gentrification that gained traction in North Carolina and Louisiana restaurants of the 1980s, and the artisanal renaissance that reconnected farmers and cooks in the 1990s.

The Potlikker Papers is a work of remembering through food, an attempt to gather sometimes lost narratives to tell old stories in new ways. Many of the people recalled here are unsung players in the Southern pageant, previously denied their roles in the definition, reinvention, and redemption of the region.

L ike the place I claim, my motivations are complicated. Born in the Clinton, Georgia, home of Confederate brigadier general Alfred Iverson Jr., I began grade school as the civil rights movement refocused on feeding our less fortunate brothers and sisters. I now live and work in Mississippi, the state that birthed novelist William Faulkner and activist Fannie Lou Hamer. After a sloppy run through college and a detour through a series of corporate jobs, I returned to school to earn a master's degree in Southern Studies at the University of Mississippi. I wanted to reconcile my profound love of the South with the deep anger that boiled in me when I confronted our peculiar history.

In Oxford I met a man from California who studied the front porch as a social space in 1930s Alabama and a woman from Mississippi who documented the impact of the Association of Southern Women for the Prevention of Lynching on 1930s Georgia. My horizons broadened, my understandings deepened. But I didn't find a way to burrow in until I recognized that farmers and cooks and waiters have been activists, too, fixed on forging their own newer South.

I've drawn on those lessons while directing the Southern Foodways Alliance, a not-for-profit that documents and studies the diverse food cultures of the changing American South from a base at the University of Mississippi's Center for the Study of Southern Culture. Charged with exploring and explaining the South to residents and critics since its 1977 inception, the center has served as a progressive force in a region reckoning with its past.

Today, my SFA colleagues produce films about oystermen and collect oral histories of fried chicken cooks. We edit collections of scholarship on Jim Crow foodways. We publish journals and audio programs that tell sometimes difficult stories of Southern pasts and presents. We profile Kurdish kabob cooks in Nashville and stage symposia on the Latino South. We direct oratorios and folk plays that confront issues of class and gender. We stage suppers of squirrel stew in wainscoted Charleston dining halls. And we ask questions about who we are and how we got here, about who cooks, who cleans, and who earns a seat at the welcome table.

There are hosts of ways to tell the story of the South through food. Bowls of hoppin' John, mixed with pearlescent grains of rice and dank brown cowpeas, bespeak an antebellum past when plantation agriculture fueled the slave trade and peas provisioned ships for the Middle Passage. Mississippi Delta–style tamales, unwrapped from their shucks and doused in hot sauce, launch stories about late-nineteenth-century Mexican migrations, commissary diets, and boom-and-bust cotton economies.

I wrote my graduate school thesis about the Potlikker and Cornpone Debate of 1931, which began when Julian Harris, an editor at the *Atlanta Constitution*, published an Associated Press story about the sale of highway bonds by Governor Huey Long of Louisiana. Long credited the sale to a supper of potlikker and cornbread, which he served the lead investor in a financial syndicate. In an editor's note, Harris, who crumbled his cornbread into potlikker, questioned Long's habit of dunking. In response, Long telegrammed Harris. And Harris telegrammed Governor Franklin Delano Roosevelt of New York, who vacationed at Warm Springs, Georgia. The debate was on.

From mid-February to early March, movie reel viewers joined the conversation, ladies' groups gathered to dunk and crumble, and the *Constitution* received more than six hundred letters to the editor, including a diatribe about regional differences from Dudley V. Hadcock of the Arkansas State Chamber of Commerce in Little Rock, a treatise on race by a mental hospital patient in Milledgeville, Georgia, and a query from an eighty-five-year-old Confederate veteran who addressed the relative merits of dunking and crumbling when he asked, "Does it not depend in a great measure if the users have two sets, upper and lower teeth?"

In addition to passionate letters, readers wrote playlets, songs, and poems. "Ode to a Crumbled Pone," by George L. King of Atlanta, may have been the best: "I've eaten many luscious fruits, I've tasted many sweets / I've been in many hot disputes, about the choicest eats / I've dined on tongue of nightingale, at manus I'm some picker / But how I wish I were a whale, facing cornpone and potlikker."

Readers used potlikker to speak of women's rights, class divisions, and the failings and successes of Emancipation and Reconstruction. They discussed diet and nutrition. Rekindled Southern patriotism, stirred by World War I, surfaced. So did economic concerns. Potlikker, the debate made clear, nourished a poverty-wrecked South, mired in the Great Depression, and served as a symbol that broadcast beliefs about its future.

I first tasted potlikker at Mary Mac's, the dowager tearoom in midtown Atlanta, famous for crackling cornbread and peanut butter pie. As a boy in the 1970s, I ate lunches at Mary Mac's during family pilgrimages to the big city. Later, I wrote a magazine profile of Lester Maddox, the governor of Georgia who rose to prominence as a pistol-wielding segregationist restaurateur and fell while performing in a biracial musical duo called the Governor and the Dishwasher. (When they performed together on the 1970s nightclub circuit, Bobby Lee Fears, a convicted felon who had once sung with the Ohio Players band, wore a ketchup- and mustard-splattered busman's coat.) For our interview, I met Maddox at Mary Mac's. He had recently weathered a bout of prostate cancer and an AIDS scare, which had driven him to adopt a macrobiotic diet. But Maddox made an exception that day, ordering baked chicken, cornbread dressing, and potlikker. Afterward, he stopped on the street to do deep-knee bends and prove his virility.

Like great provincial dishes around the world, potlikker is salvage food. During the antebellum era, slaveholders ate the greens from the pot, setting aside the potlikker for enslaved cooks and their families, unaware that the broth, not the greens, was nutrient rich. After slavery, potlikker sustained the working poor, black and white. "I lived on what I did not eat," Richard Wright wrote. "Perhaps the sunshine, the fresh air, and the pot liquor from greens kept me going."

In the rapidly gentrifying South of today, potlikker has taken on new meanings. In search of a dish that represents the region, chefs and writers have reclaimed potlikker. The glossy food magazine of the moment recently published a recipe for potlikker noodles with mustard greens. National Public Radio reported that a Washington, D.C., chef reduces collard potlikker to a low gravy, tosses the liquid with black-eyed peas, and pours the sauce over grilled fish. A chef in Athens, Georgia, recently introduced a dish of poached mountain trout in boiled peanut potlikker. Inevitably, he called the broth "nutlikker."

D ecade by decade, food narratives illumine history. On the long march to equality, struggles over food reflected and affected change across the region and around the nation. Once thought retrograde, Southern food is now recognized as foundational to American cuisine. Southern cooks who labored in roadside shacks now claim white tablecloth temples where they cook alongside new immigrants. This ongoing ascent has been tumultuous. And it has powerfully driven national conversations about cultural identity.

Beginning in 1955, home kitchens were sites of drama, from which black women drew strength and plotted change. Georgia Gilmore, a cook and midwife, fueled the Montgomery Bus Boycott with sales of her fried chicken and cakes. Conflict in the 1960s over restaurant service made clear the differences between black beliefs about everyday dignity and white ideas about property rights. During the civil rights movement, restaurants were battlegrounds and bunkers, places of conflict and communion. Lunch counter sit-ins, which ignited at a Greensboro, North Carolina, Woolworth store in 1960, demanded the nation's attention and foreshadowed the twenty-first-century embrace of food as creative expression and political activism.

In the 1960s, America faced down poverty. On the porches of Kentucky cabins, in the fly-swarmed back rooms of Mississippi shacks, politicians witnessed hungry children with distended bellies. And activists plotted strategies to feed them. As the 1970s dawned, struggles over food remained in the spotlight. Black farmer co-ops devised responses to poverty. Instead of integration, Black Power advocates aimed for independence from white power and money. Black restaurants served as clubhouses for progressive leaders and showcases of black art and craft.

When hippies went back to the land in the 1970s, quitting California or New York to stake claims to rural and communal lives, many chose the South. To escape a society they believed corrupt, a new generation farmed old crops (sorghum) and new crops (soybeans) in the hills of Tennessee, the mountains of West Virginia, and the hollers of Arkansas. The path forward took many circuitous turns. As the nation suburbanized, fast-food chains, led by Kentucky Fried Chicken and followed by dozens of imitators including black analogue Mahalia Jackson's Fried Chicken, sold Southerners on newfangled versions of traditional dishes from fried chicken to biscuits to muffulettas.

In 1976, when Jimmy Carter won the Democratic Party nomination, Fritz Hollings, a senator from South Carolina, said, "Now we can rejoin the Union." As all eyes turned toward Carter's hometown of Plains, Georgia, Americans stocked up on grits and runner peanuts. And the press proclaimed that a *true* New South had arrived. After the vogue for soul food peaked and then played out, Edna Lewis sketched a black pastoral in the 1980s. The cooking of black Southerners contained multitudes, the Virginia-born granddaughter of slaves said, setting a standard that future generations would recognize as the beginnings of the farm-to-table movement.

Wealthy and educated urban Southerners of the 1980s and 1990s nurtured their Southern identity. Loosed from the choke hold of racism and the fallout from Jim Crow, no longer defined by opposition to the North or obeisance to the indefensible, Southerners assigned deeper meanings to regional music, literature, and food. Writers and chefs led the charge. Craig Claiborne, a son of the Mississippi Delta, emerged as an expatriate kingmaker who introduced two new prototypes: the scholar-chef, Bill Neal of North Carolina; and the sensualist interpreter of regional cooking, Paul Prudhomme of Louisiana. At a time when women struggled to define their roles in an evolving South, television personality Nathalie Dupree offered women a way back to the kitchen and taught new arrivals that a command of grits and greens could be a passkey to belonging.

In the 2000s, Southern products from grits to ham to moonshine gained new relevancy and value. After a long slide in popularity, bourbon was reborn as a frontier beverage. It represented much that was admirable about the American South. As Americans rediscovered artisanal goods, they even transformed Coke, the ultimate commodity. Mexican Coke, sweetened with cane syrup, emerged as an artisanal beverage in the 2000s.

As a new generation of chefs revived American cooking, Southern cuisine became America's signal food system. Working out of Pawleys Island, South Carolina, and Birmingham, Alabama, and a dozen towns and cities in between, they shepherded the American regional food movement. By the 2000s, cooks and chefs in Charleston and New Orleans emerged as economic assets and tourist draws. Pitmaster flourished in the that era, too. Barbecue, a dark and mysterious art traditionally practiced in tumbledown Southern shebangs, became the obsession of

Brooklyn entrepreneurs who built neo-joints and engineered distribution from digital front porches.

Studies of the South in the 1960s, when children starved for want of enough food, exposed racism and its impacts. Within a generation, bodies that once bloated from hunger ballooned from cheap calories. Against that backdrop, activists in the 2010s debated the value of black creativity and enterprise. And a black female chef worked a reinvented Savannah, Georgia, lunch counter where her grandmother would not have been able to claim a seat.

Women and men who quit sharecropping to take industrial jobs sweated and suffered through dehumanizing days and nights on chicken disassembly lines and in hog barns. Faced with these realities and the news that a sort of slavery was still practiced in the tomato fields of Florida, Southern activists summoned the gumption that once drove civil rights–era activism to develop national models for redemption and reconciliation.

Despite inhospitable immigration laws, a true new Southern cuisine flourished in the 2010s, driven by recent arrivals who came in search of agriculture and construction jobs and stayed to reinterpret chicken cafés and fish joints. As the Taco Circuit displaced the Chitlin Circuit, the best cooks in cities like Charlotte and Houston revealed themselves to be men from Texcoco who dished cow cheek barbacoa in corn tortillas and women from Oaxaca who peddled raja tamales from street carts.

America has long reacted with vigor to the South because the nation recognized the worst and best of itself here, beginning with the version of our country that music documentarian Harry Smith called "the old, weird America," including the poverty-wrecked and racism-ruined South that H. L. Mencken parodied and Edward R. Murrow exposed, and concluding with the dynamic South of today, where change is constant, new traditions gestate, and many peoples and cultures belong.

Over the last sixty years, wrenching changes transformed the South, beginning with the black freedom struggle and concluding with the assimilation of new immigrants. New traditions blossomed. Cultures showed new facets. As changes accreted, new layers precipitated a newer South. As the region stepped from the mire of poverty and beyond the long shadow of Jim Crow, natives and new arrivals, blacks and whites and browns, forged vibrant cultures. Food traditions, from potlikker and cornpone to barbacoa and frijoles, brought that dynamism into focus.

To apprehend how Southerners have fed themselves and others gains us a necessary glimpse of remarkable lives, a kitchen-eye view of the revolutions and evolutions that have shaped the region. Those stories reveal a people's history, embedded in the crops we grow, the dishes we cook, and the tables where we gather. In these *Potlikker Papers*, complex narratives reveal how and why Southern food has become a shared culinary language for a nation now fixed on finding new meaning in its meals.

Freedom Struggles

1950s–1970s

Georgia Gilmore fueled the 1955—56 bus boycotts and fed the civil rights movement from her Montgomery, Alabama, kitchen.

Kitchen Tables

T here comes a time when people get tired of being trampled over by the iron feet of oppression," Martin Luther King Jr. shouted from the pulpit of Holt Street Baptist Church in Montgomery, Alabama, on the night of December 5, 1955. "There comes a time, my friends, when people get tired of being flung across the abyss of humiliation, where they experience the bleakness of nagging despair." Unspooling metaphors and similes, quoting scripture from memory, the twenty-six-year-old called an audience of his elders, weary from a long day of work, to its feet. Men in blue cotton work shirts, their names stitched in cursive across the breast, shouted support. Women in lace-trimmed maid uniforms shrieked assent. Following the arrest of Rosa Parks four days before, black Montgomery had joined a battle. Almost a century after the demise of the Confederacy and the failure of Reconstruction, they took up a fight for social justice and civil rights that should have been won with the surrender of Lee at Appomattox.

Georgia Theresa Gilmore, a cook, midwife, and mother of six, stood amid the pews that night for the first meeting of the Montgomery Improvement Association, when Rosa Parks rose to silently acknowledge applause, and black citizens pledged to quit riding city buses until their rights were ceded. Five thousand African Americans crowded the sanctuary, the balcony, and the basement annex. To get close, black citizens of Montgomery abandoned their cars in the streets and walked to Holt Street. Bundled against the cold, they listened via parking lot–mounted loudspeakers as King pledged to "work and fight until justice runs down like water, and righteousness like a mighty stream." Driving nearby, whites stopped to eavesdrop and marvel at what was to come.

For the better part of a year, Gilmore brought food to the Monday night mass meetings, where preachers delivered speeches and activists plotted strategies to desegregate the buses that ferried maids and cooks to their jobs in the brick bungalows and columned homes of Cloverdale and the Garden District. For that first meeting, she collected fourteen dollars to buy chickens, lettuce, and white bread and packed a hamper full of fried chicken sandwiches. Along with her friends, she sold sandwiches in the parking lot and on the front steps of the church to hungry men and women who were determined to remain in those pews until the last words had been shouted from the pulpit. When ushers passed hats that night to gather a collection, men with mended coveralls on their backs and women with holes in their shoes crowded forward to drop bills, shouting, "Here, let me give."

In October 1954, more than a year before police arrested Rosa Parks for refusing to give up her bus seat, Gilmore had begun her own boycott after a Friday afternoon rush hour confrontation with a white driver who shouted her down for entering the front door of the bus and drove off before she could walk around back. At an early mass meeting, Gilmore introduced herself to King. He made it clear that the boycott was part of a larger freedom struggle. "He told all about the good things you should do for one another," Gilmore said, "and how with a better education you could be a better person." Night after night, as preachers fed the audience inspiration for their fight, Gilmore fed the men and women who traded pocket change for sandwiches. And she plowed the profits into the MIA. In the process, her home kitchen became a locus for change.

By February 1956, more than three hundred cars and wagons served forty-plus pickup and drop-off spots, driving laborers from their homes to jobs across town. This alternate transportation system, devised to put pressure on white Montgomery, required money for gas and insurance policies, and, after a while, new sets of brakes and tires. Gilmore, who lived on the same street as Rufus Lewis, architect of the boycott transportation system, organized a group that eventually sold fluted pound cakes and sweet potato pies to beauty parlors and laundries, to cab stands and doctor's offices. They fried fish and stewed down greens and sold plates of pork chops and rice that mothers and fathers bought and toted home from church to sons and daughters. For Gilmore and her friends, raising funds became a second job.

She called her group of black cooks and bakers the Club from Nowhere and explained the promise this way: "We had a lot of our club members who were hard-pressed and couldn't give more than a quarter or half-dollar, but all knew how to raise money." Progressive white Montgomery could support the cause, too, sidestepping the rebuke of conservative friends and neighbors by purchasing cakes and pies instead of making outright donations.

In the city where, less than one hundred years prior, the secessionist states convened to establish the Confederate States of America, Gilmore organized black women and told them that the knowledge they nurtured as domestics in white kitchens was valuable. She offered these women, many of whose grandmothers were born into slavery, a way to contribute to the cause that would not raise suspicions of white employers who might fire them from their jobs, or white landowners who might evict them from the houses they rented. While some black women avoided Jim Crow indignities by avoiding whites, black cooks and maids didn't have that option. They lived in a white-dominant world. Cooking in their own homes, selling food to their neighbors, these black women won some independence. Joining together, they gained a scrim of anonymity. "It was like, 'Where did this money come from?'" Betty Gilmore, younger sister of Georgia Gilmore, told me, years later. "It came from nowhere."

During the mass meetings, maids and cooks rose from the pews to testify about their mistreatment in white homes. After suffering decades of abuse, those women steeled for a fight. "I'll crawl on my knees, before I get back on them buses," said one maid. "I'll walk twenty miles before I ride them." Another maid said, "Honey, I have washed and ironed clothes until my legs and body ached." Her body hurt more than ever, now that she walked back and forth to work, but she didn't mind: "I still ache but my mind is now at peace with God, because we're doing what's right and right will always win out."

Glennie Mae Cox told a typical story. When she handed a bus transfer to a white driver, he refused to accept it. When she objected, he cursed her and said he "hated niggers." A white passenger said, "It is a beautiful day, isn't it?" The driver replied, "It sure is, pretty enough to beat a nigger." When black domestics quit the bus system, they delivered a forceful message to whites. "It'll teach them how to treat us," a maid named Beatrice Charles said. "We people, we are not dogs or cats."

When Gilmore stood before a mass meeting to announce how much money she had collected that week, she sang "Shine on Me" or "I Dreamt of a City Called Heaven." As she high-stepped down the aisle with her contribution, the congregation erupted in shouts and applause. Inspired, another group began raising gas money for the black-run cab and shuttle services.

A rivalry developed. On the west side of town, Inez Ricks of the Friendly Club fried fish and baked cakes. All across town, Gilmore and Ricks and a dozen or more other women baked and sold cakes and pies. Layered with Christian scripture, the stories they told of work in white homes were motivational. Early in the struggle, Inez Ricks wrote King to tell him that God was with them. Telling the truth about the trials they faced was the righteous path, she said, because lies didn't pay well.

To get to their jobs during the boycott, women walked as many as two miles each day. Men rode mules instead of buses. Gilmore, who often walked, never flinched: "A lot of the times some of the young whites would come along and they would say, 'Nigger, don't you know it's better to ride the bus than it is to walk?'" And Gilmore would say, "No cracker, no. We rather walk."

When the county government of Montgomery prosecuted King and eighty-nine other members of the MIA in March of 1956, claiming the boycott was an unlawful conspiracy, Ricks told the packed courtroom about the time a driver had twisted and turned the wheel of a bus, trying to throw her to the floor. Georgia Gilmore, her eyes hooded with contempt, spoke more fiercely, testifying as a defense witness on the second day of the trial. "I don't know the driver's name. I would know him if I saw him. He is tall and has red hair and freckles, and wears glasses. He is a very nasty bus driver," she told the packed courtroom. "I put my money in the cash box and then he told me to get off. He shouted I had to get on in back. I told him I was already on the bus and I couldn't see why I had to get off."

In its boldness, Gilmore's testimony compared to that of Mose Wright, the great-uncle of Emmett Till, who, six months earlier, testified against one of the white men who lynched his fourteen-year-old nephew. Standing tall in a Mississippi Delta courtroom, Wright dared to point at the white man and say "Dar he." Gilmore, whom King called an "unlettered woman of unusual intelligence," showed the same courage when she turned to the judge and said, "When I paid my fare and they got the money, they don't know Negro money from white money." The audience gasped when Gilmore told the courtroom what a white driver said to her mother: "You damn niggers are all alike. You don't want to do what you are told. If I had my way, I would kill off every nigger person." The next day, the *Pittsburgh Courier* published a second-page picture of Gilmore, dressed in a formal black suit, flanked by attorneys Fred Gray and Orzell Billingsley Jr. Gilmore told the court that Montgomery bus drivers were the "meanest, nastiest" people in the world. In the black world she was a star. In the white world she became a pariah.

As a girl, Gilmore had learned to milk cows and feed hogs and slaughter chickens, which her mother kept on a small farm in Montgomery County. Employed first as a tie changer on the railroad, where she laid track, Gilmore put six children through Catholic school during the years before the *Brown* decision filled black citizens of Montgomery with hope for an integrated future.

By 1955, she worked at the National Lunch Company, a meat-and-three downtown. Gilmore served as a cook, winning a reputation for sweet potato pies and fried chicken. Her sister Alice Gilmore ran the steam line. Mark Gilmore, her son, washed dishes. An ordinance required that restaurants maintain separate entrances and erect seven-foot dining room partitions to prevent the races from mixing. But across the city, black laborers and white bureaucrats alike sat down to noonday lunches of collard greens flavored with pig tails, sweet potatoes drenched in syrup, and fat slabs of meat loaf.

White women worked the counter at National Lunch, passing plates of fried chicken to waiting white customers, but black hands always grasped the stewpots and skillets, just as black hands had long knife-scraped feathers from butchered chickens and stripped stems from mess after mess of collards. Until her bosses learned that she was involved in the boycott that agitated for better treatment for black riders, that hand was often Georgia Gilmore's.

It's unclear whether the proprietor of National Lunch fired Georgia Gilmore, or whether she left on her own, knowing that her testimony would lead to her dismissal. Rather than seek another job where she would work for meager wages and a share of the leftover cornbread and greens from the pots and pans she stirred and scrubbed, instead of working for the sort of boss who paid her, in part, with the gizzards and feet she cut from the chickens she fried, Gilmore went into business for herself. King, who lived just three blocks away, and who admired her fortitude and her pork chops, fronted some of the money to expand her kitchen and furnish it with stew kettles and roasting pans. He told her, "All these years you've worked for somebody else, now it's time you worked for yourself."

When the boycott came to a successful close five days before Christmas in 1956, fifty thousand black citizens returned to riding city buses. They had held out for more than a year. In that time, as empty city buses trundled by, white citizens got a glimpse of the black resolve that would sustain the movement all the way to Selma and across the Edmund Pettus Bridge. The MIA had won. Blacks no longer had to ride in the back, or give up their seat at the whim of a white passenger, or suffer abuse at the hands of a white driver.

At the final, celebratory mass meeting in 1956, Georgia Gilmore sang "Swing Low, Sweet Chariot" and "This Little Light of Mine." "Weary feet and weary souls were lightened," she said. "We didn't have to walk no more. Even before Martin Luther King got up there and told us it was over, we knew it was over and we knew we had won."

Georgia Gilmore inspired black citizens of Montgomery. And she worried whites, who clung to the idea that, through daily intimate exchange, black cooks and maids became members of their family. Domestics worked for love, whites came to understand, but that love was for their own black families.

If the maids and cooks and yardmen and drivers were speaking out, if women like Georgia Gilmore, who had so much to lose by speaking their minds, were no longer willing to accept the lot they inherited, then change was surely on the horizon. "I'll never trust any nigger again in life," a white Montgomery man said after he saw his black chauffeur driving, on his day off, in a bus boycott auto pool.

G ilmore was a big woman with a swaggering personality, who showed no fear in the face of white bigotry. She drew her strength from her family, her church, and her community. When police beat and arrested her son Mark Gilmore in 1957 as he crossed whites-only Oak Park, she took the city to court. When a white store clerk refused to sell her grandson a loaf of bread and a box of laundry detergent, she marched to the counter, took a pistol away from him, and whipped him with it.

Gilmore heard Martin Luther King Jr. when he preached nonviolence. She believed in the principle. But her practice, which hinted at the "by any means necessary" ethic Malcolm X would soon drive, was more radical. "It didn't matter who you were. Even the white police officers let her be," Thomas Jordan, pastor of Lilly Baptist Church, said. "The word was, 'Don't mess with Georgia Gilmore, she might cut you.'"

Time at table in her house restaurant offered respite in the midst of turmoil. Georgia Gilmore was the surrogate mother to her community, the big woman with the big heart, who talked trash like she was playing the dozens. From 1956 onward Gilmore, emboldened by the support of King, ran a restaurant and catering service out of her modest brick home. "It wasn't a real restaurant," her son Mark Gilmore told me, when I toured her house years later. "She didn't call it one. Everybody just said they were going down by Georgia's to eat." For customers who didn't have time for a true lunch break, Gilmore delivered. Toting wire baskets stacked with pork chop plates, her children traveled to laundries, barbershops, and the administrative offices at nearby Alabama State College.

When movement people visited Montgomery, their first stop was often her kitchen. As they crossed the threshold, Gilmore might call from the kitchen in a growling voice, "Come here you little whore and get your food! I don't want to hear any of your mess. I got a big bowl of buttermilk and some corn bread for you to crumble into it, just like you want." Reverend Al Dixon got that treatment. Gilmore called him "whore." Under her roof, she called Martin Luther King Jr. "heifer." King loved her stuffed pork chops and stuffed bell peppers, said Mark Gilmore. "When she fixed rice, every grain would stand off to itself. He couldn't get enough of her potato salad." During his late-career return to the governor's office, a reconciled George Wallace, who had once promised "segregation now, segregation tomorrow, segregation forever," got the Gilmore treatment, too. She called him "Guvs."

Gilmore's house became a clubhouse for King, who, as his fame rose, even as white restaurants integrated, gravitated to the kitchen tables of friends. He wanted pigs' feet and collards, the foods that sustained him in his youth. Far from home, he longed for the comforts of family. When King arrived in Montgomery during the 1965 march from Selma, he beelined to Gilmore's kitchen for pork chops. Later, when city building inspectors tried to declare her house unsafe, and her insurance company refused to write a policy, King stood up during the middle of lunch service to declare he would help save her home restaurant. Threatened whites recognized that Georgia Gilmore's house on Dericote Street served as a clubhouse for progressive black Montgomery. So did King.

Like the *paladares* that arose in Cuba after the revolution, house restaurants were key to the informal economy in the black South. Designed to thrive beyond the reach of the white system, they provided black women income that was independent of white dollars. As the struggle for black voting rights and economic parity gained momentum, Georgia Gilmore's home became an executive dining room for the civil rights movement.

Half her customers ate standing up in the kitchen, as Gilmore pulled casseroles of macaroni and cheese from the ovens and baskets of fish from a stovetop fryer. Seated on the deep freezer, tucked in her dining room, men took breaks from postal routes to eat stews of chitlins and hog maws with sides of coleslaw. Women from a nearby laundry ate lunches of chicken wings and green beans. Even during the winter, Gilmore rarely turned on the heater, relying, instead, on the oven stacks to warm the house. As she cooked, Gilmore watched soap operas, cried at the heartbreak, cussed her faithful, and doled slices of pineapple upside-down cake to regulars.

At a time when blacks and whites did not dine easily together in public, they elbowed together into Gilmore's kitchen, lined with white laminate counters, to order from menus she printed in pencil on notebook paper. "I just served 'em and let 'em talk," Gilmore said, channeling the democratic ethic of the day.

That sensibility won converts beyond Montgomery, too. Mark Gilmore said that King and Lyndon Baines Johnson ate deviled eggs, served from carnival glass platters, at her twelve-seat oak trestle table, draped in a white tablecloth and set with hot sauces and pepper sauces. In her green tile–floored kitchen, crowded around a double oven and a side-by-side refrigerator, Robert F. Kennedy may have joined King for strategy sessions fueled by pork chops, collard greens, and 7UP cake. Aboard Air Force One, John F. Kennedy likely ate her fried chicken and peach cobbler.

Gilmore's house restaurant, which straddled the divide between a dining hall and private club, defined a welcome table ideal that would emerge as a primary metaphor in the civil rights movement. After she stepped away from her job at National Lunch to claim her own business in the underground black economy, her success hinted, too, of the moves to come during the Black Power stage of the civil rights movement, when, instead of angling for the integration of white spaces, African Americans created black spaces.

President Johnson, dressed in a somber blue suit and a thin blue tie, stood before a joint session of Congress on November 27, 1963, secured reading glasses on the bridge of his nose, leaned his lanky frame into the rostrum, and declared, "No memorial oration or eulogy could more eloquently honor President Kennedy's memory than the earliest possible passage of the civil rights bill for which he fought so long." Five months earlier, John F. Kennedy had called for a bill that would desegregate restaurants and other places of public accommodation. Five days earlier, Kennedy had died from a rifle shot to the head. "We have talked long enough in this country about equal rights," Johnson said. "We have talked for one hundred years or more. It is time now to write the next chapter, and to write it in the books of law."

Listening in the presidential box above, with their children Lynda and Luci, Lady Bird Johnson nodded. Seated behind were Zephyr Wright, the family cook, and her husband, Sammy Wright. Interrupted thirty-two times by applause, President Johnson delivered an eloquent plea for national resolve in the face of "the foulest deed of our time." He recognized that one of the keys to passing the civil rights bill was to leverage the Kennedy legacy. He recognized, too, that the bill would require more intimate salesmanship, a narrative that brought the argument home and shifted the action from lunch counters to kitchen tables.

Over the next months, to win votes and coerce opponents, Johnson moved the narrative from public forums to private spaces. He made the politics personal by inviting congressmen, business leaders, and the American people into his home. Time and again, Johnson told stories about the Jim Crow indignities suffered by Wright, the cook who served his family for the better part of three decades. When Johnson assumed the presidency, she had taken over the second-floor family kitchen, leaving the French chef René Verdon to direct state dinners and other formal occasions. (Verdon resigned in 1965 after being asked to prepare a cold dish he described as "already bad hot.")

At dinner in the White House, in the halls of Congress, at barbecue lunches on his Texas ranch, Johnson told the story of Wright, the black woman from Marshall, Texas, who deserved better than Jim Crow offered. Sketching the prejudices she endured, asking audiences to share his moral outrage, Johnson modified details of the story each time to suit his listeners.

Called to the White House cabinet room for a meeting with business and labor leaders, including Henry Ford, Defense Secretary Robert Mc-Namara heard a version set in Oklahoma. Frustrated because he could not get the men to agree to lobby for the passage of the Civil Rights Act, Johnson pounded the table that day, and then, in a flash, went soft. "You all know Zephyr," he said casually, as if everyone knew the Johnson family cook by her first name. In this version of the story, Johnson, Lady Bird, and Wright were driving from Texas back to Washington, as they passed through a small town.

"Lyndon, would you mind stopping at the next gas station?" Lady Bird said. "I would like to relieve myself." They stopped, used the bathroom, got back in the car, and drove on. About half a mile down the road, Wright asked, "Would you mind stopping by the side of the road?" She needed to relieve herself. "Goddamn it, we went to the gas station to relieve ourselves," Johnson replied, frustrated, until Wright confessed, "Mr. President, they wouldn't let me in."

As the men in the White House took stock of his words, Johnson pounded the table again and growled, "Damn it, gentlemen, is that the kind of a country you want? It's not the kind of a country I want." The tack, McNamara noticed, as he scanned the faces of the power elite, was very, very effective.

In time, Johnson's colleagues adopted the story of Zephyr Wright as their own. Leonard H. Marks, director of the U.S. Information Agency during the administration, told a version in which Wright served an informal lunch in 1950s Washington. Johnson, then a senator from Texas, told her to ready the car for the drive back home. The family would join later. In this version, Wright refused, telling Johnson that, when she and her husband drove cross-country, they could not stop at most gas stations to use the bathroom like Lady Bird and the Johnson daughters did. "I have to find a bush and squat," Wright said. "When it comes time to eat, we can't go into restaurants. We have to eat out of a brown bag. And at night, Sammy sleeps in the front of the car with the steering wheel around his neck, while I sleep in the back. We are not going to do it again."

Johnson told those stories often during the run-up to the Civil Rights Act of 1964 vote. In his telling, he sometimes included a dog in the mix. And he often loaded the car down with different passengers, including Helen Williams, the Johnson family maid, and her husband, Gene Williams. Traveling the Jim Crow South with the family dog, Little Beagle Johnson, was too degrading, too demeaning, too much, Helen Williams told Johnson: "We keeps going until night comes, until we get so tired that we can't stay awake anymore. We're ready to pull in. But it takes us another hour to find a place to sleep. You see, what I'm saying is that a colored man's got enough trouble getting across the South on his own, without having a dog along."

Back when Johnson was vice president, he had buttonholed Senator John Stennis of Mississippi: "You know, John, the other day, a sad thing happened. My cook, Zephyr Wright, who has been working for me many years—she's a college graduate—and her husband drove my official car from Washington down to Texas, the official Cadillac limousine of the Vice President of the United States. They drove through your state and when they got hungry, they stopped at a grocery store on the edge of town in colored areas and they bought Vienna sausages and beans and they ate them with a plastic spoon. And when they had to go to the bathroom, they would stop, pull off on the side of the road, and Zephyr Wright, the cook for the Vice President of the United States, would squat in the road to pee. And you know, John, that's just bad. That's wrong." "And there ought to be something to change that. And it seems to me that if the people in Mississippi don't change it voluntarily, then it's just going to be necessary to change it by law."

The Zephyr Wright story reduced a national issue to a personal one. It moved the argument from the Senate chamber to the cloakroom and then to the kitchen. The Zephyr Wright story worked on the other side of the divide, too. When civil rights leader James Farmer, a fellow Texan, asked Johnson how he came to be such a strong advocate for the desegregation of restaurants, Johnson told a dog version of the story, in which Lady Bird asked Wright to carry the beagle back to Texas on her drive home. Farmer, a black activist, got the same point all audiences did: This issue was personal for Johnson. And if Americans would look deep in their souls, they, too, would recognize that the Jim Crow system was morally bankrupt. "Damn it, gentlemen, is that the kind of a country you want?" Johnson would say, his voice rising to the cause. "It's not the kind of a country I want."

The injustice of that roadside bathroom break seemingly broke Johnson's heart each time he told the story. And it called into question his belief that the woman who cooked weeknight suppers for his family and chastised him for his erratic diet, the black woman who seemed to love his white daughters like they were her own, was in practice a member of his family. When Johnson signed the Civil Rights Act of 1964 into law, the president acknowledged the debt he owed to the family cook.

Wearing a satin dress and white gloves, a stylish purse slung over her arm, Zephyr Wright gathered in the East Room with Robert F. Kennedy and Martin Luther King Jr. as Johnson sat down to sign the legislation into law. Looking up from his desk, with a clutch of fountain pens in his left hand, Johnson motioned to Wright, handed her one of the first pens that he used to sign the bill, and said, "You deserve this more than anybody else."

O ver the next two generations, the battles that linked Georgia Gilmore and Zephyr Wright transformed the South. Through kitchen table diplomacy, these women and thousands of others drove change, using the power they earned as black servants in white homes. Like mammy figures from a Southern past, who straddled the gap between the everyday subservience that was expected of them and the full participation in American life they earned, these women emerged as powerful symbols in a newer South.

The kitchens run by Gilmore and Wright were clubhouses where whites and blacks identified problems and solutions. They were everyday sources of black wealth and surety. The stories Southerners told about their struggles framed the civil rights movement to come and made clear that kitchens were not always places of comfort. By sharing narratives about injustices, the women who controlled those kitchens defined a new grassroots activism that depended on local people to drive federal interventions. At a moment when they had seemingly little leverage, cooking afforded brave black women intimate and essential power. Martin Luther King Jr., the great black orator, grasped the narrative power. So did President Johnson, the master of the Senate.

As the battle for equal rights moved from home kitchens to restaurant dining rooms, men took on larger roles, and the stakes, which escalated during lunch counter confrontations, grew larger and more public. If Gilmore and Wright challenged the myth that blacks were content, the next generation of activists leveraged their time at table to subvert the whole of the Jim Crow system.

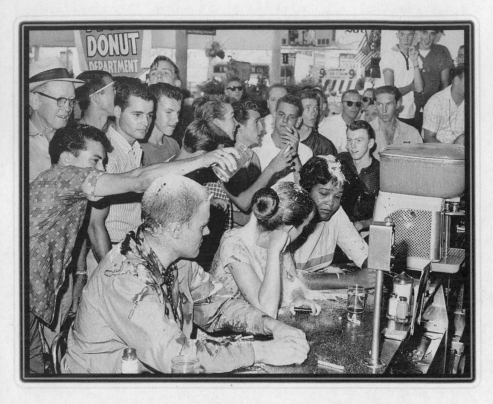

During a 1963 sit-in at the Woolworth lunch counter in Jackson, Mississippi, activists John Salter, Joan Trumpauer Mulholland, and Anne Moody suffered mental and physical abuse.

Restaurant Theaters

T his is Booker Wright," a television narrator with a smooth baritone said as the black-and-white scene cut from the dining room of a Greenwood, Mississippi, restaurant where a self-possessed group in suits and ties smoked cigarettes and talked about the race problem. "The white men we've just seen and heard think he's a carefree, hardworking Negro. But what does he think?"

The young black waiter in the starched white dinner jacket looked nervous. Coiled with energy, he filled the screen, bouncing from foot to foot. Wright twisted and bobbed. He swiveled left and right, as if his torso were fixed to a gyroscope. His voice screeched and cracked. As the camera rolled, Wright reeled off the menu of steaks, shrimp, oysters, and soft-shell crabs, singsonging their deliciousness like Harry Belafonte calypsoing bananas. And then, in a rush of syllables, he reeled through his own hopes and fears.

During a 1965 visit to the Mississippi Delta, an NBC television crew had persuaded a tenured waiter at the 1933 vintage restaurant Lusco's to speak his mind in the cotton market town of Greenwood. When Wright opened his mouth, he spoke with candor, knowing the act was radical, recognizing that a national television audience would see his face and hear his story, knowing that white and black locals would rally to his words, acknowledging, on some level, that his monologue was an act of self-immolation.

As perspiration beaded his forehead, an audience of two women smoked cigarettes, drank beers, and cut Wright incredulous stares. Delivered from the front room at Booker's Place, the cross-tracks café and juke he ran when he wasn't waiting tables at Lusco's, this was tragic theater, based on grievous testimony. The women wanted to look away from the scene. Like the audience that eventually watched on NBC, they could not.

Booker Wright wore black pants and a black bow tie when waiting tables at Lusco's. He draped a folded white towel over his left arm. "Some people is nice, some people is not," he said of his customers, all of whom were white and many of whom were cotton planters and factors who made their fortunes from black labor. "Some call me Booker. Some call me John. Some call me Jim." His voice rising to a falsetto, Wright shouted, "Some call me nigger!"

"All that hurts," Wright said as he acted out the roles of a servile black waiter, smiling placidly, and a domineering white patron, seething with privilege. "But you have to smile . . . although you're crying on the inside. Although you're wondering, 'What else can I do?'" Wright had recited the menu and slung platters of pompano for decades. By 1965, the burden of his nightly performances for the gentry proved too heavy to bear. The smile on his face broadcast welcome. But that veil came with a price. "The meaner the man be, the more you smile," Wright said, his voice buoyant with emotion, his face contorted as if to ask, *How did I learn this calculus? Why do I tolerate this system?*

Beneath the glare of the lights, Wright came alive. Looking into the lens of the camera, he said that, although he bucked and scraped and grinned for white patrons, he wasn't carefree. Like many black Southerners, he was deeply angry. He was afraid. He was close to broken. His story laid bare the duality of Southern life, the Janus-faced lie that Jim Crow coerced. "We took care of them," said the wife of a planter who had always asked for Wright when she dined at Lusco's. "And they knew us, knew our family and tended to us when we were growing up. . . . In the nicest way, you felt like they belonged to you."

The system was corrupt. Relations across the color divide were toxic. Though the realization was slow to come for many whites, Wright's monologue made clear that, no matter what some whites wanted to believe, blacks were not content. His television appearance made the abstractions of the civil rights movement concrete. He brought home big-picture politics to the small screen and the small town. The white gentry had regarded him as an Uncle Tom, a doting servant. When he spoke, Wright stepped out of that role. He forced whites to step out of theirs and grapple with reality.

NBC broadcast Wright's plaint in May 1966 as part of the hour-long show *Mississippi: A Self-Portrait*. His monologue, which you may stream on the Web, emboldened Delta blacks to speak out and risk white retribution. Robert Hauptman, a black Greenwood native, told me that Wright spoke for all blacks. "It was an angry statement. We were backed up like a cat against a wall, and wouldn't take no shit anymore."

The next month, Stokely Carmichael, who rose to lead the Black Panther Party, stepped onto a truck bed at a Greenwood rally, jabbed his fist in the air, and led the crowd in a chant of "BLACK POWER." Carmichael had arrived in the Delta that spring to rally voters to the cause of James Meredith, who integrated the University of Mississippi in 1962, and had recently been shot in the back while walking the state on what he called a March Against Fear.

Activists had employed "Black Power" before. This was different. This time, Carmichael used it as a bludgeon. "We begged and begged, we've done nothing but beg," he said. "We've got to stop begging and take power." As the crowd roared in agreement on that summer evening, Carmichael's voice spiraled from a plea to a guttural shout that recalled Wright's televised moment. "The only way we gonna stop that white man from whipping us is to take over," he screamed, tapping frustrations that had accumulated over years of nonviolent responses to brutal white resistance. "We been saying freedom for six years and we ain't got nothing. What we got to start saying now is Black Power. Black Power. We want Black Power. We want Black Power."

Carmichael's words were clarion. But he was less bold than Wright. The Student Nonviolent Coordinating Committee (SNCC) employed Carmichael to speak those words. He was a premeditated activist. Wright, instead, plunged in without much forethought and without any backing. He claimed his own power. Wright's command was subtle, intimate, and insistent. In Greenwood, it carried more weight. His gravitas came from speaking truths that white and black Southerners often chose to ignore or deflect.

As he came to the close of the monologue, Wright gestured toward the economic problems that civil rights movement leaders would later tackle. "I'm trying to make a living," he said, looking straight into the camera, alternately smiling and frowning. "I got three children. I want them to get an education. . . . Night after night, I lay down and I dream about what I had to go through. I don't want my children to have to go through with that. I want them to be able to get the job that they're qualified for. That's what I'm struggling for."

B lack waiters in the South straddled two worlds. They were proxy house servants whom middle-class whites called members of the family. In black communities, waiters who worked in white restaurants were often proud wage earners, taking home tips that compared to postal service and funeral home salaries. But money earned waiting tables came with promises of subservience. False intimacy, reenacted nightly at restaurants like Lusco's, bred discontent.

Lusco's was a Jim Crow theater, where white-jacketed waiters played the parts of faithful retainers to the cotton gentry. Wright was not the only star on the roster. Richard Hunt, always smiling, showing his gold tooth, worked at Lusco's for thirty-five years. Illiterate, he could take an order for a twelve-top without writing it down. His performances were scripted. And so were Wright's. Engaging a waiter was akin to booking a piano player and requesting a song. "People would approach Booker and ask him to recite the menu," a longtime patron told me. "He would rattle out that menu, fast like an auctioneer. And they would always say, 'Say it again, Booker, go through that again.'"

Factors, planters, businessmen, fading dowagers, and courting couples dined at Lusco's in curtained booths. Converted from a store to a restaurant in 1933 by Sicilian immigrants from the town of Cefalù, Lusco's was where Delta men came to escape their wives and their debtors, where Delta women came to celebrate their second divorce with their third fiancé. The restaurant, set in a neighborhood dominated by blacks and immigrants, cultivated its exclusivity. People of color were unwelcome. So were patrons deemed lower class. From the 1930s onward, Marie Correro, daughter of the founders, sat in a rocking chair at the restaurant entrance and handpicked customers. Menus, recited by the waiters without mention of prices, reminded patrons that if you needed to know the cost, you didn't belong in a booth.

Greenwood rose to prominence in the early twentieth century as the nation's dominant long staple cotton market. By 1965, the city was already infamous for intolerance. SNCC activist Bob Moses called Greenwood the "iceberg of Mississippi politics." Tom Brady, whom *Time* magazine called "the philosopher of Mississippi's racist white Citizens' Councils," made his "Black Monday" speech there in 1954, denouncing the Supreme Court decision in *Brown v. Board of Education of Topeka*. Byron De La Beckwith, who lay down with his rifle in a field of honeysuckle to shoot and kill NAACP Mississippi field secretary Medgar Evers in 1963, called Greenwood home. A plaque at the police station honored

Tiger, a German shepherd that had charged civil rights protesters that same year.

Wright paid for his time on television. In the aftermath of the broadcast, he lost his job at Lusco's. The family probably did not fire Wright. As was the case with Georgia Gilmore, dismissal wasn't necessary. After saying his piece, after revealing his anger and hopes, Wright couldn't return to bucking and scraping for cotton plutocrats. And his patrons couldn't pretend to be unaware of what he said or the pride that Greenwood blacks took in his bravery.

Booker Wright's bold stance proved catalytic in that peculiar Southern moment. Like Gilmore, who leveraged what she had learned as a cook to serve the cause, Wright used the skills he learned at table to tell a story of oppression and hope that captivated a national television audience. Their paths to respect were limited. No matter. Both of these Southerners, a woman working behind the scenes in the kitchen, and a man working the front of the house for an audience, cooked and served food and drove change.

D efenders of segregation thought their cafés and barbecue huts and diners were extensions of their homes. They ran their restaurants like they ran those homes, treating white customers as guests and telling themselves they treated black cooks, bussers, and waiters like family. On that basis, white restaurateurs built reputations for warm hospitality, until the sit-in movement exposed the realities of life below the line mapped by Mason and Dixon.

If Lusco's was a Citizens' Council clubhouse, where the gentry gathered to prosecute their mores and privileges, the Silver Moon Café in Selma, with its spittoon trench beneath the counter, was a bunker where the threatened, working-class whites of Alabama plotted violent resistance. The four white men who killed James Reeb, an activist who heeded Martin Luther King Jr.'s spring of 1965 call to march on Montgomery, spent the evening of the murder at the Silver Moon.

Before they accosted the white Unitarian minister in the street, shouted "You want to know what it's like to be a real nigger!" and clubbed him to death, they hunkered in Silver Moon booths. Elbows on the table, they plotted violence and downed beers. Less than three weeks later, the Klansmen who killed Viola Liuzzo gathered in the booths at the Silver Moon to rehash the murder of Reeb. Afterward, they chased her car into the countryside, pulled alongside, and shot the white civil rights activist in the head.

Set alongside a tire plant on the seedy side of town, the Open House was the Athens, Georgia, analogue. By the 1960s, when Blanche Guest took over operations, years of cigarette smoke had rendered the white brick dining room walls beige. The floor was a checkerboard of red and white tiles. Seven red vinyl stools faced a scarred linoleum counter. Guest, who looked like a cross between Minnie Pearl and Elly May Clampett, worked the grill and the cash register, serving food that was greasy and generous. Goat meat omelets arrived with buttered white toast and grits the consistency of spackling. Burgers, fried on a flattop alongside strips of bacon, tasted as much like pig as they did cow.

During the early-morning hours of July 11, 1964, Lt. Col. Lemuel Penn, a black Army Reserve officer, traveling from Fort Benning in Georgia to his home in Washington, D.C., was killed near a bridge north of Athens. A shotgun blast blew out the back of his head. The Klan singled him out for the color of his skin and the out-of-state license plate bolted to his bumper. Before they spotted his car, the white men charged with shooting Penn had spent their night shuttling back and forth between the Open House and the garage owned by Blanche's husband, Herbert Guest.

The terrorists had heard that activists planned to make Georgia a testing ground for the Civil Rights Act of 1964, which President Johnson had signed into law less than two weeks earlier. James Lackey, a member of the Klan Security Patrol who drove around town with KKK placards fixed to his car, confessed, "We thought some out-of-town niggers might stir up some trouble in Athens." Almost ninety FBI agents descended on Athens that summer to investigate. Agents questioned college students who said they purchased amphetamines from Herbert Guest. They interviewed a man who spoke of buying bootleg whiskey from him. Another claimed that the Guest garage, four blocks from the Open House, was a way station for the transport of prostitutes from Athens to Jacksonville, Florida.

Athens had erupted in violence during the 1961 desegregation of the University of Georgia, when a mob of white students hurled bricks and bottles before police dispersed the crowd with tear gas. By 1964, the city was again a flash point. Throughout that spring and summer, peaceful black teenagers and hooded white thugs from Clarke County Klavern 244, United Klans of America, Knights of the Ku Klux Klan, clashed at the new uptown location of the Varsity drive-in. As coeds ate chili dogs and onion rings, Klansmen, draped in white robes, their eyes barely visible through slits in pointed masks, walked a picket line opposite black activists.

Accounts of that summer in Athens almost always mentioned the Open House, which the FBI identified as a "hangout for rabid Klansmen." That June, Local 244 terrorized residents of an Athens housing complex, firing shotguns into the air and into the back door of an apartment. They struck a nineteen-year-old black man in the eye and a thirteen-year-old black girl in the lip. Herbert Guest was arrested in the first round of shootings and charged with disorderly conduct. One of the accused triggermen dredged up an alibi. He claimed to be drinking coffee at the Open House, run by Blanche Guest, a member of the Ku Klux Klan Ladies Auxiliary.

The Open House was a regular stakeout sight. On the evening of July 19, FBI informants tallied a filling station employee, a drive-in theater worker, several college students, a midget, two state patrolmen, one Athens policeman, and a man who bragged of "hitting and killing a nigger with his car." It was a typical night. FBI agents eventually arrested Herbert Guest on federal charges of violating Penn's civil rights. Almost two years later, two safety patrol members were convicted on civil rights charges.

The murder of Lemuel Penn has remained officially unsolved. While Herbert Guest was never convicted in the Penn case, he did serve time for the sale of amphetamines, a turn of events that compelled Blanche Guest to rethink her business options. When he headed for the federal penitentiary in late 1966, she closed the garage and bought the restaurant her husband and his cronies called home. In the years that followed, the Open House transitioned from a Klavern hangout to a late-night frat boy purgatory, where the racism that white kids spewed was less vitriolic and more insidious.

By the early 1980s, I was one of those frat boys, who arrived after the parties began to peter out in search of grits and grease, in hope that a plate of eggs and biscuits might stymie my hangover. At her counter, with a couple of sausage patties and a pool of grits before me, I chose to believe that a place like Blanche's had been washed clean of past taints. Like so many whites, I chose to avert my gaze from that ugly history, until it was impossible to look away.

With stainless backsplashes, vinyl spinner stools, and long slabs of elbow-polished linoleum, lunch counters were designed as everyman spaces, where lawyers and laborers might sit side by side to eat flattop-fried burgers and crinkle-cut fries and drink sweaty tumblers of tea. They were modern places. They were city spaces in a rapidly urbanizing South.

If house restaurants like the one Georgia Gilmore ran were urban outposts for farmhand cooking, serving pork chops and collard greens

and cornbread, lunch counters were streamlined and efficient predeces-
sors to the fast-food restaurants of the 1970s, serving dishes that were
more broadly American than Southern. The setting had nothing to do
with home and everything to do with commerce. After finishing a lunch
counter meal, diners did not linger and talk about the weather. They
pivoted toward the register, paid their tab, and walked out the door,
twirling a toothpick in their mouth.

At their best, these modern restaurants reflected democratic ideals.
The symbolism of the long unbroken table was important to Southerners. Many had been schooled from infancy in Last Supper imagery. Sharing a meal signaled social equality. And no eating space promised more
democracy than the lunch counter, where diners stooped to take their
seats and eat with people of other sexes and, eventually, other races. The
problem was, for much of the South's history, neither the people who
owned lunch counters nor the people who patronized them were at
their best. Until the summer of 1964, many restaurants reserved their
seating for whites, while black citizens ate their burgers and fries standing up, or at a cordoned section of the counter, or after walking around
to the back door.

The role of lunch counters in the social life of the region had begun
to change in February 1960, when four black freshmen at the Agricultural and Technical College of North Carolina walked into an F. W.
Woolworth Company store in Greensboro, North Carolina, and requested coffee and doughnuts. Protesters demanding equal treatment
had staged previous actions in Southern border cities like Baltimore and
Oklahoma City. Activists in the tobacco citadel of Durham, North Carolina, had agitated for service as early as 1957. But this protest struck hard
where Jim Crow reigned, and it was sustained by students who showed
no fear.

Waitresses refused the students that day. Instead of accepting the decision and leaving, or heading downstairs to a stand-up counter where
blacks could order hot dogs, the students remained in their seats. A

larger group of students, dressed in pressed suits and starched dresses, and looking far more composed than the protesters who gathered to heckle them, returned the next day. By day four, white students from the Women's College of the University of North Carolina joined. All took their place on spinner stools at the counter and ordered food that never came. The Greensboro Woolworth store was the civil rights movement equivalent of Fort Sumter. Shots were fired there. Lines were drawn. Ground was taken and given. A future was grappled.

Within two weeks, students in eleven cities had staged sit-ins, mostly at downtown department stores. They were organized and insistent. Students in Nashville, wary of violent reprisal, developed protocols: "Do show yourself friendly on the counter at all times. Do sit straight and always face the counter. Don't strike back, or curse back if attacked. Don't laugh out. Don't hold conversations. Don't block entrances." The prospect of violence was persistent. During classes staged by black college students in Orangeburg, South Carolina, activists learned, "To protect the skull, fold the hands over the head. To prevent disfigurement of the face, bring the elbows together in front of the eyes."

At the 1960 founding of the Student Nonviolent Coordinating Committee in Raleigh, North Carolina, Ella Baker said that sit-ins were not just attempts to eat in prohibited spaces. They were not mere tests of flawed laws and corrupt morals. Sit-ins focused on something "bigger than a hamburger." Activists wanted to rid America of racial segregation and discrimination. "Not only at lunch counters, but in every aspect of life."

By April of that year, restaurant sit-ins spread to seventy-eight cities, including Rock Hill, South Carolina, where students from Friendship College, arrested in an attempt to integrate the downtown McCrory's, refused to put up money for bail and fund a system they believed corrupt. They opted, instead, to serve thirty-day sentences of hard labor at the York County Prison Farm. "Jail No Bail," the tactic they developed, spread through the movement. By the end of 1960, more than 70,000 men and women, boys and girls, had joined sit-ins and picket lines, mostly in the South. And more than 3,600 had been hauled off in squad cars and cattle trucks, bound for county jails and work farms.

S egregationists were not bound by the same codes of behavior. Faced with the prospect of living integrated lives, they often retaliated with violence. In 1961 at a Woolworth counter in Columbia, South Carolina, a white man stabbed a young black man, Lennie Glover, then studying theology at Benedict College. After a Houston, Texas, sit-in, three whites beat a black man with a chain, carved the initials *KKK* in his chest, and hung him upside down from an oak tree.

In May 1963, an integrated group, led by college students, ordered lunches at a Woolworth counter in downtown Jackson, Mississippi. After waitresses used a rope to close off the counter, white students made a noose out of the rope and tried to force the noose over the heads of ac-tivists. While a mob of protesters threw salt and pepper in their eyes, women students asked politely for menus so that they could order cheeseburgers. Angry white high school students dumped mustard on their heads and stubbed lit cigarettes on their forearms while male activ-ists, dressed in button-downs, politely requested slices of apple pie.

The next year, when the Chapel Hill Freedom Committee recruited University of North Carolina and Duke University professors to join black activists and integrate Watts Restaurant on the outskirts of town, Jeppie Watts, a white co-owner of the Chapel Hill restaurant, kicked one of the young black protesters who tried to claim a seat. When he dropped to the floor, she straddled his head and urinated, screaming a kind of af-firmation, "Anybody that'd let somebody piss on them!" The next night, Watts met the next wave of protesters at the door, poking them in their groins with sticks, yelling, "This is how we get the hogs to move."

Other merchants responded with passive strategies. Instead of serv-ing integrated crowds, department store and drugstore managers in cities like Knoxville, Tennessee, unscrewed the seats from their lunch counter stools and tossed them in rubbish heaps. If they couldn't control who sat on their stools, then no one would have the pleasure. In Durham, North Carolina, E. J. "Mutt" Evans, a progressive white Jew who served six terms as mayor, worked the reverse angle. Ordered to quit serving blacks and whites together at the lunch counter in his department store, he ripped out the seats and raised the counter height so that all stood together and ate together.

Restaurants weren't the only public spaces where the prospect of mixed race eating offended, revealing skewed moral standards. Clark Foreman, a civil rights advocate who had worked in the Roosevelt administration, told the story of a white girl from his home state of Georgia who would visit her mixed-race child at the orphanage, but declined an administrator's suggestions that she lunch with him. "Well I couldn't do it. Eat with niggers?" The complexities of interracial eating called to mind the complexities of interracial sex: Appearances mattered.

When President Johnson signed the Civil Rights Act on July 2, 1964, he outlawed discrimination and segregation in places of public accommodation. Many hotels and theaters and restaurants integrated that first week. In Birmingham, a black chauffeur named J. L. Meadows sat for dinner at the Town and Country restaurant at the Dinkler-Tutwiler Hotel, billed as a "Dispenser of True Southern Hospitality." Before ordering, he said, "I've been driving white folks down here for 21 years, and now I'm going to eat where I've been taking these white folks."

In Danville, Virginia, where policemen had water-hosed and clubbed black high school students the previous summer, a white restaurant owner resigned himself to a new reality. "Last year we fought them because they were breaking the law," Cy Shiap said. "This year, I'd be breaking the law if I refused to serve them. If the law says feed them, I feed them. While I don't like it, I'm not going to break the law." On

July 5, the Sun-n-Sand Motel in Jackson, Mississippi, a pop culture icon catercorner from the state capitol, graciously seated a black diner at an aquamarine banquette, but closed the swimming pool.

The resistant minority was noisy. Jimmy's Restaurant in Montgomery, Alabama, desegregated, but the white owner fired his white waitresses and hired black waiters to deliver fried chicken to the tables. He didn't want white women to wait on black men, whom he thought of as inferiors at best and sexual predators at worst. An old white customer at a late-night diner in Chattanooga, Tennessee, shot and killed a young black customer who reached across the counter in a recently desegregated restaurant and supposedly said to a waitress, "Hey baby doll, how about a cup of coffee?"

While cameras whirred, Lester Maddox of Atlanta wielded a pistol to repel the July 3, 1964, integration attempt of his Pickrick Cafeteria. For posterity he published "If I Go to Jail," an audio recording of his press conference on free enterprise and property rights, which he said the new civil rights law undermined. Like many white business owners of the day, he claimed persecution, telling reporters, "The life that I have lived and the torment that has been mine since yesterday, would make death itself seem sweet." Instead of submitting to the shackles of big government, Maddox declared, "Is life so dear, peace so sweet, and money so valuable, as to exchange it for slavery? I say not."

Canny white segregationists took advantage of a bill amendment that excepted private clubs. In Mississippi, one hundred businesses converted to so-called key clubs in the first two months, including the Robert E. Lee Hotel in Jackson. Key clubs flourished in the northern reaches of the region, too. Soon after the Dutch Bucket Tavern in Norfolk, Virginia, became a private club in 1963, membership topped five hundred. A week after the civil rights bill passed, membership passed seven hundred, but the price of membership remained the same: one nickel. Some of the chosen received membership cards. Others got actual keys to front doors.

Across the region, most of the restaurants were clubs in name only, relying on what was called a paper bag test to screen admittance: Patrons with skin lighter in color than a paper bag sat down. Otherwise, it was backdoor service, takeout, or denial. Some responses were comparatively sophisticated. The owners of the Emporia Diner in Virginia developed a two-menu system. Blacks got menus with higher-priced fried chicken, until a Baltimore woman, Swannie K. Howard, brought suit in 1964.

Segregationists leveraged their stances to gain fame. The most well known included Maurice Bessinger of Maurice's Piggie Park in Columbia, South Carolina, who integrated his barbecue restaurant after losing a U.S. Supreme Court battle, but continued to fight through the 1970s, when he served as president of the National Association for the Preservation of White People and ran a losing campaign for governor while sometimes wearing a white suit, riding a white horse, and distributing flyers that declared, "You are white because your ancestors believed in segregation."

Like Laurie Pritchett, the Albany, Georgia, sheriff who adopted the nonviolent strategies of black activists to tamp down strife and divert violence, Bessinger deployed civil rights movement tactics. "Our strategy is counter reaction," he said, explaining the protests he organized in 1964 to defend Jim Crow Columbia. "As a result of our picketing, we are holding the line on integration. All the hotels were going to integrate in December, but we stopped that with our pickets. Two of the theaters which integrated now are negotiating with us to go back to segregated business if we'll pull off our pickets."

Just as restaurants served as stages where students publicly protested mistreatment, restaurants provided resistant whites with venues where they could publicly profess beliefs. Instead of integrating, L. J. Moore of New Bern, North Carolina, locked the doors and bulldozed his barbecue restaurant in 1967. Down the road, he built a new place with walk-up window service only. The proprietors of Ayers Log Cabin Pit Cooked

Bar-B-Que in nearby Washington took a cruder tack when they agreed to serve blacks, but posted a sign by the register, "ANY MONEY FROM NIG-GERS GIVEN TO THE KKK." When Brownie Futrell was a boy, he asked his father, publisher of the local newspaper, what the sign meant. "It means we can't eat here anymore," his father told him. A progressive white son of the South, Futrell had to wait a long time before pondering a return. The sign remained in place until 1970, when the U.S. attorney general filed suit to force its removal.

By the time the 1960s gave way to the 1970s, most of the clubs had closed or reopened as honest restaurants. But not all. Over a fifty-plus-year career that ended with his death in 1984, Dinty Moore of Shaw, Mississippi, never served a black man or woman at his Shady Nook café. For the first thirty years, that policy didn't require active enforcement. But during the summer of 1962, as tensions mounted in nearby Oxford over the integration of the University of Mississippi, Moore began selling keys to the café for a dollar and calling it the Shady Nook Key Club.

A smiling white face, glimpsed through a one-way mirror, became the passkey for coverall-wearing Friday lunch customers who came in search of gravy-drenched hamburger steaks and high-crown yeast rolls. White Sunday afternoon diners, dressed in church clothes, arrived to eat deviled yard eggs, fried Biloxi oysters, and homemade banana cream pie. While the town of Shaw declined, as locals moved north for jobs, cotton gins closed, the tax base shrank, and the roofs on abandoned downtown buildings collapsed from neglect, Moore refused to integrate his restaurant. Each day, he staged a pageant that asked viewers to believe that Booker Wright had never spoken his mind, and the Civil Rights Act of 1964 had never passed.

During the tumultuous 1960s, restaurants were backdrops for change, stage sets where black and white Southerners negotiated an integrated future before a national audience. As the civil rights movement gained momentum and the struggle for civil rights begat a demand for black power, everyday people claimed leadership roles. Black waiters and waitresses, once submissive, once without voice, pushed for change and spoke in opposition.

Hospitality, learned at table with whites, served everyday activists well. Their closeness to white families and their previous dependence on white dollars gave their testimony added strength. "Always learn to smile," Booker Wright said to the camera that day in 1965, his round face crinkled in a forced smile, his white teeth flashing. "The meaner the man be, the more you smile."

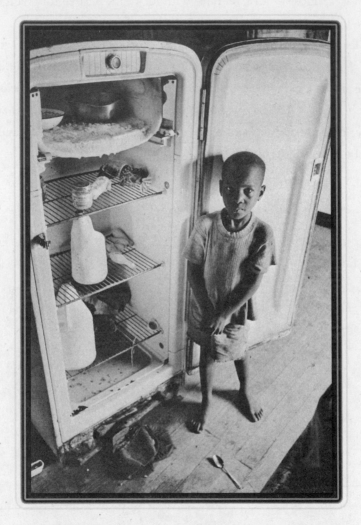

Poverty in the Mississippi Delta of the 1960s was stark and gut-wrenching, as captured in the face of an unnamed child near the town of Belzoni.

· 3 ·

Poor Power

The children of Issaquena County ate breakfasts of grits, rice, and commodity butter. They skipped lunch. "In the evening, it's those beans, those commodity beans, boiled with meat and sometime without meat or sometime with butter cut up in the beans to give it a little flavor," Unita Blackwell told the world in 1967. Born into a sharecropping family in the Mississippi Delta, Blackwell began the 1960s in a three-room shack, chopping cotton for three dollars a day. When she took a job in 1967 with the National Council of Negro Women, she turned America's attention to the starving children of her native region. And she turned up the volume.

Forty million of the 180 million Americans lived in poverty at the close of the prosperous 1950s. Food aid to foreign countries was central to foreign policy, but domestic policy often overlooked the needs of American citizens. By the mid-1960s, when the federal government introduced new hunger programs as part of President Johnson's Great Society initiative, more than half of all black Americans lived in poverty. And most of those poor black Americans lived in the South.

Arrested more than seventy times in her voting rights work with SNCC, Blackwell recognized that economic justice was the next battle to join. As the cotton industry had mechanized over the last generation, farm jobs in the Delta atrophied and welfare rolls bulged. Earlier that year, a one-dollar federal minimum wage went into effect on larger farms. The intent was to raise wages for workers who remained employed. Instead, planters, who calculated that spraying chemicals on cotton fields was cheaper, laid off croppers. Instead of paying black laborers to pull in crops, landowners used federal loan programs to buy tractors and combines and mechanize planting and harvest.

A recent change in federal assistance programs, aimed at increasing the buying power of poor people, exacerbated problems. As states dropped commodity assistance programs and adopted the new food stamp program, civil rights attorney Marian Wright made it clear that even the minimum family expenditure of two dollars per head per month was too high for unemployed Delta farmworkers. This early example of welfare reform, like many of the poverty fixes that would follow, made matters worse, not better, for the nation's poor.

Before the switch to food stamps, poor families ate biscuits baked with surplus flour. Children drank condensed milk with weekday breakfasts. After the switch to food stamps, families dropped out of governmental programs. When Sunflower County moved to food stamp sales, welfare program participation plummeted from more than eighteen thousand commodity recipients in the spring of 1966 to less than eight thousand food stamp users in 1968. At a time when it didn't seem possible, Delta residents went hungrier, children starved.

"There is absolutely nothing for them to do," Wright told the United States Senate Poverty Subcommittee on April 10, 1967, at a hearing at the Heidelberg Hotel in Jackson, imploring the men to travel north from the state capital to meet the starving citizens of the Delta. "There is nowhere to go, and somebody must begin to respond to them. I wish that the senators would have a chance to go and just look at the empty cupboards in the Delta and the number of people who are going around begging just to feed their children." Wright wanted the senators to meet men like Locket Mayze. When he stopped to talk with a visitor in the spring of 1967, Mayze could not remember when he last had a dollar to his name. Other than the time a friend had given him a hog's head, Mayze could not recall when his wife and eight children had eaten anything but surplus commodities.

Two senators accepted her invitation to take a Delta tour at the close of the hearings. One was Robert F. Kennedy of New York. Dressed in a blue suit, a striped silk tie pulled tight against his neck on a warm April day, he stooped in a dimly lit cabin, patted a young boy on the head, and asked what he had eaten for breakfast. Molasses, the black child answered. No grits, no eggs. No biscuits, no butter. Just the leavings from refining sugar, the bottom of the barrel, the lees in the three-M diet of meat, meal, and molasses. That diet had wrecked a previous generation, riddling sharecroppers with the nutritional deficiency pellagra. By the late 1960s, even that diet was beyond the reach of many poor Southerners.

Fifteen people lived in that first shotgun cabin Kennedy visited near Cleveland, Mississippi. At the second stop, Kennedy spied a child on the floor in the fly-swarmed back room of a shack that stank of mildew and urine. Barely two years old, the boy wore a dirty diaper and chased grains of rice and crumbs of cornbread across the floor. Kennedy placed his hand on the child's swollen stomach. For two minutes, the senator tried to rouse the boy. Kennedy poked and pleaded. He smiled and cajoled, while the baby continued to chase those table leavings around a plank board floor that crawled with rats and roaches.

Distraught, Kennedy made his way to the back where Annie White, mother of the boy and five other children, washed the family clothes in a metal tub. She couldn't afford to buy food stamps, even at the steepest discount, she told him. She was hopeless, seemingly helpless. For a moment, so was Kennedy. With tears in his eyes, he turned to a reporter and said, "My God, I didn't know this kind of thing existed. How can a country like this allow this?"

The experience radicalized the senator. Shared with crowds in stump speeches, sketched for reporters who wanted to comprehend the fierceness of his convictions, that experience helped awaken America to the problem in its midst. When Kennedy returned home to Hickory Hill, the family estate near McLean, Virginia, he walked in as his wife and children ate dinner. Ashen-faced, he told them, "In Mississippi a whole family lives in a shack the size of this room. The children are covered with sores and their tummies stick out because they have no food. Do you know how lucky you are? Do you know how lucky you are? Do something for your country."

During the early years of the movement, activists leveraged press coverage of sit-ins and marches and church bombings to pressure and win passage of landmark legislation. The struggles of the poor didn't promise that sort of drama. But as reporters canvassed the Mississippi Delta and the Black Belt of Alabama, they came back with horrific tales.

In 1967, a journalist discovered a woman and six children living in a shack alongside the Mississippi River near the town of Greenville. It was past two in the afternoon when he arrived. No one in the home had eaten that day. Four of the children had slept most of the day and night on the floor, their lips and legs covered with scabs and open sores. The smallest had a distended stomach, topped by a recently tied umbilical knot.

To shine a light, CBS produced two television documentaries, set largely in the South. *Harvest of Shame* focused on the tomato, bean, and sugarcane fields of Florida. Broadcast the day after Thanksgiving in 1960, the documentary introduced viewers to mothers who couldn't afford milk to feed their children and day laborers who traveled to work in open trucks, packed like cattle on the way to slaughter. Set in Texas, Virginia, and Alabama, and out west on a Navajo reservation, *Hunger in America* opened to close-ups of hungry boys and girls and a monologue. "Hunger is hard to recognize in America," Charles Kuralt, a native of North Carolina, said in the 1968 film. "We know it in other places like Asia and Africa. But these children, all of them, are Americans. And all of them are hungry," he said as the camera lingered on children who looked well scrubbed, well cared for, perfectly ordinary.

They were not. A quick cut to a hospital scene in Alabama revealed a white doctor trying to pump life into the lungs of a small black child. "Hunger is easy to recognize when it looks like this," he said as the camera panned over a tiny, contorted body with exposed ribs. "This baby is dying of starvation," the narrator said as a medical technician disconnected the life-support system. "He was an American." A pause followed. "Now he is dead."

As the decade advanced, revelations mounted. At the invitation of a Catholic nun, Fritz Hollings, the U.S. senator from South Carolina, stared down poverty in the Little Mexico neighborhood of Charleston in 1968. As with Kennedy, his tour became an altar call and a media event, from which he emerged chaste, aghast, ashamed. The next week, Hollings toured a black neighborhood near the capitol in Columbia where a single outhouse served thirty-eight families. By 1969, Hollings, who had previously voted against civil rights legislation, led his own poverty tours to call attention and spur legislation. On the Atlantic coast, he met a young child so ill that he coughed up worms.

Many white Southern politicians feared that government poverty programs might loosen their financial stranglehold on the black underclass. Hollings, on the other hand, argued for public assistance programs. Speaking in Timmonsville, South Carolina, he pointed out that, within forty miles of where he stood, forty farmers had received more than $40,000 each in federal subsidies the previous year for leaving their land idle. "This doesn't affect the character of the farmer," Hollings said, lay-

ing on the sarcasm. "He's still as red-blooded, capitalistic, free enterpris-
ing, and patriotic as ever before. But give the poor, little hungry child a
forty-cent breakfast and you've destroyed his character. You've ruined
his incentive. You've taught him bad habits. You have developed a drone
society."

Not all Southerners bought these arguments. Congressman Paul
Rogers of West Palm Beach followed a tour of poverty-wrecked farm
camps in Florida, driving a pale blue Lincoln Continental plastered with
a sign that announced, "I FIGHT POVERTY. I WORK." Senator Strom Thur-
mond of South Carolina agreed. The poor were just lazy: "You had
them back in the days of Jesus Christ, you have got some now, and you
will have some in the future. You will always have some people who are
not willing to work."

"I have called for a national war on poverty. Our objective: Total victory,"
President Johnson announced in April 1964 as he walked through the
front yard of the home where Tom Fletcher, his wife, and their eight
children lived in Inez, Kentucky. Fletcher, who had never finished ele-
mentary school, had been out of work for two years when Johnson
squatted on a pile of lumber to listen to his life story. He told Johnson
that his two oldest children had already dropped out of school. And he
worried that the others would, too.

Johnson recognized an opportunity. On whistle-stop tours that winter and spring, the president worked to mainstream narratives about
hunger. He had grown up among the poor. As a young man, Johnson
taught students of Mexican descent in Cotulla, Texas, who came to class
without breakfast. "Somehow you never forget what poverty and hatred
can do when you see its scars on the hopeful face of a young child," he
said. If Johnson was going to end poverty and meet other Great Society goals, he had to convince white voters that the problems were not
just black and brown. To that end, the White House shot and packaged

videos to appeal to crossover voters, showing faces that were mostly white.

The Fletcher home, with its asphalt siding and tin roof, proved that the American dream had failed whites as well as blacks. Inspired, Johnson aimed to help all Tom Fletchers: "They were black and they were white, of every religion and background and national origin."

In August 1964, Congress passed the Economic Opportunity Act. Pouring nearly a billion dollars into job training, youth employment, adult education, migrant farmworker services, and rural economic development, the legislation declared: "It is the policy of the United States to eliminate the paradox of poverty in the midst of plenty in this nation." Great Society programs benefited Fletcher. He won a job on a federally funded road crew, cleaning trash and sling-blading brush from the Martin County roadside. Taking advantage of a new training program, he studied auto mechanics, earning enough to buy sets of teeth for his wife and himself.

The short-term gains Fletcher made didn't translate for all Southerners. Especially in the old plantation belt, state and local governments refused to fund or selectively enacted new programs, leaving many of the neediest beyond the reach of these new governmental lifelines. By 1968, pressure built as a coalition of poverty advocates massed in the Mississippi Delta town of Marks, seat of the poorest county in the nation. Weary from negotiation, they rejected judicial and legislative paths to stanch poverty and, instead, took up the Poor People's Campaign that Martin Luther King Jr. had been planning when he was assassinated in April of 1968.

Few remembered that the full name for the 1963 March on Washington had been the March on Washington for Jobs and Freedom. Ralph David Abernathy, who became president of the Southern Christian Leadership Conference (SCLC) on King's death, committed to making that link explicit when he organized the Poor People's Campaign. This time, organizers would not just stage speakers on the National Mall.

This time, they would invite poor people to camp on the National Mall and inhabit a living history museum of poverty.

O n a May morning in 1968, Coretta Scott King stood on the second-floor balcony of the Lorraine Motel in Memphis with her back to room 306, where her husband had been assassinated less than a month before. Alongside her stood Ralph Abernathy. "I dream of the day where not some but all of God's children have food," she told the crowd that swelled in the parking lot below, "where not some but all of God's children have decent housing, where not some but all of God's children have a guaranteed annual income in keeping with the principles of liberty and justice."

After the speeches concluded, Abernathy told the crowd it was time to focus attention on the Mule Train then organizing seventy miles south in Marks, Mississippi. "The moment has come," he said. "The day of weeping has ended. The march has begun." Planned for more than a year, the campaign took shape quickly in the weeks after King's death, as SCLC operatives dispatched telegrams that spelled out why the march had to proceed: "The late Martin Luther King Jr.'s last dream was to turn the poorest county in America—Quitman County, Mississippi—from a 'dungeon of shame to a haven of beauty.'"

Caravans planned to travel across the nation, converging on Washington, where they would camp alongside the Lincoln Memorial in a settlement called Resurrection City. As conceived by Marian Wright, who would remain on the front lines of poverty work throughout her life, and executed by Abernathy, the journey was as important as the destination.

Most traveled in chartered buses and vans. The group that departed from Marks staged a kind of rolling protest theater, clip-clopping down highways in wooden-spoked wagons, topped by canvas bonnets, marked with slogans. Painted in black on white, they read, "DON'T LAUGH FOLKS:

JESUS WAS A POOR MAN." And, "EVERYBODY'S GOT A RIGHT TO WORK, EAT, LIVE."

After seemingly interminable delays, the Mule Train set off on May 7 from Quitman County, where the legend atop the courthouse read, "OBE-DIENCE TO THE LAW IS LIBERTY." The departure point had been inspired by a King visit in 1966, when he preached at the funeral of a friend and took a tour of Marks with Abernathy. When they visited a primitive school-house at lunchtime, meeting the gaze of wide-eyed and silent children, King and Abernathy recognized that almost all of the students were un-derweight. Children who had appeared bright-eyed were actually bug-eyed, their cheekbones hollow from hunger. They were starving.

Progress out of Marks was slow. One of the fifteen mules died from tetanus after a nail pierced a hoof while the animal was shod. Another died from a broken neck. One wagon slid into a deep highway ditch after being startled by a car horn. Once the Mule Train reached Atlanta, pas-sengers boarded trains for the remainder of the journey, joining thou-sands of protesters in Washington. Weakened by the long journey, limping mules and rickety wagons followed in freight trains.

Things got no better once the buses, cars, and trains reached Wash-ington. It rained seemingly all month. Mud on the National Mall turned so thick that it sucked overshoes off the feet of campers who walked the muck that runneled between tents. After King's murder, movement leaders adopted stronger language and showed less patience. Black citi-zens had waited for 350 years, Abernathy said when asked why organiz-ers hadn't waited for better weather before beginning the encampment.

More than seven thousand people made homes that summer in Res-urrection City. Canvas tents and plywood shanties stretched along the Reflecting Pool from the shadow of the Lincoln Memorial to the base of the Washington Monument. For the most part, lawmakers looked the other way. Instead of responding to arguments that Abernathy and his lieutenants made, instead of blaming Congress for being nonresponsive, observers tended to blame the Poor People's Campaign. "The poor in

Resurrection City have come to Washington to show that the poor in America are sick, dirty, disorganized, and powerless," Calvin Trillin reported, "and they are criticized daily for being sick, dirty, disorganized, and powerless."

Activists won some of the fights. The Johnson administration expanded the commodity food program. The Agriculture Department earmarked funds for free and discounted school meals. But the more lasting efforts were homegrown. The most emboldening work would occur after the poor returned home and realized that government might not be their best hope for deliverance. They might, instead, have to secure their daily bread by banding together, beyond the gaze of white America.

I f this society of yours is a 'Great Society,' God knows I'd hate to live in a bad one," Fannie Lou Hamer, the voting rights activist who led the Mississippi Freedom Democratic Party at the 1964 Democratic National Convention, wrote to President Johnson two years later. She recognized that the promises he made to America weren't likely to affect the Mississippi Delta, where she was born and raised. Like Unita Blackwell and Marian Wright, Hamer believed that black Southerners would not achieve full citizenship until they claimed sovereignty over their diet. She argued that raising your own crops was key to fixing the problems, saying food "allows the sick ones a chance of healing, the silent ones a chance to speak, the unlearned ones a chance to learn, and the dying ones a chance to live."

Hamer didn't trust the welfare system, which she believed was destroying black families. She believed, instead, in the agrarian ideal that Virginia farmer and statesman Thomas Jefferson touted in the 1700s. She adopted the yeoman farmer stance that the Fugitive Poets of Vanderbilt University honed in the 1930s, the belief system that writer and farmer Wendell Berry of Kentucky began to test in the 1970s. Hamer regarded landownership as elemental to a thriving society and believed that faithful stewardship of the soil was man's highest calling.

With these ideals top of mind, she founded Freedom Farm in Sunflower County in 1969 on sixty acres of land, acquired by paying off the tax debt of a black landowner. Hamer believed the need for land was urgent. "We must buy land immediately, or our people will die forgotten," she told Northern supporters. Writing to funders, she pointed out the profound irony that so many starved in the Mississippi Delta, the place playwright Tennessee Williams described as the "richest land this side of the Nile Valley." Hamer aimed to foster a kingdom of God on earth, a communal society inspired by the book of Acts (2:44–45): "All who believed were together and had all things in common; they would sell their possessions and goods and distribute their possessions to all, as any had need."

Freedom Farm aimed to give farmers land to work and poor families food to eat. That simple tack was brazen. Across the region, many whites saw cooperative farms and livestock shares as threats to their political and economic power. In reprisal, white banks called in loans, white families fired housekeepers, and night riders torched crosses. In December 1967, fifty black farmers met in a church in Wilkes County, Georgia, to plan a vegetable marketing cooperative. Later that night, arsonists burned their meeting place to the ground.

The Mississippi Delta was an especially toxic place. During the mid-1950s, as the Brown decision loomed, Senator James Eastland spoke to thronging white crowds. Threatened by the black majority, his supporters distributed flyers that read: "When in the course of human events it becomes necessary to abolish the Negro race, proper methods should be used. Among these are guns, bows and arrows, sling shots and knives: We hold these truths to be self-evident that all whites are created with certain rights, among them are life, liberty, and the pursuit of dead niggers."

A plantation owner who chaired the Senate Judiciary Committee and often ran Mississippi like a cotton fiefdom, Eastland recognized that his success as a farmer depended on a submissive black labor force. Hamer refused to heel to the man who liked to say that the best plantation fertilizer was the owner's foot.

With the help of singer Harry Belafonte and the Madison, Wisconsin, group Measure for Measure, Hamer acquired six hundred more acres of Delta farmland by 1971. She planted snap beans, squash, butter beans, peas, and cucumbers. Any family could work for a few hours and take home a bushel of produce in exchange. More than 1,500 people arrived regularly to pick their own vegetables in crews she called self-helpers. "You can give a man some food and he'll eat it," she liked to say, quoting a parable. "Then he'll only get hungry again. But give a man some ground of his own and a hoe, and he'll never go hungry again."

Hamer also planted more than one hundred acres of cotton, the same crop her mother picked, the same crop her grandmother picked. Obeisance to that crop and the ways it was grown, harvested, and sold had held her people in penury. For a farm that was always short of money, however, cotton was a cash crop, and cash kept bankers and their foreclosure notes at bay.

From its beginnings Freedom Farm struggled. Hamer's problems were monetary. They were also cultural. Between 1940 and 1969, the rural economy shifted from family farms to industrial farms. Inspired by manufacturing models and abetted by the USDA, this reinvention pushed more than three million farmers and their families off the land, including more than half a million African Americans.

At a time when many left the Delta for manufacturing and service jobs in cities, when few could feed themselves from what they grew, Hamer struggled to persuade blacks to stay and farm. For black Southerners, those linkages to the land were tangled. By the late 1960s, freedom meant release from the demands of agriculture. It meant measuring work by the punch of the time clock, not the weight of a bale.

Not all poor blacks chose to leave. Even as planters mechanized cotton production and cut black jobs, some white landowners continued to provide black laborers with free or low-cost housing in shotgun cabins. Whites shared hocks and heads from hog killings. Whites allowed black families to glean the fields they had once worked. This Delta social contract was a meager take on the old promise of noblesse oblige.

As a child, working cotton fields in bare feet wrapped with rags, Fannie Lou Hamer had gone hungry. Her parents had fallen into sharecropping after a jealous white landowner poisoned their two cows and three mules. She knew the struggle to gain control of the farm economy would be long and hard. Fannie Lou Hamer's father was a Baptist preacher, a juke runner, and a bootlegger. Her enslaved grandmother, Liza Bramlett, gave birth to twenty-three children. All but three resulted from a rape by a white man.

Lou Ella Townsend, Hamer's mother, was one of those three. Townsend scavenged scrap cotton from picked-over fields and tended a backyard garden. When Townsend worked the fields, she kept a gun in her lunch pail to protect her children. Townsend washed clothes in exchange for milk and butter. To feed her family, she cut the leafy tops from sweet potatoes and beets and cooked them like turnip greens.

Poverty haunted Hamer. Her daughter Dorothy died in 1967 after a long series of illnesses rooted in childhood hunger. When Dorothy was a teenager, doctors fed her glucose to stave off malnutrition. Even late in life, after Hamer achieved a measure of fame, the family cupboards were often empty of canned goods. And Hamer's freezer was often bare except for a couple of possum carcasses. After Hamer's cancerous left breast was removed, she couldn't afford money for a prosthesis. "You know what I got in here?" she said, gesturing to her chest during a conversation. "Some socks rolled up."

Like her mother, who had worked as an itinerant hog slaughterer, Hamer regarded livestock as a solution to poverty and hunger. She conceived the idea for her Pig Bank with Dorothy Height, chair of the National Council of Negro Women. The idea behind the Pig Bank, a complement to Freedom Farm that Hamer originally called the Oink Oink project, was bold.

Beginning with fifty Yorkshire gilts and five boars, she gave pregnant pigs to families who agreed to return two of their offspring to the bank and keep the other piglets as dividends. Poor families butchered those dividends once they reached an acceptable weight.

Height, who helped finance the project, and who brought in a hog farmer from Iowa to consult, got positive feedback quickly. Instead of buying meat and lard from a country store, women across the Delta wrote to her about going a year without store-bought pork.

In 1969, when Hamer founded Freedom Farm, nearly 70 percent of the people in her native Sunflower County lived on an income of $1,000 a year or less. By most governmental measures, they were no better off four years later. Despite the grim numbers, the Pig Bank showed promise. In the first year, thirty-five families who had received a pregnant gilt from Hamer handed over two pigs from their own litter to other needy families. By year two, one hundred families slaughtered pigs in the fall, froze the meat, and roasted hams for winter suppers.

Hamer was delighted. "Child, we cured our own meat this year," she bragged. "We can have ham and we can have biscuits and you got a good meal. . . ." A Cooperative Gardening Project followed. "When you've got 400 quarts of greens and gumbo soup canned for the winter, nobody can push you around or tell you what to say or do," Hamer said, explaining the idea. Good housing was part of the plan, too. Tapping into FHA loan programs, Hamer helped seventy families build homes by 1972.

On a winter day in 1973, Hamer, dressed in a housecoat, her hair in curlers, cut into a dividend from the Pig Bank. "The one kind of remark that means the most to me is the one I hear frequently on really cold mornings," she said as she slipped a slice of home-cured ham into a skillet. "You'll see two men walking out their front doors. One will kind of stop, look around, and say, 'Phew! I didn't realize how cold it was outside.' Every place they had lived before, it was just as cold inside as it was outside."

Freedom Farm inspired Delta spin-offs, including a sewing co-op in Doddsville, a clothing boutique in Drew, and a plumbing company in Moorhead. But by the mid-1970s, her Freedom Farm and Pig Bank had lost momentum. Hamer's health suffered, managers of the project fumbled, and her right-hand man dropped dead of a heart attack.

The larger problem, though, was perception. Hamer preached the differences between the white-owned plantations where she was raised and the interracial cooperative farm she organized. Hamer argued that Freedom Farm and Pig Bank subverted that past. Her farm was a site for renewal and reclamation. To many blacks in the Delta, though, the land that Hamer farmed was tainted. And so was the labor it required.

Translation problems plagued her efforts. White funders grasped the promise. But many black farmers and the children of black farmers failed to grasp the difference between cropping cotton for white planters and raising beans and corn for a black co-op. The differences seemed subtle, the farm labor just as strenuous, the financial rewards just as slight. Freedom Farm failed to prove an anchor for black Delta natives who, like their grandparents and uncles and aunts, floated north to Memphis, St. Louis, and Chicago.

As stories of poverty mounted and efforts to correct the inequities gained some traction, denial remained pervasive among some of the white and wealthy. Asked about the problem of hunger, Mississippi governor Paul Johnson said in 1967, "All the Negroes I've seen around here are so fat they shine."

When the Tufts-Delta Health Center opened that same year in the Delta town of Mound Bayou, Bolivar was the second-poorest county in the country. The staff quickly recognized that hunger would throttle the diagnoses and treatments they planned. Before patients could recover from any illnesses, they had to recover from starvation. Working with area residents, intent on raising their own food, the clinic founded a co-operative farm, comparable to Freedom Farm.

Jack Geiger, the white founder of the center, had arrived in the Mississippi Delta in 1964 during Freedom Summer. Along with his colleagues, he dug wells and outhouses. They screened windows and plugged holes in roofs. They created a bus system, badly needed in the largely rural Delta with its far-flung towns. They staged canning and cooking classes where local women learned nutritional lessons. They called their approach "community health action." "Our concept of health is to make social change, to build institutions that can make social change, and to keep it going," Geiger said.

For the rural poor, "the recent national focus on the environment must seem a bitter irony," he told the Senate Select Committee on Nutrition and Human Needs in 1967. "The rural poor have been drinking dirty water, fighting the elements, living amidst society's garbage long before the nation became concerned about smog on Park Avenue, industrial pollution in Lake Erie, or the exhaust fumes from automobiles on the Los Angeles freeways." To address the worst kind of malnutrition, Geiger began issuing prescriptions for food.

The solution was simple, heart-wrenching, and effective. Geiger prescribed food for children whose families couldn't afford it. Unemployment at the time ran about 80 percent among the black Bolivar County population. The average black family of four lived on $900 in annual income. Those same families collected water in used pesticide barrels. And they shot squirrels for meat.

Geiger, who had studied in South Africa during medical school and came away inspired by that country's community health practices, was a realist, fixed on pragmatic solutions. His prescriptions—which stipulated quantities of milk, vegetables, meat, and fruit—could be filled at local grocery stores. Bills went to the health center, which paid them out of the pharmacy budget.

When the Office of Economic Opportunity reprimanded Geiger, instructing the doctor that its funds could be used only for medical purposes, he replied, "The last time I looked in my textbooks, the specific therapy for malnutrition was food."

As it was with so many of the antipoverty initiatives that emerged from the 1960s and 1970s, the South served as both the locus for the problem and the genesis of a solution. Geiger's holistic approach to addressing poverty and its effects would, in the decades to come, prove prescient. Fifty-plus years later, when the federal government again embraced food prescriptions, his effort, like the agricultural experiments of Fannie Lou Hamer, would look resolutely modern.

You see those houses over there," Fannie Lou Hamer said on a spring day in 1970, sweeping her hand wide in the general direction of Senator James Eastland's plantation. "We paid for them. Me, my husband, my daddy, and his daddy before him. All the black people working in these cotton fields for next to nothing all these years paid for them. They belong to us." In the years ahead, a succession of black Southerners would make complementary cases. Facing down poverty and hopelessness, they, too, recognized that the first step to feeding their people was the acquisition of land.

Early in her Freedom Farm work, she pushed hard for the redistribution of acreage that was not being farmed by Eastland and other subsidy-dependent plantation owners. As she grew older, Hamer grew more intolerant of inequities and more radical in her resolve.

A trip to Guinea awakened her to the sins of colonialism. "We've got to hook up with all the other non-white peoples of the world," she said. "We're going to need them if we're going to make it." After a visit to the restored slave market in Charleston, South Carolina, where she glimpsed an advertisement that read "Crippled but a good breeder" and noticed that the stump on which slaves stood to be sold was well polished, Hamer said, "They has robbed us of our heritage, stolen our names, and stripped our men of their dignity. . . . America owes us a debt."

Who owned the South? Who should control the means of production? And who should speak for the South's people? Answers were tough to come by. The persistence of poverty in the "best fed nation on earth" made it clear that, while civil rights movement victories had changed where and with whom Southerners ate, food access would continue to be a political issue in the region. As the 1970s unspooled, the debts Hamer accounted continued to accrue.

The Black Panthers established the People's Free Food Program to feed
both children and the elderly. What they began in California
informed efforts across the nation.

Black Power

F arish Street was the black mecca of Jim Crow Mississippi. On Saturdays, farmers and their families traveled to the Jackson neighborhood to buy dry goods and visit cafés where fried fish and cold beer came cheap and jukeboxes blared rhythm and blues. Women in floral cotton dresses shopped for canned goods at the Jungle Food Store, men bought Tuf-Nut coveralls from the Famous Bargain Store, and children played tag in alleyways. Afternoon moviegoers crowded into the Booker T. By night, drinkers caroused down neon-pulsed streets. And families ate fried chicken suppers at the Home Dining Room.

After desegregation, Farish Street slowly emptied, as black buying power dispersed across once segregated cities. Beale Street in Memphis nose-dived. Deep Ellum in Dallas followed. The unintended consequences of the Civil Rights Act of 1964 included the decline of black business districts. "Desegregation was great for the black race," Geno Lee, the fourth-generation proprietor of the Big Apple Inn told me, years later, when I stopped by his Farish Street café for a pig ear sandwich. "But it was horrible for black businessmen." Black consumers took their grocery shopping and five-and-dime splurges to the white suburbs. They took their meals in white restaurants, where owners were, after a time, willing to sell them platters of catfish, bowls of spaghetti, baskets of hamburgers and fries.

Urban renewal condemned and bulldozed blocks of homes and businesses, decimating black business districts like Hayti in Durham, Treme in New Orleans, Frogtown in Savannah, and Overtown in Miami. Elevated interstates, erected in their place, cut residential neighborhoods in half and rendered streets unwalkable. Melvin Van Peebles distilled the anger many felt toward white-controlled government programs that broke apart black neighborhoods. "Chicken ain't nothing but a bird," he declared in *Sweet Sweetback's Baadasssss Song*, a 1971 film meditation on black poverty, sexuality, and the radical responses that desperation inspired. "White man ain't nothing but a turd."

By the 1970s, soul food, like soul music and soul power, was cultural currency. Food choice emerged as a means to construct black identity and express black mores. Blacks debated the value and worth of soul food and proposed alternate labels. In honor of Paul Laurence Dunbar, the African American dialect poet, Ishmael Reed called hog jowls and pone bread "Dunbar food." Helen Mendes, author of *The African Heritage Cookbook*, claimed a broader African identity when she referred to blacks from various backgrounds as "Soul people."

Instead of dismissing soul food, Mendes said that the cuisine connected African Americans with their history and with a global band of brothers and sisters. In an age when air travel linked all points of the globe, and African countries finally shed their colonial governments, she recast the African diaspora as a cosmopolitan gelling of many peoples and many tribes into a definable aesthetic. Mendes described soul food as a cultural expression of "Black international society" that spanned the Atlantic from West Africa to the Americas.

While black America puzzled through a complicated relationship to the foods that sustained their communities during Jim Crow, white America fell for collards and pone, embracing soul food as a roster of exoticisms that offered a glimpse of black life. In *Vogue* Gene Baro described the fetish as "white sympathy for the black drive to self-reliance." Three months before Fannie Lou Hamer told another *Vogue* writer about her vision of reclaiming the land her forebears worked, Baro explained the soul food phenomenon to that magazine's readers: "It is as if those who ate the beans and greens of necessity in the cabin doorways were brought into communion with those who, not having to, eat those foods voluntarily now as a sacrament."

Activist and author Eldridge Cleaver wanted none of this. "You hear a lot of jazz about soul food," he wrote from jail, where he was serving a sentence for attempted rape. "Take chitterlings: the ghetto blacks eat them from necessity while the black bourgeois has turned it into a mocking slogan. . . . Now that they have the price of steak, they come prattling about Soul Food."

Vertamae Grosvenor, author of the cookbook-cum-memoir *Vibration Cooking*, was riled, too. When *Time* dismissed soul food as antebellum plantation throwaways, Grosvenor defended agrarian Africa and its American descendants. In a letter to the editor that presaged arguments against industrial agriculture, she wrote, "So you white folks just keep on eating that white foam rubber bread that sticks to the roof of your mouth, and keep on eating Minute Rice and instant potatoes, instant cereals, and drinking instant milk and stick to your instant culture. And I will stick to the short-lived fad that brought my ancestors through four hundred years of oppression."

B lack nationalists offered alternatives. They didn't aim to reinvent society after the fall of segregation. They aimed to leave the system. Separatism was not just about living apart. It was about finding purpose

in the absence of whites. Taking control of diet was key. Growing, cooking, and eating natural foods was a means of community activism, they
argued.

Black physicians joined black nationalists to speak against soul food,
which they linked to a slavery diet of offal and leavings, scarcity and
want. "We cannot continue to disregard what we eat as if our diet has no
effect on our health status," Dr. Therman E. Evans wrote in *Ebony* magazine in 1972. "In fact what we eat is both directly and indirectly related
to every major illness we know of, including heart disease, high blood
pressure, cancer, diabetes, and infectious diseases."

Vegetarian diets were vogue, especially among African Americans
working in politics and the arts. *Ebony* bid "Farewell to Chitterlings."
Members of Earth, Wind & Fire sang along. Black movie star Cicely
Tyson became part of the "vegetarian vigilante" then "steaming, cream-
ing and pickling their way across this meat-infested region determined
to stave off America's open-mouthed nutritional suicide." Musician Taj
Mahal called hamburgers a "real vulgarity." A decade after African Americans had won the right to eat in white-owned restaurants, the ironies
were rich. "It is a paradox to be sure," the *Ebony* writer observed, "the
astounding aspect of an American black flinging away his barbecue bone
for a celery stalk."

Dick Gregory, the comedian turned activist who later experimented
with a fruit-only diet, rejected soul food in favor of "soil food." He ate
only things that grew out of the ground. Black nationalists urged African
Americans to adopt a whole foods diet. Some grounded the appeal in
beliefs that West African diets before the colonial era were also vegetable
based.

Muslims made the strongest arguments for independence. Elijah
Muhammad challenged Nation of Islam members to "take their mouths
out of the white man's kitchens." He said that black men and women
had to develop a self-sufficient society that did not rely on white farms,
white systems, or white consumers. He spoke of job opportunities. And

he delivered a Three Year Economic Savings Program that called for black people to "pool their resources by contributing $10 a month to help fight against poverty, want, unemployment, abominable housing, hunger and nakedness of the 30–40 million black people in America." A system of farms, mostly in the South, where land was cheap and labor was plentiful, would grow the raw materials for clothing and food. On farms, black nationalists would fuel the revolution.

Despite his advocacy for poor blacks, Senator Fritz Hollings drew the line at black nationalism. He regarded the rise of Black Panther–sponsored free breakfast programs in California and the promise of Muslim farm initiatives in the Deep South as threats to the system. Hollings challenged his audiences to harness their outrage about hunger or black radicals would leverage the desperation of poor and impoverished people to foment a revolution. "The Black Muslims have already begun," Hollings warned. "They preach separation and anti-Semitism and recently acquired several large farms in Alabama. There they are raising food on a thousand acres in order to supply produce for the stores they operate in northern cities."

Vertical integration, by which a company or organization controls the supply chain from production to consumption, had long been part of the black Christian church. During the middle years of the twentieth century, the United House of Prayer opened beauty salons, barbershops, and cafeterias that served Southern parishioners. Bishop Daddy Grace stocked those cafeterias with coffee from the church's Brazilian plantation and chicken from its Cuban hatchery. This time the scale was different. By 1975, the Nation of Islam farmed more than fourteen thousand acres in the Deep South.

Muslims cropped corn, string beans, apples, tomatoes, okra, and soybeans. They raised chickens, cows, and sheep. In the urban North, they owned and operated dairy and meat-processing plants. Elijah Muhammad supervised restaurants, a clothing factory, and a small bank. The Nation of Islam operated Your Super Markets, which stocked vegetables canned at a Nation of Islam farm in Bronwood, Georgia. After centuries of living in a white world, this black world looked attractive and secure. Life off the white grid promised prosperity, even peace.

Food was central to the beliefs and practices of the Nation of Islam. Eating the right thing was a spiritual practice. To aid that practice Muhammad published *How to Eat to Live*. African Americans had not previously been able to control their bodies or those of their families. During the time of slavery, blacks were chattel. In the Jim Crow era, black men and women were perceived as sexual and physical threats.

It's common to think about kitchens as places of comfort where family ties were nurtured, but kitchens were also places of violence. When white women ceded their kitchens to black maids and cooks, they left those black women vulnerable to white men. In white kitchens, the same spaces where black women baked skillets of cornbread and stewed down pots of greens, white men raped black women like Fannie Lou Hamer's grandmother. Acts of violence like these reinforced black instincts to leave the kitchen, just as rape amid the crop rows had driven blacks to quit the fields. The Black Power movement, and the rise of the Islamic religion and Muslim identity, promised a reclaiming of the black body, a regaining of control through diet.

"Eat food that Allah (God) has prescribed for us," Elijah Muhammad wrote. He prohibited field peas and black-eyed peas, crops associated with slave provisions and sharecropper subsistence. Sweet potatoes, often called yams and just as often linked to West Africa where a tuber by that name is beloved, were not allowed. "Sweet potatoes were never good for any human to eat," he declared. "They are good for hogs, but not for you."

Wallace Fard Muhammad, who said he came from Mecca to found the Nation of Islam, shared a recipe for bean pies with Elijah Muhammad and his wife in 1930s Detroit, where many black Southerners gathered. It spread wherever Muslims worshipped. Sold on street corners by

Nation of Islam supporters, bean pies became icons of black life in Chicago and Detroit. For a new generation of Southern migrants, dinner after a long day of labor ended not with a slice of pale gold sweet potato pie, but with a small tin of pale brown bean pie, made from mashed navy beans, enriched with evaporated milk and butter, spiced with cinnamon, and baked until custardy.

If the first step for black Southerners was to wrest control of their bodies, the next step was to take back their farmland. Four centuries of enslavement and Jim Crow had wiped clean many of the black signatures on American farming. One million African American farmers owned land in 1910. And they owned more than fifteen million acres. By 1969, black farmers owned only six million acres. In the triumphalist version of that story, rural blacks moved to the urban North and West in search of better jobs and more opportunities. Pulled north by the pledges of black newspapers like *The Chicago Defender* and job contracts offered by labor recruiters, they rode the Illinois Central, known to generations as the Chicken Bone Express, fleeing Jim Crow and his henchmen, arriving to claim jobs in stockyards and at manufacturing plants. They drove the Lincoln Highway to California, where the sun-spangled port of Oakland promised union jobs and affordable bungalow housing. Escape from farm life was the goal. Factory jobs were the prizes.

During her Senate poverty subcommittee appearance in 1967, Marian Wright had shared a different story, in which black migration was driven by a pernicious white push, not a sustaining black pull. She said that federal reform of the welfare system, along with the shift to farm mechanization, was draining the rural South of black people. Blacks did not leave their farms on their own. They were being forced off the farms they scrimped and saved to purchase during the late nineteenth and early twentieth centuries. As farms mechanized, twentieth-century USDA farm policies restricted black access to capital. The removal of black men and women from farms was purposeful.

The steep decline of black farmers fueled a kind of second Redemption in the 1960s and 1970s. During the first Redemption, an organized effort following the Civil War to excise black- and Republican-controlled governments from Southern states, white and moneyed Democratic leaders regained the reins of government. This time, the white power grab focused on farms. During this second Redemption, wealthy whites grabbed black farmland.

As black activists finally gained access to the ballot box, white planters in black majority farming districts including the Mississippi Delta, the Alabama Black Belt, and the Plantation Corridor of the Carolinas disinvested state and local dollars and reclaimed black lands for white use. While the fight for civil rights won sympathetic coverage in Northern newspapers, and the hand-to-hand combat of demonstrators and police during the 1960s played well on network television programs, struggles over land took place out of sight, in the back offices of bank vice presidents and middling government bureaucrats, where discrimination was harder to pinpoint but no less destructive.

Property was more than a means of production. For a black man or woman whose parents or grandparents had been traded and sold as property, the ownership of land was a bulwark against threats. For emancipated black farmers the allure of owning farmland, the rewards of working their own property, and the legacy of bequeathing that property to heirs had been great.

From Reconstruction forward, black farmers had banded together to wrest a living from the land. The Colored Farmer Alliance, organized in Houston in the late 1880s, published a newspaper, ran academies, and operated cooperative exchanges in port cities including New Orleans and Charleston. Members secured mortgage loans and bought goods at reduced prices.

In Memphis, black consumers joined in 1889 to found a cooperative called the People's Grocery, across the street from a white-owned store. Three years later, whites perceived the threat of black economic independence to be so great that a mob lynched three of the owners, including co-op president Thomas Moss. Shot in the head and neck, his final words, reported by Ida B. Wells in her Memphis newspaper *Free Speech*, foreshadowed black migrations to escape Jim Crow terrors: "Tell my people to go West, there is no justice for them here."

Instead of merely selling goods in local markets, black farmers in the South of the late 1960s adapted Nation of Islam strategies to develop city outlets where black expatriates clustered. By 1969, Black Markets Incorporated operated two co-ops in Washington, D.C., and planned a chain that would purchase directly from black-owned canneries and black farmers. The Federation of Southern Cooperatives acted as a go-between for small black businesses. Founded in 1967, the Federation brought together twenty-two different co-ops of mostly black farmers. The situation was dire. Between 1940 and 1969, as farmers came to rely on machines and chemicals, nearly 600,000 African Americans left their farms.

The Federation of Southern Cooperatives tapped the vein Malcolm X exposed when he challenged the goals of desegregated lunch counters, theaters, parks, and public toilets. Sitting down next to white folks on a toilet was no revolution, he preached from a Detroit pulpit in 1963: "Revolution is based on land. Land is the basis of all independence. Land is the basis of freedom, justice, and equality."

To gain capital and, eventually, power, co-ops spun off businesses like the Acadian Delight Bakery in Lake Charles, Louisiana, which baked brownies, fruitcakes, and pralines. To stimulate sales, the black-owned company packaged its pecan-studded cakes in metal boxes that recalled cotton bales. Success bred detractors. A reporter for *The Councilor*, house magazine of the White Citizens' Council, printed a recipe for

"Poverty Fruit Cake" that translated as a critique of Acadian: "Stir the gullible public to a frenzy. Soak the nuts in cheap wine. Mix all light and dark ingredients to a mulatto blend. Baste with Sargent Shriver. Heat quickly and serve while the odor is strong."

In the 1970s, the Federation reached beyond the Deep South, spreading its message of black enterprise and collaboration. The Episcopal Church of Kentucky funded the Breathitt Rabbit Producers. The Kentucky Mountains Feeder Pig Cooperative, which met above Callahan's Hardware in the town of Jackson, partnered with the Heifer Project, then headquartered in St. Louis, to make good on a livestock grant of thirty gilts and six boars, much like the one that birthed Fannie Lou Hamer's Pig Bank.

The Federation dispatched members to Wisconsin and Nova Scotia and Saskatchewan to study how other co-ops worked. On the coast of South Carolina, the Bluffton Oyster Cooperative brought together black watermen, who shared a shucking house and sold their harvest under a branded label. The Southwest Alabama Farmers Cooperative Association, a ten-county alliance of more than one thousand members, grew and sold one million pounds of vegetables in its first year. Purchasing farm supplies in bulk, it cut hard costs almost in half and doubled the price it commanded for peas and cucumbers.

Organizers took their cues from the civil rights movement. Church ministers planned strategies. Voter drives and co-op member drives dovetailed. Responding to boycotts by white vegetable brokers who resented black farmer participation in the civil rights movement, the Grand Marie Vegetable Producers Cooperative formed in Sunset, Louisiana. Grocers in Washington, D.C., sold Co-Op Sweets brand sweet potatoes.

Linkages between the larger movement and the farmer co-ops proved strong. At the second meeting of the Federation of Southern Cooperatives in 1969, Fannie Lou Hamer spoke. In 1970, Ralph David Abernathy, organizer of the Poor People's March, stepped to the podium.

Farmers, like grocers, took chances. In 1969, Shirley and Charles Sherrod helped found New Communities, a 5,000-plus-acre farm near Albany, Georgia. White neighbors claimed they were Communists. The Sherrods fought off challenges from Georgia governor Lester Maddox, who dismissed the farm as "Sharecropper City" and refused to sign off on a grant. They suffered through three years of crop-killing drought. At every turn, institutionalized racism reared its horned head. When the Sherrods requested an emergency loan during the drought, a Farmers Home Administration supervisor told them they would get it "over his dead body."

During the 1970s, the USDA, under the direction of Earl "Rusty" Butz, helped drive the removals. In addition to denying black farmers loans, local operatives in states like Alabama openly ridiculed black farmers who attempted to secure capital for new efforts. Butz, for his part, called on farmers to "Get big or get out." Industrial agriculture was the future. Family farmers "must adapt or die," he said.

Instead of planting a cash crop for market and a garden patch for family, the USDA encouraged farmers to plant soybeans and corn from "fencerow to fencerow." Butz was no friend to black farmers. He didn't think they were industrious enough for his new-style agriculture. Exposing the underlying racism that befouled the USDA for much of the twentieth century, Butz told a joke in 1976 that compelled his forced resignation from the Ford administration. All black men want, he said, was "first, a tight pussy; second, loose shoes; and third, a warm place to shit."

Co-ops, founded on Black Power principles, helped stanch the losses that the USDA drove. By the mid-1970s, the Federation claimed 120 members. And complementary efforts thrived like the Freedom Quilting Bee in Alabama and a Channel Catfish Training Program in Mississippi, designed to teach black farmers how to convert from cotton and soybeans to aquaculture. Cooperatives helped farmers plant fruit orchards, process and can vegetables, and jointly market goods to wholesalers and consumers. Leslie Dunbar, director of the Field Foundation, called their work "boot-strap reconstruction." Ezra Cunningham, a black farmer and activist from Monroe County, Alabama, who served as a Federation organizer, made clear the stakes: "You can't eat freedom. And a ballot is not to be confused with a dollar bill."

As black farmers tried to earn a living while holding on to their land, black restaurateurs leveraged the new soul food chic that ranged from Harlem, where diners at the Red Rooster washed down chitlins with Champagne, to Atlanta, where Rev. Willie James Stafford of the Free For All Missionary Baptist Church (who favored maroon jumpsuits and packed a revolver), opened Soul on Top of Peachtree atop a downtown skyscraper. "I'm giving the people pleasure and I'm creating jobs for them," he said in 1972, explaining what it meant to claim a perch on top of Peachtree Street, "and I'm throwing the money right back in the Black community."

Black restaurants served black customers as clubhouses. Leah Chase built the reputation of her husband's family restaurant by serving her New Orleans neighbors and courting political and civil rights figures. Early in her career Chase managed boxers. Later, her dining room was a gathering place for black progressives and musicians. Ray Charles ate gumbo at Dooky Chase's and cut a song to make clear his devotion. Lena Horne came for fried chicken. Sara Vaughan ate stuffed crabs. Breaking the color line, playwright Tennessee Williams taxied down Orleans Avenue to eat lemon ice-box pie.

Constance Baker Motley, the attorney who represented James Meredith in his federal appeal to gain admission to the University of Mississippi, arrived before court to eat breakfast. When union organizer Jim Dombrowski, a founder of the Highlander Folk School, met with Godchaux Sugar Company employees, he claimed the upstairs at Dooky's.

Before retiring to a friend's home to eat crawfish or boiled crabs on newspapers, spread on the hardwood floor, Thurgood Marshall, the eventual
Supreme Court justice, swung by Dooky's for gumbo.

Chase recognized that neither her famous customers nor the black
chefs who worked in restaurants across New Orleans saw value in traditional dishes like fried chicken. "I don't think they realized their worth
because they never put emphasis on anything they had," Chase said,
speaking of the intricate Creole dish gumbo z' herbes and of the women
who were expert at cooking it. "They never thought it was good enough.
They never thought it was something to make over. It was just what we
do. Like the ladies who sew, the men who do the carpenter work, just
what we do you know. They didn't put any value on themselves or on
their work."

By the mid-1970s, Rudy Lombard, who led the desegregation of
New Orleans restaurants in the 1960s, recognized that, if black workers
were going to see value in their labor, new frames for that work had to
be constructed. He reached this realization in the midst of the Black Arts
Movement of the late 1960s and early 1970s, which the critic Houston
Baker described as an "attempt to construct a chrysalis of blackness."
That cloak, he said, might allow artists to "grasp the essence of the black
American's reality."

Published in 1978, the year after New Orleans elected Ernest "Dutch"
Morial the first black mayor of the city, *Creole Feast* was a political manifesto, masquerading as a cookbook, draped in a black chrysalis. "Black
involvement in the New Orleans Creole cuisine is as old as gumbo and
just as important," Lombard wrote. "French, Spanish, Cajun, Italian—all
these ethnic groups live in New Orleans, but they are not running the
best kitchens of the best restaurants of the city. The single, lasting char-
acteristic of Creole cuisine is the Black element."

Too many writers ascribed a "secondary, lowly, or nonexistent role to
the Black hand in the pot," Lombard explained. Too few recognized that
New Orleans culture, food, music, architecture, ceremony, and belief

were based on African knowledge and traditions. If the chefs who ran the kitchens at Antoine's and Galatoire's were not going to get the pay they deserved from employers or the accolades they deserved from customers, Lombard aimed to canonize them himself.

To make his case, Lombard interviewed fifteen black chefs including Nathaniel Burton, with whom he partnered on the recipes. (Toni Morrison, who had already written *The Bluest Eye* but was still working at Random House, served as editor.) Lombard gave the chefs voice and space to share the lessons they learned in city kitchens. Leah Chase held forth on how to avoid a gravy that roped on the heat. Austin Leslie of Chez Hélène talked through how to cut up a chicken into twelve pieces instead of the customary ten.

Sherman Crayton, who began cooking at Arnaud's in 1936, confirmed Lombard's argument that the problems of Creole food were rooted in attribution: "They say it is a mixture of Spanish and French, but the only people who seem to know all about it are neither Spanish nor French, they're Blacks." Lombard worked to frame the lives of these chefs in a way that bestowed honor. He accomplished that with a subtitle, *15 Master Chefs of New Orleans Reveal Their Secrets*.

Jacques Pépin, the celebrated French-born chef, made the arguments advanced by Crayton and Lombard when he told his biographer that, on arrival in the United States in 1959, he was most impressed by the old guard African American chefs he met, the men and women who worked in the grand hotels and fine dining rooms. He thought they had the same gravitas, the same experience-honed talent that Frenchmen exhibited.

Pépin expected those black men to emerge as the stars, and was surprised when they did not ascend to the firmament during the American culinary renaissance of the late twentieth century. He didn't understand why they failed to get their due. As the years advanced and Southern food gentrified, his question would linger in the air, nagging and unresolved.

O ther writers followed the lead of Lombard and Burton, including Idella Parker, whom *Cross Creek* author Marjorie Kinnan Rawlings of Florida had referred to as her "perfect maid." When Parker wrote her own book, she sounded a Black Power tone: "I am *not* perfect, and neither was Mrs. Rawlings, and this book will make that clear to anyone who reads it. . . . Many of the recipes in the book were mine, but she only gave me credit for three of them. . . . All I ever got from the cookbook was an autographed copy, but in those days I was grateful for any little crumb that white people let fall, so I kept my thoughts about the cookbook strictly to myself."

Bobby Seale, who had helped found the Black Panther Party for Self-Defense in 1966, focused his attentions on food, too. Inspired by the rhetoric of Malcolm X and the end of colonialism in Africa, Seale, like other Panthers, argued that power would allow blacks to gain "land, bread, housing, education, clothing, justice and peace."

Many onetime activists ran for office and were elected. Others retreated to the safety of churches. Segregationists Lester Maddox in Georgia and Maurice Bessinger in South Carolina had proved in the 1960s that restaurants could be bases of operation for political gain. By the 1970s, black activists worked the inverse.

Seale imagined a career in food that would include a television show, backed by a funk band, presented before a live studio audience. He wrote a cookbook inspired by the skills he learned growing up on the Texas Gulf Coast. *Barbeque'n with Bobby* had a neon orange cover and brimmed with aphorisms, concoctions for vinegar mops, and a recipe for pork ribs that Seale perfected at Black Panther cookouts in Oakland. Reflecting the move toward healthy eating, Seale included sugar- and salt-free "Hickory Hocked Black-Eyed Peas" and "Honey Seasoned Turnip Greens." Seale, who had served jail time for his Black Panther activism,

did not retire his ideologies when he quit the barricades. In the dedica-
tion to his book, he pledged, "They used to holler: 'Free, Bobby! Free,
Bobby! Free, Bobby!' "Now, they're going to yell: 'Bobby-que! Bobby-
que! Bobby-que!'"

The 1970s was a time of sharp contention. The decline of black business districts challenged triumphant views of the civil rights revolution. Revolution, Malcolm X said, was based on land, and land was what
black Southerners needed. Efforts of Muslim farmers and co-op members to wrest a living from lands to which their forebears had once been
shackled begged questions about who owned the South's farmland and
who ought to work it.

As the Black Power movement gained momentum and the Black
Arts Movement gained patrons, whites and blacks came to see the value
of everyday labor. Born as romantic views of the Old South faded, these
voices democratized American ideas about why food mattered, which
cooks were worthy of respect, and how to define a cuisine.

Terms for the diet of black Southerners fell in and out of favor. From
soul food to soil food, from the cooking of "Black internationalist society" to the cooking of the "vegetarian vigilant," differing views about
what black Southerners should call their diet illuminated opposing narratives embedded in Southern food and set the stage for knitting the region back together during the Carter ascent.

Rise of
the Folk

1970S & 1980S

All worked the sorghum harvest at The Farm near Summertown, Tennessee.

Landed Hippies

I can't put my attention into a city scene anymore," Stephen Gaskin told the bangled and bell-bottomed hippies who gathered at his feet in Sutro Park for a Sunday morning service in February 1971. "Because the worst thing happening on the planet is the cities. Like the cities are the major cause of warfare, poverty, totalitarian police state, whatnot. All those things are functions of being crowded up in cities. . . . After the services the caravan is to take off to Tennessee and get a farm. Because what you put your attention into you get more of, and I need more trees, more grass, more wheat, more soybeans, more healthy babies, more good-looking sane people, people that can work."

Gaskin stood with his back to the fir- and palm-framed park overlooking San Francisco Bay, blew a tremulous horn note, and led the crowd in a long *Ommmmm*. Afterward, a couple hundred hippies shambled back to their flophouses and microbuses to pack. The next morning, Gaskin led them in an Age of Aquarius exodus, bound for the Cumberland Ridge in south-central Tennessee. They would call the place they settled The Farm.

The Farm ethic took shape in a San Francisco concert venue called the Family Dog, where radical politics, acid rock, and mime troupes were draws. Set in what had been an amusement park, the Family Dog staged shows by the Mothers of Invention, the Velvet Underground, and the Grateful Dead. When Dick Gregory ran for president, he scheduled a fund-raiser there. When Timothy Leary, the psychologist behind the Harvard Psilocybin Project, wanted to reach his acid-goosed faithful, he took the Family Dog stage.

Stephen Gaskin began teaching classes in English and creative writing at San Francisco State in 1964. Two years later, the college declined to extend his contract. His lectures, extended to cover hermeneutic geometry and Masonic-Rosicrucian mysticism, had gone astral. Soon, he was teaching informal courses like Group Experiments in Unified Field Theory and Meta-PE at the San Francisco State Experimental College. His classes grew and the venues changed before he settled at the Family Dog. But the focus on religion, belief, and psychedelic possibilities remained constant during what came to be called Monday Night Class. Before the year passed, Gaskin would transplant that ethic to a wooded plot of hilly land outside Summertown, Tennessee. Before the decade was out, The Farm would emerge as a prime incubator of countercultural America.

A long-haired Marine Corps veteran of the Korean War, who sat cross-legged and open-minded before his Monday Night Class charges, he played the roles of shaman and psychedelic wayfarer. Gaskin lectured on auras and astrology and ecology. He juggled questions about morality and Tantric thought. He claimed contact buzz telepathy. "You can't define God," he said. In search of personal and universal truths, Gaskin had taken a couple hundred acid trips before reaching the conclusion, "It's easier to be God than to see God."

Drugs were key to unlocking the messages. After drinking peyote tea, followers learned to view their experiences in terms of world religions. United by contact highs, they chanted *Ommmmm* until they gasped

for breath. Gaskin preached that the psychedelic experience was a religious affirmation. Grounding his talks in Christianity and Buddhism, he
overlaid teachings with psilocybin mysticism. "When we feel high, we
feel God," Gaskin said to the paisleyed faithful, making his case for a
surreal Christian morality. He offered a blueprint to trippers: Focus here,
look for that, relate to others this way. For new arrivals who believed
that drugs were mind expanding, his lectures hinted of the possibilities.

Fame came quickly, driven by an easy charisma and an ability to fix
charges with soul-boring blue-eyed stares. Gaskin explained what was
happening to both sides of the hip-straight divide. *Kaliflower*, the San
Francisco newsletter published by the anarchistic Diggers troupe, profiled Gaskin. *The New York Times* reported that Gaskin encouraged followers to take LSD so they could expand their consciousness and sharpen
the vibrations while staying "loose, groovy, high, happy, and compassionate, to manifest the kingdom here and now. . . ." Mainline Protestant
ministers arrived to take notes and plot youth outreach. By late 1969,
Monday Night Class attendance regularly topped one thousand.

The late 1960s and early 1970s were a time of doubt and introspec-
tion, a season of mistrust and apprehension. The Summer of Love was
over. Watts was in ashes. Nixon was in the White House. The Chicago
Seven were in jail. Body bags, stuffed with American soldiers and lifted
from army transport planes, flashed nightly across television screens. Bi-
ologists discovered that DDT poisoned our bodies. Journalists reported
that the cyclamate-sweetened Tabs might cause cancer.

American cities were flash points. In response to the assassination
of Martin Luther King Jr., protesters torched city blocks in Memphis
and Washington, D.C. Police shot and killed college students in Jackson, Mississippi, and Orangeburg, South Carolina. Environmental crises
mounted. Nuclear power plant cooling towers climbed skyward on construction scaffolding. Smog choked Los Angeles. The Cuyahoga River
caught fire in Cleveland.

In the woods, Gaskin aimed to retrench and rethink. He would grow his own food and weed. He had company. By the close of the 1970s, more than one million people lived in communes or collectives or as rural homesteaders. Their parents had ditched the farm for postwar corporate jobs and ranch homes on half-acre lots. Rural life looked more promising to this new generation. The hills were alive with hippies. And with new ideas. Gaskin's ideas eventually drove shifts in American attitudes about whole earth ecology, natural childbirth, and organic, vegetarian, and vegan diets.

For a disillusioned generation, staring down the successes and failures of public protest and political dissent, channeling new ideas was a survival tact. If hippies couldn't change things, then they could drop out, bug out, split. The countryside promised communion. Spaces were emptier. Land was cheaper. Rural California, Oregon, New Mexico, and New York beckoned. It was cheaper still in the woods of Arkansas, Tennessee, and West Virginia, where, if you tramped far enough up a hill or deep enough into a cove, respite from the sorry state of national affairs awaited.

The South was the ideal destination for Gaskin. A counterintuitive thinker with a subversive sense of humor, he liked to tell people he was starting a "mental nudist colony." Rural and mountainous south-central Tennessee was one more step removed from the urban and suburban South, which was already thought behind the times. Our "contemporary ancestors," who "unconsciously stepped aside from the great avenues of commerce and of thought"—that's how an *Atlantic Monthly* writer described the mountain people he met in 1899. Three generations later, when Gaskin and his followers moved south, they brought similar expectations.

For a band of hippies, determined to apprehend their roots and return to the land, the South appeared a place both raw and pure, a fountainhead of primal American culture. Hippies in search of honest American expression studied the South. Knowledge of the region served as a countercurrency. When a Rolling Stones song came on the radio, hippies heard the drawl and screech of Mississippi natives like Muddy Waters and Howlin' Wolf. When hippies dropped the needle on a Joan Baez album, they took pride in knowing "Butcher Boy" was borrowed from the hollers of Appalachia.

The young men and women who settled The Farm and other communes claimed something not quite tamed, something almost lawless. During the civil rights movement, that lawlessness struck fear in native blacks and newly arrived whites. The South of the 1950s and 1960s was a place to escape, a place desperately in need of change. Less than a decade later, the South had become a place to return to, a place to find solace amid the strife. To kids in their twenties, looking to practice a laissez-faire lifestyle, the South broadcast a queer appeal.

At a time when the rest of the nation was fast becoming cul-de-sac suburbs, thick with ranch houses and strip malls, the mountain South of mule-plowed farms, revenuer-fighting moonshiners, and make-your-own porch music beckoned. For the young men and women who settled The Farm, those stereotypes were naively inspirational.

Resettlement transformed largely rural states. During the 1970s, the population of West Virginia, a favorite destination of kids from Washington, D.C., and the Mid-Atlantic, spiked by more than 200,000 people. John Denver channeled the national appeal of the state's rural vistas and mountain mommas when he cut the 1971 hit "Take Me Home, Country Roads."

These were purposeful Southerners. Most were not born in Tennessee or Arkansas or West Virginia. Instead, they chose to live here. They claimed this place as their own. Between 1965 and 1970, more than three thousand country communes put counterculture ideals into practice in what became one of the largest urban to rural migrations in the nation's history.

Communes flourished at Tick Creek and Red Worms in the North

Carolina Piedmont. Twin Oaks in central Virginia helped pioneer the commercial production of tofu. At Doobie Planation in central Arkansas, organic farming was the focus. Some Arkansas groups applied gender politics to the hippie aesthetic. Upstate at Huckleberry Farm, and later at the purposefully ambiguous-sounding Ozark Women on Land and the Ozark Land Holders Association, lesbian farm women purchased plots of "Goddess earth" in an attempt to "buy her back from the patriarchy." Queer activists, like Black Power advocates before them, aimed to go their own way. Tennessee, with laws that recognized a religious organization as a group that ministered to a flock, was a hotbed. Short Mountain, a radical faerie commune in Cannon County, between Chattanooga and Nashville, claimed its land soon after Gaskin and his crew. A nearby collective, calling itself Door Ajar, farmed land near the town of Temperance Hall, Tennessee.

At about the same time Gaskin landed in Tennessee, Wendell Berry of neighboring Kentucky began preaching the gospel of small farms and local foods. Berry was a farmer who wrote and a writer who farmed. Fond of calling agribusiness promoters "pornographers of farming," he denounced capital-intensive agriculture as complicit in the "farmer-killing and land-killing economy." Like Gaskin, Berry was inspired by the Amish and their "uncanny instinct about limits, about the connection between the spirit and tools."

Berry took solace from the family farm, from the ancient rhythms of making a crop. But he wasn't a provincial. Early in his career during a creative writing fellowship at Stanford University, he studied alongside Ken Kesey, architect of the LSD-fueled bus ride that became a symbol of the psychedelic 1960s and an inspiration for Gaskin's caravan across the nation.

Encouraged by the American Academy of Religion, Gaskin had previously traveled to lecture at colleges and churches on a seven-thousand-mile, four-month, forty-two-state speaking tour, beginning in October 1970. Driving a retrofitted school bus that heralded "Out to Save the World," trailed by a cavalcade of twenty-plus brightly painted buses, bread trucks, and camper vans, he called the production the Astral Continental Congress. Fifty more vehicles and 150 more adults joined him along the way.

Midway through the trip, the community gelled. Traveling in buses, heated by woodstoves with jerry-rigged chimneys, the tribe gathered nightly in prayer circles to hold hands, trip, and smoke. Gaskin told them that marijuana was a sacrament. "We believe that if a vegetable and an animal want to get together and can be heavier together than either or one of them alone, it shouldn't be anybody else's business." Groupthink took hold. Instead of continuing to roam, the collective would buy a tract of farmland. During a prime-time television report on their travels, Walter Cronkite asked Gaskin how they would determine where to settle. The vibes will be right, Gaskin told him.

In Tennessee, the vibes were right. When the power brokers of Nashville learned that a band of hippies were descending, they didn't brace for attack like the editors of the Columbia, Missouri, newspaper who announced with a blaring headline, "THE MONKEYS ARE COMING." The city laid out the equivalent of a communal bedroll, reserving a campground on Percy Priest Lake near the construction site where the Opryland theme park would soon rise from pastureland.

During their weeklong encampment that March, hundreds of locals arrived nightly, some to ogle the longhairs, others to talk philosophy, smoke, and sing. In a music store on Lower Broadway, Nashville's driveway of the down and out, the vibes got better. A young woman who had read about them in the paper, and whose family owned acreage that was not being farmed, told Gaskin they could squat on their land for the winter. After returning to San Francisco for money and recalibration, Gaskin and his followers made a second eastern pilgrimage that winter.

A month later, 320 Gaskin followers stood blinking in the Tennessee sun, reckoning their new life. Some danced. Some dove naked into the woods. Others lit joints. In the weeks that followed, they pitched army surplus tents. They fixed plyboard lean-tos on buses. And they began gathering on Sundays for lessons led by Gaskin. "The Caravan was spiritual boot camp, and I like to think of our new commune as my ashram, my monastery," he told the collective, as swirls of pot smoke haloed his backlit head. "I am a spiritual teacher, a teacher of change, and this farm is my school of change. I am the roshi, the abbot, and if you live here, I will be your spiritual teacher. . . ."

What they attempted seemed new. These children of the Haight aimed to liberate themselves from contemporary ills. But the place they claimed came with a queer and confounding history. Just thirty miles south in Pulaski, six Confederate veterans had founded the Ku Klux Klan on Christmas Eve 1865. By the time Gaskin and his followers arrived, the city had distanced itself from the Klan activity of recent years. The current Klan were the night riders behind the murders of Goodman, Schwerner, and Chaney, the local Chamber of Commerce said. They were racists who exploited the name and the sustaining service of the original Klan, which was a mere fraternal organization.

Members of The Farm joined aesthetic and spiritual forebears in Tennessee. Since the 1940s, Amish farmers had worked the area, building a religious farming community that Gaskin and his followers recognized as a model. More recently, nearby Nashville had emerged as an organizing center during the civil rights movement, the place where John Lewis, Diane Nash, and James Bevel developed the policies and tactics that drove restaurant desegregation. But the surrounding countryside still looked intimidating to hippies who often arrived with scenes from the 1969 film *Easy Rider* unspooling in their heads.

Gaskin was determined to go mainstream quickly. He looked like a longhair. But he didn't play the part of the outsider. In conversation with locals, he quoted Jesus, swallowed his consonants, and went long on aphorisms. Making note of their tie-dyed clothes and back-to-the-land work ethic, the press began referring to Farmies as the "Technicolor Amish," while Gaskin encouraged followers to think of themselves as "voluntary peasants," focused on labor and thrift, duty and service. Soon, *The Wall Street Journal* would call The Farm the "General Motors of American communes."

To become a part of The Farm, supplicants turned in their money, their cars, their inheritances. When it came time to buy property, trust fund hippies signed over thousands. Artists sold their brushes. Jewelry makers sold their tools. Kids with nothing agreed to work the land as long and as hard as Gaskin asked them to. On The Farm, all adopted a vow of poverty lifted from the New Testament book of Acts, the same passage that inspired Fannie Lou Hamer: "All who believed were together and had all things in common; they would sell their possessions and goods and distribute their possessions to all, as any had need."

The Farm was vegan before the term entered popular usage. All sentient beings were valued. Abortion was forbidden. And so was birth control, until 1978. If you could look a being in its eyes, Farmies didn't eat that beast or products made from that beast, even honey. "It's good for everybody else, it's good for the individual for health, and it's good for the soul and the spirit not to be involved in killing," Gaskin explained in *The Farm Vegetarian Cookbook*. "I understand that vegetables are alive, but . . . I've been to pig stickings, and I've been to rice boilings, and rice boilings have better vibrations than pig stickings."

Embracing a traditional relationship to food and the land at a time when many Southerners had abandoned that facet of their lives, Farmies became more Southern than the Southerners they joined. While many of their peers applied for food stamps, Farmies raised their own crops. In an age when many young people rejected symbols of authority, from the military to the church to their parents, Farmies accepted Gaskin as their undisputed spiritual and community leader.

Before the decade was out, The Farm expanded. Plenty USA, a Farm-funded charity, began addressing hunger through direct aid. Satellite communities, including the New York Farm in Franklin and the Virginia Farm near Louisa, adopted Summertown principles.

C rescent Dragonwagon acted on her idealism to claim a perch in the mountains of Arkansas. Like Gaskin, who helped fund The Farm with sales from books he wrote about his search for meaning, Ellen Zolotow of New York City wrote a book that helped finance her flight. Published in 1972, when she was eighteen, *The Commune Cookbook* chronicled how to wrap chestnuts for rumaki and make a pineapple sauce for soyballs. By the time it was released, Zolotow had quit high school and moved to a commune near Ava, Missouri, across the state line from Arkansas. The idea was to claim a small corner of the world and render it as sane as possible. Remote and unspoiled by urban intrusion, the Ozarks were thought a safe haven.

At about the same time Zolotow decamped and changed her name to Crescent Dragonwagon, Sassafras, a feminist commune near Fayetteville, began attracting lesbian farmers. On the eve of her initial departure for the Ozarks, Dragonwagon sounded a lot like Stephen Gaskin standing before his charges at Sutro Park. She pledged her excitement for the experiment, her commitment to growing food, weaving clothes, and making art. "And we will be so close to our environment and know it so well that it too will be an extension of us, as each person shall be of every person."

R espect for the individual was part of the back-to-the-land vow. While many communards rejected their own parents, they saw value in the lives and the knowledge accrued by elder rural folk. Soon after Gaskin arrived in Tennessee, Homer Sanders, who ran a lumber mill by day and a whiskey still by night, rode into the encampment on a mule. Shotgun in hand, he had planned to drive the new arrivals out. But he was soon entranced by the smiling, bright-eyed young women in long dresses. He admired how the long-haired young men in overalls worked from sunup to sundown like the women did. Sanders even tried some of their drugs, sipping marijuana tea to help with migraines. When Sanders heard about psilocybin, he said, "Give me some of those mushrooms. I'm going to go home and tie my leg to a tree and try some."

Quiet conversations with Gaskin converted Sanders. When the long-hair made clear his knowledge of the Bible and his intent to live in peace and farm with vigor, Sanders took him at his word. At the post office, the bank, the feed and seed, Sanders spread the word that the kids were all right. A genius with his hands, Sanders was missing some of his teeth and part of his tongue. When he talked, people leaned in close to hear. Later that year, Sanders introduced Gaskin to a moonshiner who sold them a thousand-acre parcel known as Black Swan Ranch. Instead of being mere squatters on borrowed property, the Farmies were now landed.

Sanders taught Farmies how to grow and grind and boil sorghum. He put them to work at his wildcat lumber mill. A band of Farmies harvested oak trees from the woods and planed logs into boards. In exchange, Sanders gave them some lumber and lots of bark-covered slabs of sawn timber. Chopped into short logs, stuffed into woodstoves, those slabs were the fuel that warmed their houses.

There was precedent for this type of cooperation. Almost a century before, the Ruskin Cooperative Association made inroads when Julius Augustus Wayland, publisher of one of the most profitable and widely read socialist publications of the day, purchased one thousand acres of hill country near the town of Tennessee City in Dickson County, sixty miles north of Summertown. In the pages of *The Coming Nation*, Wayland argued for eight-hour workdays, equal pay for the sexes, and the abolition of child labor.

With the commune of Ruskin, Wayland and his followers aimed to put their socialist theories into daily practice. The commune was self-sufficient, growing its own sweet potatoes and greens, canning surpluses beneath the protective overhang of a cave canopy, serving meals in a communal dining hall. Like the Farmies who would follow three generations later, Ruskinites forbade alcohol. Money was no good. Health care was free to all. Profits from the magazine and the canning operation drove the building of a hotel, a theater, and more than thirty homes.

To build a community that would last, Farmies went native. In the spring of 1972, Gaskin and a Church of Christ pastor from Summertown began staging public debates in a hay barn, outfitted with oriental rugs and bleachers made of bales. Bearded young men in overalls took seats alongside buzz-cut churchmen in blazers and ties. One night, a Farmie stood and spoke: "It says in there that God preaches to all creatures, not just man, all creatures." The comment, a defense of The Farm's vegetarian diet, begged a response from a Church of Christ preacher who stood to ask why, if eating meat was wrong, did Jesus give the multitude fishes as well as loaves? After a slight pause, a dozen people offered the same answer, "Because they were hungry." In that moment, the two groups began to find common ground.

The Farm shared its message through media. To deliver information about its construction and agricultural work, The Farm paid local newspapers to print single-page "Farm Reports" in which Lewis County readers learned that promiscuity was not tolerated and pregnancy outside of wedlock was not allowed. "We believe in Jesus; we believe in Buddha," Gaskin wrote to answer questions about polytheism that dogged The Farm. "Some people don't think you can do that; we think you can."

Gaskin continued to stage classes, shaping the lives of his members in a way some compared to the Shakers, who had once farmed opium in nearby Kentucky. Detractors, who associated communal living with the murderous rampage of Charles Manson, compared The Farm to a cult. Gaskin confronted those suspicions. "What we've done in Tennessee has shown them that our minds ain't blown," he wrote. "We're okay. We can still figure out a tractor. We keep the toilet paper dry most of the time. We're like a heart transplant, and we ain't been rejected."

Local people trusted Farm members, Gaskin said, because Farmies told the truth and because their checks to the feed and seed store didn't bounce. If rain threatened and a neighbor farmer needed to get in his hay, men from The Farm came running. For construction projects, The Farm loaned out laborers. They laid the bricks for a holiness church. Ina May Gaskin, wife of Stephen Gaskin, began a midwife practice that would teach generations of American women the virtues of natural childbirth.

Five years into this rural experiment, The Farm emerged as a kind of laboratory for the American counterculture, where hippie ideals and capitalist ingenuity cross-pollinated. Instead of rebelling against prevailing American ideals, Gaskin and his followers made good on them. Working with efficiency, industry, and thrift, they became more American than the Americans they left behind.

Farmies made for good copy and great television. *National Geographic* published a photo spread. *Mother Earth News* did, too. *60 Minutes* rolled in with hulking video cameras. Turned on and tuned in to Gaskin's message, more than one hundred new people settled at The Farm each year. By the late 1970s, the population was well over one thousand. And more than ten thousand visitors passed through the gate each year. Life on The Farm got easier. Tents became "hents," part tent, part house with windows installed to let the sun shine in. Through the Beatnik Bell phone system, a kind of party line meets intercom, residents learned when the Soy Dairy would have milk to distribute and when the Store would receive the next shipment of matches and toilet paper.

An entrepreneurial spirit flourished. Residents of The Farm developed a Doppler fetal pulse indicator to check the health of unborn children, a radiation detector that grew popular after the Three Mile Island accident, and space heaters powered by passive solar technology. Farmies installed the landscaping at Opryland, where they had camped years before, and helped build a Kmart. Farm businesses made tie-dyed clothing. A leader in alternative energy, The Farm built solar homes, constructed a solar schoolhouse out of reclaimed and recycled materials, and built a walk-in solar food dehydrator.

While other communes like Drop City in Colorado slipped into chaos by the 1970s, Gaskin kept tight reins on The Farm. For the first decade, he brooked no dissent. When you joined The Farm you copped to him. To be a part of the community, residents acknowledged him as their spiritual teacher. Conversations with Gaskin began with a soulful stare and ended with a hug. The guidelines were stringent. No guns. No synthetic psychedelics. Bras were unnatural. Expressions of anger were not tolerated. Gaskin delivered weekly sermons, presided over burials, and performed marriages. If two people had sex, Gaskin considered them engaged. If the woman got pregnant, Gaskin married them. Not all relations were conventional. Unions of two couples, called four marriages, were common. For a time, Gaskin was in a marriage of six.

Life relied on conventions and routines. Men blew conch shells to announce communal meals. Women cooked soybeans for dinner, which they folded into corn tortillas and sprinkled with soy cheese. Prepared communally in a shack that moonshiners had once used for sugar storage, meals were served in a dining tent next door. Mornings began with what the hippies called Farmola or Mellowmeal, hot cereals of cracked wheat, cracked rye, cornmeal, soy flour, and more, sweetened with sorghum. In the evening, Farmies ate bean burgers and nut loaves. Instead of oven-frying chicken, they oven-fried gluten. Most families kept a shaker of nutritional yeast on the table, which they applied like salt.

The Farm maintained a two-way radio, which Farmies used to keep in touch with their touring rock bands, including the Nuclear Regulatory Commission. They encouraged people outside The Farm to radio them for advice on how to talk to their local sheriff or handle the water inspector: "Be in communication. We can all be in cahoots all over the country." Gaskin didn't aim to topple the government. To the greater world, he proposed alternatives. "The thing you do about a decadent empire is you don't try to tear it down, you'll get caught underneath it," he explained in *Hey Beatnik!*, a how-to manual and hippie high school yearbook published in 1974. "Just stand back and learn how to take care of yourself. Learn how to take care of some other people. Don't take over the government, take over the government's function." By 1975, co-ops across America sold that book, and hitchhikers carried dog-eared copies in their duffels.

At times, The Farm seemed like a summer camp. Before they became the memes of design catalogs, Farmies made lamps out of Mason jars and fueled them with kerosene. Farmies salvaged a junked water tower and rigged it up. The bakery turned out hot whatnot bread six days a week. On hikes, they captured rattlesnakes, which they refused to kill and turned over to forest rangers.

N ot all went well. During a bitterly cold second winter, tucked into army surplus tents and crammed in buses and vans, Farmies subsisted on wheat berries and not much else. The next spring, after eating watercress that grew downstream from an outhouse, dozens came down with hepatitis. Early into the experiment, after locating a marijuana patch on the property, the county sheriff arrested Gaskin and three others on drug charges. The tip came from a local who said he saw naked commune members playing flutes in the style of Pan.

While the outside world focused interest on sex and drugs, The Farm focused on growing crops to feed its own. Work began with a pair of Belgian mares and a plow. Gaskin and his crews soon added tractors to the mix, working toward a balance between ideals and realities to "have a stoned connection with the dirt and the plant force and at the same time have a sane enough use of the technology that we can feed ourselves."

Gangs of young workers raised soybeans and corn, sweet potatoes and watermelons. When workers on The Farm recognized a market for sweet potato slips, they planted acres. They grew snap beans and snow peas because they didn't need shelling. They grew tomatoes by the ton as a cash crop. They contracted out labor to a pimento farmer, who sold to a packer, who sold jars to home makers of pimento cheese. They called their work a yoga and thought of hoeing as meditation.

The second year in Tennessee, Farmies planted 140 acres of sorghum, which they harvested by hand. Work was tougher than expected, but they approached the project with a romantic fervor, swapping stories of how sorghum making had been a Southern tradition for generations, how communities used to join together for a collective harvest, how mules used to power the mills, and how a hardwood fire was ideal for boiling sorghum juice down into syrup. The Farm went with propane. And they soon built a gravity-fed mill, using a government brochure schematic.

Farmies harvested cane and cooked syrup for their neighbors. And they split the profits. By year three they went commercial, selling bottles of "Old Beatnik Pure Lewis County Sorghum," affixed with a label that showed a couple dozen bright-faced and long-haired hippies in the midst of a harvest. An advertisement read, "In the South, it's home, country, mother, apple pie, God, and sorghum." Locals arrived to ogle their new neighbors and buy sweetener. Soon, health food stores across the South and across the nation stocked their syrup as well as their books.

From soy ice cream to tempeh, The Farm developed or popularized many of the foods that fueled the American counterculture. Under the umbrella of Farm Foods, they managed the Good Tasting Nutritional Yeast company and a tempeh spore business. Adopting techniques pioneered in Indonesia, Farmies grew spores on sterilized pieces of sweet potatoes. Inoculated in test tubes, the potatoes lent a sweetness to tempeh made from their spores.

Soybeans proved the great sustainer. Early in his experiments with drugs, Gaskin had a psychedelic vision of soybeans in which he saw them as the vegetable that would feed hungry people in the decades ahead. When Gaskin settled his tribe in Tennessee, they planted soybeans. Within a few years, they cultivated 150 acres. By 1972, The Farm produced soy milk for babies and children. *Yay Soybeans!*, a free recipe booklet, showed how to roast whole soybeans into soy nuts and soy coffee, grind soybeans into flour, stuff soysage, and toast soyola.

There was regional precedent for this innovation as well. Madison College, a Seventh-Day Adventist school, just north of Nashville, had begun producing soy foods under the label Madison Foods by 1918. Soy Bean Meat came first. Four years later, they were canning soybeans and producing two other meat substitutes, Nut Meat and Savory Meat. Like The Farm, they aimed to share their meatless diet with others, opening a Vegetarian Cafeteria and Treatment Room in Nashville.

At the Soy Dairy on The Farm, workers pulverized beans with an electric coffee grinder and cooked them over a gas burner. Using a top-loading washing machine, they extracted soy milk. Cooked milk and bean pulp flowed to a lower level where the milk was bottled for drinking or strained and rendered into tofu.

After adopting more modern technology, The Farm developed one of the first commercial soy ice creams, Ice Bean. By the early 1980s, Farm Foods was taking out full-page ads in *Vegetarian Times* to sell peanut butter–flavored soy ice cream sandwiched between two carob-coated honey wafers.

The back-to-the-land movement inspired a new educational movement, which began in the mountains of north Georgia in the late 1960s and spread through the nation, inspiring more than two hundred projects in the United States and abroad. Eliot Wigginton and his eighth-grade English students at the Rabun Gap–Nacoochee School in north Georgia practiced what came to be called cultural journalism, and published their interviews in *Foxfire*, named after the blue green glow of lichen that grows in the damp forest understory. That school journal eventually inspired a Broadway play and a made-for-TV movie.

Beginning in 1966, students interviewed their elders and their parents. The first issue, published the next year, included an interview with the local sheriff, who told of how he captured the bandits after a bank robbery. By 1970, the students hit on the formula that would make the program famous, when they interviewed Arie Carpenter, who lived high on a ridge in nearby Macon County, North Carolina.

A wiry woman with a mischievous glint, Carpenter insisted that Wigginton help prize the eyes from a severed hog head as she prepared souse meat. During her interview, she talked about picking blackberries and strawberries and about raising Irish potatoes, which most Americans now know as white potatoes. Carpenter was a font of food recollections. "You ever eat any corn pones that was raised?" she asked the interviewer, who transcribed her reverie phonetically. "It's made out a'cornmeal. Now it's another hard job, and I love it better'n a cat loves sweet milk, I sure do."

Doubleday published that interview in 1972 in the first *Foxfire* book. First-month sales topped 100,000 copies as hippies, back-to-the-landers, and voyeuristic middle-class folk read about how to shoe horses, plant crops by the signs, stone-grind corn, and scald bristles from hogs. Over the next decade, Doubleday sold more than two million copies.

Similar projects sprang up as close as Atlanta, where a group of young people collected oral histories of the Appalachian women who lived in a neighborhood called Cabbagetown. Originally built as company housing for the Fulton Bag and Cotton Mills, and staffed by immigrants from Appalachia, the area had begun a long slide toward slum when the mill was sold in 1957.

Two decades later, when the students began to record oral histories, they got to know the women of Cabbagetown by collecting recipes for crackling bread, butterbean dumplings, and black-eyed pea sausage. The resulting 1976 book, *Cabbagetown Families, Cabbagetown Food*, linked Appalachia past and present.

The *Foxfire* and Cabbagetown projects tapped the same American hunger for rural ways and farm means that Stephen Gaskin recognized. *Saturday Review* called *Foxfire* a "fine example of Emersonian self-reliance and compassionate anthropology that would have charmed James Agee and Oscar Lewis." By the time Jessica Tandy starred in a made-for-television movie of the same name, a generation of Americans had gained a library of manuals for boiling soap from lard and boiling hominy from corn. And a generation of mountain children had discovered a range of honest ways to connect with their parents and grandparents and neighbors.

After the mid-1970s, the growth of new farm communes slowed. Divisions among idealists were rancorous. Life in a tent or a hent seemed like an adventure at the six-month mark. At the three-year mark, the adventure was often over. Summers were mosquito plagued. During the winter, northerly winds ripped tents from poles. Communes imploded, as member rolls bloated and income streams flattened. But The Farm endured.

Over the following decades, mainstream America adopted the innovations that The Farm introduced to the hippie community. Amid the oil crises of the 1970s, solar energy proved an atractive alternative to fossil fuels. Soy ice cream became a grocery store staple. Sandwiches of wheat bread, sprouts, and tempeh became deli counter standards. And burritos stuffed with rice and beans, it turned out, tasted nearly as good as burritos stuffed with beef and cheddar.

At a time when farming was vogue among dropout idealists, the hippies who worked The Farm put agrarian principles in practice. Two generations before, the twelve Southerners who signed the manifesto *I'll Take My Stand* had made a comparable case when they argued that the "culture of the soil is the best and most sensitive of vocations," and should "enlist the maximum number of workers."

On The Farm, new-generation agriculturalists made good on the promises of old agricultural ideals. These purposeful Southerners proved that the region so many had recently rejected, the South that so many recognized for poverty and racism, was a place with a future as well as a past.

By adapting the knowledge of neighbors like Homer Sanders, Gaskin and his followers set a stage for the next phase in the region's history, in which Southern entrepreneurs built fast-food businesses based on traditional dishes like fried chicken and biscuits and sold those newly packaged foods to suburban folk who were grasping for claims to the American mainstream as well as tastes of the farms they had left behind.

Colonel Sanders and Kentucky Fried Chicken
emerged in the 1970s as American icons.

· 6 ·

Faster Food

D ressed in a double-breasted white suit and a black bolo tie, tucked
in an almond leather high back, Harland Sanders welcomed a
guest to his walnut-paneled office at the white-columned Kentucky Fried Chicken headquarters in suburban Louisville. When the visitor pulled out an Egg McMuffin as part of a taste test, Sanders dispatched
small talk before lifting the top from the sandwich like a cavalryman in-
specting an unexploded grenade. "The only way I like eggs is to take two
of 'em, break 'em in a dish, and then take half an eggshell of cold water
and add it to the eggs," he said. "Then beat it up with 'em. No milk ner
cream—and your eggs will be tender, fluffy, tasty. . . . An old darky
cook in Georgetown, Kentucky, learnt me that years ago." Sanders almost smiled at the recollection. "Never tasted eggs like that in my life."

As the visitor set down a breakfast of scrambled eggs, sausage patties, and hash browns, purchased from a nearby McDonald's, the Colonel reached inside his coat, pulled out a gold-colored spoon, and poked
at the scrambled eggs. "Rubbery," he said. "Over-cooked. There's the
potatuh. Instead of fryin' it, why, they've put paprika on it to give it the

color. And that sausage there is just a piece of hamburger." When the Colonel critiqued a Filet-O-Fish, he pointed at the bun with his extended middle finger, making a sign that left no doubt of his impression. A young man who assisted Sanders with media relations handed the visitor a pamphlet of the "Colonel's Other Recipes." Sanders grumbled and pointed to a photograph of a platter of sauce-covered chicken. The legend read, "This authentic recipe was served by the Colonel at the Sanders' neighborhood barn dances years ago." The Colonel shot the young man a piss-and-vinegar glance of rebuke. "That barbecued chicken," Sanders said. "That's a bunch of shit."

After Sanders sold his company and his secret recipe of herbs and spices in 1964, businessmen John Y. Brown and Jack Massey made plans to franchise and expand. In his paid role as their living mascot, Sanders made sales visits to far-flung outposts. Flush with cash and somewhat famous after appearing on the TV show *What's My Line?*, Sanders often hit his mark, generating press and boosting sales from Atlanta to Salt Lake City. Just as often, he proved a murderous critic, who couldn't stomach that the crust on the birds his successors now sold by the bucket tasted like a "damn fried doughball put on top of some chicken."

Asked about the company's new products, Sanders said, "They really gag me, that's what I think of them." He referred to the corporate version of his gravy, prepared for a succession of corporate owners including liquor conglomerate Heublein, as wallpaper paste and sludge. After a particularly bad spoonful, he asked a franchisee, "How do you serve this God-damned slop? With a straw?" It was as if Sanders recognized his own role in subverting the traditional food on which he built his reputation and fortune.

Ray Kroc and the McDonald brothers invented American fast food. Set in Illinois and California, that narrative is useful and concise but it's incomplete. Harland Sanders and the Southern men and women inspired by him fueled the growth of fast-food franchises and determined the contents of fast-food menus. At a time when fast food was new,

Sanders was a fitful ambassador of the possibilities. Although he drove around Louisville in a two-tone silver Rolls-Royce with his smiling face embossed on the driver-side door, he didn't appear happy.

Sanders recognized that the changes he introduced, beginning with pressure-fried chicken, resulted in that slop. Caught between the old and the new, like the South from which many fast-food businesses sprang, Sanders chafed and fretted. He bitched and moaned. Sanders had made a deal with the devil, and, by the 1970s, he was beginning to wonder if the terms on which he sold his soul were as favorable as they first seemed. His dilemma was Southern, it was American, and it was modern.

B efore the 1970s were over, America began to complain, too. Health studies revealed the paucity of nutrients and excess of calories in the average fast-food meal. Calvin Trillin and other cultural spelunkers began to celebrate small-town restaurants like crawfish shacks and bemoan their replacement by anywhere fried fish chains. Skillet fried, not pressure fried, became the chicken grail. Wood-fired barbecue, cooked slowly in a traditional manner, drew praise instead of gas-fired barbecue, cooked quickly and efficiently.

From the mid-1960s through the mid-1970s, however, franchise food was alluring. Electric cookers, marketed as Bar-B-Q Kings and Bar-B-Q Slaves, offered franchises push-button solutions to stoking fires and tending pits. For entrepreneurs, the faster-cheaper-better mantra was aspirational. And no business better represented American aspiration than Kentucky Fried Chicken.

Back when he was a one-man show, Sanders sold the future by romanticizing the past. To hustle that newfangled pressure-fried chicken he wrapped himself and his products in an Old South mantle. His bleached white goatee signaled plantation rigueur. His mouth-full-of-gravel accent bespoke oak-shaded authenticity. That white jacket conjured mint julep–sodden afternoons on the veranda. His title was an honorific, bestowed by the governor of Kentucky. It referenced the sort of Confederate hero worshipping that many white Southerners still clung to more than one hundred years after the Civil War ended.

Early in his career, Sanders cut deals with restaurateurs who paid a royalty of five cents per bird for the right to add the Colonel's chicken to their menu. To show his appreciation and drive sales, the Colonel escorted his wife, Claudia, to parties in their towns. She wore a hoopskirt and curtsied on cue. He squired. If he felt spry, Sanders also did what he called "colonelizing": "I'd take off my apron, dust the flour off my pants, put on my vest, long-tailed coat, and gold watch chain, and go out into the dining room and talk to the guests."

After they bought his name and face, Jack Massey and John Y. Brown continued to foster the cult of Harland Sanders. To telegraph their devotion to the founder and the brand, Massey and Brown wore string ties at work and posed for company photographs with their bolos cinched tight around their necks. That devotion paid off. Kentucky Fried Chicken went public in 1966. By the end of 1967, the company had opened more than three hundred franchises. By the close of 1968, six hundred more sold striped buckets of chicken, blazoned with the Colonel's smiling face.

To mark the company debut on the New York Stock Exchange big board in 1969, Sanders dressed in his best whites, handing drumsticks to floor traders and posing for the press. Kentucky Fried Chicken's red-striped rectangular buildings were soon more plentiful than the McDonald's arches. Thanks to an advertising campaign that cost the company more than $9 million in 1968, the slogan "Finger-lickin' good" became a pop culture phenomenon. Musician Lonnie Smith used that title for an album of songs, recorded in a style he called "soul organ." When Sanders wrote an autobiography, he called it *Life as I Have Known It Has Been Finger Lickin' Good*.

By 1970, Kentucky Fried Chicken opened franchises in Mexico. To commemorate the debut, the company commissioned a Herb Alpert–inspired jazz album, *Colonel Sanders' Tijuana Picnic*, fronted by a picture of a white-suited Sanders with a bucket of chicken in his lap and silver-handled black cane in his hand.

A s Southerners moved from farms to small towns and eventually cities, they adapted traditional dishes that were born of frugality, using new designs, packaging, and distribution. Innovations came early. Ham sandwiches on white bread, wrapped in wax paper, were quick-serve country store standards, sold over the counter in Virginia, Kentucky, and Tennessee by the 1940s. A generation later, Lumbee Indians in North Carolina sold collard sandwiches of hoecakes stacked with greens to textile plant employees.

Made with low-cost processed cheese and pimiento peppers, which thrived in the summer heat of the South, pimento cheese became the default sandwich spread for working-class folk in the Carolinas before fast-food chains opened. Entrepreneurs sold sandwiches of white bread and cheese spread from dope carts wheeled through fabric mills. A generation later, textile mill commissaries bought fresh sandwiches from Duke's Sandwiches of Greenville, South Carolina, and quart tubs of pimento cheese from Star Food Products of Burlington, North Carolina.

Along with the corrupt society that had gunned down its leaders, doubled down on the war in Vietnam, and left the poor to starve in Appalachia, counterculture leaders rejected sliced and bagged white bread, frozen peas, plastic cheese, white sugar, and the buckets of fried chicken that American consumers adopted in the post–World War II years. Working-class and middle-class Southerners, on the other hand, embraced cheap convenience foods and fast foods in the 1970s as if they were long-denied birthrights. Often too poor to buy big-ticket American consumer products, they bought low-cost buckets of fried chicken for Saturday church socials and two-piece boxes for Tuesday lunches.

Southerners with lower incomes were ideal fast-food customers. A burger, a sleeve of fries, and a shake promised a sugar rush, a full stomach, and temporary middle-class status. Fried chicken promised all of that plus a tether to their rural past, when yardbirds pecked for grain and the first step in frying chicken for dinner was wringing a bird's neck before breakfast. As factory jobs expanded and farm jobs shrank, Southerners adopted restaurants that served passable versions of the foods that Southern women, liberated from tending skillets of hot oil, could buy for their families on the drive home from work.

Entrepreneurs in the South made fast food their own. Long John Silver's, the fried fish chain, began far from the ocean in Lexington, Kentucky. Captain D's sold its first plank of fish and chips in suburban Nashville. A generation before, the Pig Stand chain, founded in 1920s Dallas, popularized drive-in service across the nation. Its model may have served as an inspiration for McDonald's, which included barbecue pork and beef sandwiches on early menus.

Just as religious beliefs affected Southern social patterns, they informed business practices. At Chick-fil-A, founded in suburban Atlanta, Christianity set the tone. While other fast-food chains operated seven days a week, Baptist founder S. Truett Cathy declared that Sundays were for religious worship and family. As downtown shopping districts began to atrophy, Cathy opened counter service Chick-fil-A restaurants in suburban malls. Customers who arrived on Sundays for fried chicken sandwiches and lemonades came upon shuttered fronts and freestanding signs that suggested they spend the afternoon in church or at home with family.

W hen Jerry Clower, the fertilizer salesman turned comedian, stepped to the stage in 1973, he wore a leisure suit, white shoes, and a look of playful contempt. After praising his mother's cathead biscuits, which she had made from scratch by cutting lard into flour in a big wooden bowl, he let loose: "There are some fancy women in Yazoo City, Mississippi, what wop them biscuit across the counter. They go to the supermarket, back to the dairy case, and buy these here little old cardboard tubes or sleeves full of biscuits. And the instructions say you are to WOP them on the counter. Every morning about seven-fifteen down there on Swayze Street it sounds like a young war, WOP, WOP, WOP, WOP, WOP, WOP. Them womens cooking them biscuit. I want to get the news out, I do not eat them kind of biscuit."

Clower's young war pitted modernity against housewifery. Tipping his hat to the NAACP, and anticipating the Society for the Revival and Preservation of Southern Food that Edna Lewis and Scott Peacock would found in Atlanta two decades later, Clower announced the National Association for the Society of Hand Squashed Biscuits. He suggested that canned biscuits were new sorts of foods, subversions of tradition, backed by Northern capital and sold by outlander marketing schemes. Canned biscuits were a horror visited upon the South, Clower said, a development that was not an improvement but a degradation. The audience roared approval.

Clower got the humor right. Tapping a vein of chauvinism exposed by the departure of women from home kitchens for service jobs, he sounded the grievances of men who believed the needs of their families were being neglected. But the North versus South frame didn't hold. Canned biscuits and rolls had been developed by Southern companies that recognized there was money to be made selling traditional culture back to a rapidly changing region. Instead of suffering through the industrialization of American food culture, Southerners helped lead the revolution. Along the way, Southerners aimed to keep up appearances. That's what canned biscuits promised. Convenience foods allowed consumers to serve foods that reflected the region's past but could be produced at low cost with new efficiency.

Biscuits went industrial early. Lively Willoughby of Louisville, Kentucky, began selling biscuit dough via bicycle delivery in 1929. By 1931, working with the Ballard and Ballard firm, he developed a pressurized foil sleeve for storing par-baked quick breads. Frozen rounds of biscuit dough, known in the industry as pucks, were on the market by the 1940s. Even when ready-made biscuits were assembly line stamped outside the South, Southern caricatures sold them. Morton Frozen Foods dominated grocery freezer cases by the 1950s, selling bags of Old Kentucky Recipe biscuits, printed with a drawing of a silver-haired, string tie–wearing white plantation boss who struck a pose similar to the one Harland Sanders made famous. The aproned black woman who presumably baked the biscuits was nowhere to be seen.

As convenience foods became everyday indulgences, another round of fast-food restaurants followed. Inspired by a scouting trip to the first North Carolina location of McDonald's in Greensboro, Wilber Hardee opened a walk-up burger business in Greenville across from East Carolina University in 1960, selling charcoal-broiled hamburgers, fries, and apple pies from a sleek, tile-blanketed restaurant. Success came quickly. By 1963 the company sold stock to the public. Franchises opened across the region. Before McDonald's was a small-town constant, before Florida-born Burger King arrived, Hardee's was often the first fast-food restaurant to open in smaller markets.

Until Harland Sanders began traveling the country in a Cadillac, with a pressure fryer he called Bessie in the trunk, Southerners believed that traditional foods were not adaptable to modern imperatives. Fried chicken was a symbol of hearth and home, not fry baskets and drive-throughs. A cast iron skillet was elemental. Calvin Trillin, who sussed out great foods as a journalist on small-town assignments, channeled that belief when he wrote that a "fried chicken cook with a deep fryer is a sculptor working with mittens." Hardee's pioneered the market for breakfast biscuits, served at a drive-through. Before Hardee's, biscuits were the burger antithesis, the product of women like Jerry Clower's mother, who learned to bake catheads on wood-fired stoves, not grill cooks who wore grease-stained aprons, sported paper skiffs, and absentmindedly flipped patties.

In the early 1970s, Hardee's franchisees Jack Fulk and Mayo Boddie of North Carolina began baking biscuits from scratch and selling them to morning commuters. What began as a way to get more operating hours out of businesses that had previously been idle before lunch evolved into a staple of the industry. If the McDonald's Egg McMuffin was an American food without a regional identity, the Hardee's biscuit was a regional food with national aspirations. The trick was this: Hardee's made scratch biscuits. No canned biscuits, no frozen biscuits, no conceits. The buying public was skeptical. So Boddie hauled a stainless steel table to the front of the kitchen where an aproned woman rolled and cut dough while onlookers watched, creating a postmodern theater for a traditional craft.

By 1977, Fulk and partner Richard Thomas opened their own chain, Bojangles' Famous Chicken 'n Biscuits. As Hardee's and Bojangles' expanded, a generation of Southerners began detouring through drive-throughs on the way to school and work for biscuits that were rooted in a romantic vision of an American past. Biscuitville, a smaller chain based in Greensboro, North Carolina, exploited the gap between public perception and quality, touting its biscuits as both the perfect fast food and the antithesis of fast food. The first camp held that a sausage biscuit is nothing more than an early-morning, grab-and-go burger in a flour sack dress. The latter claimed that a truly great biscuit depended on the learned touch of the individual baker. With fast-food biscuits, both were true.

In 1978, Boddie launched a media campaign, designed to play up the grandmotherly roots of the newest industrial food, in which a woman with a thin and reedy voice told radio listeners, "You know I'll never forget the morning my grandchildren asked me to take them to Hardee's for breakfast. 'What's the matter,' I said, 'don't you like Grandma's homemade biscuits anymore?' Little Tom looks at me real cute and says, 'We like the biscuits at Hardee's better.'"

As Hardee's and its inheritors spread across the region, the idea of what a biscuit should look and taste like changed. Low-crowned biscuits, the kind often made at home, began to fall out of favor. By the time I became a Hardee's regular in the late 1970s, high-crowned fast-food biscuits, jacked up with shortening and stuffed with what the company called country fried steak (but which looked like a battered and fried burger), were the standard by which I judged morning commute meals.

As Southerners deconstructed, industrially reconstructed, and rolled out biscuits across the region, entrepreneurs saw possibilities in other vernacular foods. When Don and Dolores Dissman opened Schlotzsky's sandwich shop in Austin, Texas, they built their business around a variation on the muffuletta, a sandwich of cold cuts and cheese and olive salad, piled on a round seeded loaf that bakers in Sicily called a muffaletta. By 1977, that first location spawned a chain. Schlotzsky's was a made-up name, coined to sell sandwiches, but the sandwich it was based on was real, and it came with a compelling backstory.

The Lavoi family of New Orleans claimed to have begun stacking sandwiches of mortadella, salami, provolone, and giardiniera by 1901, wrapping these muffalettas in pages ripped from the *Picayune* newspaper, and selling the rounds from a wooden pushcart in the French Quarter at the corner of Royal and Dumaine. Around the same time, Sicilian immigrant Salvatore Lupo, owner of Central Grocery on Decatur Street, probably began selling a similar sandwich, stacked on a round seeded loaf, wrapped in butcher paper, to Sicilian immigrants who worked the port, unloading banana boats from Central America.

Wrapped in butcher paper or newspaper, born of the Lavois or the Lupos or another Italian merchant family, muffalettas became icons of Italian American commerce. By around 1927, proprietors of Fertitta's Delicatessen in Shreveport, Louisiana, began making an olive salad–

garnished sandwich they called the Muffy, stacked with bologna and ham instead of salami and mortadella. Though the Fertittas sometimes claimed that Schlotzsky's borrowed their formula, the Dissmans said Central Grocery was their inspiration. So did Joe Tortorice, who founded Jason's Deli in 1976 in Beaumont, Texas, and sold his own variation.

Unlike shrimp or oyster po-boys, which required access to cheap Gulf seafood, cooks could build muffulettas on ingredients easily sourced far from the point of origin. By the 1970s, as entrepreneurs shifted from single-location family businesses to multiple-location franchises, restaurateurs adapted folk foods that were previously thought too odd, too singular, for sale to Middle America. Except for the hamburgers stuffed with deep-fried pineapple slices that country singer Conway Twitty hawked in the late 1960s, the most unlikely food to go mainstream in that era was the Schlotzsky. In the age of Orville Redenbacher's popcorn television commercials, the odd name was part of the appeal. If it sounded that queer, it had to be good. Not everyone thought the word had resonance. Early market research showed that customers were more likely to associate the name with a Polish plumbing supply house.

By 1981, one hundred stores across the South and beyond sold the Schlotzsky's variation, made with lunch meat, stacked on house-baked sourdough rounds, smeared with marinated black olives and yellow mustard. As the chain grew, Schlotzsky's aired television advertisements that featured Austin musicians. New Orleans–inspired sandwiches, it turned out, could be sold to a backbeat of Texas swing. And Southern culinary culture isolates like muffulettas were as salable to the masses as music.

Throughout the 1970s, when a spate of Southern companies studied their business plans and followed their lead, the restaurant to copycat was Kentucky Fried Chicken. Eddy Arnold, the singing Tennessee plowboy, lent his name to a fried chicken café. Little Jimmy Dickens, who recorded "Take an Old Cold Tater (And Wait)," opened a restaurant. Maryland Fried Chicken, Ozark Fried Chicken, and Cock-A-Doodle of America followed. To document the phenomenon, Homer and Jethro cut "There Ain't a Chicken Safe in Tennessee." And Billy Edd Wheeler recorded "Fried Chicken and a Country Tune." Over a banjo backbeat he sang: "They started a bunch of corporations / Everybody got into speculation / Chicken stock was so alarming / Nearly made Dow Jones go back to farming."

Owing to the success of Colonel Sanders, fried chicken was the entrepreneurial grail. Al Copeland, born in the working-class New Orleans suburb of Arabi, was a next-generation Harland Sanders. When he was a boy, his family lived in a public housing project, relying on welfare. Copeland never forgot being poor: "I know what it is, and I don't want it." Two years after he dropped out of high school, he ran a Tastee Donuts franchise. While another restaurant down the road packed in the customers, Copeland struggled. "Here I was in a donut shop, breaking my butt, and Kentucky Fried Chicken came in at 11, closed at 8, and was doing four times the business," he explained. "I said if I can come up with a better-tasting fried chicken, I can beat these guys."

Copeland opened his first takeaway, Chicken on the Run, in 1971, advertising service "so fast you get your chicken before you get your change." It failed quickly. He reopened with spicy fried chicken and a new name, Popeyes. Though early advertisements featured a Popeye cartoon character, Copeland told reporters that the Popeye Doyle character in the movie The French Connection inspired the name. Copeland didn't use an apostrophe, he said, because he couldn't afford one.

Six years after he began selling franchises in 1977, he founded Copeland's of New Orleans, a casual dining chain that expanded as far as Maryland. Specialties included the Crash and Burn cocktail, a tip of the hat to his love of racing speedboats and Lamborghinis and his habit of taking spectacular chances. As the chain expanded, Copeland proved

a genius marketer who understood the value of celebrating home
state talent. Popeyes booked Dr. John to sing "Love that chicken from
Popeyes" and followed with Fats Domino and Jerry Lee Lewis.

Copeland sold Louisiana as much as he sold fried chicken. Specifically, he sold Cajun Louisiana, even though he was from suburban New
Orleans, known for Creole cuisine. Like many who merchandized Creole and Cajun culture when America couldn't distinguish between the
two, Copeland varied messages to suit the market. He sold Bourbon
Street in a 1978 campaign that promoted "chicken that's as tempting as
the French Quarter itself." At other times he sold the cooking of his in-
laws, the LeComptes. "They cooked like you couldn't believe," he said.
"Crawfish etouffée. Smothered chicken. Broiled crawfish. Spicy fried
chicken." Along with traditional sides like coleslaw and baked beans,
Copeland added dirty rice, flavored, as an honest Cajun might, with
chicken gizzards.

Like Sanders, he brought his outsized personality home with him.
Each Christmas season, his light displays, often topping a million bulbs,
drew crowds. So did his weddings. For his fourth trip down the aisle,
Copeland transformed his mansion into a fairy-tale castle, haloed by a
snow machine, decked in ten thousand white roses, with four Christmas
trees spinning upside down. The local newspaper called him "Louisiana's homegrown Liberace."

The success of Kentucky Fried Chicken inspired the nation. Rumors
spread through Nashville and Louisville of employees who became
overnight millionaires when their stock split. (By 1970, Sanders's personal secretary was worth more than $3 million.) Wealth created during
those early years fueled the broader fast-food industry. Ray Danner, who
opened Captain D's, was an early Louisville franchisee. Dave Thomas,
who became a millionaire when Kentucky Fried Chicken bought back
his high-performing franchises, founded Wendy's.

If Kentucky Fried Chicken was the gold standard, Minnie Pearl's was RC Cola to their Coke, an also-ran business that aimed to sell "How-dee-licious Chicken and Grand Ole Extries You'll Go For." The Minnie Pearl's chain promised to deliver rural tastes to urban customers. Looking to the growth of the chain, Sarah Cannon, the persona behind Pearl, promised, "I will still be saying 'Howdy!' to all my friends and neighbors." "It's going to be real good country fried chicken. Not a city chicken in the lot." A daughter of wealth, Cannon played up the conceits she honed while performing at the Grand Ole Opry and later on the television show *Hee Haw*.

Restaurant designs for Minnie Pearl's were based loosely on the colors of Cannon's signature hat, crowned with plastic flowers and dangling a buck-ninety-five price tag. Early sales of franchise licenses exceeded sales of fried chicken. By 1968, John Jay Hooker, the Nashville businessman who brought the company to market, had sold the rights to almost three hundred franchise stores. Only five of those had begun frying. By that fall Hooker and his brother had sold the rights to eight hundred, but only forty were in operation.

A few weeks after Minnie Pearl's went public in May 1968, Hooker and his Performance Systems colleagues announced that their company had purchased a 50 percent interest in another fried chicken enterprise. But there was a problem. Almost no one knew how to fry chicken. When an investor asked one of the Hooker brothers how they would teach franchisees something they didn't know, Henry Hooker said, "We can just call up General Mills or any restaurant we want and they'll get us someone who knows that any time we want."

B lack Southerners often regarded fast-food chains as blank slates. Free from the taint of the Jim Crow past, they were showcases of modern culture and commerce. Faced with the success of Harland Sanders, they beat him by copying him. When Benjamin Hooks broke ground on the flagship Mahalia Jackson's store in Memphis in 1968, he was accompanied by Ralph David Abernathy, who, earlier that year, had directed the Resurrection City camp on the National Mall. Joining him was Fred Shuttlesworth, who led the black children of Birmingham in 1963 protests that police met with dogs and fire hoses. Along with SCLC board chairman Joseph Lowery, they had come to town for the annual meeting of the organization. The grand opening was a bonus.

"Mahalia Jackson's Chicken System is the first national fast food franchise under complete colored management," reported the *Afro American* newspaper, on hand to watch the dirt turn. "It was conceived and developed to bring economic independence to the black community. Franchising, one of the fastest growing businesses in the country, is one way for black people to pool their resources and to invest in business which will keep the wealth in, and benefit the entire community." When Mahalia Jackson's Chicken opened, the chain announced a "Declaration of Negro Economic Independence."

With a roof that jutted like a church spire, a mod stained glass chandelier that dangled above double doors, and flanking signs that suggested stained glass windows, the Mahalia Jackson's prototype was a black gospel cathedral, erected in tribute to fast-food possibilities. The slogan "It's Glori-Fried, and that's the gospel truth," was overwrought. But the aim was sophisticated and current. Conceived to leverage the fame of a beloved singer, then topping the gospel charts, the chain's investors argued that black cultural life was bankable, too. Hooks, who served the company as president and the SCLC as financial secretary, framed the promise. He accepted money from white investors. But he said Mahalia Jackson's Chicken System was a "business arrangement of partnership, not plantationship." At a moment when black cultural expression was newly valued, and Black Power was vogue, this was an effort to leverage her popularity to build wealth.

The name and reputation of Mahalia Jackson resonated in the black South. In the aftermath of the 1955 murder of Emmett Till, she had reached out to the family and bought his tombstone. As the civil rights movement progressed, her voice was an essential track on the activist soundtrack. At the March on Washington she sang, "I've Been 'Buked and I've Been Scorned." At a pivotal moment in King's speech, she was likely the person who gave him the cue, "Tell 'em about the dream, Martin, tell, Martin, tell 'em 'bout the dream!"

Jackson came to cooking honestly. She was raised in New Orleans, in a neighborhood that came to be called the Black Pearl; her mother and her aunt worked as domestic servants. Jackson left school in the eighth grade to work as a cook and washerwoman. Though she was not involved in the operations of the restaurant chain, Jackson earned royalties for lending her name. With those royalties came responsibilities. When new locations went online, she appeared at grand opening ceremonies, sometimes wearing a pillbox hat and gloves.

The menu was basic. The Nitty Gritty included one piece of fried chicken and a biscuit. Soul Bowls translated as chicken giblets and gravy over rice. Inspired by Kentucky Fried Chicken, which sold fried chicken in pasteboard buckets, plastered with an image of a white-suited Harland Sanders, Mahalia Jackson's Chicken System sold buckets of legs and thighs and wings, plastered with an image of the gospel singer, her mouth parted in song, flanked by stylized church window ovals. Slaw, biscuits, and sweet potato pies rounded out the menu.

Most stores were planned for the South. But Mahalia Jackson's also courted an audience in the urban North, where many black Southerners had moved during the Great Migration. Chicago franchisees were early adopters, opening two units paired with gas stations. Cleveland and Detroit followed. "We've used black people in the entire scheme," Hooks explained. "In architecture, in construction, and in advertising, we mean to be a black business."

Outlets were licensed only to black investors or to partnerships in which blacks owned 50 percent or more of the venture. The black press touted Mahalia Jackson's Chicken System as an example of "American free enterprise's endeavor to promote Negro ownership of businesses." Mahalia Jackson's promised great profits. By June 1969, Hooks announced a second line of restaurants, Mahalia Jackson Parlors, serving gumbo, "soul food that is extra fancy," and burgers dressed with soul sauce.

I f you don't like Gold Platter, you ain't got no soul," singer James Brown declared at a 1969 press conference that announced his new restaurant chain. Blacks from the South had long peddled food on street corners as part of the informal economy. Men cooked ribs on oil drum smokers in Birmingham parking lots. To raise money for grade school trips, young girls in Savannah sold what locals called "thrills": Dixie cups of frozen Kool-Aid. Women from small-town Arkansas fried whiting and sold hot sauce–drenched fish sandwiches from Chicago apartment kitchens. But this was different. This generation of entrepreneurs fixed on securing bank loans and developing business plans and reasserting a black economy.

Brown went into business with a group of white Georgia businessmen from Macon. Black wealth creation and black job opportunities were aims for the Gold Platter chain. Brown shared plans for a training center that would teach the skills needed to work his restaurants. Along with making franchisees rich, Brown said Gold Platter would teach business strategies they could carry into black communities.

These were tough years. The Poor People's Campaign had failed to gain traction in activist circles or garner the undivided attention of President Johnson, whose Great Society programs were undercut by escalation of the Vietnam War. For black Southerners, franchise entrepreneurship was one way out. Like Mahalia Jackson, Brown was an ideal salesperson. When a reporter asked about competition, Brown said, "There ain't any. This is pioneer, like Daniel Boone and Davy Crockett. And it's so big that you as an American can't be out of it. You've got to be in."

To develop black separatist financial ideals for a new generation, Brown made a play for federal money. "It's a little like the black capitalism Mr. Nixon is stressing," Brown said. "We have what he wants, now we'd like his help with some government self-help financing for people who want to go into the business." That tack didn't work. Underfunded from the start, the Gold Platter chain never grew beyond two trial locations in Macon.

But Brown didn't give up on the possibilities of growing a food business to achieve black economic parity. Along with retired pro football player Art Powell, he founded Black and Brown Trading Stamps as an answer to S&H Green Stamps, the loyalty program that promoted a sort of grocery store prequel to frequent flyer programs. Test marketed in Oakland, California, the idea was to reward consumer loyalty to black-owned businesses through trading stamps blazoned with portraits of black American icons. The first and likely only stamp the company printed bore the smiling face of Soul Brother Number One: Brown himself.

B y the early 1970s, as public schools desegregated, the region no longer defined its character by the black fight for integration and the white defense of segregation. Life at its best was no longer lived on the farm, tilling the soil your forebears broke, but at the knob of a cul-de-sac in a crabgrass suburb. At a 1972 symposium on the contemporary South, historian C. Vann Woodward spoke of Henry Grady, the Atlanta newspaper editor who popularized the term *New South* in a late-nineteenth-century speech to Northern investors: "We are, in fact, still living with a progressive realization of Grady's dream of a Yankee-fied South. Every new thruway, every new supermarket, every central city is an extension of it. . . . I wonder if what the South really wants is an uncritical emulation of the North."

Tanya Tucker, who won fame when she released the gothic single "Delta Dawn" in 1972, sounded a more optimistic tone the next year. Tucker saw a South on the horizon in which ghetto shacks had been leveled to make way for wooded parks and skyscrapers. She sang, "I believe the South is gonna rise again / But not the way they thought it would back then."

Southerners recognized new value in unheralded traditions and practices. So did the rest of the nation. Southern religious views, often couched in Christian evangelical terms, gained purchase across the country. Southern sports, like stock car racing and roughhouse college football, gained new fans. And Southern foods, from fried chicken to biscuits, became American foods, whether they were prepared by an apron-clad grandmother with a cirrus of gray hair or a corporate employee dressed in a polyester uniform with her name stitched across the breast. "That a change is now in course all across the South is plain," Stark Young wrote in I'll Take My Stand, back in 1930, "and it is as plain that the South changing must be the South still."

The spread of fast food did not rob the South of character. Instead, the advance of fast-food restaurants, conceived by Southerners, marked changes, bringing into relief the ways the region adapted to suit new needs and new lifestyles. In an era of convenience foods, the South emerged as a packager of American regional tastes and traditions. Instead of aberrations, forced on the South by outsiders like McDonald's, fast-food fried chicken, fast-food biscuits, and reinvented muffuletta sandwiches were the products of insiders, fixed on reinventing the traditional practices of the region and selling the nation on their bona fides.

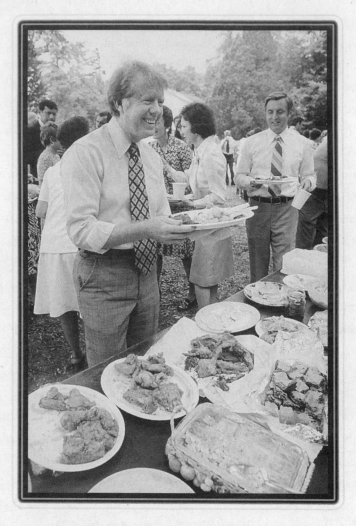

During the run-up to his 1976 election, Jimmy Carter and his
Peanut Brigade volunteers pressed the flesh and feasted
at church suppers across the nation.

· 7 ·

Carter Country

The orchestra played "Happy Days Are Here Again" when the Ohio delegation put Jimmy Carter over the top on the night of July 15, 1976. Labor activist Mazie Woodruff danced through the North Carolina delegation, jabbing a sign into the air that read, "PEANUT BUTTER IS LOVE. SPREAD SOME AROUND TODAY." Aaron Henry, an aging activist from Clarksdale, Mississippi, wrapped his black arm around the young white neck of Ross Barnett Jr., son of the segregationist former Mississippi governor. "Is this the New South?" someone asked above the roar as Henry, jubilant, shouted, "That's right! That's right!" Lillian Carter reached up and placed the palm of her hand against the cheek of her son as if to say, "I'm proud of you."

The Democratic Presidential Convention of 1976 played like a television commercial for the New South. Southerners were bow-chested. After watching Martin Luther King Sr. lead the convention audience singalong of "We Shall Overcome," Larry King summed up the mood: "Ol Southern boys around the world, recognizing the nuances and shadings of home, lurched to their collective feet, spilling right smart amounts of bourbon branch water over the rims of their gold goblets or jelly glasses, and with wet eyes huskily proclaimed: 'We ain't *trash* no more.'"

New pride emboldened moderate and progressive white Southerners who had grudgingly accepted their role as national embarrassment. Roy Blount Jr. said, "I was like a man who goes from being half eat up with hookworms to catching nice speckled trout with them." Battered by depictions of their region during the civil rights movement era and realizations of their own culpability, they refashioned their regional identities. So did black Southerners, who, by the 1970s, began to glimpse the possibilities of integrated lives.

My parents were Carter people. Our family plastered green-and-white JIMMY CARTER FOR PRESIDENT stickers to the bumpers of our Mercedes sedan and our VW station wagon. In 1976, the year our former governor ran for president, we drove downstate to his hometown of Plains, Georgia. We visited Hugh Carter's antique shop and took pictures of his worm farm sign, circled the perimeter of the Plains Baptist Church, and caught a softball game between the press corps and Carter's campaign staff. At the railroad station, converted to a campaign headquarters, we bought buttons, flags, and coffee mugs. On the way home, I hunkered in the backseat, reading pamphlets and pinning GRITS AND FRITZ buttons to my army surplus jacket.

During the short-lived American flirt with Carter, his wide smile became a meme. So did his morality. In those early post-Watergate days, the nation took solace in his agricultural roots and religious fortitude. *Hail to the Teeth*, a Carter-themed comedy album, included a final track, "Lust but Not Least," that referenced a *Playboy* interview in which Carter confessed that, while he had never committed adultery, he had lusted in his heart. Inspired by Carter's ascendance, the nation thrashed its way through the cultural thicket that was the South and gained a peek at its own future.

In the 1970s, as the world discovered Plains, the nation began to grapple with a baffling range of Southern stereotypes including Carter's born-again little sister Ruth Carter Stapleton, an evangelist and faith healer; his good-ole-boy little brother Billy Carter, who ran a filling station, moonlighted as a lobbyist for Libyan oil interests, and once urinated in broad daylight on an airport tarmac; and his steel magnolia mother, Miz Lillian, who had previously taught contraception as a Peace Corps volunteer in India. Along with those discoveries came grits stirred orange with cheese, boiled peanuts eaten from brown paper bags, and, eventually, Billy Beer in pull-tab cans.

Every other newspaper article in the mid-1970s pointed out that Carter was a peanut farmer. Tony restaurants that previously served coq au vin introduced peanut soup. *The New York Times* ran articles on peanuts that read like spoofs. Readers learned that Jack Springer, spokesperson for the National Peanut Council, also represented the National Broom and Mop Council. They learned that, while Virginia peanuts were the largest, Carter raised smaller runner peanuts in Georgia. Southerners yawned. Outlanders called mail-order houses in south Georgia to get runner peanuts shipped their way.

Grits were suddenly courant. By January 1977, as Washington readied for Carter's inauguration, Yolande Fox, a former Miss America from Mobile, Alabama, said that everyone in Washington had begun thumbing through cookbooks, in search of grits recipes. "A lot of it is kidding, but I'll tell you, a lot of it is dead serious, too," she said. "I'm going to have some cheese grits myself in about a half hour." Restaurants advertised dishes made from ground corn as "Georgia ice cream," cooked until creamy and scooped into footed bowls. Democrats in the Northeast minted Carter-Mondale buttons with a subscript that read "New Jersey's Diet, Grits and Fritz." In this small-d democratic moment, Americans adopted grits as a food of the people, a simple porridge, cooked by simple folk. Grits also managed to be somehow exotic like the South itself, worthy of study and instruction, ripe for stereotype.

Playing to that hype, Plains residents published at least four cookbooks during the Carter administration, thick with grits casseroles and peanut brittle and homespun bon mots. They read like attempts to cash in on the Carter phenomenon, and, at a moment when everyone else seemed to be telling their story, they read like attempts to grab the mic, written by a community that longed to speak for itself. *Plains Pot-Pourri*, from the Junior Woman's Club, featured congealed salads. *Ruth Jackson's Soulfood Cookbook*, an homage to black life with an overall-blue cover, included a requisite chitlin dish.

Not everyone bought the notion that Southern foods and Southern peoples were odd and in need of explanation. "I don't see any excitement about anything," Alice Lee Roosevelt Longworth, the ninety-two-year-old daughter of President Theodore Roosevelt, said. "What's so special about these Georgians—they don't wear queer clothes, they don't wear masks, they're not hermaphrodites."

Denatured white Southern culture flourished during the run-up to the 1976 election. By the late 1960s, *The Beverly Hillbillies* and *Hee Haw*, which spoofed and celebrated rural Southerners, had become prime-time hits. Since Appomattox, Southerners had been selling a New South that, South Carolinian Edwin De Leon promised in 1870, "sits in the seat of the dethroned king, exhibiting a lustier life, and the promise of greater growth and strength, than did its predecessor." By the mid-1970s, the South was more than the sum of its antebellum past and less backward than the Clampetts would have viewers believe.

Change rocked the region. As interstate migration into the South transformed who lived there and who claimed the place, white conservatives grew nostalgic for a past that had faded or maybe never was. In Atlanta, the city that became the financial and cultural capital of the region, whites indulged that nostalgia in restaurants comparable to the spaces where black students staged protests in the early 1960s. But these restaurants were not lunch counters, constructed for quick weekday meals. They were pageant restaurants, run like latter-day Cycloramas for Old South recidivists.

As the South urbanized, Aunt Fanny's Cabin in suburban Atlanta gained fame for fried chicken and rosin potatoes, cooked in pine tree sap, served in a country manor accessorized with tchotchkes and primitives. For the pleasure of whites, a crew of black women in calico gowns sang gospel music and shook Mason jars for tips. And a squadron of black boys worked the dining room with menu boards yoked over their necks, singsonging "Howdy folks, what'll it be?"

By the 1960s, when the centennial of the Civil War and the peak years of the civil rights movement entwined like combatants in an awkward headlock, the Johnny Reb's restaurant group was in its neo-Confederate prime. Johnny Reb's Dixieland, one of the four Atlanta restaurants in that group, erected a sign, topped with two mannequins dressed in butternut gray, muzzle-loading what appeared to be an actual cannon. Outlined in lightbulbs, the legend DIXIELAND blinked beneath.

A portrait of Lt. Gen. Nathan Bedford Forrest, CSA, dominated the menu front, which opened to reveal a chicken giblet soup, said to be handed down from the wife of Gen. Robert E. Lee. Guests ordered sirloins Shermanized (burned to a crisp), Lincolnized (warm, red heart), and Stonewalled (rare). Across town, Johnny Reb's Canteen stationed an unattended cannon above the awning and sold "Confederate" fried chicken. "It's new, it's different," promised newspaper advertisements, seemingly unaware that pegging a century-old Confederate ideal was, instead, retrograde.

Pittypat's Porch, which opened three years after the Civil Rights Act of 1964 passed, was the invention of A. J. Anthony, a Czech immigrant. Set in a onetime Atlanta funeral parlor, the restaurant printed menus on church fans, which Southerners were accustomed to waving at funerals. Fried chicken and roasted venison arrived on pewter plates. Brunswick stew came in souvenir skillets. Mint juleps were guaranteed to make you "feel like a plantation owner." Ankle breakers, named after Stonewall

Jackson, who Anthony said fell and shattered his ankle after downing a half dozen of the drinks, arrived in ceramic jugs with skull-and-bones stoppers. Anthony missed some of the marks. Until at least the mid-1970s, menus misspelled the word *y'all*, inserting the apostrophe between the *a* and the first *l*.

Mammy's Shanty, which, in addition to an Atlanta flagship, ran a Pickaninny Coffee Shop next door, printed menus that were pithy narratives of Louisiana turkey and rice à la Alexandria. The listing for the Georgia cracker sampler plate suggested tourists who longed to have another go should "Save your Confederate money like the rest of us." Mammy's teleported chicken shortcake Natchez from a day when "crinoline and hoop skirts were in vogue and Jean Lafitte was pirating around New Orleans." Guests learned that Lafitte wasn't looking for gold. "No suh, he was looking for a Natchez Negro Mammy who could make Chicken Shortcake. This old recipe has been handed down from the Good Old Days."

James Earl Ray, who murdered Martin Luther King Jr., ate at the Shanty. He told investigators that he met Raoul, the "real" shooter, there for a meal. The Shanty, which fronted its early menus with kerchiefed mammies and watermelon-eating children, printed a more subdued scene by the 1970s. A washed-out watercolor of the restaurant dominated the foreground. In the background, the skyscrapers of Atlanta loomed, symbols of ascendance and urbanity.

A hundred years ago, a Northerner in the South was called a carpet-bagger," Roy Reed of *The New York Times* reported. "Ten years ago, he was called a meddling integrationist. In 1976 he is being called to come and have dinner." In the 1970s the divide between North and South faded as the Sun Belt in general and the South in particular boomed. As that red clay wall came down, so did distinctions between Yankee and Confederate, between urban and rural America. Many

Northerners adapted quickly. Reed reported that by 1976, every city in the Sun Belt had "some transplanted Yankees who have adopted open collars, drawling speech, and bourbon mixed with Coca-Cola."

Richard Nixon noted the shift. After he took the oath of office in 1969, the California Republican changed his voting residence from New York to Florida, saying, "The time has come to stop kicking the South around." Nixon recognized that the Sun Belt economy was booming. And he calculated that conservative white voters, threatened by the civil rights movement and lured by a pro-business platform, would adopt his party. He figured right. When Nixon traveled to Atlanta in 1972, a ticker tape parade greeted the president and his wife, Pat Nixon.

Almost a decade later, as the Carter presidency fizzled, Ronald Reagan took the podium at the 1980 Neshoba County Fair in Philadelphia, Mississippi, to announce his candidacy for president. As voters licked their fingers clean of fried chicken grease, waved Confederate battle flags, and took flask swigs of bourbon, he talked of restoring states' rights. His aim was to woo white, conservative Democrats, who believed the party had deserted them.

Blacks and whites recognized the racial coding. Both recalled the horrific 1964 murders of three civil rights workers in their county. Both remembered how the demand to leave the South alone so that it could manage its own affairs had become a grail for recalcitrant and racist white Southerners who brooked no intrusions from Northern activists or government bureaucrats. When the election results came in that November, white Southerners played to type. Reagan carried every state in the former Confederacy except for Georgia.

Reagan recognized that such views were not restricted to the South. More than eight million whites had left the rural South for the industrial North from 1940 to 1970 during the latter phase of the Great Migration. As the 1980s unspooled, those migrants transplanted evangelical Christianity, conservative politics, and cheese grits across the nation. The rest of the country held fast to its stereotypes of the South as the American

other, a cultural and economic backwater. But when no one was looking, the South colonized the North. And the North adopted Southern
political and cultural mores as if they were its own.

Between 1970 and 1990, the South's population exploded by 40 percent. With that demographic shift, Southerners and South watchers declared that the long-heralded New South had at last arrived. *Ebony*
magazine documented the vogue for "rhapsodic litanies on the New
South," a region that had "turned its back on the horrors of the past; a
South that was too busy to hate, a South that was hard at work outdoing
the Yankees, a South of hustle and bustle, of new buildings, new roads
and new factories."

Country music became the soundtrack of truck stops and car dealer-
ships and roller rinks. It blasted from eight-track tape decks mounted in
four-wheel-drive pickup trucks and cassette decks embedded in the
burled walnut dashes of sleek Mercedes sedans. The integrated Muscle
Shoals sound had served the civil rights movement as a soundtrack. By
the 1970s, America was listening to Charlie Daniels and Loretta Lynn
sing of lost loves and lost places, paeans to a South that was no longer
the South they knew.

Their lyrics spoke to the anxieties of country people who now lived
in cities, family men who had strayed far from Momma. They spoke,
too, to the good life and prosperity possible in this newer South. The
Charlie Daniels Band recorded "The South's Gonna Do It" in 1974. Eight
years later Hank Williams Jr. released "If Heaven Ain't a Lot Like Dixie,"
and answered the hypothetical by answering "I don't wanna go."

That same year, when I was doing more dancing than studying at
the University of Georgia, a similar instinct drove twelve bands from the
burgeoning Athens scene to pose for a *People* magazine photo shoot in
New South promoter Henry Grady's hometown, beneath an obelisk
honoring a Revolutionary War hero, alongside a memorial to the Confederate dead of Clarke County. The photograph spoke to the yield of

small-town creativity, not the promise of industry. But the frame was the same. Here was another New South. Like the ones that came before, this New South came into best relief when glimpsed against a backdrop of the Old South.

B ack when most of America still viewed the South as a bulwark of tradition instead of a dynamo of change, Jane and Michael Stern, authors of the pioneering restaurant guidebook *Roadfood*, pushed an eight-track Merle Haggard tape into the dash. As the Hag serenaded them with songs of working men, they cruised Southside Virginia in a Chevy Suburban with calico curtains, passing clapboard houses shrouded by oak canopies. An old man wearing overalls waved from his front porch. Michael leaned his head out the car window, driving by way of scent. "I smell biscuits," he said, steering Jane toward a café, fronted by mud-splattered pickup trucks and bracketed by planters of pansies.

They ate country ham, eggs, grits, and homemade cherry preserves that morning. Driving the backroads that William Least Heat-Moon later called blue highways, they found their calling. Romantics, the Sterns searched for an unvarnished America that forever waited, just around the next bend. The narratives played like Saturday westerns in which the Sterns were the new sheriffs in town: "The waitress stood before us, order pad in hand. 'We don't get too many strangers passing through here since the interstate was built.'"

Though their books, beginning with *Roadfood* in 1978, covered the whole nation, they lavished attention on the South. The Sterns met while graduate students at Yale University. He was a suburban Chicago boy, studying art history. She was a New York City native, studying art. Jane Stern, nurtured as a child by a black woman with Southern roots, had long cultivated a taste for country ham, biscuits, and Coca-Cola. In search of cathead biscuits, wobbly gelatin, candied yams, smothered pork chops, and seven-layer caramel cakes, the Sterns drove the nation. They sought homey local foods that were off the radar and off the menu for many Americans. They were not foodies, Michael Stern said. "We are relativists. We examine food in its context, what it means to people, where it is served."

Prejudices, informed by religion, education, race, and class, showed through. "People are so accustomed to using food as a source of social expression, to show how hip they are," they told a reporter. "Our book really says that, hey, it's okay to be retarded once in a while." For the Sterns, poverty was often an atmospheric grace note that heightened a louche appreciation of Southern taboos. The Sterns described an Arkansas barbecue restaurant as a "shack scarcely bigger than an outhouse" and a "dump of the first order." The pit house, they took pains to say, backed up against a garbage mound.

Other members of their generation found themselves by traipsing through the woods, toward wilderness escape. Stephen Gaskin, their contemporary, gave up on America, and on the military-industrial complex that drove the national economy. The Sterns, instead, saw virtue in small-town crab houses and big-city pie houses. Like antique pickers in search of face jugs and quilts, or Spanish explorers in search of the lost Mayan city of gold, they ranged the backcountry, trumpeting the riches that provincial folk harbored.

The Sterns were fabulists. Sausages were turgid with juices and forever close to bursting, conversation was palaver, arguments were colloquies, and sweet tea was salubrious. Like many who trafficked in stereotypes, the Sterns were both attracted to and repulsed by the South. They struggled to puzzle through the tensions. In the first-edition mash-up of *Roadfood and Goodfood*, they wrote of a "fat man who sauntered up to us in a bar in Mobile, Alabama, the one we pegged as the worst sort of redneck, who instead of killing us as we expected, took us out to dinner in an oyster restaurant we would never have found by ourselves, then wouldn't let us leave until we Yankees got a taste of Southern hospitality, which meant filling up our car's back seat with his homegrown watermelons, his wife's hot pepper jelly, and enough home brew quince wine to keep our car fueled up to California and back."

Once converted to the region, they were zealots. The Sterns referred to their favorite restaurants as shrines, and they began to think of themselves as pilgrims on a sacred journey: "We had no Bible to direct us, but we did have a few roadfood reverends on whom we could always rely for veritable sermons of where to eat and what to eat when we got there." The Sterns were vigorous advocates for regional food. When chef Wolfgang Puck, who rose to fame in Los Angeles mixing and matching French and Italian and Chinese cuisines, published his own American food treatise, Jane Stern called him out: "The thing that makes me maddest is that chefs think they are inventing American food. What do they think the American people have been eating for 200 years?"

Readers valorized the Sterns, ascribing to them a sort of anthropological approach that would, in the years to come, look prescient. When I first began traveling to eat in the 1980s, their writing was inspirational. But as I read more deeply, my devotion to the Sterns faded.

Just before John Egerton published *Southern Food* in the summer of 1987, the Sterns wrote to his editor at Knopf, claiming that Egerton had plagiarized their work, and that many of the restaurants he wrote about were their discoveries. The gambit was a colonial power grab for ownership of a place, its peoples, and its institutions. It also served as a new measure of the value that Americans were beginning to associate with the working-class restaurants that the Sterns celebrated.

Instead of debating their claims, Egerton calmly and coolly proved them false. One evening, after we enjoyed a glass of Tennessee whiskey, John handed me a stack of letters from that confrontation and suggested that I might want to save them for posterity. Until I began writing this book, I didn't realize what purpose that correspondence might serve.

C alvin Trillin, a reporter posing as a tongue-in-cheek provincialist, worked the other side of the equation. Traveling the country for *The New Yorker*, writing of small-town murders and human nature, he saw through the stereotypes about the South, revealing the narratives embedded in barbecue and fried chicken. When he began writing about the working-class foods of his Kansas City youth, Trillin argued with subtle humor for a rejection of fast food and corporate food.

These were bleak times. Pizza Hut had expanded its red-roofed chain east of the Mississippi. Stouffer's dinners of French bread pizza, boil-in-bag spaghetti with tomato sauce, and creamed spinach casserole were freezer-case standbys. White Southerners, who had fled to the suburbs to avoid integrated classrooms and restaurants, had not yet taken stock of what they left behind. There was much to dislike about what they carried forward.

Locating honest cooking reflective of place and tradition was difficult, Trillin told his readers. To find a good restaurant in a new town he said, "I sneak up on an unsuspecting hotel desk clerk, yank him by the necktie, and ask him where he went to eat the night after he got home after his two-year tour in Vietnam." Local dishes were hard to suss. But Trillin had measures: "I try to stick to regional specialties and the cooking of any ethnic group that is represented by at least two aldermen on the city council."

His first food book, *American Fried*, published in 1974, tapped the zeitgeist for honest Americana. Instead of adopting the countercuisine of brown rice, tofu, and tamari, Trillin argued for vernacular foods. He rejected "La Maison de la Casa House" restaurants where the specialty was "Frozen Duck à l'Orange Soda Pop," in favor of fried chicken from the Kansas City roadhouse Stroud's and barbecue from the crosstown smoke shack Arthur Bryant's. Trillin waged a one-man war against continentalism, challenging readers to reevaluate the foods of their youth.

His playful boosterism inspired a generation of writers. And he emboldened a generation of eaters. Trillin, who had traveled the region to report on the civil rights movement, inspired Southerners to appreciate
anew specialties like crawfish and catfish, mutton and maque choux.

He introduced the nation to the joys of unsung eater's towns like
Breaux Bridge, Louisiana, and Owensboro, Kentucky. Channeling a new
respect for African American knowledge and expertise, while poking
subtle fun at a new generation of white Americans who fetishized the
working-class foods of black women and men, Trillin wrote, "Going to a
white-run barbecue is, I think, like going to a gentile internist: It might
turn out all right, but you haven't made any attempt to take advantage
of the percentages."

Reared on a truck farm outside the city of Amite in northern Louisiana, beyond the bounds of Cajun Country, Justin Wilson had worked
as a safety engineer before he began recording Cajun comedy albums
and writing Cajun cookbooks. Fond of bolo ties, red suspenders, and
country aphorisms, he played the role of a bayou Colonel Sanders. "What
I love mos' about Cajun cookin' is the imagines what they done put into
it," he wrote in the introduction to his spiral-bound first book. "You see,
my frien', although some Cajuns is rich as thick cream, mos' of them
Cajuns ain't got the money to buy them fancy cuts of meat and high
price' vegetables. An' that's where the imagines comes in."

When he hit public television in the 1970s, Wilson sloshed sauterne
in every other dish. Oyster chowder, scallop chowder, seafood gumbo,
corned beef, backbones and turnips, broiled shrimp, mustard greens,
rabbit étouffée, squirrel stew: All got the treatment. So did shrimp à la
Mexicana. And shrimp fried in pancake batter. When cooking macaroni
and cheese, he advised, "Here's where you' nose come in handy. When
you mixes that wine with them egg, you gonna know it's right when the
mixture done smell jus' like eggnog at Chris'mus' time."

Wilson achieved fame in the 1970s and '80s, when his shows were afternoon constants on public television stations. As his Nielsen numbers rose, the lines blurred between his personality and the person he played for the cameras. Wilson talked about how cayenne pepper relieved sinus congestion. "It'll open up your sciences!" he shouted in an early show. Wilson howled and barked and smiled and clowned his way through episodes in which he served as a sort of court jester and explainer in chief for Cajun culture, the sort of character the Sterns tracked. Not everyone appreciated the bombast. His speech, rendered in print phonetically, reminded some Cajuns of the demeaning dialects that Joel Chandler Harris of Uncle Remus fame had once ascribed to black Southerners.

Early in his career, when Wilson was still cutting comedy albums like *I Guar-Ron-Tee* and *The "Wondermus" Humor of Justin Wilson*, James Domengeaux, chair of CODOFIL, the Council for the Development of French in Louisiana, attacked the budding television star for slinging a kind of Cajun doggerel. Founded in 1968, the same year that James Brown climbed the *Billboard* charts, chanting "Say It Loud—I'm Black and I'm Proud," CODOFIL channeled the identity politics of the day to showcase Cajun language and culture in positive ways.

Like the Southerners before him who peddled a Dixie illumined by moonlight and shaded by magnolias, like the Southerners after him who sold a New South as the cradle of the civil rights movement, Wilson made no apologies for his shtick. But he put some limits on the liberties he would take. "You' common sense gonna tell you what goes good with what, an' when, too," he wrote. "You gonna know you don't put you' sawmill gravy on them prunes."

B y the time Trillin began traveling and eating for a living, Buster Holmes, the new Orleans red-beans-and-rice cook, was already a star. A native of downriver Plaquemines Parish, he arrived in the city at about the same time as the Flood of 1927. After working as a longshore-man, Holmes opened a restaurant where he fed dockhands and musicians. The Olympia Brass Band considered the restaurant a clubhouse. Preservation Hall artists regarded Buster's as the staff canteen. In the Musician's Union directory, Dixieland trumpeter Kid Sheik Colar listed the restaurant phone as his home number.

Perched at the corner of Burgundy and Orleans, the building was painted pink and black. Newspaper clippings covered plaster walls. Two fluorescent tubes hung from the ceiling. A blue neon Pabst beer sign buzzed. "The place is seedy and shabby—so much so that it seems contrived, like a Hollywood version of a restaurant for down-and-outs, in the depths of the French Quarter," wrote a newspaperwoman who channeled the slumming style of the Sterns.

By the late 1960s, when blacks could finally eat in white restaurants and whites felt comfortable walking in the front door of black-owned cafés, Buster's had become the city's most favored and most integrated Creole soul lunch spot. White hippies, black civil rights activists, and tourists from New York ate side by side at the counter, in sight of the stove bank where pots of turnip greens, pork backbones, beef stew, and red beans burbled.

All mopped their plates with quarter loaves of cottony po-boy bread. Some smeared the bread with margarine, which the counter woman troweled on every plate. If the Holmes cookbook is to be believed, margarine was also one of the secrets to the creamy mouthfeel of his red beans. Published just a couple years before he shuttered the restaurant in the early 1980s, the cookbook documented the people who lived on his side of the Quarter like Hustler, the produce vendor, and Slow Drag Pavageau, a jazz guitarist who claimed that voudoun priestess Marie Laveau was his aunt. Along with two recipes for red beans and rice, one of which called for a sauterne wine soak of the beans, Holmes included recipes from his country youth like nutria sauce piquant and marsh hen.

Like Mama Louise Hudson of Macon, Georgia, who fed the Allman

Brothers greens and beans and cornbread when they arrived hungry in her town, and Mama Lo Alexander, who cooked eggplant casserole, suc-cotash, and stuffed pork chops for two generations of University of Flor-ida students, Holmes fed all who crossed his threshold, even if they couldn't afford to pay the meager bill. That relationship, between a black man or woman with a talent for cooking and a white boy or girl with a taste for home, fueled its own set of stereotypes that spanned beloved communities who gathered to take sacrament and wayward white flocks ministered by black caretakers.

The election of Jimmy Carter as president in 1976 signaled that, after banishing the region to the woodshed for more than a century, Amer-ica had finally called the South to the table. To mark the occasion, politi-cians made speeches about redemption, country musicians cut albums that celebrated rural life, and the proletariat sat down to a bounteous spread of grits and peanuts. Inside and outside the region, writers and thinkers issued proclamations about its integrated present and bright fu-ture. Many reached easy conclusions about complex issues that had yet to be resolved. On the campaign trail, Carter himself played to the stereo-types when he told cheering audiences, "Come January, we are going to have a President in the White house who doesn't speak with an accent."

As the Carter years gave way to the Reagan era, Americans adopted the stereotypes. The maximalist writings of Jane and Michael Stern, bal-anced by the subversive, everyman humor of Calvin Trillin, rendered the South a bastion of traditional foodways populated by singular char-acters, from a cigar-chomping red-beans-and-rice cook in New Orleans to a storyteller who played a Cajun buffoon for television shows.

Tensions over who should speak for the South, over whose version of the story best represented the people who lived in the region, carried forward into the following decades as writers and chefs began to rede-fine the foods of black Southerners.

Homecoming at Bethel Baptist Church near her birthplace in Freetown, Virginia, was the highlight of Edna Lewis's year. Lessons she learned there drove the modern American food movement. Edna Lewis (right).

· 8 ·

Black Pastorals

Threading cornfields and pastures and stands of pine, Edna Lewis and her sister Jen Ellis drove the sinuous asphalt roads of Orange County, Virginia, in the 1980s and 1990s. They passed one of the two houses that their grandmother Lucinda Lewis, a skilled mason, helped build by molding and laying bricks. Born a slave, she had come to Orange County when a white landowner purchased her for $950. The sisters steered alongside Bethel Baptist Church, which their grandfather Chester Lewis, also born into slavery, helped found a century before. They talked of how he hosted the first school in the county for blacks and recruited a black college graduate to teach in a classroom in his own house. Skirting a stand of fruit trees, they drove past a meadow where their brother Lue Stanley Lewis tended cattle and pigs.

As the sisters traveled in and around the Freetown community, they talked of church suppers and Emancipation Day feasts. They spoke of fall hog-killing breakfasts and spring wheat-threshing dinners. They recalled suppers of corn pudding and country ham. The sisters talked of the Great Depression into which they were both born, and of the dismal institution of slavery, which their grandparents escaped. They spoke of the Jim Crow poll taxes that had once pushed blacks off voter rolls. And of the 1963 March on Washington for Jobs and Freedom that had offered a hint of what was possible when black folk banded together.

Speaking of their shared past, the Lewis sisters conjured a rich and varied place where black farmers controlled their own destiny and agriculture was not demeaning work that shackled black Southerners. Instead, over the decades after freedom came, Lewis and her family had embraced agriculture. They found joy among the furrows and reveled in the pleasures of the table.

More than a century after Emancipation, as America stitched together the frayed tethers that connected the land and the larder, their stories inspired Americans who cast about for meaning in a world they believed bereft. At a time when chefs and educated eaters looked to France for inspiration, Edna Lewis argued, in her quiet way, that all true paths of self-discovery led home. Before Americans bandied the term *farm-to-table*, she lived by that credo. In the process she honed a black pastoral, a rural idyll, which resonated for generations to come.

Born in 1916 on Thomas Jefferson's birthday, twenty miles from Monticello, Lewis spun a narrative that was bucolic. As William Faulkner illuminated northern Mississippi, and Randall Kenan mythologized eastern North Carolina, Lewis made a study of Freetown, beginning with *A Taste of Country Cooking*. Published in 1976, her book arrived as the nation celebrated its bicentennial and renewed a commitment to reckon with its past. *Roots*, Alex Haley's novelized exploration of African culture and its imprint on America, arrived the same year. (When ABC showed a *Roots* miniseries the following year, it won a bigger audience share than the previously most-watched broadcast, *Gone with the Wind*.)

Lewis drew inspiration from her extended community and her family. Orange County had been an early center of black entrepreneurship. From the mid-1800s onward, African American women there peddled food to the trains that paused in the county seat of Gordonsville to take on water and coal. Before the Civil War, women earned their freedom with profits made selling fried chicken, coffee, and fried pies. After the war, when writers referred to Orange County as the "chicken-leg center of the universe," black women supported their families and "built houses out of chicken legs." Called "waiter carriers" by locals, these women cooked the food, delivered it on trays balanced on their heads, and passed lunches and dinners through the open windows of passenger cars.

Beneath starched white aprons, these black entrepreneurs wore brightly colored frocks. They wrapped their hair in multicolored bandannas. The women who worked the Gordonsville station flaunted their independence and their entrepreneurship. A century later when Edna Lewis stepped onto the national stage, she garbed herself in West African–inspired batik and dangled oversized pendants from her ears in a style that echoed the Gordonsville flair.

O range County gave Edna Lewis gravitas. In a rapidly urbanizing America, her knowledge of native plants and heritage breed animals, learned on the family farm, set her apart. Memories of Freetown did more than connect her to kin. Edna Lewis's rural life became her greatest asset. At a time when grocers sold the virtues of California-raised peas, frozen and bagged and available in any season, as consumers fell for Florida tomatoes, picked hard and green and ready for transport, Lewis introduced a counternarrative. Even chickens have a season, she said. During the late spring and early summer, when the feed was sweet, their flesh was firm and their size was ideal for frying.

A generation before it became vogue among young chefs, Lewis valorized smallholding. She suggested that Jeffersonian agriculture, practiced on a minor scale, was practical. If her family could flourish under the thumb of Jim Crow, then the American experiment was worth another look. Farming might be a way forward. A connection to the land that yielded pleasing food and drink might not be frivolous. Instead, as the nation urbanized, as life quickened and daily pleasures diminished, it might be elemental. America had pawned much of its culinary heritage, M. F. K. Fisher wrote when *A Taste of County Cooking* was published. But, with Lewis leading the charge, she said that heritage could be reclaimed.

Like many Southerners past and present, from the Georgia writer Carson McCullers to the Alabama musician Sun Ra, Lewis found an audience for her narrative after leaving home. First in New York City, then in North Carolina and South Carolina, and finally in Atlanta, she interpreted her youth for an audience that longed to hear rural tales. In the telling, Orange County stood in for their home places. "Growing up, we always gathered wild things to eat," she recalled. "My brothers would pick watercress by the burlap bag full and hang it in the meat house to keep. Watercress would grow up under the snow and, after the snow melted and before the watercress bloomed, we would pick it too."

Wherever she lived, Lewis brought her South with her. When I worked in Atlanta in the early 1990s, I took classes from Lewis and her protégé, the Alabama-born chef Scott Peacock. I learned how to fry a small chicken in a big skillet of butter infused with country ham. Under her gaze, I pulsed butter with shrimp to make a paste that melted luxuriously over a bowl of grits. Later, as a graduate student, I interviewed Lewis about the ways she bridged the Virginia of her youth and the New York of her midlife prime.

Country food fueled her peregrinations, Lewis told me: "After people had gone off up north, we would send a big box of ingredients up to New York or Pittsburgh, a big cardboard box full of fresh ground cornmeal with eggs submerged in the middle, so that when they opened it up, they could have country eggs and cornbread. After I moved north, my sister would can watercress and then put it in a box full of cornmeal with maybe some ham and farm fresh eggs and ship it to me in New York City. I'd open it up and have a whole Southern meal."

Lewis returned to Orange County to source ingredients. She returned to reconnect with family and neighbors. And she returned to tramp the woods, to forage for tastes that others thought lost. "I just hope people will like my cooking," Lewis said before a New York City dinner she provisioned with churned buttermilk, hauled from South Carolina. Her humility was honest. And it was attractive. Admirers flocked, first to the dinner parties she staged for the New York City creative class in the post–World War II years, later to the restaurant kitchens she directed from the 1950s through the 1980s.

Lewis meant many different things to many different people. Friends and admirers called her pure, virtuous, and regal. The fashion photographer Karl Bissinger referred to her as an African queen. Molly O'Neill, the food writer, referred to her as the grandmother of everyone's dreams. Acolytes told stories of how she had milked her own cows back in Virginia, made her own baking powder, and could determine when a cake was ready by listening. "When it is still baking and not yet ready, the liquids make bubbling noises," she wrote. "Just as the cake is done, the sounds become faint and weak. . . ."

Her admirers valorized the communal attributes of Freetown. And so did Lewis, who said that rural life required that neighbors cooperate. "If someone borrowed one cup of sugar, they would return two," she explained. "If someone fell ill, the neighbors would go in and milk the cows, feed the chickens, clean the house, cook the food and come and sit with whoever was sick."

Lewis championed agrarian lifestyles. "We never bought anything from stores except sugar and kerosene," she said, explaining that necessity was the mother of purity. Alice Waters, who got to know Lewis when they cooked together at New York City benefits in the 1970s, regarded this grandchild of freed slaves as an advocate of organic foods and seasonal diets, an "inspiration to all of us who are striving to protect both biodiversity and cultural diversity by cooking real food in season and honoring our heritage through the ritual of the table."

Edna Lewis's true talent was holding a gazing mirror up so that

America might better see itself. By sharing what she had left behind when she departed Orange County as a teenager, Lewis helped America apprehend a way back and forward at once. Her rhapsodies of rural Virginia were harbingers of the Slow Food movement that Waters would champion, previews of the broader Southern renaissance that would gain momentum in the 2000s.

After she left Virginia as a teenager, before she settled in New York City, Edna Lewis landed in Washington, D.C., where she worked as a cook at the Brazilian embassy. Once she arrived in Manhattan, she ironed clothes for a laundry and worked as a prop stylist and a window dresser. As a young woman in Freetown, she had sewn her own frocks. After she settled in New York City, Lewis began sewing the batik dresses for which she became known. Early in her New York days, she sewed an outfit of "real whory clothes for a young model, real cute, for the cover of *True Story* magazine." The woman was Marilyn Monroe.

Her politics reflected the complicated times in which she lived. As a young woman, she campaigned vigorously for the 1936 reelection of Franklin D. Roosevelt. Along with her husband, Steve Kingston, a merchant marine and cook, she petitioned for the release of the Scottsboro Boys, young black men who were falsely accused of gang-raping a white girl in Alabama. During her early years in New York City, the *Daily Worker* employed her as a typesetter. Before the Voting Rights Act of 1965 instilled hope for a long-deferred democracy in which black citizens could participate, she joined the Communist Party because she believed it was the only political group agitating for equality.

Lewis found her way while cooking in a New York City restaurant, remembered for combining Southern ingredients and French techniques, a tack that would, a generation later, describe the ethos of many American restaurants. When Johnny Nicholson and Lewis went into business together in 1948, she was about to take a job as a domestic, cleaning and cooking for a white family. Instead of returning to that work, which Lewis had been forced to do when she first arrived in Washington, D.C., she became a partner in a business that became a beacon of postwar possibilities.

Decorated in what Nicholson described as a "fin de siècle Caribbean of Cuba style," Café Nicholson, on the ground floor of a midtown brownstone, served as a canteen for the creative class and a backdrop for fashion shoots. Nicholson was the Barnum of the social set, presiding with a parrot named Lolita on his shoulder. Lewis was understated, quiet. Her approach, like her cooking, was straightforward. "As a child in Virginia, I thought all food tasted delicious," she said. "After growing up, I didn't think food tasted the same, so it has been my lifelong effort to try and recapture those good flavors of the past."

Café Nicholson employed a conceit that foregrounded the current white tablecloth aesthetic. They printed no menu, relying instead on the seasons and the availability of good produce and meats to determine the dishes. "We'll serve only one thing a day," Johnny Nicholson said to Lewis, as they schemed their opening. "Buy the best quality and I don't see how we can go wrong." Long before farm-to-table was a marketing concept, Lewis challenged chefs to learn "from those who worked hard, loved the land, and relished the fruits of their labors."

Nicholson imagined a "place where truck drivers eat and the food is really great." It didn't work out that way. Paul Robeson became a regular. So did Truman Capote, who sometimes came bursting into the kitchen, wearing slacks and penny loafers, looking for biscuits, which Lewis did not serve. Tennessee Williams, who lived across the street, took his morning coffee at the café. He sometimes walked Lewis home after work. Greta Garbo dined in the courtyard with her two poodles. After dinner one evening, William Faulkner asked Lewis where she had trained in France. She delighted in telling him that she had never left the country.

Lewis rose to fame cooking elemental and elegant dishes like roast chicken, which Clementine Paddleford, the reigning national critic of midcentury America, described as "brown as a chestnut, fresh from the burr." She baked a chocolate soufflé that was "light as a dandelion seed in a wind." She-crab soup bobbing with roe, panfried quail atop a bale of spoonbread, lemon pies bouffanted with meringue, and chocolate cakes scented with coffee: Edna Lewis cooked food—first at Nicholson, later at Gage & Tollner in Brooklyn—that was rooted in the South but could not be accurately categorized as soul food or country cooking.

Lewis actively rejected the term *soul food*, which she found limiting. Her cooking was an act of recollection, a remembering of tastes and smells by a woman who delighted in the colors of wildflower petals and liked to stand in the middle of a cornfield to sniff the tasseled stalks. "This week we have been having beans and squash out of the garden, and they're the best I've ever tasted," she told a visitor to the family farm. "And I said to my sister, you know, in the city you put a lot of spices and herbs on food, but you really don't need it. I don't think people realize that. Food is so good out here."

Her career was scattershot, reflective of bohemian sensibilities and the sad realities of black employment in Jim Crow America. Before Lewis opened a restaurant in Harlem that closed in less than a year, she tried and failed to raise pheasants with her husband in New Jersey. After detours to take jobs at Fearrington House, a country estate near Chapel Hill, North Carolina, and Middleton Place, a former rice planation near Charleston, South Carolina, Lewis became a freelance advocate for the revival of the foods of her youth. As she grew older, and her memories of Freetown began to fade, she dedicated herself to reviving a cuisine she believed was slipping from her grasp.

Norma Jean and Carole Darden, authors of the 1978 book *Spoonbread and Strawberry Wine*, traced their ancestry directly to slavery, too. Freed when he was eight, their grandfather Charles Henry Darden made

his way to Wilson, a tobacco market town on the eastern flank of North
Carolina, where he became the first black undertaker in the state. That
vocation landed the family in the upper tier of black America. The
Darden sisters collected recipes that revealed middle-class life, which
might otherwise have been lost in the rush to embrace all black cooking
as soul food.

Memories of shelling peas and beans with beloved aunts and uncles
drew Norma Jean and Carole Darden home to research their book. They
gathered recipes from Grandfather Darden, who brewed strawberry and
watermelon wines; Grandfather Sampson, a farmer and chicken cook
whose father may have been a white plantation owner; and father Bud
Darden, who talked them through the recipe for the sweet potato biscuits his mother packed in family lunch pails. Cousin Thelma shared her
tipsy cake recipe. Hilda Lockett allowed them to include her heaven
cake. Aunt Lizzie shared pecan waffles and cousin Artelia revealed the
secret to her tea biscuits. "We had our first draft done before Alex Haley
published his book," Norma Jean Darden said, making note of the family history reclamation work then going on across the region.

Along with Lewis, the Dardens expanded national ideas of what
black food might be. Soul food was an important part of the story, they
said. But neckbones and turnip greens, cooked first in rural cropper shotguns and later in urban hotbed flats, were not the whole tale. Vertamae
Grosvenor made a bigger grab when she said that her kitchen was the
world, not the plantations of the South or the ghettoes of the North. "It
seemed to me while certain foods have been labeled 'soul food' and associated with Afro-Americans, Afro-Americans could be associated with all
foods. . . ."

Edna Lewis aimed to capture what she believed was being lost by
unwitting neglect and by a rewriting of American culinary history
that excluded all black narratives except for the poverty-riddled ones.

Later in her career when students in her classes heaped praise, Lewis deflected their attentions, saying, "Why, that wasn't anything but field food." That sounded like false modesty. But Lewis meant it. Her people were farmers. And the foods she championed were what sustained them in the fields. "In the South, you didn't have to be rich," she said, sketching a broad definition of middle-class life. "There was always something good to eat."

Working at Café Nicholson, Lewis began to write and to develop the recipes that formed the core of her masterwork, *The Taste of Country Cooking*. Judith Jones, the Knopf editor who published Julia Child, shepherded Lewis into print. With Child as her model, Jones built a stable of amateur women cooks. Expatriates, compelled to reproduce the foods and the places they left behind, these women wanted to keep those memories and tastes alive.

Jones signed Claudia Roden, who grew up in a Sephardic family in Cairo and began cooking after her family moved to London. Her aim in *A Book of Middle Eastern Food* was to "rejoice in our foods and summon the ghosts of our past." Madhur Jaffrey, a native of Delhi, was an actress who moved first to England and then America. To reacquaint herself with the cooking of her mother, she wrote *An Invitation to Indian Cooking*, which Jones edited and Knopf published. *A Taste of Country Cooking* was Jones's first attempt to apply that rubric to American food.

Lewis's prose was lyrical and romantic: "I will never forget spring mornings in Virginia. A warm morning and a red sun rising behind a thick fog gave the image of a pale pink veil supported by a gentle breeze that blew our thin marquisette curtains out into the room, leaving them to fall lazily back. Being awakened by this irresistible atmosphere we would hop out of bed, clothes in hand, rush downstairs, dress in a sunny spot, and rush out to the barn to find a sweet-faced calf, baby pigs, or perhaps a colt." Her words were deeply grounded in place. She offered a child's-eye view of the community she had called home. "A stream, filled from the melted snows of winter, would flow quietly by us, gurgling softly and gently pulling the leaf of a fern that hung lazily from the side of its bank," she wrote in *A Taste of Country Cooking*. "After moments of complete exhilaration, we would return joyfully to the house for break-fast." To a generation of serious American cooks, Lewis offered a way to appreciate American food that did not begin with burgers and end with apple pies.

After publishing Lewis's first book in 1976, Jones signed more authors for what came to be called the Knopf Cooks American series. She published books about New England and West Coast cookery. The South became a specialty. Jones commissioned *Biscuits, Spoonbread & Sweet Potato Pie*, the second book by Bill Neal, chef-owner of Crook's Corner in Chapel Hill, North Carolina. She published *Preserving Today* by Jeanne Lesem, who grew up in Depression-era Arkansas eating her mother's pickles and preserves. For Jones, Jeanne Voltz wrote *The Florida Cookbook: From Gulf Coast Gumbo to Key Lime Pie*.

The success of Lewis and her inheritors set the standard in American food publishing for a generation of writers and readers. In the decades to come, Southern chefs would lead the revival of American regional restaurants. And Southern writers like Lewis would lead a reawakening of research into regional foodways. Together, they drove the next phase in the evolution of the region. By the 1980s, a South that had been defined by poverty and racism, by neglect and ignorance, gentrified as Southerners saw new value in old ways.

Edna Lewis feared for the future of regional food and drink. And she wondered aloud whether the contributions of African American cooks would ever gain recognition. "Southern cooking is about to become extinct," she said. "It's mostly black, because blacks—black women and black men—did most of the cooking in private homes, hotels and on the railroads." In 1992, Lewis gathered with John Egerton, Marie Rudisill, Eugene Walter, and others for a Southern food festival on the

Florida Gulf Coast at a new urbanist enclave called Seaside. Egerton brought his beaten biscuit brake. Scott Peacock, who had recently left his post as chef for the Georgia governor, arrived to assist Lewis with the Frogmore stew, pig ear salad, and benne seed biscuits.

Over a long and boozy weekend, Walter gave interviews from the bedroom of his bungalow. Rudisill regaled all with sotto voce tales of how her nephew Truman Capote, a childhood friend of Harper Lee, really wrote *To Kill a Mockingbird*. At one point, all pledged to write a collaborative book with Walter as editor. Edna Lewis turned in her essay. In an exchange of letters with Walter, Lewis wrote, "For me the South is not just food. It is beauty, love, hate, art, poetry, and hard work. I love what is good about it. It is what makes us who we are."

By 1993, Lewis had moved to Atlanta, where she and Peacock made plans to offer classes through a local gourmet grocer, for whom they developed a line of packaged foods including baking powder biscuits and stewed butter beans. At about that same time, they founded the Society for the Revival and Preservation of Southern Food. For a magazine spread, they posed in a rice field, Lewis in a rocking chair, Peacock standing behind her. To outsiders looking in, they were the odd couple of Southern cuisine, one black and aged and straight, the other white and young and gay. Considered another way, they were a harbinger of a reconciliation that was still on the horizon, a joining together of black and white, a living embodiment of the welcome table ideals advocated by activists in the 1960s.

Lewis and Peacock dreamed of a school for Southern cooks who had become untethered from their forebears. "The philosophy of the school will be to teach children the historical and cultural perspectives of Southern food," said Peacock, who became her caretaker when they moved in together in suburban Atlanta. Peacock didn't cotton to the New South dishes then becoming popular. "That doesn't mean butter bean salad with cilantro and snow peas," he said.

They both derided the tendency to prop any protein on a pool of grits and call the resulting construction Southern. Char-grilled lobster on grits with lemongrass sauce was not born of the South, he said. Too few people were using regional produce and cooking seasonally, she said. Over the next three decades, a new generation of chefs rededicated themselves to the Freetown ideals recollected and practiced by Lewis over a long life in the fields and behind stoves.

Gentrification

1980s & 1990s

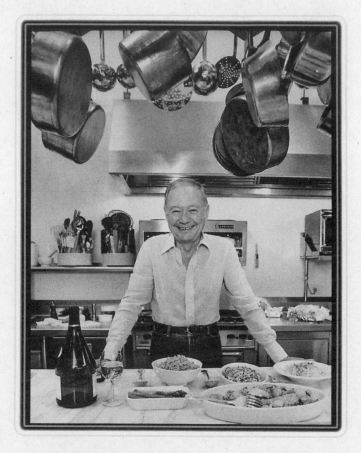

Craig Claiborne transformed his Long Island home kitchen into a writing studio and recipe test kitchen.

Kingmaker and Kings

Paul Bocuse, the Michelin-starred French chef, arrived at Craig Claiborne's Long Island home to bone and stuff squabs with foie gras and truffles. Diana Kennedy, the British chronicler of Mexican cuisine who taught Americans that ant eggs were edible, came to teach him how to make tortillas. Paul Prudhomme lugged a cooler of crawfish from Cajun Country to his house overlooking Gardiner's Bay.

Half-moon glasses perched on his nose, a black IBM typewriter in reach, mannerly Claiborne documented their work and recipes as food editor of *The New York Times*. A native of Mississippi, he thrived on Long Island, where his kitchen served as a studio for *Times* stories. In the 1970s and early 1980s, Claiborne was the kingmaker of the American food world, more influential than James Beard or Julia Child. In the pages of the *Times*, America tracked Gardiner's Bay comings and goings and chef coronations.

Born in 1920 in the Delta, Claiborne left the South halfway through his sophomore college year. He never lived there again. But he didn't leave the region behind. Expatriate Southerners clustered in his orbit.

James Villas, the North Carolina–born *Town and Country* writer who shared his love of luxury ocean liners and French cuisine, lived down the road. Willie Morris, the Mississippi native who moved north to edit *Harper's*, compared the Hamptons to the Delta, where he, too, was born. The land was flat and the potato plants reminded him of young cotton. "You know who's sick and who's died," Morris said, "and you know each other's children and dogs."

One December night in 1973, after they drank themselves sentimental on Scotch and sodas at Bobby Van's bar in Bridgehampton, Morris and Claiborne talked of home, of Faulkner and the blues, of Claiborne's mother's cooking and Morris's high school football triumphs. Morris, who shared a complicated relationship with the Delta, and who had already published a memoir that plumbed those depths, told Claiborne that he must reclaim the place of his birth. At that point, Claiborne hadn't been back to Sunflower County in almost twenty years. Even when his mother died in 1966, he declined to attend the funeral. You have to write about the place that made you, Morris told Claiborne: "Hell, you and B.B. King are the only two people anybody ever heard of outside Sunflower County." (In his drunkenness, Morris forgot Fannie Lou Hamer, born three years before Claiborne.)

Before the night was over, Morris suggested that Claiborne write his own book. More than eight years passed before Claiborne actually traveled home. But he did begin an autobiography, *A Feast Made for Laughter*, which he dedicated to Morris. Drawn back to Sunflower County, finally, in 1981 by the death of his uncle and the chance to see his sister, Claiborne figured he could get some newspaper work done, too. Mississippi had begun to convert cotton fields to catfish ponds. And Claiborne, who grew up attending fish fries, saw an opportunity for eating as well as reporting.

With his sister, he walked the grounds of their old Sunflower home, an audiocassette recorder in hand, reminiscing about the days before the family lost its fortune, when the Claibornes were so wealthy that they threw barbecues for the community, serving a whole lamb, whole pigs, and sides of beef to anyone who smelled the smoke. After that visit, when Claiborne returned to Long Island, he flew north with coolers of frozen catfish filets, packed by Delta farmers, anxious to spread the news of their cotton-to-aquaculture transition.

Back on Long Island, Claiborne and his cooking and writing partner Pierre Franey developed recipes for catfish meunière, catfish in white wine sauce, catfish baked with cheese and almonds, and fried catfish with hushpuppies and tartar sauce. In addition to returning with inspiration for his *Times* column, Claiborne came home to New York with a sense that the South of the 1980s might welcome him.

A Feast Made for Laughter was a dark memoir in which Claiborne revealed how his mother emasculated him and hinted, in a seeming dream sequence, that his father and he may have fondled each other. The 1982 book made clear to Morris and everyone else why Claiborne had a hard time returning. Publication was cathartic. At a reunion of his father's family that year in Brownsville, Tennessee, a matriarch approached to say that she had a bone to pick with Claiborne. But it was not about the seeming incest. Instead, she took issue with his wish to be cremated when he died. "You've got to be buried *here* in this cemetery," she said, "next to your grandmother and grandfather."

Claiborne's family story was archetypal: When cotton prices dropped by half during a 1921 plummet of agricultural markets, Luke Claiborne, a land speculator, cotton gin operator, and banker, lost nearly everything. From their comfortable home in the village of Sunflower, where Kipling and Shakespeare lined the bookshelves, opera records stocked the phonograph machine, and a baby grand piano dominated the living room, the family moved to a succession of lesser dwellings in nearby Indianola.

The solution, once they settled, was a New South standard, dating back to the early years of Reconstruction when Confederate widows wrote and sold charity cookbooks to purchase artificial limbs and crutches for survivors: Mother pulled the family out of the ditch.

By 1922, Kathleen Claiborne converted their white clapboard home into a boardinghouse and took responsibility for the family finances. Like Mary Bobo, who started serving drummers in Lynchburg, Tennessee, in 1908, and Sema Wilkes, who began feeding the railroad men of Savannah, Georgia, in 1943, the food at the Claiborne family boardinghouse became the draw. *Liberty* magazine reported in 1948: "The six paying guests, all bachelors, said there wasn't much point in getting married when Miss Kathleen's food was so good."

Time in the kitchen was formative. Like Truman Capote, who grew up in the Monroeville, Alabama, kitchen of his aunt Sook, Claiborne was not a rough-and-tumble boy. He didn't slosh in the gumbo clay to hunt ducks like other white sons of the gentry. He found refuge in his mother's kitchen among black cooks. When they fried chicken or simmered a pot of black-eyed peas, Claiborne was at their skirt hems. For his birthday, Blanche, whose ample bosom he said was a "marvelous thing to lean against," baked coconut cakes, with frosting spread "over and around and between the layers like thickly tufted snow-white chenille." Claiborne loved the women who nurtured him but didn't know their last names. Typical of the day, he couldn't convey respect without insult, writing, "I am convinced that given the proper training in the kitchen of a great French restaurant, any American black with cooking in his or her soul would be outstanding."

Claiborne enlisted in the navy after college as World War II came to a close. In Morocco, he learned to steam couscous. During the Korean War, Claiborne worked his way through the *Joy of Cooking*. After discharge, on recommendation from a banquet manager at the Peabody Hotel in Memphis, he enrolled in the École Hôtelière de la Société Suisse des Hôteliers near Lausanne, Switzerland, where he earned certificates in classical French cuisine and banquet service. Returning to America,

Claiborne flacked Waring blenders and worked as a receptionist at *Gourmet* magazine before plotting his ascent to the *Times*.

Like many of his generation who were gay or recognized they were somehow different, Claiborne loved and loathed the South in sometimes equal measure. But as he made the leap for a job at *The New York Times* in 1957, Claiborne wrapped himself in the mantle of Mississippi. When managing editor Turner Catledge, a native of upstate Ackerman, asked where he had attended college, Claiborne replied "Missippi State," eliding his consonants and amplifying his drawl.

As they talked, Claiborne laid it on thick for Catledge, who had graduated from that school when it was called Mississippi A&M. Claiborne, who transferred to the University of Missouri as a sophomore, said that he, too, had lived in the Starkville dorm that everyone called Polecat Alley and let it slip that he had pledged KA fraternity.

When Craig Claiborne joined *The New York Times*, food coverage was restricted to the so-called women's pages. As the first male to edit the food pages of a major American daily, he foreshadowed a shift in American attitudes about food (and a shift in the ranks of food writers, from women to men). Like the chefs and restaurateurs he wrote about, Claiborne put food in its historical and cultural contexts. He marked the personalities and craft behind the dishes.

Claiborne revered French food and French service. He cultivated a taste for foie gras and loved to sink a mother-of-pearl spoon in a tin of caviar. Claiborne liked to tell admirers that, before he took the position, quiche was newfangled on this side of the Atlantic. For the *Times*, Claiborne traveled the globe. In 1974, he reported from Paris, Amsterdam, Tokyo, Osaka, Bali, and Singapore. That same year, five months before the South Vietnamese government fell and American troops evacuated, he filed a story from Saigon focused on, among other dishes, pho, the beef broth and rice noodle soup. A writer for *The New York Times Book Review* argued that Claiborne had done more to "shrink the globe and end isolationism than all the politicians in Washington."

Writing for the *Times*, Claiborne popularized a star rating for restaurants that became the standard across the nation. More important, he redefined cooks and chefs as personalities, drawing Bocuse and Kennedy and Prudhomme out of the kitchen and into his reach. Claiborne treated them like they were stars, worthy of profiles, with smart things to say about the broader culture as well as cooking.

Claiborne saw new value in American food. "Regional cooking is the down home staples of an area that in years gone by received little attention," he said, "because people were under the delusion that it had to be French to be food." In search of honest American food, Claiborne explored his native South. As he returned to his roots in the 1980s, the region began to embrace its foods. Claiborne traveled to Dallas to interview Stephan Pyles and report on his quail with goat cheese and black-eyed peas vinaigrette. Claiborne revisited *Cross Creek Cookery* by Florida novelist Marjorie Kinnan Rawlings. Of Mrs. Wilkes in Savannah, he wrote, "There is something warm and peculiarly congenial about a Southern boardinghouse. (I should know, I grew up in one.)"

Claiborne's absence from the region could be telling. His 1987 book *Southern Cooking* included recipes for catfish this and barbecue that and spanned the genre from cheese straws to chitlins. But Claiborne's po-boy recipe called for salami and cheese and pepperoncini, a likely conflation of the muffuletta. Reared among black cooks, he still could not find the words to praise their knowledge and labor, describing Creole cookery as a marriage of "innocent Spanish" and "bastardized French."

The great regional cuisines of the country were Southern, Claiborne declared after reacquainting himself with his native foods, naming the best as Cajun, Creole, Soul, Tex-Mex, and barbecue. Two of the chefs he championed would lead the regional food revolution of the 1980s, instilling pride in the long-beleaguered South and helping America recognize the value in regional foods, from the clambakes of New England to the hot dishes of the Midwest.

Throughout his life, Claiborne remained conflicted about his birthplace and his people. He began to reconcile with the region while writing about two Southern chefs.

Paul Prudhomme was the maximalist, who hunted and fished and cooked like the manly Delta boys whom effeminate Claiborne idolized as a youth. As a Cajun proselytizer, he sold the world on tasso, andouille, and turducken. Claiborne did more than write glowingly about the chef. In the early days of K-Paul's, Claiborne asked Prudhomme if he planned to renovate, taking into account the crush of crowds that was then descending. When Prudhomme said he wasn't sure what he was going to do, Claiborne told him, "If you don't have the money, I'll lend it to you!"

Bill Neal, the whip-smart aesthete, likely reminded Claiborne of his younger self. Before Claiborne called on Bill Neal in Chapel Hill, shrimp and grits was a working-class fisherman's breakfast, rarely eaten more than fifty miles from the Atlantic coast. From Neal, a generation of Southern chefs would learn that good cooking required research. They would learn, too, that the best cooks brought broad artistic sensibilities to their work.

It took me many years to understand that it was the use of local fresh products that was the single most important factor in good eating," Paul Prudhomme explained in a recollection of his youth that could have come from the mouth of Edna Lewis. "We had no refrigeration, so we'd go out in the fields to get what we needed. When we dug up potatoes, within two hours they'd be in the pot, cooked and eaten. I couldn't seem to get a potato to taste like my mother's until I realized that it wasn't anything that was done in the kitchen—it was just the freshness of the potato that made it completely different."

Prudhomme did more than trumpet farm goods. He conceived and popularized blackened redfish, the dish that led to the decimation of the Gulf of Mexico redfish stock. Demand proved unrelenting. "If customers come to my restaurant and find that there is no blackened red fish available, they sulk like children," he said in 1981 at the height of the craze.

Prudhomme also helped popularize the modern Cajun persona. Like its city neighbor New Orleans, Cajun Country was thought a place apart. A travel writer in the 1950s called southwestern Louisiana as "foreign a country as any to be found on another continent, where Main Street may be a bayou, and the postman must be a motorboat pilot." By the time Prudhomme came on the scene, Cajun culture was already on the upswing.

Justin Wilson was not the only popular figure to play the Cajun card. Edwin Edwards, the libidinous Cajun whom detractors called the Silver Zipper, won the governorship in 1972 with the slogan Cajun Power, printed on posters that showed a white fist clenched around a red crawfish. The suggestion was that working-class Cajuns, like the working-class African Americans who adopted Black Power as their mantra in the late 1960s, were a besieged people and Edwards was fighting for their autonomy. Eventually, that new pride begat cayenne-flavored Cajun brand beer, brewed in Milwaukee by Pabst; blackened Cajun Cola sold under the slogan "because some like it hot"; and a Cajun edition of the San Francisco magazine *Bear*, which promised a "celebration of unshaven masculinity."

When Ella and Dick Brennan hired Paul Prudhomme to run the kitchen at Commander's Palace in 1975, he was the first American-born chef to hold that position since the restaurant was founded in 1880. The Brennans didn't hire him to tap the budding Cajun phenomenon. They hired him as lunch chef and told him to run the day kitchen. He quickly threw out the interchangeable French menu that every New Orleans restaurant seemed to have served since Jean-Baptiste Le Moyne mapped the city.

Long before the move became a marketing conceit, Prudhomme

stocked the Commander's pantries with local goods, inspired by his mother's kitchen, sourced by his nephews. For his menu of playfully re-imagined Louisiana dishes, one might trade for tasso with a friend, another would shoot a brace of ducks, and a third might harvest spring greens. Like Edna Lewis, he cooked the food of his ancestors, but he was not limited by that food. Trout almandine got a blanket of Louisiana pecans instead. Prudhomme ditched crabmeat imperial in favor of crabmeat and corn bisque. Prudhomme didn't like to hear his cooking labeled Cajun. He preferred to call it Louisianan. Or American.

The shift away from pretentiousness and toward localness continued at K-Paul's, which he opened in 1979 with his wife, K. Hinrichs, as a French Quarter café. Long before other chefs developed restaurants that were downscale in price but sacrificed nothing in quality, K-Paul's earned a national reputation as a no-tablecloth restaurant that drew on an impeccable larder. Prudhomme purposefully ran the sort of place where his family back home in Opelousas felt comfortable.

Before trendy restaurants in Brooklyn adopted Mason jars, before the restaurant chain Po Folks served sweet tea in them, Hinrichs filled those jars with vodka steeped with hot peppers and sold the drinks as Cajun martinis. Instead of fighting the belief that Cajun food was necessarily spicy, Hinrichs and Prudhomme gave the public what it wanted. And Prudhomme did it while wearing a button on his white hat that read "TOTALLY HOT!" Before Thomas Keller earned his reputation for dish conceits like oysters and pearls and coffee and doughnuts, Prudhomme served roast beef with debris, a sauce made from threads of roast beef and gravy, and Cajun popcorn, made from deep-fried crawfish tails.

A great showman, he knew how to leverage that playfulness for public theater. Prudhomme was at the center of a 1979 dinner that was the food equivalent of the famous Judgment in Paris wine tasting, in which American bottles were declared better than French. The occasion was the first anniversary of *Food & Wine* magazine. Chefs flew to New York City from France and Italy and California. Prudhomme stole the show with a dessert of plank board Cajun cottages, made from chocolate, filled with strawberries, surrounded by coconut "grass" that Prudhomme dyed green. When waiters arrived with bowls of heated grocery store strawberry ice cream and poured it over the top, guests gasped and shouted and clapped as their cabins collapsed. Alice Waters, who had served a restrained lunch course of baked garlic, crusty bread, and goat cheese, came away smitten.

Taking note of his girth and flair, *Newsweek* called Prudhomme the "Pavarotti of American chefs." *People* called him the "Guru of Gumbo." *The New York Times* described Prudhomme as a "Cajun Buddha," a "self-made deity of let-the-good-times-roll cooking." Compared to the minimalist French style that Waters and others nurtured in the Bay Area, this was brawny and resolutely American.

Prudhomme gave good copy. "That's one of those kick-you-in-the-pants dishes, boy, I'll tell ya," he said of his mirliton stuffed with fried oysters and topped with hollandaise. "It has so many tastes, and every bite whops up on something else." Claiborne was an early champion. "Although a good many of the meals of my Mississippi childhood were Cajun, Creole or soul food, I would have been hard put, until recently, to make an elaborate distinction between what is Cajun and what is Creole," he wrote. "But my solution was simple: Go to the undisputed pontiff and grand panjandrum of the Cajun and Creole cookstove, that genial genius of massive girth, Paul Prudhomme."

The American food renaissance was in its infancy in 1981, when Prudhomme came north to visit Claiborne at his Long Island home. The youngest of thirteen children, Claiborne described him for readers as a rarity, a "celebrated, internationally known chef who just happens to have been born in the United States." In the age of French epiphanies, Prudhomme was a different sort of chef, inspired not by the grandmothers of Provence or the bouchon cooks of Lyon, but by his parents.

Enthralled by the chef and his stories of growing up near Opelousas, Claiborne reported that Prudhomme's father, a sharecropper, grew his own corn, which the local miller cracked for chicken feed, cornmeal, and grits. Prudhomme's mother made jambalaya and gumbo on Fridays. After his brothers and sister went dancing, they came home late to hot chicken-sausage gumbo. "Mother was a highly resourceful woman," Prudhomme told Claiborne. "She could take a couple of hens out of the yard, hens that were too old to lay eggs, and make enough food for a dozen or so children." When Claiborne curated the foods served for the 1983 Williamsburg, Virginia, World Economic Summit, Prudhomme joined other Claiborne protégés—including Mexican expert Zarela Martinez, who had roots in El Paso, Texas, and barbecue pitmaster Wayne Monk of Lexington, North Carolina—to blacken messes of redfish for the masses.

Before pop-ups were common, Prudhomme scheduled summer residencies in media capitals. In the summer of 1983, he closed his New Orleans restaurant and took his crew on the road to San Francisco, where rock promoter Bill Graham turned over the keys to a shuttered nightclub. The overbooked restaurant turned away as many as five hundred guests a night. In the summer of 1985, he closed temporarily in New Orleans to open in New York City, where he served blackened tuna because redfish had become too scarce and expensive.

To ensure that the copycats who followed his recipes got it right, Prudhomme introduced Louisiana Cajun Magic spice mix, a blend of seven spices, herbs, and salt that recalled Colonel Sanders's eleven-ingredient mix. His cookbook included three pages of detailed instruction on how to make a proper roux, and two pages of color photographs of light brown to almost black versions. Prudhomme, who wore chef whites and walked with a cane, referred to the cooked slurry of flour and fat as "Cajun napalm" and directed novice cooks to be "certain that any possible distractions—including children—are under control."

His food was unbridled, unmediated. In a moment when America longed to reacquaint itself with its frontier roots, Prudhomme's version of Louisiana food promised a rusticity then in retreat. At a time when the average consumer felt disconnected from the natural world,

Prudhomme offered a path through the suburban hedgerow to a sylvan America.

Not long after the Ritz Café opened in Los Angeles with a menu of blackened redfish and other newfangled Cajun dishes, one of the owners reflected on their success. He was packing them in, he said, because Americans had developed a stomach for "gut food." By 1989, Prudhomme entered the expansion game himself, opening a permanent restaurant in New York City. After an initial rush of business, things didn't go well. "Cajun food is dead," a *Village Voice* writer declared, and "Paul Prudhomme is its undertaker." By that time, London boasted two Cajun-style restaurants. And the hottest new restaurant in Amsterdam was Riekje Sluizer's Cajun Louisiana Kitchen.

As Prudhomme's imitators grew legion, so did the liberties they took. The American gut wanted something more refined, it seemed, and the Ritz in Los Angeles stood ready to deliver a dish of foie gras atop blackened pasta, made by stirring a Prudhomme-inspired seasoning mix into the dough. Late in life, faced with the various ersatz Cajun dishes that were being sold as genuine, he doubled down on his Louisiana Cajun Magic spice mixes, which he sold as a brand of authenticity, available for purchase on grocery store shelves.

O n a spring morning in 1985, Craig Claiborne rapped at the screen door of a one-bedroom apartment in the college town of Chapel Hill, North Carolina. Bill Neal, the thirty-four-year-old chef at Crook's Corner, a local bistro with a pig sculpture on the roof, escorted the *New York Times* editor into a narrow galley kitchen. Both native Southerners with complicated sexual identities, they had gotten to know each other the prior year when Claiborne traveled North Carolina to document the work of traditional barbecue pitmasters including Wayne Monk. After the men exchanged pleasantries, Neal began boning quail, shelling shrimp, and shredding cheddar cheese to mix with grits. Claiborne, who had eaten dinner on the patio at Crook's the night before and knew what he wanted to taste that day, pulled up a stool, placed his battered IBM on top of the water heater, and captured what the young chef cooked.

In a roundup of North Carolina fine dining restaurants, Claiborne did not stint praise: "Traditional ham-and-grits-and-red-eye-gravy style food is not as easy to come by in the region as it once was. But make no mistake, it still exists and the most talked-about proponent of it is Bill Neal, the young chef at Crook's Corner in Chapel Hill." Tucked in a shebang that had been a taxi stand, a fish market, a filling station, and a hobo home, the restaurant was a Chapel Hill standard, where construction workers drank beer and college students courted over oyster stew and chocolate soufflé cake.

Two weeks later, Claiborne crowned Neal the future king of the Southern food fraternity in a second North Carolina love letter, appended with recipes for hoppin' John capped with shredded cheddar and sautéed shrimp over a bed of cheddar grits. (Authenticity in the 1980s accommodated shredded cheddar.) "Bill Neal, considered by many to be one of today's finest young Southern chefs, takes a decidedly historical approach to cooking," wrote Claiborne. "That is because he considers the regional dishes of this country as important and worthy of preservation as the nation's monuments and architecture."

Like Julia Child before him and Frank Stitt after, Neal said that time in France compelled his epiphany. He was at home there. Southern life translated beautifully into the French. "My tie to the land had been just as great," he said, "the tiny radishes my sister grew in late February were as eagerly anticipated as Argenteuil asparagus." Travel in France served Neal as a sort of graduate school. The grandson of farmers, he had begun his culinary education on trips to New Orleans with his wife, Moreton Neal. They met in a French class at Duke University. When he was nineteen, her mother took them to dinner at Antoine's in New Orleans. For a young man raised on a farm diet of pork chops and mashed potatoes, soufflé pommes frites and crabmeat salads were revelatory.

"It was like watching Helen Keller discover language," Moreton Neal said of their dinner of trout almandine at Galatoire's. Self-taught, Neal talked his way into restaurants in the Triangle, first as a baker, then as a line cook. Like Claiborne, he cooked his way through Julia Child's work and mastered brioche. Together with Moreton, he opened La Residence, a French country restaurant on a former dairy farm outside Chapel Hill. An emphasis on Southern food came later, after he and Moreton divorced, as Neal translated their travels to France and New Orleans at Crook's Corner. "I realized my food always had been telling who I was, when, and where; how I felt about my family, and how I related to nature," Neal explained. "I saw it first in the lives of people whose language, customs, and culture were foreign. . . ."

Famously dismissive of cooking schools, he turned away CIA graduates Ben Barker and Karen Barker, who went on to open Magnolia Grill in nearby Durham. Instead, Neal hired a ragtag crew at Crook's. Robert Stehling, who would go on to open Hominy Grill in Charleston, arrived shoeless to apply for a dishwashing job. John Currence, who opened City Grocery in Oxford, Mississippi, in 1992, took a dishwashing job at Crook's to earn bucks between band gigs. Gene Hamer, who eventually became Neal's lover and his partner in Crook's, studied business, forestry, and horticulture before he began his restaurant career. (His first gig at La Residence was to assemble cookie plates and mix drinks.)

Neal's path to epiphany was typical for the day. But his attitudes about the South were not. Instead of dismissing Native Americans as accidental agronomists and the descendants of slaves as interpreters of European recipes and techniques, he paid down debts of pleasure and labor that his forebears had accrued. "There has been an interaction among African, Western European and Indian food, which can be seen in all true Southern dishes," he said, sketching a broad and inclusive definition of the region. "One aspect may dominate, usually the African influence, but interacting with the other two major forces in the Southern area, you get Southern cooking." When a writer called for a Fourth of

July recipe, Neal delivered "Battery Fried Fish with Peanut Sauce and Stuffed Okra" and told her the name was born of the Reconstruction era: "After the Civil War, fish fries and all-day picnics were a Fourth of July tradition with Charleston blacks, who were allowed free access to the Battery on this day alone."

At a time when Southern college towns were magnets for artists and musicians, and IBM investment in nearby Research Triangle Park drove the creation of high-tech jobs and middle-class wealth, Chapel Hill was the nucleus of a future-tense South. A thinking chef, Neal emerged from the Triangle at a moment when Athens jangle rockers R.E.M. arrived to record their first songs at Mitch Easter's studio and rock clubs like Cat's Cradle drew new wave and punk and rock idealists. Restaurants like Crook's attracted rock and rollers and gay boys and girls. They were safe havens in a gestating Southern bohemia.

One year after Crook's opened in 1982, Neal pulled back from the kitchen to write. He holed up in the stacks at the University of North Carolina, searching for food references in the novels of Eudora Welty and Thomas Wolfe. Neal traveled to Charleston to read plantation day books and receipt collections at the South Carolina Historical Society. Recognizing the roots of Brunswick stew as a hunter's dish, he developed a recipe that included rabbit.

Neal took his work seriously. But he didn't cotton to the staid trappings adopted by most restaurants. On the night Claiborne came for dinner, a chain saw–carved giraffe with eyes made from green plastic apples stared out from a window. In love with the odd name, as well as the good taste, Neal served Claiborne muddle, a fish soup from the North Carolina coastal provinces, with eggs bobbing in the broth.

The timing of his 1985 book, *Bill Neal's Southern Cooking*, was good. New American cooking was ascendant. Great Chefs of France events, staged by the Mondavi Winery in Napa, had introduced America to the Troisgros brothers and Alain Chapel, champions of nouvelle cuisine. That French movement, which began as a rebellion against butter sauce–

sodden traditional dishes and matured into an embrace of terroir and simplicity, spurred two domestic rebellions. First, American chefs rejected the Americanized French food that had come to be called continental cuisine. Then they reinvigorated American food.

Neal benefited from the timing but rejected the movement. When Stephan Pyles opened Routh Street Café in Dallas in 1983, the chef focused on what was then called New American cuisine, which often translated as fancy meat loaf. By the summer of 1986, when Claiborne arrived to try his honeyed fried chicken, Pyles had tightened his approach. "I like to think I'm trying to redefine and refine things that I grew up with," he said, citing a roster of tamales, enchiladas, tostadas, and fried chicken. "If I can make it more sophisticated, using a lot more fresh herbs and so on, I'll feel like I've accomplished a great deal."

Neal didn't like what he heard. "The new American cuisine is nothing more than a commercial flash in the pan, made up by restaurateurs and trend-setters," he said. Neal was moving away from sophistication, toward elemental cooking, genuinely based on the crops grown in the region and the people who claimed that place as home. At a moment when a cap of goat cheese was considered a sophisticated topping for a roasted chicken breast, Neal resuscitated older dishes that had fallen out of favor. That said, he was not immune to the lure of fashion. By 1985, when Claiborne came to dinner, he already served a blackened rib eye inspired by Paul Prudhomme.

Shrimp and grits, a traditional fisherman's breakfast, proved his money dish. It was a stir-fry, really, a toss of shrimp, bacon, mushrooms, and scallions. Served on a base of grits, Neal's version was an ideal restaurant dish. Prep could be done in advance and the toss could be finished to order. A base of grits meant a low food cost. Plus, it was a curiosity that sounded as odd to many American diners as chicken and waffles would sound a couple decades later when the nation began puzzling through that dish. By the time Neal wrote a revised edition of his book in 1989, in which he explained that shrimp and grits was a popular combination from Wilmington, North Carolina, down to the northern Florida coast, Crook's served more than ten thousand plates each year.

Like Prudhomme, Neal knew how to sell the foods of his native region. When journalists called, he gave good copy. Neal knew the value of context, of culture, of personal recollection. "Quail is absolutely my favorite food," he told a reporter in 1985. "My father always hunted. I remember reaching into his pockets to get the still-warm birds. . . . Grandma would clean them, momma would cook them, and we would all eat them."Asked about his favorite fish, Neal talked of catfish stew, describing how the men in his family nailed fish to a tree and stripped the skin from the bones of writhing carcasses.

By the close of his life, Neal shifted his focus to horticulture, a reorientation that preceded the current vogue of farmer-chefs by a generation. He recognized that while fried chicken and barbecue appealed to outlanders, Southern cookery was a vegetable-driven cuisine built on corn and greens and okra. With his friend Barbara Tolley, who earned her doctorate while working at Crook's, Neal began writing a vegetable cookbook.

In the months before his death of AIDS-related complications in 1991, Neal also tried his hand at fiction, writing a story about a Depression-era Carolina farm, delivered in the voice of a girl. All were part of what he called "my affirmation of an active Southern heritage." Like Southerners before and after him, Neal used food to shape narratives of his people and his place.

Craig Claiborne went north to find himself. But he could never shake the South. That place made him. In the generations to come, Prudhomme and Neal inspired two chef schools that would become national models: the maximalist home cooking champion and the scholar aesthete. Like Claiborne, many of their peers had to travel beyond the South before they could appreciate the region. But these new-generation Southerners didn't stay gone. Like Neal, they returned home. They reclaimed their region.

At a time when the South still suffered from the stereotypes it earned during the Jim Crow era and the civil rights movement, these chefs recognized that, if they wanted to change the region, they could do it at the table. As the South continued to urbanize and dining moved from homes to restaurants, they led in ways that were unexpected. They would help the South see itself anew. They would help the region reveal its better self.

Salute to Southern Chefs, Charleston, South Carolina. (Back row, from left)
Marcel Desaulniers, Louis Osteen, Bob Kinkead, Mark Militello, Mark Abernathy,
Grant Noe, Ben Barker. (Middle row, from left) Elizabeth Terry, Jose Gutierrez.
(Bottom row, from left) Frank Stitt, Stephan Pyles.

Generation Grits

I think that food in America can be all those things that we envy other cultures in being," Paul Prudhomme said to cheers at the first Symposium on American Cuisine, staged in Louisville, Kentucky, in 1982. "Our restaurants have a huge task ahead. And it's translating the heritage of American food from every region of this country that's in our homes into the restaurants. That's not an easy task. It's going to take more than this room full of people. It's going to take more than ten times this room full of people, but we have to do it because it is our heritage and because it's the right and proper way to live—to accept the responsibilities of who we are and what we are and carry on."

Before the conference concluded, Ella Brennan, who had already hired Emeril Lagasse to succeed Prudhomme in the kitchens at Commander's, invited the group to reconvene in New Orleans the next year to celebrate the centennial of her flagship restaurant. The conversation that second year got testy. Speaking on a program that also included Chez Panisse veteran Jonathan Waxman, an architect of what came to be called California cuisine, James Villas declared war on the emergent trend in which chefs topped greens with foie gras, truffles, and walnut oil. If chefs do not stay true to regional roots, he said, they will make a "further mockery of our food." America has many regional styles of cooking but no coherent national one, Villas told attendees. The problem was research and understanding: "No cuisine is less explored or appreciated than our own."

Conceived as public relations gambits, the first two editions of the Symposium on American Cuisine drew attendees who aimed to define American food culture. Some said that the term *cuisine*, borrowed from the French, wasn't appropriate for an American enterprise. Lidia Bastianich said the exercise was easy as petting a porcupine. Larry Forgione argued that it was more important to establish regional restaurants than to attempt broader, American restaurants. Michigan restaurants shouldn't rely on Florida pompano, he said, when the Great Lakes teem with whitefish, perch, and trout.

Over the following decade, Forgione got what he wanted. Jasper White reinvigorated the seafood cookery of New England when he opened Jasper's on the Boston waterfront in 1983. New World cuisine, with its mango ketchup and yucca fritters, emerged from Florida. By 1984, New Texas cuisine gained momentum, led by Dean Fearing of the Mansion on Turtle Creek in Dallas and Robert Del Grande of Café Annie in Houston. To the consternation of traditionalists like Villas, grilled salmon with chili pepper, swaddled in avocado puree, was soon omnipresent. Egg rolls, stuffed with black beans and avocados and drizzled with chipotle mayo, followed.

Merican consumers embraced dining out as a leisure activity. Chefs stepped out of French shadows. Cooking schools blossomed. *The Official Foodie Handbook* sold like hoecakes. "The young urban professionals have arrived," *Newsweek* announced. "They're making lots of money, spending it conspicuously, and switching political candidates like they test cuisines."

Gourmet foods became markers of status for a new leisure class that aimed to best Europe. Afflicted by what the French called nostalgia for the mud, the middle class ate down the ladder where their forebears began. In the 1960s, Southerners thought fried chicken, tonged hot from a cast iron skillet, was a mundane indulgence. By the 1970s, whole hog barbecue, cooked over hickory coals in a tin-topped brick pit, was an anachronism. As the South urbanized, as wealth broke through the thick amber of poverty, as national chains spread and families shopped at suburban strip malls instead of downtown department stores, fried chicken cafés dwindled or switched from skillets to pressure fryers. Barbecue joints shuttered or shifted from coal-fired pits to electric ovens. Biscuits became drive-through ballast for morning commutes.

Southerners feared losing foods they thought birthrights. Americans, who had long dismissed grits and greens, recognized that regional foods were imperiled. Writers sounded warnings and chronicled the dishes in decline. The survival of regional foods and customs was merely token, Raymond Sokolov wrote in a series of articles that resulted in a 1981 book. They were "gastronomic invalids," victims of a "food-delivery system that is highly regulated and built to serve faceless millions in the most convenient, efficient way."

Home-cured country hams, which could not be sold across state lines, no longer served Kentucky tobacco farmers as a second source of income. Few markets in Cajun Country still sold the sausages of pig offal, pig blood, and rice known as boudin rouge. The process appeared irreversible. "Barring the advent of a totalitarian government on the order of the Khmer Rouge, we are not going to see significant numbers of people returning to the land," Sokolov wrote just one decade after Stephen Gaskin and his followers had settled The Farm. "No one is seeding new beds of Olympia oysters or pressing for the legalization of moonshine. History has taken its inexorable toll."

Against these odds, America began to claim a cuisine. Mark Miller, a Chez Panisse graduate, recognized the awakening: "The United States had been moving away from Europe and defining itself for a very long time, in literature and poetry with Walt Whitman, in philosophy with the Transcendentalist movement, in music with jazz, and in art with abstract expressionism. There was a sense that America had arrived and was mature. What was the one art form left to develop? Our cuisine."

Much of the work began in the white tablecloth restaurants of the South in the late 1970s and early 1980s. Patrick O'Connell and Reinhardt Lynch opened the Inn at Little Washington in a retrofitted garage in rural Virginia. The first menu in 1978 featured frog legs niçoise. Within a couple years, O'Connell, who famously wore Dalmatian-print chef pants and aspired to Michelin-starred opulence, was larding timbales with Maryland crab and crusting lamb racks with native crop pecans. In 1979, Louis and Marlene Osteen opened a restaurant at Pawleys Island Inn near Charleston, South Carolina. Marlene pursued vanguard California winemakers. Louis stepped away from swordfish with olive butter, toward brown oyster stew with benne and barbecue duck with Vidalia onion jam.

Before she opened Elizabeth on 37th in Savannah in 1981, Elizabeth Terry dug through archives, reading garden notebooks and cookbook manuscripts that she translated into shrimp with country ham in red-eye gravy and shad stuffed with shad roe. She studied how to stone-grind grits and salt-cure hams. She learned that pioneers salted and smoked fish for preservation. In a housewife recipe for fish, wrapped in paper and buried in coals to roast, she recognized a rudimentary pompano en papillote. At the Georgia Historical Society, she read the minutes of the antebellum Madeira drinking societies that proliferated in that port city.

America has long struggled with culinary identity. Does the nation possess one cuisine, many cuisines, or none at all? To have a cuisine, a nation requires engaged eaters who recognize a canon of dishes and defend it from bastardization. But American cuisine had been built on bastardization. Pizza, layered with tomato sauce and maybe some cheese, was born of Italy. By 1983, Americans layered pies with barbecue chicken, smoked salmon, and blackened shrimp. Fried chicken was a farm woman's dish, perfected by cooks of African descent. By 1986 a Dallas chef marinated his birds in berry vinaigrette and drizzled the finished dish with honey. Signal American dishes were honed through the adaptive reuse of native goods and the inventive sampling of immigrant traditions.

An interrogation of American culture had begun long before, in the late nineteenth and early twentieth centuries. As the nation knitted itself together after the Civil War, we went searching for the great American novel. When America looked for its cuisine, critics often didn't like what they found. Cooking in the United States was a primitive affair, the *Chicago Tribune* reported in 1910, sounding a recurrent theme: "Compared to French cooking, it is a string quartet." A headline summed up the state of affairs: "DISCOVERED, AMERICAN RESTAURANT; CHANCES ARE IT'S THE ONLY ONE ALIVE."

So-called foodies reserved laurels for the kind of home cooking Mark Twain advocated. During a long European tour in 1878, he famously compiled a list of the signal foods he missed while abroad. Twain pined for early ash-roasted rose potatoes, hot corn cakes with chitterlings, for fried oysters, stewed oysters, and frogs. Twain wanted a pluralistic American cuisine built on regional dishes that could be adopted across the nation. He was not alone. "Can't the Western woman learn to bake her pot of beans after the Boston method," Mary Parmelee asked in a 1905 issue of *Table Talk* magazine, "and the Northerner to boil rice as light and as snowy white as on the plantation?" Her approach sounded modern. A century later, it would begin to be realized.

It's common to peg modern American culinary consciousness to the rise of California cuisine. Many participants refer to what transpired in the 1970s and 1980s as a revolution, citing various places of agitation including Ma Maison in Los Angeles, the Astroturf-carpeted patio restaurant where Wolfgang Puck courted the Hollywood elite, and Chez Panisse, the craftsman bungalow in Berkeley, where Alice Waters preached a sensualist dictum of mace and mesclun. Asked why and how California begat the American food revolution, chroniclers answered with rhapsodies about long growing seasons that yielded exotic broccoli varieties, fresh fenugreek, heirloom watercress, and mandarin oranges that "would have made M. F. K. Fisher's mouth water."

Unlike the traditional cuisines of France, Japan, or the American South, rooted in home cooking and community events, California cuisine began in restaurants. "There was no California cuisine at somebody's house," said Gary Jenanyan, who programmed 1970s Napa Valley chef events. "No one said, 'We're going to Joyce's house for California food.' No one asked, 'Are we going to have Italian or Californian tonight?'" California cuisine was a lifestyle. Southern cuisine was a constellation of peoples and places, a vocabulary of dishes drawn from the life experiences of cooks and, eventually, chefs.

Speaking at that fractious second Symposium on American Cuisine in 1983, the French critic Christian Millau said that, owing to the rise of industrial foods and to a seemingly unshakable obeisance to French dining, American chefs were not interpreting the diversity of their various regional cuisines. His plaint came just as the nation was ready to prove him wrong. The host of New American restaurants that opened in the early to mid-1980s served as de facto academies for new consumers. Following the leads of the chefs, they ate Texas game, tossed Virginia dandelions in vinaigrette, and sucked the heads from Louisiana crawfish.

When Frank Stitt opened Highlands Bar and Grill in Birmingham in 1982, Southerners in general and Alabamians in particular did not embrace provincial cookery. The clientele who first claimed Highlands did not celebrate crops plucked from Alabama soil and fish pulled from

Alabama waters. They wanted lamb chops with mint jelly and foil-wrapped baked potatoes. Local grandees required buck-and-scrape retainers who telegraphed their subservience with downcast eyes and muffled assent. Customers didn't know how to dine back then. They didn't know how to tip.

Stitt made it his mission to win them over to his place, to their place, to their common foods. After a flirt with French bistro food, he introduced hoppin' John with lump crabmeat. And roast pork rack with Tennessee whiskey glaze. He sold them on their own provender. "When the first peaches of the season arrive, I want trumpets to play," Stitt explained. "I want horns blasting. I want people dancing in the streets when we harvest our first Alabama strawberries." Back when bacon-wrapped filets were the height of sophistication, the burghers of Birmingham didn't know what to make of Highlands, which opened with a line out the door for crab cakes and speckled trout meunière.

Born and raised an hour north of Birmingham in Cullman, a one-time "sundown town" where blacks could work but were expected to depart before nightfall, Stitt had left the South of his youth to escape the strife that hung like a pall over the region. First came Tufts University outside Boston, then the University of California at Berkeley where, inspired by the writings of Richard Olney and Elizabeth David, he cadged a kitchen gig. A stint at Chez Panisse followed. And, finally, an invitation to the South of France, where he worked as Richard Olney's assistant and shopped the markets with Jeremiah Tower. In France, Stitt had what he called "an Alabama epiphany." He realized that much of what he valued in French life—a reverence for place, a belief in the possibilities of agriculture, a respect for the formalities of the table—were also Southern virtues. Back home, Stitt leveraged that past for Alabama's future.

His maternal grandmother had churned farm milk for butter. His maternal grandfather once tended a smokehouse and plowed the red clay hills with mules. When Stitt opened Highlands he drew on that farm experience. And he drew on the strength of his family. To raise start-up capital, his mother mortgaged her home. He called, too, on the promise of Birmingham, still reeling from the lunge of Bull Connor's police dogs and the closure of the steel mills that had employed the city's working classes.

When Highlands opened, a new restaurant didn't seem noteworthy. But for a city pursuing an identity other than "Bombingham," the slander it earned during the civil rights movement, the rise of Birmingham as a restaurant city proved a fiscal and image boon. At the time Highlands debuted, the owners of Old Plantation Barbecue, down the street, tended a crop of cotton in the parking lot. A sign invited diners to "WATCH THIS COTTON GROW." A second sign, mounted on the roof eave, proclaimed, "YAS SUR, IT'S COOKED IN DE PIT." Highlands offered a different narrative. The restaurant became a showcase for post-segregation Alabama, run by a son of the gentry, employing black waiters and cooks who took pride in their work and took home good paychecks instead of leftovers.

Like Paul Prudhomme, who introduced andouille and tasso and other rustic country foods to the city repertoire and forged a new kind of Louisiana cuisine, Emeril Lagasse drove a restaurant renaissance that reshaped ideas about New Orleans. A young man of Portuguese descent from Fall River, Massachusetts, with a culinary school degree, he foretold a new kind of New Orleans and a new kind of South, no longer insular, now more accepting of outlanders, now more attractive to migrants.

"You give this country twenty or thirty more years," Satchel Paige, the Negro League baseball superstar, said in 1965, "everybody's got any sense is going down South." He was talking about black Southerners returning to the region. But as the economy grew and Jim Crow's grip withered, new arrivals like Lagasse, with no ties to the region, claimed the South, too. He was brash and smart. He was curious. Each Saturday,

Lagasse visited Ella Brennan to leaf through the latest books and magazines, talk food, and drink wine. After Sunday brunch service, Lagasse
went in search of second line parades, hoping to glimpse the magnifi-
cent plumed costumes of the Mardi Gras Indians. On days off, he fished
for drum and redfish in the Gulf. At lunch, he snuck into Uglesich's, the
grand joint near Lee Circle where Anthony Uglesich had begun cooking
in a similar freewheeling style, serving dishes like angry shrimp sautéed
with chili paste and voodoo shrimp with fermented black bean sauce.
He partnered with chef Frank Brigtsen to raise hogs and quail and rabbits across the state line in Mississippi.

   After seven years with the Brennans, Lagasse opened his own place,
Emeril's, in the Warehouse District. It was a bold move. Stretches of the
neighborhood lacked streetlights. Homeless squatters had recently lived
in the derelict grocery warehouse he renovated. At this flagship restaurant, Lagasse deconstructed and polished New Orleans classics like barbecue shrimp, pulling the heads, swaddling the tails in a butter sauce
made with house-aged Worcestershire, serving the dish with diminutive
buttermilk biscuits. He conceived new dishes like redfish filets crusted
with andouille sausage crumbs, joyful conceits that played like sly jokes
among a fraternity of insiders then subverting the canon. He developed
a Tuesday red bean soup, made with the leftovers from Monday night
red beans and rice. Payoffs came quickly. Gene Bourg, restaurant critic
for the *Times-Picayune*, fell for the choupique caviar with crème fraîche
and a corn crêpe, the duck and wild mushroom étouffée, the gumbo of
rabbit and wild mushrooms, saying, "It amounts to a manifesto, aimed
at radically altering the way we think of Creole cooking."

   Lagasse modernized New Orleans cuisine. He attacked the insular-
ity. He dug deep into Southwestern cuisine, then gaining momentum in
Texas. His repertoire soon included crawfish rellenos with red bean
sauce. And pork chops with green mole cream sauce. With his second
restaurant, NOLA, which opened in 1992, Lagasse sold New Orleans on
the notion that Vietnamese chicken wings stuffed with fish sauce–

doused pork and shrimp was not ethnic food but future-tense New Orleans cooking, reflective of immigrants then making their homes on the Gulf Coast. By 1997, Lagasse sold America on this newer New Orleans via a late-night television show, *Emeril Live*.

Susan Spicer opened Bayona in the French Quarter less than a week after Emeril's. Serving dishes that replotted map points, she made an internationalist argument. Since New Orleans had long defined itself as a city of trade, she believed the food in its best restaurants should reflect the many peoples and places that intersected when it was the second-busiest port in nineteenth-century America. In the hands of Spicer, that worldview translated as lunch sandwiches of smoked duck, cashew butter, and pepper jelly. Dinners skittered across North Africa and roped in hot sauces from Vietnam. But Lagasse proved the star player. He became a kind of proxy for the rest of the United States, which longed to claim the city as its own but didn't know the difference between a second line and a second breakfast.

His first book, *Emeril's New New Orleans Cooking*, introduced reinventions of traditional dishes with Chinese, Portuguese, and Mexican flourishes. Black-and-white photographs grounded the book in New Orleans: po-boy shops with misspelled menu boards; shellacked alligator heads with hot sauce bottles mounted amid the teeth; shelves of Café du Monde beignet mix boxes; and crawfish boils on the banks of the Mississippi. Lagasse delivered the novelty expected from new guard chefs as well as the pomp and funk and tradition that locals and curious tourists demanded.

B lack cooking is not what it was twenty years ago," Darryl Evans crowed when elected to the U.S. Culinary Olympic team in 1990. "We still cook collard greens, but we don't cook them as long as we did. Instead of flavoring with pork rinds, we might do it with duck breast or some style of sausage. Cornmeal is still used, but it's now polenta." Over the previous generation, black chefs had alternately adopted and rehabilitated and rejected soul food. Restaurants like Soul on Top of Peachtree had opened in downtown Atlanta, on the thirtieth floor of the Bank of Georgia building, but closed quickly. The restaurant promised a fashionable place to sup on pigs' feet, collards, and cornbread, but the best-selling entrée was spaghetti and meatballs. That was the problem: Soul food seemed good to think, but, especially among the upwardly mobile, soul food was not always thought good to eat.

By the late 1980s, after a stint at a chic city club and a detour to a restaurant where he served ginger-larded whole catfish drizzled with black bean sauce, Evans led the kitchen at Anthony's, an antebellum mansion restaurant on a wooded three-acre plot in the tony Buckhead neighborhood. Founded by the same Czech immigrant entrepreneur who opened Pittypat's Porch as an ersatz *Gone with the Wind*–themed tourist claptrap, the restaurant played the moonlight-and-magnolias card. Early on, Anthony's dressed its waitresses in hoopskirts and printed references to the "War of Northern Aggression" on menus.

Evans took joy in assuming the reins of a onetime plantation mansion. He reinvented the staid continental-ish menu. Fusing New South and Old South, Evans served chicken livers in the manner of a foie gras torchon. He fashioned hoppin' John into croquettes. He paired tuna tartare with watermelon. He plated striped bass with goat cheese–stuffed ravioli and Georgia caviar. A black man in a pleated chef's toque, commanding a kitchen brigade in a former plantation manse, he signaled that a change had finally come.

Evans showed the generation of black chefs who would eventually follow him to Atlanta, eager to claim a space on the kitchen line alongside a black man, that a career in food was possible. Two generations after civil rights movement protests revealed the ways that black relationships to farming, cooking, and eating were toxic, Darryl Evans showcased an Atlanta that was rapidly becoming the hometown for black American dreams. He drew black men and women into the kitchen and said these ingredients and this South were theirs to interpret.

When the centennial Olympics arrived in Atlanta in 1996, the *Journal-Constitution* published a gatefold profile of Louis Osteen of Charleston. Skillet in hand, wearing starched chef's whites, he stood at the white porch balustrade, framed by a background of stooped live oaks and a foreground of white rocking chairs. The genteel promise of the Old South was alive and well in that New South moment. And Osteen was the darling of his class, an idealized good ole boy, the sort of character Roy Blount Jr. would have dreamed up if he hadn't already existed: big boned, full of bonhomie, comfortable leaning hard into a bar, the sort of chef who quoted A. J. Liebling on gumbo, cited Marshall Frady on George Wallace, and delivered symposia speeches on American culinary identity. *The New York Times* called Osteen the "spiritual general" of the new Charleston chefs. *Esquire* said his drawl was "rich as praline candy."

Osteen was a new sort of Southerner, running a new sort of restaurant, constructing a newfangled regional identity. Chefs and other creative folks were rooting around in the region's basement, looking for representations of the South that could be revived and polished and presented. One answer was Southern restaurant cuisine. Like all aspects of life in the South, it was burdened by the region's peculiar past. But over the past generation, the worst of that taint had been scrubbed clean. Many lunch counters, where blood was spilled and salt tossed in the eyes of student protesters, closed. The counters that remained open continued to serve burgers and fries, which weren't, after all, distinctly Southern foods. The most intransigent barbecue joints integrated.

Born in upstate South Carolina, Louis Osteen cooked in Atlanta for a French chef before he settled on Pawleys Island. Along with his wife, Marlene, he transformed a sandwich shop in the back corner of an antique store into one of the most influential American restaurants of the 1980s. Like those of Frank Stitt, who opened Highlands Bar and Grill in

Birmingham three years later, Osteen's early menus of veal mousse–stuffed lamb ribs and scallop mousse–stuffed trout were more broadly French than explicitly Southern. By 1985, the same year Edna Lewis took a job as chef-consultant at nearby Middleton Place, Osteen had focused his field of vision. Grilled South Carolina squab with sage dressing and crawfish and giblet gravy was in heavy rotation. So was roasted duck with local honey.

The cooking he turned out was not specifically Lowcountry. That retrieval of a more specific history and marketing of a more specific terroir would come later. In the 1980s, Osteen, like most Southern chefs of his generation, worked a broader rubric. He focused on the South because he recognized that his region needed to be rehabilitated and that, between the four walls of his restaurant, he might be able to craft a new narrative.

The Osteens were savvy marketers, aware of the press that Bill Neal had garnered for his shrimp and cheese grits, haloed with bacon and mushrooms. Never one to stint, Louis Osteen tripled down on the possibilities. He served roasted duck over stone-ground grits. He fried flounder and tucked it alongside a pool of grits. He cooked grits to a polenta-like porridge and fried squares of mush in the Italian style.

But he didn't leave the Old South tropes behind. Playing to the tourists who were his summer bellwethers, he planted tiny rebel flags in his mesquite-grilled grouper filets and béarnaise-topped tenderloins. Osteen sampled the Old South and the New, straddling the two worlds. "Secession never went down so easily," *The Atlanta Journal-Constitution* reported. Working the same angle, CNN proclaimed in 1996, "Low-country cuisine will never be gone with the wind in this Southern seaport."

B ill Neal's signature dish, shrimp and grits, went national in the 1980s. By the close of the 1990s, it was a Southern dish on the verge of becoming an American phenomenon. As the dish spread, a second wave of New Southern chefs took liberties, often overlaying Lowcountry and Louisiana ingredients. Georgia Brown's in Washington, D.C., added Cajun andouille sausage to the sauté, a newly typical mash-up of the two most broadly celebrated subregions of the South.

The restaurant Charleston in Baltimore added Cajun tasso. In Chicago, Soul Kitchen conceived an Herbsaint-perfumed shrimp and grits that was Creole inspired instead of Cajun. Down the road from Charleston, South Carolina, where the dish first made landfall, the Atlanticville Café served grits topped with shrimp stewed in a sauce of dark beer, veal stock, and something called Montreal Steak seasoning.

As the various borrowings and marriages grew bolder, chefs mixed and matched the flavors of three and sometimes four different regions or countries in a way that showed little respect for origins. The popular term was *fusion*. Mark Miller called it "cultural strip mining." These developments drove the stratification of Southern food, in which the divides were not South versus North, or black versus white, but middle class and upper class versus everyone else.

By the 1990s, the people most likely to identify as Southerners, the people who broadcast their ethos by reading *Southern Living* magazine and eating in this new generation of chef-driven restaurants, were educated white urbanites who believed themselves unburdened by the racism of previous generations. They were solidly middle class, often upper middle. Southerners who made more than $60,000 per year were more than nine times as likely to positively identify with the region as residents who made less than $20,000.

From those ranks came the diners who claimed the tables at Highlands and Anthony's. On the lower end of that spectrum, consumers bought Southern kitsch, from Jeff Foxworthy albums to White Trash brand white chocolate–covered pretzels. On the top end of the educational and economic spectrum, they went looking for a rawer and more honest South. They didn't read Foxworthy's spiritual sire Lewis Grizzard, who wrote books like *Elvis Is Dead and I Don't Feel So Good Myself* and ranked his favorite restaurants on a scale of one to five bowls of turnip greens. After being introduced to the possibilities of regionally grounded fine dining, they went deeper.

They went questing for folk art. They traveled to eat. A new generation of Southerners claimed the foods of the region as their own. And many discovered they didn't really know how to cook the foods they valorized. They sought education from a generation of women who were then writing books and developing television shows that aimed to recapture the vitality of a beleaguered cuisine.

*At Rich's Cooking School in Atlanta, Georgia, Nathalie Dupree (far right)
mentored women chefs and entrepreneurs including (left to right)
Shirley Corriher, Kate Almand, and Anne Galbraith.*

· 11 ·

Cooking School

W e were poor," Margaret Lupo, proprietor of Mary Mac's, the last female-owned tearoom in Atlanta, said as Nathalie Dupree crumbled pale brown cornbread into a white china cup on a winter day in 1986. "It's a poor cuisine." Over a midmorning snack of brothy potlikker at Lupo's restaurant, they spoke of beaten biscuits, once the labor of the enslaved, and about how poverty imprinted the foods of whites as well as blacks. Lupo talked of backyard chickens and kettle-rendered lard, of communal stews cooked with hog heads and medicinal teas steeped from hog feet and scurvy grass. Dupree talked about how, as women moved to cities and suburbs, cooks struggled to reproduce farm dishes handed down through oral traditions.

Dupree explained that the South was a complicated place, best glimpsed through a study of home kitchens, where black and white women had worked together for three centuries. Coinciding with the debut of her public television show, New Southern Cooking, the conversation relied on many of the same pastorals Edna Lewis sketched in A Taste of Country Cooking. But as Dupree talked through dishes she planned to demonstrate on the show, from grilled duck slathered with muscadine jelly to turnip green soup perfumed with ginger, she defined Southern food in modern ways. Women no longer had to cook, Dupree said. Now they chose to cook. When they did, they created new narratives and carried forward old ones.

To women in the 1980s and 1990s, Nathalie Dupree communicated a subversive feminism. Less than a decade after Julia Child swanned into American living rooms, espousing the Life Bourguignonne, Dupree emerged as a second-wave women's libber, determined to sidestep what Betty Friedan called "the problem that has no name." Dupree taught the South to cook again. A generation after women stepped away from kitchens to begin careers, she offered a way back. In addition to teaching them to roll and cut biscuits, she convinced women that knowledge learned working the biscuit bowls of mothers and grandmothers had value beyond the home. She told them that the commercial kitchen was one of the places they belonged.

When culinary epiphanies were vogue, Dupree had glimpsed her own way forward while living and traveling in Europe. By the time she returned to the States in 1971, Dupree had earned an advanced diploma from Le Cordon Bleu in London, operated a dessert kitchen out of her Mayfair flat (delivering lemon soufflés via taxi to wealthy matrons), and run the kitchen at a restaurant in Majorca, Spain. As Dupree traveled Europe, she saw new value in the South she left behind. Even as she cooked her way through the classic French and Spanish repertoires, Dupree longed for a taste of green beans, cooked with ham hock. She pined for tomato relish, made from the red-ripe fruit of a Virginia summer.

In 1972, she opened a restaurant, Nathalie's, southeast of Atlanta near Social Circle, Georgia, the hometown of her second husband. As they prepared for the opening, she and David Dupree lived in a trailer on his mother's wooded property. To raise money, she delivered newspapers, flinging them across the seat and through the open driver-side window of her Vega. The opening menu, in what had recently been a machine shop warehouse, was a three-course prix fixe of dishes like iced cucumber soup with shrimp, pork tenderloin with mustard sauce, and sweetbreads with brown butter.

Set across from the Tri-County Cattle Auction Barn, in sight of a drive-in movie theater, near a rural bus transfer station then said to be the busiest in the nation, Nathalie's opened in the rear of an antiques store. The vibe was equal parts *Green Acres*, which had ended its prime-time television run two years earlier, and *Diet for a Small Planet*, the Frances Moore Lappé argument for a vegetable-driven diet, published that same year. As Lappé would have it, Dupree sourced her vegetables from nearby farmers. And she grew backyard crops of Jerusalem artichokes, fennel, and garlic. As Eva Gabor would have wanted it, a community theater staged earnest musicals in the same building, and Dupree set the tables with red-striped napkins, family china, and heirloom silverware.

The ladies-who-lunch liked to know that Dupree tended plots of herbs that she stirred into vinaigrettes and grew pots of pansies that she scattered as salad garnish. The restaurant drew Atlantan Andrew Young, the civil rights movement veteran and future UN representative. Members of the Rich family, who ran what was then the largest and most influential department store in the South, also made the trek. Nathalie Dupree's Social Circle idyll was, however, short-lived. David and Nathalie Dupree divorced after David told Nathalie he was gay. These kinds of splits were common among creative couples in the closeted South of the 1970s.

In 1975, Dupree moved to Atlanta to found Rich's Cooking School. A generation of Georgians, native and adopted, learned to cook in the twenty-stove basement kitchen of the flagship downtown department store. Following the advice of Julia Child, Dupree designed the curriculum around participation. Hundreds of women forged their professional culinary careers under Dupree's gaze, including television personality Virginia Willis, who proved her mettle by whipping egg whites into tight meringues that Dupree tested by suspending bowls over her head and waiting for the drip that never came. Novelist Pat Conroy was one of more than ten thousand students who learned to truss chickens and whisk vinaigrettes from Dupree. When Bill Neal and Moreton Neal were running La Residence, their neo-French restaurant outside Chapel Hill, Bill Neal took Danish pastry classes from Dupree.

Rich's Cooking School was a social boot camp for spouses of relocating corporate executives. Dupree was the teacher of record for city-dwelling locals who lacked the time and knowledge to cook. Divorcées reentering the workforce signed on, too. At Dupree's suggestion, Betty Talmadge, ex-wife of Senator Herman Talmadge and sideshow star of the Watergate hearings, staged Magnolia Suppers at her columned home, said to be the inspiration for Twelve Oaks, the Wilkes plantation from *Gone with the Wind*. To cement the theme, Talmadge kept a donkey on the property, which she named Assley Wilkes.

Dupree began by teaching French cuisine. Flyers for the first round of classes in 1975 promised tutorials on oeufs aioli, pommes mousseline, and lamb Breton. For a text, she used Child's book *Mastering the Art of French Cooking*. When a pupil lost her way, Dupree called out, "Look it up in Julia." At a time when continental cuisine was au courant, Dupree taught her charges veal Italienne and chicken chaudfroid, dishes that had more to do with pretension than tradition. Early in her tenure, Dupree introduced the Atlanta gentry to pan-sautéed kidneys, a dish she learned in London. She thought her choice would broadcast sophistication. Instead, Dupree recognized she was trying too hard to prove herself. "The whole Rich's store, from top to bottom," she said, "smelled like baby's diapers."

Her home dining room table, as well as her school kitchen, became a draw. At a time when the urban South was awash in faux French and Italian restaurants and the creative class wanted a salon, the culinary and literary elite gathered at Nathalie Dupree's Atlanta home. When the Italian cooking teacher Marcella Hazan came through town, Dupree hosted her. Paul Prudhomme and Julia Child got the Dupree treatment. Child got too much of it. After eating one of Dupree's grits roulade in the Rich's kitchen, Child extracted a promise that, on her next visit, she would eat "good old Southern food." So that she could cook the food she missed in Atlanta, Child lugged home a copy of *Southern Cooking*, the 1928 book by Henrietta Dull.

A focus on traditional Southern food came later, as Dupree recognized that many of the women in her classes couldn't fry a mess of okra without soaking the kitchen in skeins of grease. Kate Almand, a daughter of mill hands who had worked in cotton mills herself, taught Dupree, the teacher. From Almand, who worked first as a dishwasher in Social Circle, then as a prep cook at Rich's, she learned to roll and shape biscuits by touch and then to teach that touch to others. Dupree quickly recognized the possibilities resident in Southern food. To sell an early book, *The Cooking of the South*, she distributed flyers that read, "Putting the glory back in Grits & Glory."

Through television shows and books, Dupree argued that Southern cooking should be considered a cuisine. "People go all the way to Italy to study how to make pasta with Giuliano Bugialli," said the woman who, in the 1960s, had gone all the way to London to learn how to stew a proper coq au vin. He moves his hands, she said, in the same way a Southern cook shapes biscuit dough. "It's just that no one ever bothered to say that making Southern biscuits was a technique worth learning."

When Dupree thought it useful, she played the Old South card. She spoke to white, privileged, and recalcitrant readers when she wrote in *New Southern Cooking*, her 1986 breakout book, "The poverty and humiliation resulting from the War Between the States and the Great Depression fixed us in time. Our desire to preserve, hold on to, and remain set in our ways is reflected in our politics and customs and in the soul food that became a trademark and mainstay of Southern cooking. Much of it came from former slaves who were our cooks."

But she didn't limit her work to romanticism. To research that book, she dug into the archives at the Atlanta History Center and traveled to Mount Vernon to sift through the papers of Martha Washington. For a crab pie recipe, spiked with Madeira, she traced the history of that beverage in Savannah. In the headnote for grilled chicken kabobs basted with soy sauce, Dupree documented the lives of Chinese immigrants who arrived in Augusta, Georgia, in the 1870s to build canals and stayed to operate laundries and grocery stores.

Dupree found her voice when talking class and gender. Inspired by her working-class mother, and by a grandfather who edited a union newspaper, Dupree spoke out for women's rights, agitating for better pay and honest attribution. After speaking to a men's group one night, Dupree sat down the next morning to reflect. The person who decides what and when and where food will be eaten wields power, she wrote. "I know this because I'm a Southern woman and for us the only place to wield power was in the home—more specifically in the kitchen. Blacks knew this too. Keep a white man happy, be you slave or woman, and your lot in life will be better—you may even be able to get some of what you want."

I n January 1986, White Lily, the biscuit flour miller headquartered in Knoxville, Tennessee, bankrolled a cooking show, *New Southern Cooking with Nathalie Dupree*. An everywoman who would go on to host eight more television series on public television and, later, the Food Network, Dupree lost ingredients in the midst of tapings. She burned herself while the cameras rolled. During one taping, a crawfish escaped and skittered across the set. At a moment when fealty to farmers' market produce was a budding mark of sophistication, Dupree told viewers that she shopped at the grocery store. To the consternation of the gourmet clubs blossoming across the region, she presented a cheater grocery store cake on a *Today* show cooking segment.

In a very modern twist, Dupree wrote her book as a companion to the television series. With recipes for turnip green pasta, herb-fried rabbit, and sweet potato and bourbon soup, the book came out that fall. Aware of what South she was selling, and how her food might be perceived as ersatz, Dupree joked that she should have called the book *Fried Watermelon, Poke Sallet, and Lady Peas.* Her riffs on tradition were bold for the day. When she visited Albany, Georgia, that spring, the newspaper reported that she did scandalous things with native victuals. Dupree added coriander seeds to greens, made red-eye gravy with Coca-Cola instead of black coffee, and rolled a tablespoon of ground black pepper into the dumplings for her chicken and dumplings. "Of course, if that is too much zing for you," a local columnist reported in a breathless tone that hinted she had been scandalized, "you can cut down on the pepper."

The television show did more than build an audience. It gave her a platform to speak to the South. Early in her career, Dupree had adopted progressive and contrarian politics. She had served as a precinct captain for John F. Kennedy in 1960 and a national committeewoman for the Democrats in 1966. Raised a Christian Scientist, she once volunteered for a bloodletting experiment, because she needed the money and because it went against the church teachings about medical intrusions. She was one of the early television personalities to mix food and politics; for a 1985 taping, she wore an AIDS ribbon, a daring move at the time for a woman whose audience skewed middle-class conservative.

Three years later, when the Salman Rushdie book *The Satanic Verses* was banned in some countries and Ayatollah Khomeini of Iran issued a fatwa ordering Muslim believers to kill the author, the publisher, and bookstores that sold his book, Dupree helped plan an Atlanta publication party for Rushdie. In the dustup that followed, she defended the rights of Muslim protesters who spoke in opposition to her stance. And then she presumably served all who gathered celery boats stuffed with pimento cheese.

Dupree wrote books for kitchen shelves, not coffee tables. But she didn't limit her reach to kitchens. Before chefs became brands who made their money doing things other than cooking, Dupree developed corporate consultations. She led the charge to adopt the French food processors marketed under the Cuisinart label. Krystal, the Chattanooga, Tennessee, hamburger chain, inspired by the success of Hardee's, contracted her to help them bake better biscuits. The Richmond Marriott opened a restaurant, Nathalie Dupree's, with a menu of dishes like smoked pork chops atop Mississippi caviar made with marinated black-eyed peas. Shuttling back and forth from Atlanta, in a manner that would, a generation later, become customary for superstar chefs, Dupree was the marquee draw.

No matter her successes, Dupree was never satisfied with her status. She thought her talents were underappreciated, her shows underfunded. "My show is a hit in Hong Kong and I can't even get an appointment here with Coca-Cola," she said in 1994, when her fourth show *Nathalie Dupree Cooks* was the second most popular cooking program on public television behind *The Frugal Gourmet*. "You'd think somebody would want to sponsor us. But no. Kroger told me they didn't want a national show, then the national people told me I'm too regional."

Dupree was a model for the New South, an entrepreneur who aimed to reinvent cooking and transform the work of blacks and women into a vocation worthy of respect. When she was in her prime in the late 1980s and early 1990s, she broadcast success, posing for publicity photos in a crisp apron, brandishing a whisk. "I think the American woman is the best home cook in the world," Dupree said. "She is quite better than the French woman who is used to picking up a pâté at her corner store. . . ." Dupree knew how to gin up press. When she flew to New York City in 1991 to appear on *CBS This Morning*, Dupree told the gossip columnists at the Atlanta newspaper that she planned to stow her ingredients for the demo in her carry-on: "It's an exciting life. I travel with chicken, asparagus, and my underwear in a suitcase."

R onni Lundy, the Kentucky-born cookbook author and Appalachian foodways advocate, did not buy the reigning narratives about Southern food. She rejected Old South tropes based on plantation mythologies. Her people were hardscrabble subsistence farmers and coal miners, not cotton plutocrats, she said, and their stories were worthy, too. At an early Southern Foodways Symposium, she stood to say that beaten biscuits were the conceits of gentry homemakers, who could hire help to do their labor. She declared loudly and often that cornbread should never contain sugar. That was cake, Lundy told the smiling and nodding faithful. Cornbread was the everyday sacrament of her people, one that it was unwise to sully.

She spoke often and with some fierceness of Appalachia. "The culture of my people has been systematically denied, from jokes about 'Li'l Abner' and poor white trash to the 'Dukes of Hazzard' and 'Deliverance,'" Lundy said. "At worst those depictions were hostile and condescending, at best they were cruel and flat-out wrong." Born in Corbin, Kentucky, the "sundown town" where Harland Sanders built his first restaurant, Lundy lived a hippie life in Colorado and New Mexico before settling in Louisville in the 1980s. Music was her first gig. As the newgrass movement took hold, Lundy documented the ascent. She saw parallels in an underappreciated music, then in renaissance, and the foods of her forebears, awaiting their own rebirth. Lundy sang the praises of beer cheese and stack cake. She claimed coal camp spaghetti as a totem of Italian migration to the region.

Lundy suffered no fools. Weary of the WASP epiphanies enjoyed by seemingly every chef and food writer from Julia Child forward, she railed against easy stories of "gastronomic defloration" that began on cobblestone lanes somewhere in France. Like Edna Lewis, Lundy took her cues from home. Inspired by the same instincts that drove Eliot Wig-

ginton, she saw value in the ways of Appalachia. Even as the rest of the
South urbanized, her South remained rooted in farm traditions. Her
people valued home kitchen stoves, not hooded restaurant fry banks.
In the same manner that Nathalie Dupree celebrated the cooking of
women, Lundy mythologized her mother and her aunts, her grandmother and her neighbors.

At about the same time Dupree began to explore the country roots
of Deep South cooking, Lundy began to interview country and bluegrass musicians. Like the women before her, who baked and carried
their goods to sell at country stores, Lundy baked and carried to the
music festivals then sprouting across the region. The exchange was simple. She cooked fried chicken or shuck beans, stack cakes or buttermilk
pies, and musicians talked to her, not like she was a journalist who had
come to plumb their secrets but like a long-lost cousin who wanted to
get caught up on what had happened since they last saw each other in
church. To get Bill Monroe to sit for an interview, she baked him a stack
cake. When she first met Dwight Yoakam, they talked fried squirrel.
Lundy didn't question how a boy from Columbus, Ohio, came to eat
squirrel. She recognized that his people, like hers, had taken the so-called
Hillbilly Highway north during the Great Depression. And they arrived
with a taste for fried squirrel and a talent for country music still intact.

From a base in Louisville, she reviewed new guard restaurants that
showcased Kentucky like Lilly's, where Kathy Cary served reinvented
classics like eggs Derby, stuffed with sweetbreads and country ham, and
sandwiches smeared with Benedictine spread, a cucumber and cream
cheese mix born of a Victorian-era Louisville tearoom. But that was city
food. Lundy's heart was really in the hills. In the books she wrote, beginning in 1991 with *Shuck Beans, Stack Cakes, and Honest Fried Chicken*,
Lundy portrayed Appalachia as a place where people still sun-dried apples on corrugated tin, strung shuck beans between the sun-bleached
front pillars of clapboard cabins, and jarred pickles and preserves in
rock-walled root cellars.

Those dishes were not mere affectations. At a time when the rest of America was rethinking the virtues of domestic crafts, Lundy recognized that mountain people, her people, had never given up on those ways. Their techniques were survival gambits that yielded summer tomatoes in the depths of winter. Their recipes for hot water cornbread, handed down from mother to daughter, were cultural dowries that linked one generation to the next.

These traditional foods tasted of the mountains. And they spoke of the mountains, a place long besieged by profiteering coal companies that scalped the land of its resources, and lumber mills where men often muscled tree slabs into radial saws and drew back nubs. Like the people who made them, said grace over them, fed their families with them, these foods endured. And Lundy embraced her role as shepherd of the culture and the cuisine, offering new means to value her people and her place, new lenses to see the value of the old ways they kept alive. While much 1980s attention focused on racism and the divisions it drove, she looped the conversation back to class, and to the poverty that President Johnson confronted in 1964 on a front porch, just 140 miles northeast of where Lundy was born.

B y the 1980s, *Southern Living*, published in Birmingham, Alabama, was the most profitable magazine in America. The first-issue greeting in 1966 from editor Eugene Butler promised a magazine of "good Southern living ideas and qualities." In the pages of this New South paragon, Bombingham disappeared. What's past was past. *Southern Living* focused on the good suburban life to come. Never mind what Faulkner had to say on the subject. The magazine promised a South free of "dirty air, filthy water, growing crime, traffic jams, noise, and tension." On that pledge, *Southern Living* delivered.

By 1968, the year that nearly 7,000 poor people camped on the National Mall to protest poverty, *Southern Living* circulation shot past

500,000. By 1980, the year Ronald Reagan tapped states' rights narratives to displace Jimmy Carter as president, *Southern Living* circulation topped two million. The magazine was among the top fifteen magazines in the nation, measured by advertising revenue. As Americans embraced Southern cultural expressions, from food to music, the magazine emerged as a cultural bellwether.

"Advocacy journalism isn't our bag," executive editor John Logue explained in 1977, when memories of Bull Connor's water cannons and paddy wagons were still vivid. "We are out to save the South, but one front yard at a time." *Southern Living* leveraged the media weariness of white Southerners, still reeling from negative portrayals of the region during the civil rights movement. The editors recognized that, starved for positive reflections of the place they loved, they would embrace a magazine that celebrated social and cultural activities like cooking and gardening and sports.

An outgrowth of the magazine *Progressive Farmer,* which had struggled in the 1960s to maintain an advertising base as families moved to suburbs, *Southern Living* defined a New South in new terms. The Southern economy had been agricultural. And *Progressive Farmer* had served that South. Now the region was diversifying and urbanizing. Families moved from farms to cities and suburbs. Restaurants desegregated. The Democratic Party pulled back the curtains on voting booths.

Southern Living offered a peek of the new world that middle-class white Southerners would soon inhabit, a becalmed region of peace and prosperity, of inground pools and gas-fueled barbecue grills. Full of neo-colonial house plans, how-to-prune-a-magnolia gardening columns, and recipes for squash casseroles, the magazine stoked the egos of newly middle-class white consumers with an instructional manual, delivered in a monthly digest, on how to "live a more enjoyable life in the South by making better use of your growing incomes, your leisure and your mental and physical assets."

Southern Living was not the first magazine to frame a newer South through soft-focus features. *Uncle Remus's Magazine*, which Joel Chandler Harris began publishing out of Atlanta in 1907, had promised to rid the region of the "provinciality that stands for ignorance and blind prejudice, that represents narrow views and an unhappy congestion of ideas." But *Southern Living* was the first national magazine to grab the attention of the region.

The magazine sold food as a deracinated symbol of the good life, packaged and merchandized in a manner that was safe and cloistered, as tidy and tasty as a deviled egg enveloped in waxed paper. Between the covers of *Southern Living*, the white middle-class women of the South read a serialized cookbook, full of stories rooted in a rural past that pointed to a suburban future. The term *gentrification* describes the reappraisal of undervalued assets, repackaged and resold with such vigor that previous holders of such property can no longer afford the purchase. Or better yet, they can almost afford it. *Southern Living* sold readers a gentrified South that was more palatable, more enjoyable, and just beyond their comfortable reach.

S outhern Living editors framed cuisine as the most conservative cultural expression, a totem of identity that had survived social upheavals and demographic intrusions and remained true to its turnip greens and cornpone roots. That was somewhat true. But something else was going on, too. For all the conversations about tradition and heritage, for all the paeans to the past, the cooking of the South transformed in the 1990s.

In the move from farms that faced dirt roads to split-levels poised at the tops of cul-de-sacs, the South changed dramatically. By the late 1980s and early 1990s, the New South of Nathalie Dupree, with its grits roulades, turnip green pasta, and messages of female empowerment, had gone mainstream. Ronni Lundy had instilled the women of Appalachia with pride in their home cooking. And *Southern Living* had emerged as a national brand. Gentrification is often dismissed as a negative cultural force. In a region that had long undervalued its people and its products, these developments had some positive effects.

Southerners began to recognize that food, like music, was a cultural process, worthy of new appraisal. Far from static, Southern foodways would prove, over the coming decades, to be the most dynamic cultural facet of the region. As restaurants became reliquaries of culinary history, chefs became primary interpreters of dishes like shrimp and grits and hoppin' John, and cities staked their tourist appeal on the strengths of their culinary scenes, the brogan-shod authenticity of their farmers, the local signature of their restaurants, and the glossy magazine smiles of their chefs.

New
Respect

1990s–2010s

Glenn Roberts of Anson Mills began his career searching out old varieties of corn, before moving on to repatriate Carolina Gold rice.

Artisanal Pantry

The good stuff, Glenn Roberts noticed, grew taller. The best stuff was twice the height. Driving a Lexus down South Carolina back roads in the mid-1990s, wearing a polo shirt and a bright cotton sweater, searching for moonshiner corn, Roberts trained himself to spot heirloom varieties. When he found a patch that looked promising, he field-tested it, which is to say he pulled to the side of the road, tramped through the crop rows to harvest his prize, fired a camp stove he kept in the trunk, boiled an ear, and tasted. He did all of this to source the best corn for grits, that most elemental of Southern staples. "When Carolina gourdseed corn is fresh," he said, "the aromas fluoresce."

Roberts, who founded Anson Mills in Columbia, South Carolina, in 1998, made his reputation by sourcing corn from farmers who grew their own, saved kernels instead of buying seed from stores, and made their own hooch beneath the light of the moon. Owing to a polymath-on-speed persona and an insatiable curiosity about antebellum food-ways, Roberts came to be regarded by farmers and chefs across the country as a font of agricultural and cultural knowledge.

By the early 2000s, he emerged as the fire-and-brimstone fundamentalist of an artisan grain revival that began in the South and spread nationwide. After a long flirt with continental cuisine, a new generation of chefs was digging into regional bedrock to revive a cuisine they gauged moribund. In search of building-block ingredients, they warmed quickly to the stories Roberts spun of farmers and almost-lost heirloom corn.

His tales of moonshiner stashes sounded fantastic. But they were true. And they were widespread. Junior Johnson, who rose to fame in the 1970s as a stock car driver, talked about growing up in a moonshiner family that farmed its own corn and saved seeds, not in an attempt to nurture endangered varieties but because buying corn from the feed and seed store aroused revenue agent suspicions. Inspired by the stories of moonshining families and the corn varieties they nurtured, Roberts ditched his career in architectural restoration, donated his suits to charity, and began milling in earnest.

On a shoestring, he rented a derelict metal building behind a Columbia car wash, installed granite millstones that looked like set pieces from a stage production of *The Canterbury Tales*, and accessorized them with a Rube Goldberg assemblage of sleeves and spouts to sift and sort his grain products. To ensure that the fragile flavors of the milled corn were not muted by the humid local climate, he ground in an oxygen-free environment and shipped products the same day they were packed. After discovering archival evidence of an antebellum yellow dent that was milled frozen, he began freezing his corn before he ground it.

By the early 2000s, Roberts was a steam punk evangelist bent on leveraging the past for the future. An unapologetic wonk, Roberts wore his gray hair in a Beatles-style mop and held forth on the virtue of shatter-milling grains to ensure optimal facet exposure and even cook times. When he spoke of flavor, he cited the retention of phytochemicals and flavonoids in his grinds. At conferences, he began questions with preambles like, "During the golden age, when the Dutch market export system flourished . . ." In casual conversation he might begin a story about his mother, who raised Roberts in California and returned often to her native South Carolina, by saying, "When I was playing classical French horn . . ." or "When I was driving tractor parts and rare berries and guavas and white peaches cross-country in a reefer . . ."

Roberts came by his obsessions honestly. His family was so serious about rice cookery that when he was young, his mother dictated that until he mastered the proper technique the rice he cooked would be served only to the pets. At a time when most Southerners resigned themselves to grits as grocery store pablum, vanguard chefs embraced Roberts's vision for artisan grains with the zeal of the newly converted.

Attracted to both the ancient and modern narratives embedded in the Anson Mills story, white tablecloth devotees drove his success. Much of that business came from beyond the South. Early in Roberts's career, Thomas Keller of the French Laundry in the Napa Valley of California began buying his grits. By 2004, Charlie Trotter cooked Anson grits nightly at his Chicago restaurant. When morels were in season, Trotter served them stuffed with yellow corn grits. He floated lamb shanks, marinated in curry apricot mustard and braised for six hours, on pools of garlicky Anson grits.

Supermarket grits are industrially processed hominy, Roberts told his customers, made from corn that has been de-germinated, bleached, dried, and finely ground in roller mills. All that processing came with a price. Absent the natural oils and flavors, grocery store grits tasted like countrified farina. They were gruel with the flavor and texture of dampened sawdust. At their best, industrially processed grits tasted like the butter and cheese that cooks stirred into the pot. At worst, Bette Midler told a Charleston, South Carolina, audience, they tasted like "buttered kitty litter."

Roberts believed that if he led with grits, he could sell chefs on old varieties of rice and other goods that had fallen out of favor during the midcentury drive toward industrialized agriculture. Cowpeas, sieve beans, and sorghum followed. And then benne, farro, buckwheat, and emmer. What began as an effort to return honest grits made with corn sourced to the Southern table evolved, expanded, exploded, and then catapulted him to the forefront of the American grain revival.

When Roberts spoke of antebellum rice production, he quoted from eighteenth-century Venetian farm journals and talked about the impact of intercropping sequences on Italian rice husbandry. And he hastened to tell his audiences that, before the Civil War, the daily ration for an enslaved laborer was the amount of grain that an average thirteen-year-old boy could grasp in his fist.

Like the moonshiners he tapped for seed, Roberts trafficked in an agricultural conservancy grounded in the eighteenth century. When chefs took up the charge to renew a plundered Southern larder, he became a franchise player. When Roberts talked about his work, he got so excited that many chefs, unable to keep up with his synaptic firings, recorded his instruction in notebooks. Sean Brock, who would become one of the prime interpreters of Roberts's research and planting experiments, and who would come to call him Obi-Wan Kenobi, began recording their telephone conversations so that he could replay them later and fully absorb the knowledge and experience he shared.

I f I do the job right, my grits should taste like corn tasted one hundred, two hundred years ago," Roberts told me one afternoon, as we drove south out of Charleston, past a roadside plaque that memorialized the 1739 Stono slave rebellion and the stricter slave code that followed. "This is not about culinary one-upmanship," he said as egrets arced toward tree nests. "This is all about breathing new life into traditional foodways." Roberts telegraphed the time travel possibilities when he named his coarsest Anson grind "antebellum," as if to say here is a taste of the past, steaming on contemporary plates.

The grits that Roberts milled tasted like cracked corn, with a pronounced floral nose. He worked only with viable seed corn. Carolina Gourdseed, John Haulk Yellow Dent, Bloody Butcher Red Dent: The varieties Roberts farmed and milled suggested an American past that most thought lost. Sweet, with a bass note that hinted of the dank earth in which the ears grew to maturity, they proved to be signal artisan goods in the Southern culinary revival. Roberts also packaged hominy, which Native Americans had made by soaking corn in a lye bath made from wood ashes. To achieve a similar effect, he retrieved wood ash from the barbecue pits at Piggie Park in Columbia, operated by Maurice Bessinger, the onetime Columbia segregationist.

The previous thirty-odd years had been interesting for grits eaters. In the late 1960s, the national media touted grits as a black dish. Bluesman Little Milton had tapped the zeitgeist when he sang, "If grits ain't groceries / Eggs ain't poultry / And Mona Lisa was a man." Smaller producers of grits like War Eagle Mill in Arkansas grew from weekend diversions to thriving businesses in the 1980s. Inspired by chefs who recognized their virtues, and by vague recollections of what their forebears ate, consumers savored tastes that hearkened to the years preceding World War II, when towns in the upland South boasted a mill, and fresh ground corn was an everyday indulgence.

By the early 1990s, grits claimed a place in better Southern restaurants. Chefs cultivated relationships with small millers across the region and conceived newfangled dishes. At Highlands Bar and Grill in Birmingham, Frank Stitt developed a grits soufflé with country ham. At Chez Philippe in Memphis, Jose Gutierrez steamed grits couscous, which he topped with roasted lamb. The innovation was evident. But artisanal mill goods like the ones that Anson would introduce in the late 1990s were not yet readily available.

When Elizabeth Terry published *Savannah Seasons* in 1996, her red rice recipe dictated Uncle Ben's brown rice and Italian sausage. The grits she favored came from health food stores, not backwoods mill operators.

Eight years later, when Artisan published *Frank Stitt's Southern Table*, he specified Arrowhead Mills yellow grits for his soufflé. They were ground in the Texas panhandle, and Stitt bought them from the Golden Temple, a Sikh-run store down the street. Legs of lamb, which Stitt stuffed with greens and garlic, came from Jamison Farm of Pennsylvania.

Though Stitt had long served Cullman sweet potatoes, raised back home by friends of his family, and he had extolled the virtues of the quail he shipped from his first wife's home state of South Carolina, the pork Stitt braised in bourbon and served in a belly-shoulder combination at Highlands came from Niman Ranch in California. He purchased chickens from Amish farmers in Pennsylvania and confided that he hoped, soon, to buy birds from neighbors in Alabama.

The California food movement of the 1970s had emphasized ingredients. Ranchers made backdoor deliveries of beef to Chez Panisse in Berkeley. Oystermen traveled to Ireland to study aquaculture. Chefs encouraged artisans to embrace French cheese-making techniques and Italian salumi-curing methods. The collective work was more about invention than revival. In the South, the revolution came later, but when it came Southerners leveraged local and regional traditions instead of overseas ones.

The Southern artisan movement relied on moonshine. And on history. In the embrace of traditional goods and heirloom crops, America discovered that some Southerners had never given up on techniques and ingredients that dated to the early years of the republic.

"Jesus turned the water into wine, I turned it into likker." After Popcorn Sutton Moonshine debuted with backing from country music star Hank Williams Jr., that slogan overlaid advertising images of the fabled moonshiner. Dressed in overalls, he looked defiant. The light was stark, the background unfocused. Sutton wore a crumpled hat, tangled with ferns that had seemingly caught in the crown during a roll on the forest floor with revenue agents. His face was craggy, his eyes doleful, his hair gray and long and unkempt. Rendered on a billboard, glimpsed from the window as traffic coursed the highway, Sutton resembled a daguerreotype from an indeterminate Appalachian past.

The scene suggested the late-twentieth-century South, when moonshine became a hip flask accessory for authenticity seekers. Sold at a conservative proof, the unaged whiskey that bore Sutton's name came in Mason jars, reassuring consumers in search of honest Appalachian goods that a semblance of the real thing sloshed inside. That photograph also conjured a turn-of-the-previous-century scene, when writers flocked to the mountain South to catalog a vestigial past and locate a simpler present amid the hills and hollers of Appalachia.

"When we see them from the car window, with curious eyes, as we are whirled toward our Southern hotel, their virtues are not blazoned on their sorry clothing, nor suggested by their grave and awkward demeanor," reported a magazine writer who coined the term *contemporary ancestor* for the people he met during an 1899 tour of Appalachia. "They are an anachronism, and it will require a scientific spirit and some historic sense to enable us to appreciate their situation and their character."

If natives of the mountain South were roughhewn throwbacks in a twentieth-century America, moonshine emerged in the twenty-first century as the frontier antecedent of American whiskey. Sipped from a jar, corn whiskey was the contrarian uncle who lurked in the back of the national liquor cabinet, the rude, young, law-flouting spirit that never grew up.

As Americans shopped for goods that reminded them of a past when baseball bats were not milled in China and Korean cars were not assembled in Alabama, Kentucky bourbon emerged as a symbol of American excellence, an elemental product perfected over three centuries. Bourbon led the expansion of markets for handmade Southern goods. Dresses stitched of organic cotton by home seamstresses under the direction of designer Natalie Chanin of Florence, Alabama, appeared in the pages of *Vogue*. Vinyl blues records, pressed in Memphis on steam-driven machines by Fat Possum Records of Oxford, Mississippi, became best sellers in Portland record stores.

Crafted from the same native grain that Glenn Roberts ground for his grits, bourbon was the essence of America, literally distilled. After declining for nearly thirty years, American whiskey sales increased more than 30 percent in the latter 2000s, as the Southern culinary renaissance gained momentum and a broader American culinary rebirth followed. Super-premium whiskey sales doubled. Pappy Van Winkle, aged ten, fifteen, twenty, even twenty-three years and made in Kentucky under the direction of third-generation distiller Julian Van Winkle, dominated the market. His success inspired new distillers. As craft distilling boomed, moonshine, its little brother, attempted a transition from lowest common denominator drunk fuel to aspirational artisan beverage.

To feed the vogue, industrial distillers rushed faux country products to the market, repackaging grain alcohol as moonshine. Made in monstrous column stills, neutral spirits took on the flavors of whatever was added, from blueberries and raspberries to doughnuts and Moon Pies. The liquor that ran from those stills had been tamed. Like the South itself, even the most derivative products drew strength from the narratives embedded in the moonshining mystique, in stories of illicit goods distilled in junked car radiators, in warnings that a bad batch could render a sighted man blind or give an able worker a jake leg.

Craft distillers worked the other side of Thunder Road, valorizing the men who distilled by the light of the moon as American heroes who earned their living in the woods, extracting the essence of the kernel from bushels of corn. Troy and Sons of North Carolina produced a distillate from Crooked Creek open-pollinated corn and Appalachian spring water. Belle Isle Craft Spirits introduced flavored moonshines, distilled in Virginia from organic corn. Instead of apple pie flavoring, which had become common, or peach, which was historically accurate, Belle Isle developed roasted peanut, watermelon rind, and habanero honey infusions.

Most companies sold story as much as quality. A history of illegality became a measure of value among revisionist distillers who built brands on family moonshining stories. Tapping interest in artisanal goods and farm-to-table connections, new-generation makers fired pot stills and reframed the arrests and jail sentences of their forebears as stamps of authenticity. When distillers didn't have a forebear to celebrate, many took the same liberties that bourbon makers had taken for decades: They invented stories to suit marketing strategies.

Sugarlands Distilling Company in Tennessee, which heralded its use of a stone mill and Smoky Mountain water, banked its reputation on *Our Southern Highlanders*, a 1913 book that described its namesake as the "country of ill fame, hidden deep in remote gorges, difficult of access, tenanted by a sparse population who preferred to be a law unto themselves." Nancy Hatfield, great-great-granddaughter of William Anderson "Devil Anse" Hatfield, introduced Hatfield & McCoy Moonshine, made in West Virginia under the banner "Drink of the Devil." Some distillers did more than tell a story. When the Kaufman brothers founded Short Mountain Distillery in 2010 in rural Cannon County, Tennessee, they hired former moonshiners to staff a two-gallon backwoods-style still alongside the primary pot still where they would eventually make bourbon. In the manner of a living history exhibit lifted from Williamsburg, the two men wore overalls to work and proofed the whiskey they made by shaking a jar and reading the bead.

This return to the past happened quickly. In 1990 only 6 craft distilleries operated in the United States. By 2010, there were around 200 craft distilleries and more than 20 of those made moonshine. Five years later, more than 900 craft distillers operated. And around 150 made white whiskey or moonshine.

Popcorn Sutton, who made his name preening and flaunting and selling illegal whiskey to thrill-seeking tourists for $100 a gallon, emerged in the first decade of the twenty-first century as the poster child of the artisanal moonshine movement. A showman, he bragged about the marker he purchased for his grave, inscribed with the message "POPCORN SAID FUCK YOU."

Sutton was Hairless Joe, the comic strip character from Dogpatch who distilled Kickapoo Joy Juice. He was Snuffy Smith of Hootin' Holler, the feather-haloed cartoon chicken thief. He was Jed Clampett, the sardonic Beverly Hillbilly in the floppy hat. Sutton, who earned his name in a bar fight when he destroyed a popcorn machine with a pool cue, was outlaw musician Johnny Paycheck, flipping the nation the bird.

Fans claimed his persona as their own. To drink his goods was to traffic in the almost illicit, to flirt with danger, to live life dangerously. Legally produced moonshine promised a path to subvert the system without really breaking the law. Sutton, on the other hand, really broke the law. In 2008 federal agents raided his property in Cocke County, Tennessee, confiscating hundreds of gallons of moonshine and three one-thousand-gallon stills.

FREE POPCORN, read the T-shirts supporters wore when Sutton was arrested. POPCORN IS FREE, read the T-shirts the dutiful began wearing the next year after Sutton, unwilling to face down a prison stay, connected a garden hose to his tailpipe and slipped it through a crack in the window of a car he traded for three gallons of moonshine. By the time commercial moonshine with his name on it hit the market, and billboards with his face on them lined roadways, Sutton had been dead more than a year.

As the market for moonshine broadened, the stuff that bore Sutton's name set a standard. Embossed with his looping signature and three Xs, a mark long associated with pornography and illicit liquor, Popcorn Sutton bottles became icons of a moonshine economy that ranged from the clear and unadulterated stuff sold under the Sutton name to the peach sweet tea–flavored moonshine distilled at Short Mountain to the pickled cherry versions distilled by Sugarlands.

Moonshine went mainstream in the 2000s. Tourists raided the shelves at moonshine superstores near Gatlinburg, Tennessee. Entrepreneur Mike Haney of Hillbilly Stills in Barlow, Kentucky, constructed and shipped copper reflux stills called Hillbilly Flutes to hobbyists across the nation. Venture capitalists bet on business plans rooted in Appalachian narratives of isolated genius. Much of the moonshine effort revealed a stalling game, in which distillers plotted to make barrel-aged bourbon or Tennessee whiskey, but released moonshine products made from un-aged whiskey to quickly recoup some of their investment. Entrepreneurs could distill moonshine in one morning and funnel it into bottles by the afternoon.

At Limestone Branch Distillery in Lebanon, Kentucky, brothers Paul Beam and Steve Beam partnered with Chattanooga Baking Company to make official-issue Moon Pie–flavored moonshine. They were honest about their business plans. "It takes at least two to six years, prefera-bly four to six, for a really good bourbon," Paul Beam said, "so we had time that we had to generate income and that's why we went to the moonshine."

On a summer day in 2013, as the ferry from Williamsburg to Surry churned past the site of the Jamestown settlement, Sam Edwards III pointed out Hog Island, where English settlers once kept livestock. He told stories of his great-grandfather, Albert F. Jester, who piloted a mail boat out of Chincoteague. And he talked of his grandfather, S. Wal-lace Edwards, who sold ham sandwiches on the ferry before he built a series of wigwam-shaped smokehouses in the shadow of the Surry County Courthouse in the Tidewater region of Virginia.

Each time Edwards stepped into the cure house, he benefited from more than three centuries of experience. English settlers arrived in Surry County to discover that American Indians were already dry-curing the wild game that skittered through the forest. Settlers quickly applied those same techniques to pork. By 1750, farmers dispatched peanut-fed and salt-cured hams to England.

When his grandfather began selling hams, the elder Edwards called them Wigwams, in tribute to Native American knowledge and technique. Sixty years later, Sam Edwards III marketed his best, long-cured haunches as Surryano, a playful doff of the hat to the Serrano hams of Spain and his hometown of Surry. That wasn't his choice. A newspaper writer had used the term. And it stuck. At one point Edwards had played around with calling his cured hog jowls Jowciale, after the Italian guanciale. He even considered Samcetta instead of pancetta. Edwards liked the playfulness, but didn't like to rely on European linkage. He preferred to talk about his hams as American.

By the early years of the twenty-first century, Edwards sourced some of his hogs from heirloom stock. Fed on peanuts that thrived in the Virginia loam, they were ideal for salting and smoking. Curers in Italy dried and aged their prosciutto in crosscurrent breezes. The men and women of Spain hung their Iberico hams in cellars and rubbed them with oil to ward off insects. The modern techniques that Sam Edwards developed were, instead, thoroughly American, designed to meet standards set by his grandfather and father.

To meet the dictates of various health and agriculture departments, Edwards built a modern ham house that was temperature controlled and sealed from the elements. Knowing that a great Virginia ham emerges over at least a year of temperature fluctuation, Edwards developed a four-season system, built around four different cement-floored rooms, where the hams hung for a summer week in a hickory-choked chamber, sweating out excess liquid, before resting in a winter aging room, suspended from pinewood racks.

At about the time that Sam Edwards developed a newfangled system for curing oldfangled hams, Allan Benton, a onetime high school guidance counselor with the smile and intellect of Jimmy Carter on the campaign trail, worried if his company would survive. Trying to compete with quick-cure brands sold in typical grocery stores, he lost money. Reacting to the marketing campaigns of the National Pork Board, consumers had embraced pork as "the other white meat," a kind of livestock vodka with little distinctive taste. Benton went long and funky when most went short and bland. Regulations said that haunches of pork could be called country hams after seventy days. Benton extended his cure time, first to six months, then to one, two, even three years. And, like Sam Edwards, he began salting and smoking heirloom pigs, fed on pasture, in addition to Midwest feedlot pigs, raised on corn in confinement.

When Benton studied his competition, he discovered a clue to future success. Grocery store prosciutto, imported from Italy, sold for ten times what his ham fetched. When he tasted the two, Benton recognized that his was just as good. Maybe even better. Chefs across the nation discovered the same. John Fleer of Blackberry Farm in the Tennessee foothills of the Great Smokies introduced them to Benton's, often driving visitors forty miles down the road to his cinder block building with "WE CURE EM" painted on the side.

As demand for his bacon and ham spiraled, Benton continued to answer requests for catalogues with a handwritten roster of goods, scratched on a yellow legal pad. Customers called to hear him talk. They traded stories about how, when they received boxes of ham from Benton, the pasteboard came tagged with his greasy handprints. They smiled when he called himself a "purebred Tennessee hillbilly." His offer to ship them hams and wait on their checks reminded chefs that handshake deals were still honored in a newly digitized America. Asked about technique, he talked of the maple saltbox he and his father crafted, about the dehumidifier he jerry-rigged to draw moisture from his hams, about the rub of salt and red pepper and black pepper he applied. Pressed for a trick of the trade, Benton said, "The secret is there's no secret. Just long hours and patience."

It's common among restaurant watchers to think that the most imitated dish to emerge from Momofuku in New York City were those bao of pearly white bread stuffed with roasted lozenges of pork belly. Early in the 2000s David Chang became famous for them. That didn't suit. "Can you imagine being Neil Diamond and having to sing 'Cracklin' Rosie' every time you get onstage for the rest of your life?" he asked, weary of the repetition. Chang was more interested in persuading his customers to eat country ham. Not the traditional presentation, in which a ham is boiled in water, crosshatched with cloves, smeared with brown sugar, and roasted in the oven. That desiccates a ham, the chef said, warning that great cured pork should not be cooked, even if directions to that effect were printed on the wrapper. Instead, Chang sliced America's answer to prosciutto thin and arrayed it, raw, on a white platter with a couple slices of warm baguette and a saucer of red-eye mayonnaise, made with sriracha, sherry vinegar, and instant coffee crystals.

At the center of the platter, hams by Benton or Edwards or Nancy Newsom of Kentucky spun out from the red-eye like a rosy constellation of American excellence. Few chefs copied the red-eye gravy. But every other restaurant seemed to add a ham platter, and a third of the chefs in America seemed to begin curing their own. At a time when Walmart, born in Arkansas, often stocked its shelves with lowest common denominator products, the devotion that Chang and chefs who followed his lead showed for country ham was a boon to regionality, a reminder of the value embedded in American artisanship, a pledge of what was possible in the hinterlands.

A s America rediscovered country ham, consumers also gravitated to
brand-name products that promised both familiarity and specialization. Coca-Cola, battered by reports that corn syrup was the demon
seed of the American diet, was surprised by the stateside popularity
spike of Mexican-made and -bottled versions of its signature soft drink.
Incised with the slogans HECHO EN MEXICO and REFRESCO, bottled by
Bebidas Mundiales in Monterrey and Bebidas Envasadas in San Pacifico,
Mexican Coke became an artisanal good in the 2000s.

A quick look at the white labels plastered in seeming afterthought to
faceted green bottles revealed why: *azúcar*, which translates as sugar.
When American consumers chose Mexican Coke, they chose a seemingly less industrialized version of the most industrialized and widely
dispersed commercial drink in the history of the nation.

Born in Georgia in 1886, Coke had built its brand around sameness.
Andy Warhol once suggested that sameness was a democratizing influence: "What's great about this country is that America started the tradition where the richest consumers buy essentially the same thing as the
poorest," he wrote. "A Coke is a Coke and no amount of money can get
you a better Coke than the one the bum on the corner is drinking. All
the Cokes are the same and all the Cokes are good. Liz Taylor knows it,
the president knows it, the bum knows it and you know it."

The diffusion of the brand, fueled by the introduction of New Coke
in 1985, called those absolutes into question. While American bottlers
began sweetening Coca-Colas with high fructose corn syrup, Mexican
bottlers continued to use sugar. Among the reasons were trade tariffs
and raw materials costs. In that gap between the real thing and the realer
thing, a different sort of bootlegger exploited a cross-border market and
culinary obsessives developed fetishes.

Mexican migrants, who shopped and ate at American bodegas and taquerias, were early adopters. They recognized the heavy, returnable bottles as totems of home. They argued that a proper Coke deserved more than an aluminum or plastic container. They believed that the thick glass bottles sustained a greater wallop of carbonation. They claimed the fizzy brown water within tasted somehow sweeter, but less saccharine. They argued that Mexican-bottled Coke was somehow more caramel-y and somehow better.

When I was a boy, my friends and I convinced ourselves that we could discern a difference between Coke bottled in Macon, Georgia, the closest plant, and Coke bottled in Atlanta. We reasoned that Atlanta Coke, which we called Headquarters Coke, had more bite, that it was somehow stronger. Maybe we were right. Headquarters has long sold syrup to bottlers the world over. And Headquarters has devised advertising campaigns.

But ever since the advent of the bottling system, individual companies had sweetened and carbonated and packaged the product. As America in general and the South in particular fell hard for artisanal goods, from peanut butter made with organic North Carolina legumes to bread baked with Arkansas-raised rye, consumer demand transformed Coca-Cola, the most industrial of drinks, into an imported artisanal beverage, with a rarefied pedigree, worthy of a higher price.

In 2005, I visited Buffalo Trace Distillery in Frankfort, Kentucky, with Julian Van Winkle. Source-specific corn was on the market from Anson Mills. Another five years would pass before Balcones Distilling in Texas began marketing whiskey made from specific corn varieties. A decade would pass before Willet Distillery, in nearby Bardstown, Kentucky, began sourcing its corn from the same county where it crafts whiskey (and country hams age among the ricks). But those developments already seemed inevitable as Van Winkle and I watched the crew unload a train car of corn that Buffalo Trace would distill into Pappy and other bourbons. As the golden kernels tumbled from the hopper, I asked him what variety the corn was and where it was grown.

Van Winkle scoffed and smiled, saying it was corn and nothing more, a non-GMO commodity crop. (An advocate for the transformations possible in a toasted oak barrel left undisturbed for a generation or more, he spoke with even more good-hearted derision of moonshine, bottled straight from the still.) I had heard similar words from barbecue pitmasters. When talk turned to higher-fat heritage pigs in the 2000s, many cooks responded similarly. Good barbecue, they said, was about experience, about expertise, about the muscle memory that repeated tasks yielded. The raw product was less important. What mattered was the work of the artisan, who, over decades of training and experimentation, had devised the best means of coaxing the most flavors from commodities, whether they be pigs or corn.

That divide between nurture and nature described a schism in the farmer-artisan continuum that Southern food and drink brought into stark relief. Does honest food rely on great produce and livestock, born of heirloom seeds and breeds nurtured by farmers with a sense of agricultural possibilities and responsibilities to history? Or are the artisans who transform raw ingredients into kitchen and table goods the true heroes of the story? The answer, Americans began to discover, was a little of both.

Van Winkle didn't buy arguments that better whiskey could be made from better corn. He was suspicious of anyone who aimed to fiddle with the techniques that his grandfather had developed decades before, back when Pappy Van Winkle famously mounted a sign at his distillery that read NO CHEMISTS ALLOWED. Great whiskey, Julian Van Winkle said, was the work of a great distiller who transformed the mundane into the extraordinary by way of charred oak, time, and legerdemain. Drinking his whiskey, it was hard to argue with his logic.

As more whiskey makers entered the market with goods age old and brand new, entrepreneurs rethought the distillation of bourbon and other whiskeys. Some followed the moonshiner credo of making it fast. They flavored new-make corn whiskey with fruit concentrates better suited for jellies and marmalades. Others fiddled with the aging process. Demand for bourbons like Pappy Van Winkle, which sold on the black market for ten times its retail price, created a shortage of the charred oak barrels in which bourbon aged.

Terressentia, a South Carolina company, developed a process that cut barrel resting in favor of ultrasound and oxygenation techniques that aged whiskey in hours instead of years. Defiant of North Carolina aged its whiskey in barrels floated with spirals of oak. These innovations unsettled an industry soaked in process and tradition. But they didn't trouble Van Winkle, who believed that the value in artisan goods was measured in direct correlation to a maker's devotion to tradition.

Southerners ditched brine-injected city ham for long-cured country ham. They rejected grocery store pap for stone-ground grits. They quit relying on vodka and soda with a twist of lemon for Saturday afternoon buzzes and switched back to bourbon and branch. In the 2000s, as the region awakened to the economic and cultural promise of craft production, Southerners embraced artisan possibilities across a spectrum that connected agriculture and industry and pop culture and included moonshine, antebellum grits, three-year-old heirloom ham, cane sugar Coca-Cola, and twenty-year-old Pappy.

"This stuff is alive," Glenn Roberts liked to say, as ground corn spilled from between his millstones. Roberts was talking about how those grits retained their germ, and, by extension, their taste. There was something else in his voice, too. There was a will to nurture the system of agriculture that had yielded the corn in the first place, a belief that once-lost grains might feed a region and its peoples.

His words sounded an affirmation. And they constructed a metaphor of future possibilities in a region that had long lived close to the land and had only recently begun to regard the economic and cultural legacies embedded in its artisan goods. As barbecue pitmasters realized new value in their work, they, too, affirmed possibilities for the region. But before pitmasters climbed that ladder, chefs had their day in the spotlight.

Sean Brock, who captured the nation's attention with Lowcountry culinary revival work, tattooed his devotion to heirloom ingredients.

· 13 ·

Restaurant Renaissance

I 'd heard about it and read about it and I was excited to try it," Sean Brock said of his first taste of hoppin' John, the rice and cowpeas dish at the heart of the fabled Carolina Rice Kitchen. "It was awful." Brock was twenty in 1998, a culinary school student curious about linkages to West Africa in the dish, smitten by stories of good luck that came to New Year's Day diners who savored a bowl. A native of Wise County, Virginia, deep in the belly of Appalachia, Brock drove south to study Charleston, South Carolina, and its dishes, to enmesh himself in a storied coastal city where Africans and Europeans had, over four centuries of conflict and complement, forged one of the nation's most resonant cuisines. He arrived to learn techniques and pay respects to the cooks who honed the Lowcountry repertoire, not to disparage their patrimony. But Brock couldn't deny his palate. The peas were chalky, the rice mushy and bland. The stuff was, he said, garbage.

Like politicians who submit to interviews and answer probing questions with rote stories, chefs riding the celebrity comet repeated narratives because those stories were effective and expressed essential truths.

As Brock rose in the 2000s on a swell of rekindled respect for the South and its foods, as he moved from culinary school to take chef jobs in Richmond, Virginia, and Nashville, Tennessee, he told the story of that hoppin' John epiphany.

After he settled at McCrady's in Charleston, Brock recognized that the agricultural products on which Lowcountry cuisine were built had gone missing. He recognized, too, that owing to the trove of historical research done there over past centuries, he might reverse engineer a hoppin' John that was worth the hype. With the exception of New Orleans, which rose to new prominence along a comparable path, no Southern city other than Charleston could draw from such a deep well of culinary history.

In the early 2000s, Brock told and retold that hoppin' John story, recasting the narrative to suit his purposes like Lyndon Baines Johnson sampling Zephyr Wright's time on the Jim Crow roadways. When Brock got specific, he identified the typical building blocks of this once great dish as "Uncle Ben's rice and black eyed peas from Sysco that had been sitting on the shelf for three years and tasted like nothing." His critique of industrial agriculture could have been teleported from the neo-hippie era. This time, the answer wasn't returning to the land but bringing the farm to the city. A research dive bolstered Brock and the acolytes who followed him.

Working with a Justice League of academics and farmers including David Shields of the University of South Carolina and Glenn Roberts of Anson Mills, Brock plowed through the agricultural record, beginning with corn and rice and moving on to peas. To re-create the taste, Brock devised a three-step, three-pot, one-bowl, sixteen-ingredient hoppin' John recipe. To appreciate what he had reverse engineered, he asked diners to think of the dish as a Lowcountry history lesson. "It embodies the marriage between the golden rice seed, which crossed the Atlantic to underwrite the elaborate wealth of Charleston," Brock explained, "and the lowly cowpea, a West African native originally deemed fodder for cattle and for the slaves who had brought that rice to Carolina and grew it." To appreciate the intricacies of this revived dish, he suggested that diners needed to know this history, too.

Brock had already begun to develop a reputation for what was then called molecular cuisine. He cooked with a wink and a flourish. At Mc-Crady's, where George Washington dined after the Revolutionary War, that wink translated as cotton candy spun from country ham fat, and oysters drizzled with Mountain Dew mignonette. One bite into a quail ballotine swaddled in Dr. Pepper sauce, diners felt Brock's elbow in their ribs. Two sips into a muscadine-cucumber gazpacho, they glimpsed him in the back corner of the kitchen, wearing a tattered MAKE CORNBREAD NOT WAR hat, grinning wide like Jack Nicholson in *The Shining*.

He conceived flights of fancy like foie gras marshmallow terrines infused with licorice. Brock served pellets of barbecue ice cream made by steeping a whole pork sandwich in a mix of barbecue sauce and cream and dripping the strained concoction into a reservoir of liquid nitrogen. (On contact, the slurry formed tiny balls that looked like Dippin' Dots and tasted eerily like smoked pork shoulder.) But America didn't fully embrace Brock until the press recast him as a Southern foods revivalist, the chef who went looking for old recipes and honest ingredients, the chef who recognized that hoppin' John was a Lowcountry dowry in need of a makeover.

During the opening salvo for his second Charleston restaurant, Husk, Brock declared, "If it doesn't come from the South, it's not coming through the door." A bold statement at the time, those words were a vote of confidence for the region and its larder. In the year that followed, Brock talked about his grandmother's heirloom seed collection on the *Charlie Rose* show. *Bon Appétit* memorialized his ascent with a Southern theme issue. Blazoned with a ruddy-crusted drumstick, the cover screamed BEST FRIED CHICKEN EVER and promised recipes for potlikker noodles and devilish deviled eggs. It was a crowning moment, a nod of relevancy in the most recent Southern restaurant upswing.

Set in an antebellum home with stacked piazzas, Husk presented as an agriculture extension office, reimagined by the Disney team that designed Epcot. The only thing missing was an animatronic Thomas Jefferson, standing by the windowpaned door, holding forth on the possibilities of olive tree cultivation. Brock was a neotraditionalist who appreciated what was gained by linking place and history through food. "I talk to other chefs from other parts of the country all the time who are jealous of what we have," he said to me once, as I stared at a tattoo rendering of Jimmy Red corn running down his left arm. "They're jealous of our ingredients. They're jealous of our bourbon whiskey. They appreciate what we have. Too often we don't. I want to fix that."

To develop the Husk narrative, Brock stacked splits of hickory and oak in the hall. An oversized blackboard, mounted by the door, listed the farmers who supplied the produce and livestock. David Shields got his own listing on the board alongside artisans like Allan Benton. Slices of his ham arrived on charred oak staves from old whiskey barrels. A cupboard, tucked into the landing opposite the bathrooms, brimmed with pickled vegetables. Instead of flowers, Brock set the tables with Mason jars of brightly colored peas and beans. Dazzling red cobs of corn and wizened green spears of dried okra jutted from vases.

Brock made good on the word *husk*, which translates as the protective outer layer of a seed. He built a next-generation county fair exposition, with a laboratory kitchen for experiments in gastronomy and a dining room where he could crank the Drive-By Truckers and sing along as Patterson Hood excised the demons that drove George Wallace. Husk was a place to celebrate the South with clear-eyed vigor.

Efforts like Brock's had deep roots in the American experiment. Citizens have been alternately claiming, dismissing, and reclaiming American culinary identities since the early days of the republic. In 1921, Charles Rosenbault made the case that American food was so besieged, its future so imperiled, that the times required a "Society for the Exposition, Development, and Glorification of American Cookery." In the bright light of contemporary Charleston, as tourists thronged Queen Street to snag skillets of cornbread and plates of fried pig ears, Brock bridged the gap between Rosenbault's facetious daydream and the honest 1990s vision that Scott Peacock and Edna Lewis sketched for the Society for the Revival and Preservation of Southern Food.

Like the democratic ideal, the best American cooking has always been just out of reach. The last generation had a handle on it, Americans in general and Southerners in particular told themselves. Our parents got it right. Now all we cook is derivative and reductive. Now our cupboard goods are lesser and lack pedigree. Brock was not the first chef in the modern era to attempt a revival and claim a national stage. Paul Prudhomme told his own version of a hoppin' John story at the first Symposium on American Cuisine in 1982.

"We have a very very famous dish in New Orleans," he said to the crowd of chefs and restaurant professionals who gathered to appraise American gastronomy. "It's called shrimp creole and everybody has heard of it. You've seen it on menus all over the world if you've traveled. And every time I've tasted it, it has been universally bad. I mean, it's terrible. And I said to myself several years ago that this dish had to have been wonderful at one time for so many people to know its name, for so many people to try and do it, to copy it, to make it. And in starting to research it, I think I got down, perhaps, close to what it was in the beginning."

The secret, Prudhomme said, foreshadowing the chef and artisan movement building in the region, was in the crops and livestock nurtured, and in the knowledge accumulated by previous generations: "So what we've got to do first is documentation and we've got to document regional food and get back to that historical beginning of what that dish was and why it lasted the time that it has and why we know about it."

Charleston had long been a great food town. But until the twenty-first century, fine dining restaurants served little of that great food. Home dining had long been the bellwether. Generations of African American caterers excelled. Nat Fuller, a former slave, emerged in the mid-1860s as the premier Charleston interpreter of haute cuisine dishes like capons stewed with truffles and gâteau glacé au rhum. Lucille Grant, granddaughter of a slave, beloved for her renditions of shad roe and biscuits and shrimp and grits, was the preferred caterer to the mid-twentieth-century gentry.

Home cooking, even among the gentry, was not always rarefied. When the Junior League of Charleston sued Ernest Matthew Mickler, author of the 1986 book *White Trash Cooking*, the white-gloved ladies claimed that he lifted more than twenty of his recipes, including roast possum, from their book, *Charleston Receipts*. (They had a point; the possum recipe he attributed to Aunt Donnah, much like the one submitted to *Charleston Receipts* by Mrs. W. H. Humphreys, dictated hanging possums for forty-eight hours before skinning and trussing like poultry before cooking.)

Outside the home, corner cafés served red rice perfumed with bay leaves. Cafeterias dished okra soup, made with beef shinbone broth. But white tablecloth restaurants had recently tended more toward continental confections like the Scarlett O'Hara, a floating restaurant decked out in crushed velour and velvet. When it opened in 1973, the restaurant played up *Gone with the Wind* conceits, advertising "Rhett Butler's notorious blockade runner returns to Charleston harbor." Overt homages to the Old South were few. Instead, the restaurant aspired to a sort of European cookery defined by Frogs' Legs in Provençale Sauce Fantastique and Jellied Consommé Madrilene. (In 1979, the boat sank in Charleston Harbor, within sight of Fort Sumter.)

When Robert Stehling opened Hominy Grill in 1996, the Charleston restaurant cooking that won praise was born of hotel kitchen brigades and culinary school graduates. Their food wasn't Scarlett pretentious. It was, instead, nominally Southern, expressed by egg rolls stuffed with collards and tasso and served with peach chutney at Magnolias, which opened in 1990. If Lucille Grant served vernacular cuisine, this was veneer cuisine, rendered Southern by what chefs topped it with or placed it atop.

Stehling, who learned the trade at Crook's Corner, a restaurant that took many of its cues from home cooks, aimed to deliver riffs on what Charleston ate at home. His restaurant was casual, known for workaday dishes like shrimp bog, thick with sausage and tomatoes, and sautéed chicken livers, swamped with country ham gravy. When Hominy Grill interpreted restaurant cooking, Stehling aimed for the heart of his customers. A regular's memories of family trips to a roadhouse beyond town inspired curry shrimp, served with a relish tray and crowned with apples and bananas. To telegraph his ethic, Stehling published a staple-bound cookbook of twenty or so recipes, illustrated with simple line drawings. At a time when lavish, oversized books by Thomas Keller set the standard, Stehling self-published a cookbook that looked like it had been copied by a 4-H club and printed at the office supply store. That was the intent. The book, like the restaurant, broadcast humility. It said home.

After Stehling won the James Beard Award for Best Chef South in 2008, a few of his peers grumbled. For a good part of its existence, Hominy hadn't even opened for dinner, when Beard-winning restaurants usually showcase their finesse. Instead, Stehling drew long queues for stone-ground grits and scrambled eggs, for biscuits stuffed with fried chicken and drenched in sausage gravy, for food that, as the years rolled on and fine dining dropped its white tablecloth pretensions, looked and tasted prescient.

The response of detractors recalled what Guenter Seeger, the German-born haute cuisine chef who reigned over Atlanta for much of the 1980s and 1990s, once said about Blackberry Farm, the luxe Tennessee restaurant and resort perched on the cusp of Appalachia. "They cook like housewives," he said, revealing a prejudice born of false expectations and an insecurity that did not suit his graceful cooking.

The reinvention of Charleston and its cuisine had begun earlier, of course, before Brock had his epiphany, before Stehling drove the market for good food downscale. Hurricane Hugo, which made landfall in September 1989, was a catalyst. The storm, which cut a 250-mile path of destruction, peeled back tin roofs like tin cans, beached sloops on city streets, engulfed living rooms in pluff mud, and collapsed church spires.

The storm precipitated demographic changes in the city. The damaged Ansonborough Homes public housing project closed and was demolished. The College of Charleston expanded rapidly, drawing young white students who paid higher rents than longtime residents who worked service jobs or scratched by on fixed incomes. After the Charleston Naval Base and Shipyard closed, middle-class and working-class jobs declined sharply. Over the next few decades, as housing and jobs atrophied, the black population of Charleston dropped more than 50 percent.

By 2010, whites had become the majority for the first time in sixty years. And tourism, which grew under the leadership of longtime mayor Joe Riley, drew even more of the white and wealthy. They poured into the city, drawn by walkable neighborhoods and timeless architecture. As they settled, gentrification displaced black businesses, especially on the upper reaches of King Street, where new restaurants clustered after 2010.

Mike Lata opened the Ordinary in 2012. Set in a former bank building, the white-tiled restaurant shared King Street with a wig shop and a furniture store that sold overstuffed velour recliners. Lata had first arrived in Charleston at the behest of Glenn Roberts, then operations manager of the restaurant Garibaldi's. At a time when frozen Alaskan salmon was a standard, he built a menu at Anson, a sister restaurant, around local triggerfish and snapper. Like FIG, which Lata opened in 2003, the Ordinary was a beacon of a new Charleston in which dining out was a prime draw for tourists and a source of pride among locals who recalled the time, not that long distant, when the most heralded dishes in town were pasty she-crab soup with way too much sherry and the hoppin' John that riled Sean Brock.

As the racial and economic complexion of the city changed, and the nation stood ready to anoint Charleston a new American culinary capital, restaurants run by Stehling, Brock, and Lata weren't the only ones to gain notice. Tourists who breakfasted on oyster omelets at Hominy Grill sought out lunches of fried pork chops, red rice, and okra soup at Bertha's in North Charleston, where collards raised by Joseph Fields reached their pork-scented potential. After eating alderwood-smoked oysters with coriander crème fraîche at the Ordinary one night, vanguard tourists traveled next to nearby Bowen's Island, where roasted oysters arrived at table by the shovelful and spent shells exited through holes cut in the plank wood tables. When the press descended on the city to cover the Charleston renaissance, some correspondents devoted as much copy to red rice joints as to fine dining palaces.

Asked where he ate lunch on his day off, Sean Brock talked up Martha Lou's, a pink hutch near the docks, where seagulls circle overhead, in search of scurrying prey among the wreckage in the nearby junkyard. In Martha Lou Gadsden's kitchen, pots of chitlins and hot peppers simmered, battered aluminum pans burbled with black pepper–flecked lima beans, and hotel pans of macaroni and cheese browned. When tourists followed Brock's lead, Gadsden fed them like her own and told them stories of Mosquito Beach, where black Charleston frolicked before integration. "In the cosmology of Southern cooking, Martha Lou's is no dwarf planet," Sam Sifton wrote in a *New York Times* profile of Brock. "It is close to the sun itself."

In 2006, the year Bowen's Island Restaurant out on Folly Beach celebrated its sixtieth anniversary, proprietor Robert Barber, a minister and politician, walked onto the stage at the James Beard Awards in New York City to receive an America's Classics award. He wore a black tux. And he wore a pair of white fishing boots to honor the men and women, many of them African American, who worked the pluff mud of South Carolina, harvesting the oysters he steamed. "We should remember that we drink from wells we did not dig," Barber said that night, paraphrasing the Bible as he received his medal. "We warm ourselves by fires we did not build."

At worst, this connectivity between white tablecloth restaurants and oilcloth cafés, in which the headlong press rush toward the former supposedly benefited the latter, described a new sort of trickle-down economics, in which working-class restaurants subsisted on a sort of journalistic leftovers. At best, the linkages offered a glimpse of a new Charleston cuisine. Less stratified, more democratic, more accurately reflective of the people who claim the city, and, ultimately, more satisfying, that city and that cuisine are still in gestation.

The restaurant renaissance that Charleston experienced, beginning in the late 1990s, was part of a cycle of booms that had become routine by the latter half of the twentieth century. Every ten years, America discovered some facet of Southern cuisine, held it at arm's length to admire, and showered praise on its makers before moving on. A 1960s love affair with soul food was, at its core, a fascination with the foods of rural Southerners who moved to the urban South and the industrial North. A grits and peanuts fad coincided with the 1976 election of Jimmy Carter.

In the 1980s, when chefs like Paul Prudhomme interpreted the region and its larder, they had it both ways. They were innovators, reprising and reinventing a cuisine. And, compared with chefs in other regions, they were traditionalists, while the rest of the nation embraced fusion cuisine. John Mariani of *Esquire* set the tone when he defined Southern food in opposition to other trends including Pacific Rim, which he summarized as variants on Patagonian tooth fish with ponzu sauce and adzuki beans.

The burst of creativity that began in the 1990s proved the longest, as chefs revived the crops, livestock, techniques, and traditions that previous generations had left to wither on the vine. Instead of looking to French chefs for inspiration, this generation embraced their grandparents and the working-class restaurants that still served foods their grandparents knew. But these chefs didn't hew to those traditions.

John Fleer of Blackberry Farm braised sweet tea–marinated wild boar and fried sweet tea–brined chicken. And Ben Barker of Magnolia Grill served okra rellenos, hoppin' John risotto, and green tomato soup with crab and country ham. Anne Quatrano of Bacchanalia in Atlanta dished pork chops with tomato gravy and roasted peaches with chamomile. While they experimented, Damon Lee Fowler of Savannah, who published a book called *Classical Southern Cooking*, argued for a more hidebound South. Take ravioli, he said. "Even if it's stuffed full of collard greens, can you call it Southern? It's more like something Italian that got out of hand."

This modern restaurant renaissance flourished across the region. At City Grocery in Oxford, Mississippi, six blocks from my home, New Orleans native John Currence served countrified oysters Rockefeller, creamed with fennel-perfumed collard greens, topped with planks of crisped country ham, dusted with powdered country ham. Nashville, which earned national prominence as a pop country music mill beginning in the 1940s, emerged as a creator and disseminator of hot fried chicken. Born in the African American community as a late-night drinking corrective, it became in the 2010s the most widely adopted Southern dish since shrimp and grits, adapted by high-end restaurants and interpreted by KFC franchisees.

No city better showcased the restaurant renaissance and the headlong plunge toward gentrification than New Orleans. Like Charleston, the city reinvented itself after a disaster, as the class and race makeup of neighborhoods shifted and newcomers decamped there from the rural South and urban North. During the antebellum era, New Orleans had been a great port city, a place of entry for slaves and exit for cotton. While the gentry of Charleston entertained in their homes and on their piazzas, New Orleans had long been a grand restaurant town, a show-case of haute Creole cooking, where dishes like bananas Foster entered the American lexicon. By the second decade of the twenty-first century, as a newly creolized New Orleans assimilated a new wave of immi-grants, the city reasserted its place in the American culinary firmament.

There were one thousand restaurants in town but only fifteen dishes, served in heavy rotation. That was the old New Orleans joke. Locals knew the rotation: Sautéed drum napped with meunière and scattered with jumbo lump crab. Shrimp remoulade poised atop fried green toma-toes. Roasted duck, glazed with something sweet. But as the restaurant renaissance gained traction post-Katrina, the roster expanded. Chefs re-vived traditional dishes, nearly lost. Gumbo z' herbes, a stew of greens and pork, won a new generation of converts, who came to know the dish during Holy Thursday lunches at Dooky Chase. So did calas, fritters born of Rice Coast Africa, made from the leavings of yesterday's rice pot. Creole cream cheese, a loose clabber beloved by farmers, reentered the lexicon before Katrina, raised from the dead like a dairy Lazarus.

Newly committed after losses that came as floodwaters soaked and then rotted the city in 2005, young chefs stepped away from fine dining restaurants. Ben Wicks left Rio Mar, the fine dining restaurant where he had served as chef de cuisine, to focus on Mahony's in the Irish Channel neighborhood, where he lavished attention on the humble po-boy.

Frying Gulf shrimp instead of imports, stirring remoulade from scratch, and cooking down mirepoix for a roast beef gravy that luxuri-

ously coated the back of a ladle, he paid homage to the simple and ubiq-
uitous sandwich that historian Michael Mizell-Nelson called the "shotgun
house of New Orleans cuisine." Wicks, who made good money selling
soft-shell crab po-boys to tourists, sold locals on French fry po-boys,
drenched in that debris-rich gravy. That inclusion signaled that he re-
spected the Depression-era roots of the po-boy phenomenon, when the
sandwich became the preferred feed of striking streetcar workers.

In the move to workingman's cuisine, Willie Mae Seaton, proprietor
of Willie Mae's Scotch House in the Treme neighborhood, had inspired
Wicks. Beloved for beans and rice, wet-batter fried chicken, and cocktails
of Scotch and milk, the octogenarian had quickly evacuated to Houston
as the levees failed and the waters rose in August 2005. Just as quickly,
Seaton booked a return flight to New Orleans, intent on reclaiming her
double shotgun house and reopening her restaurant. A city official found
her on a street corner in front of the restaurant with a James Beard
medal, awarded that spring, in her purse. If Seaton was working that
hard to reopen her fried chicken restaurant, then Wicks thought he
could make an effort to uphold the city's proud po-boy tradition.

Wealthy New Orleans recovered quickly, especially on the uptown
high ground that came to be called the Sliver by the River. The work
took longer and was more arduous on the back side of the French Quarter where African American families huddled, along Lake Pontchartrain
where middle-class whites lived in ranch houses with attached garages,
and out east in Versailles where Vietnamese families worked urban
farms girded by dikes. At a time when no one knew what would become
of the city, and discussions about closing off flood-prone sections to re-
development gained momentum, when FEMA trailers littered yards and
blue tarps draped storm-damaged roofs, and the Soul Rebels played and
chanted "There's No Place Like Home" to capacity bar crowds, the fight
to save Willie Mae's became a bedrock effort.

It became clear that fine dining restaurants would reopen. As the
city took on water, John Besh of Restaurant August stowed his family in

North Carolina and texted his Marine Corps buddies to develop a plan. They cooked red beans and rice in his hometown of Slidell, across Lake Pontchartrain from the city, and served them to first responders at makeshift parking lot canteens. Like many across the city, Besh was humbled by the experience. It was the first time he had fed people who were truly hungry. In the months to come, Besh tapped government contracts to feed the troops and National Guardsmen who, after an untenable delay, poured into the city. With the profits from those contracts, he rebuilt his two restaurants and helped others rebuild their own. When volunteer work crews arrived from around the nation to help rebuild Willie Mae's, Besh and Adolfo Garcia of Rio Mar catered lunches. Besh showed a dramatic flair, draping service tables in white linen and serving gumbo and jambalaya from silver chafing dishes positioned in the gutter among debris piles and rot-leaking refrigerators tagged with graffiti.

As he rebuilt, Besh came to admire the post-Katrina resilience of the Vietnamese fishing community. And he proved an early interpreter of a Vietnamese-Creole fusion that recognized the French influence on each. He served tilefish floated tableside in a bowl of French-pressed pho broth. His newfangled shrimp Creole called for lemongrass, basil, and mint. He was not alone. By the time the city marked the fifth anniversary of the man-made disaster, corner groceries served pho, and po-boy shops stacked fried oysters on loaves baked by Vietnamese-owned Dong Phuong as well as old-guard Leidenheimer.

Just as American corporations expanded in scope during the twenty-first century, taking advantage of new scales, New Orleans restaurant groups metastasized. Before the levee failures, Donald Link owned one restaurant, Herbsaint. Seven months after the storm he opened Cochon, a Cajun Country send-up that reintroduced the city to its neighbors to the west. Two years after Katrina, that restaurant was so ingrained it seemed a classic. Cochon Butcher, an around-the-corner shop that served a muffuletta made with house-cured meats, burst at the seams. By the tenth anniversary of the storm, his group included five restaurants. Like the Brennan family before him, Link ran his group with a businessperson's efficiency. In New Orleans, restaurants served as engines of recovery during the storm aftermath. By 2010, they were beacons of the creative economy.

The demographics of New Orleans changed remarkably in the decade after the storm. The city became whiter and wealthier. Disparities grew as black waiters and bar backs and shuckers struggled to find affordable housing. Taking a page from the Charleston playbook, the Department of Housing and Urban Development tore down the Lafitte housing project, in which bussers and shuckers and waiters had lived. Ten years after the levee failures, four out of five white residents believed that New Orleans had largely recovered. Almost three out of five African American residents didn't believe they lived in the same city.

Houston, which New Orleans boosters considered the uncouth antithesis of their culturally and gastronomically rich home, emerged as a twenty-first-century creole city, thrumming with new arrivals from Southeast Asia, a destination for travelers who embraced immigrant restaurants as portals to American cultural richness. Tens of thousands of New Orleans residents evacuated to Houston, where the oil industry promised jobs and the sprawling suburbs promised affordable housing. Many of the culinary transfers worked. Boudin, the Cajun sausage popular in New Orleans, could be had in Houston, though it was sometimes spelled *boudain*. Sweet Gulf seafood and fat Gulf oysters were in ready supply. Never mind the fact that what Houstonians called bayous were, in point of fact, concrete culverts.

A new dynamism drove the New Orleans restaurant scene. By the time the city observed the tenth anniversary of the storm, transplants flocked to Red's Chinese, across the street from the avant-funk Saturn Bar, where the wontons came stuffed with crawfish and the egg drop soup bobbed with hominy. They drank sazeracs down the street at the Mayhaw Bar in the St. Roch Market. In its heyday, the market served a

working-class clientele and posted signs that read "YOUR WIFE CALLED
AND SAID TO BRING HOME SOME BOILED CRAWFISH AND PO-BOYS." When a
refurbished St. Roch opened as a food hall, Lagos, a Nigerian pot food
stand-up, sold ropy okra soup and Koreole vended fried chicken with a
soy-ginger glaze.

Concerns about gentrification were warranted. But the spike in real
estate values didn't result in the wholesale displacement or closure of
po-boy joints like Domilise's and fried chicken cafés like Willie Mae's
Scotch House. Instead, some of those restaurants became pilgrimage
sites for tourists who descended on a city that, by the tenth anniversary
of the storm, boasted 10 percent–plus more restaurants and 21 percent
fewer residents. On a typical day in 2015, the line queued at Willie Mae's
door an hour before opening, and the crowd was populated with culinary tourists.

When the Southern Foodways Alliance envisioned Willie Mae's as a
possible beacon for Treme recovery in 2005, and volunteers under the
direction of John Currence disemboweled the building and put it back
together, the reasoning was: If this little restaurant could come back,
then maybe the rest of the neighborhood could, too. By 2015, Kerry Seaton Stewart, great-granddaughter of Willie Mae Seaton, faced with daily
overflow crowds at the Treme original, opened a second uptown location. And she talked about franchising a Creole analogue to the Cajun
fried chicken that Al Copeland introduced to the nation in the 1970s.

During the nineteenth and early twentieth centuries, New Orleans
was a polyglot place. Italian dockworkers who unloaded banana boats
lived in Little Palermo. Haitian émigrés contributed the city's distinctive
house styles, the Creole cottage and the shotgun. Born of river commerce, economic opportunities drew immigrants. In the aftermath of
Hurricane Katrina, the commerce of cleaning and rebuilding drove the
economy. This time, the entwining strains were different. Hispanic construction workers and white cultural entrepreneurs dominated. Taco

trucks vended in the parking lot of the Lowe's Home Improvement Center, where locals bought plyboard for windows and blue tarps for roofs.

Post-Katrina transplants comprised more than a quarter of the New Orleans population in 2015. A sizable new creative class settled on the back side of the French Quarter in Faubourg Marigny. Co-offices sprouted with twenty-something Web designers and digital entrepreneurs, pecking at laptops and drinking café au lait. (Weary of arrivistes, detractors called the neighborhood Faux Marigny.) Equally popular was the adjacent Bywater, which became such a symbol of post-Katrina ferment that when David Kinch, the chef at Manresa in Los Gatos, California, opened a New Orleans–style restaurant near his Silicon Valley flagship, he called it The Bywater.

Chef-driven restaurants flourished in New Orleans after the floodwaters receded. Standards changed. When the levees broke, so did the barriers between fine dining and casual, between cafés that specialized in fried chicken doused with Tabasco and restaurants that staked reputations on racks of lamb with satsuma relish. The default moved from pomp to casual. Stanley, Scott Boswell's everyday café where cooks crowned soft-shell crab po-boys with poached eggs and hollandaise, packed in Jackson Square crowds. Stella, his fine dining temple, famous for foie gras and bacon sandwiches, began a long slide to closure. When John Besh reopened Restaurant August, he put red beans and rice on the Monday lunch menu. And seafood and sausage gumbo on the Friday lunch menu. As New Orleans chefs embraced traditional dishes, the rest of the nation followed.

John Folse of nearby Donaldsonville, Louisiana, and Rick Tramonto of Chicago opened R'evolution, a showcase French Quarter restaurant, in 2012. Their Death by Gumbo and Caviar Staircase recalled an era when indulgence was the best measure of excellence. But the new restaurants that generated the buzz focused less on folderol. At Pêche in the Warehouse District, Link protégé Ryan Prewitt grilled whole mangrove snappers over a live fire and dressed them with salsa verde.

Creolization showed its attributes in restaurants like Shaya on Magazine Street, where Besh protégé Alon Shaya won converts to modern Israeli fare including kibbeh nayah, made with minced beef and lamb from Two Run Farm, across the border in Mississippi. His matzo ball soup bobbed with roasted duck and was so pleasantly redolent of anise that it tasted like a drunken cook sloshed a sazerac in the pot. Magasin, a modern Vietnamese bistro two doors down from Shaya, served salmon wrapped in brown rice paper.

When Mike Gulotta, former chef de cuisine at Restaurant August, opened MoPho in 2014, he strayed from the traditional Creole formula to serve fried soft-shell crabs crowned with fermented black beans, and fried chicken and sweet potato waffles gilded with caramel nuoc mam butter. In this newer New Orleans, the best steakhouse was an Argentinean clubhouse called La Boca, where the menu read like a bovine anatomy thesis, delivered in Spanish. Caribbean foodways, long suppressed by other narratives, got their due at Compère Lapin, where Nina Compton, a native of St. Lucia, fried dirty rice arancini and doused the croquettes with sour orange mojo. This New Orleans was a more open city. Open to new arrivals. Open to new tastes.

As the restaurant scenes in Charleston and New Orleans matured, as chef-driven restaurants begat chef-owned restaurant groups, those businesses became integral to city identities. Just as Birmingham ascended on the story of Frank Stitt's biracial and becalmed Highlands Bar and Grill, the restaurants of Charleston and New Orleans emerged as modern symbols of civic possibilities.

Beginning in the 1980s, the South was the first American region to revive and reinterpret its restaurant food. Owing to the region's tragic history and long slog through poverty, Southern chefs proved anxious to reinvent themselves, too. As the 2010s dawned, and these two cities recovered from hurricanes and their aftermaths, demographics changed and the restaurant scenes democratized.

Restaurants served as reliquaries where chefs presented the best provincial cooking. They also revealed themselves to be laboratories for agricultural experiments, libraries for historical research, and fulcrums for economic resurgence. From Charleston to New Orleans, chefs led the way toward a new respect for regional American culture. In New Orleans, especially, this new vitality suggested that a truly multicultural South was finally at hand. While the region had never been accurately defined by black and white, the mosaic that came into focus in the 2010s looked and smelled and tasted like the future.

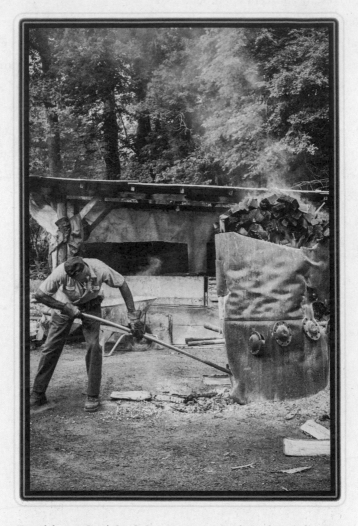

To cook hogs at Scott's Bar-B-Q in Hemingway, South Carolina, Rodney Scott and crew harvested local trees and burned them down into coals.

Pits and Pitmasters

When Sam Jones opened a $2 million barbecue restaurant in November 2015, he chose a spot on a suburban thruway on the edge of Greenville, North Carolina, seven miles from the joint his grandfather Pete Jones opened in 1947. During a 1984 renovation, Bruce Jones, a country man with an eye for spectacle, remade the Skylight Inn roof into the shape of the U.S. Capitol rotunda. When his son Sam Jones first fired the pits that November, the third-generation pitmaster took possession of a dark-timbered restaurant that was its own sort of spectacle.

Two piebald pig chandeliers, impaled with filament bulbs, hung from trussed beams at Sam Jones Bar-B-Q. When customers queued to order at the counter, they faced placards that could have been lifted from a circus sideshow. One read "LEAVE IT TO CLEAVER," another, "A MAN AMONG PIGS." Along the far wall, fixed on smoke-charred barrelheads, Jones family men stared back from sepia photographs. Standing awkwardly before the camera with, say, a shovel in hand, they looked agitated, as if stopping for a picture when there was work to be done was an insult they tasted in the backs of their throats.

Nick Pihakis, the cofounder of Jim 'N Nick's Bar-B-Q in Birmingham, helped Jones imagine what the future could be. Together, they conceived a barbecue restaurant that was not a joint but a showcase for the possibilities of the form. The Greenville location was an important place to test the idea. Fifty-five years before, in that same coastal plain college town, Wilber Hardee had opened the first location in what would become his burger chain.

A key architectural element stood outside the restaurant: a pit house, ventilated by screened windows, topped by a tin roof, with a Janus-mawed fireplace at the center and a pit array along the flanks. Day and night, plumes lifted skyward from a chimney inscribed with Sam Jones's initials. Soot-streaked pitmen wheeled into the building with gutted pigs, pale as peaches. Sixteen hours later, they wheeled out, bearing crisp-skinned beasts gone cordwain in the hickory smoke.

When Sam Jones Bar-B-Q opened, Skylight Inn became the Jones family home place restaurant. In the same manner that the original Waffle House in the Atlanta suburb of Avondale reminded patrons of the company's roots, Skylight served as a place for reflection, a shrine to family and permanence.

Detractors quickly crawled out of the woodpile. Hard-shell Baptists took issue with his decision to pour beer, while most barbecue places in this part of the state served nothing stronger than sweet tea. Elderly locals complained about the prices. In a town where sandwiches made with gas-cooked pork could be had for three bucks and change, Sam Jones's overstuffed sandwiches of wood-smoked pork ran six bucks and change.

Sam Jones felt the pressure. At Skylight, customers expected a short menu and efficient service. But when he opened a restaurant with a cathedral ceiling and a marble-top bar, customers wanted more. They wanted macaroni and cheese. They wanted salads, tossed with whole hog, cornbread croutons, and ranch dressing. They wanted warm welcomes. In a training conversation with a waiter, Jones put it this way: "Don't go walking up to a table with your head hanging down like somebody just ran over your puppy."

To weave a tether that connected what Skylight was and what the new place could be, Sam Jones employees wore Skylight Inn hats. The message was: We're family. There were aural cues, too. When customers crossed the threshold at Sam Jones Bar-B-Q, they heard the same staccato whack of cleavers on a cutting board. And they soon tasted the same whole hog that drew regulars to Skylight.

Jockeying between the two restaurants, Sam Jones straddled the past and the future. Each time he stepped into the smoke, he faced down that dichotomy. So did a whole generation of pitmasters who, beginning in the early years of the twenty-first century, thought enough of barbecue to gently reinvent it.

A generation before, when Raymond Sokolov fired those warning flares, the end appeared nigh. Regional food culture was on the ropes. Fast-food and fast-casual behemoths sprawled across the land, building burger-in-a-box hutches to feed the indiscriminate masses. When the original Leonard's Pit Barbecue in Memphis closed in 1991, John Egerton lamented the "pride of craft that is disappearing from all of American life," and declared that the fall of that craft was synonymous with the "fall of Western civilization."

But a funny thing happened in the drive-through queue. As Trillin and the Sterns serenaded eaters, and the good food movement gained momentum, and consumers talked about getting to know their local cattleman and strengthening farm-to-table connections, Americans also rejected the elitism and cost of fine dining.

Gazing into the pit at a barbecue joint was the cultural equivalent of looking under the hood of a 1960 slant-six Dodge Dart. The mechanics were straightforward and easy to understand. A peek at the inner workings reassured. To patronize an honest barbecue joint was to apprehend America's elemental past, laid bare among the cinder blocks and smolder. For a new generation of affluent consumers, fast food was anathema. And so were the casual chains that relied on central commissaries to supply far-flung networks of heat-and-serve outposts.

"Don't eat anything your great-grandmother wouldn't recognize as food," Michael Pollan told his followers. Consumers who distrusted the new industrialized agriculture system went looking for foods that met that standard and hearkened to an earlier day. That path led straight to barbecue, cooked by a newer generation of pitmasters who sourced heirloom hogs, chopped their own wood, and sourced their baked beans from Rancho Gordo.

In 2002 Danny Meyer, a St. Louis native who grew up eating rib racks and shoulder sandwiches, opened Blue Smoke, a New York City showcase of regional food culture. A triptych of photos in the men's room honored Vencil Mares of Taylor, Texas, posed with his famous bohunk sausage. J. C. Hardaway, the Memphis pitmaster whom Lolis Eric Elie, author of *Smokestack Lightning*, called the Stradivarius of the shoulder sandwich, smiled big from an oversized portrait along the dining room wall. With Blue Smoke, the man behind Gramercy Tavern and Eleven Madison Park declared that barbecue was ready for reappraisal and renewal.

The path to opening was rocky. The building inspector fought Meyer over smoke ventilation. Blue Smoke must be a fire hazard and polluter. The press fought him over authenticity. Barbecue could only be served in tumbledown joints and should only be cooked south of the Mason-Dixon. There also was the matter of the proprietor's complexion. Many of the barbecue faithful took seriously Calvin Trillin's playful observation about the validity of white-owned barbecue restaurants. Faced with the cultural faithfulness of what Meyer and his colleagues accomplished, the press eventually caved.

Removed from the homeland of barbecue, Meyer took liberties with meats and woods and sauces. "In any of the real barbecue destinations of the world, it's heresy to veer from what local tastes have dictated forever," Meyer said. Instead of hewing to one style, Blue Smoke sampled many, like a mix tape artist from the 1980s who recognized that Grandmaster Flash and Randy Newman didn't have that much in common, but knew that something good would come from the union. "The worst thing we could have done was to pretend that we were a barbecue joint rather than a New York restaurant."

In the 2000s, the growth of barbecue in New York City quickened. When Daisy May's opened a brick-and-mortar location in Hell's Kitchen, Adam Perry Lang, a veteran of Daniel Boulud's restaurants, channeled barbecue competition experience to develop a menu that included beef short ribs tagged to Oklahoma, dirty rice inspired by Cajun Country Louisiana, and bourbon-perfumed chicken impaled on a beer can and attributed to Tennessee. Mighty Quinn's, a mash-up of North Carolina and Texas, somehow accommodated a carrot salad with roasted chickpeas and tahini. By 2010 more than twenty barbecue restaurants operated in New York City. Before BrisketTown, a postmodern Texas meat market, opened in 2012, Daniel Delaney presold more than four thousand pounds of brisket over the Internet in less than forty-eight hours. Once it opened, he sold beef and tracked supply levels on the Web site istheremeatleft.com.

Meyer was not the first man to imagine a future-tense barbecue joint that collapsed the Southern map. Vince Staten, author of the road guide *Real Barbecue*, showcased multiple sauce styles at his Old Time Barbecue in suburban Louisville. In 1992, when sauces were understood to be geographic markers of patrimony, and mixing and matching of styles and sauces was verboten, Staten set the tables with six regional variants, ranging from a thin vinegar sauce of eastern North Carolina pedigree to a thick tomato sauce from western Texas.

Beginning in 2007, Louis Osteen, the white tablecloth Lowcountry cuisine champion, had touted a new kind of barbecue restaurant. At a moment when fine dining restaurants boasted theater-style kitchens, he imagined a new sort of chef table, with a splayed and coal-roasted hog as the focal point. Smoke Stack Lightning House of Barbecue for All People was an homage to Elie's book and to the United House of Prayer for All People, a black Protestant denomination with deep roots in the Carolinas. Osteen envisioned a restaurant that staged pig carcass pickings on Friday and Saturday nights and sliced hindquarters of pit-cooked beef to order. Emboldened by his 2004 James Beard Award win and by the success of Meyer, he promised a "Disney World of barbecue" on the tourist-thronged Grand Strand in Myrtle Beach, South Carolina. Osteen's vision never came true. But over the next decade, hundreds of entrepreneurs inside and outside the South made good on similar promises.

Not all great Southern pitmasters have been black. In the upper reaches of the region, in Lexington and Greensboro and other North Carolina Piedmont towns, working-class white men with their hands on long-handled shovels guided payloads of hickory coals through pit door openings. But in plantation towns, from Wilson, North Carolina, to Eutaw, Alabama, to Tyler, Texas, black men often did the smoky and infernal work that white men did not want to do. They chopped the cotton and cut the tobacco. They dug the ditches and toted the bundles of tobacco from curing barns to market trucks.

During the Jim Crow era, black pitmasters were targets of Klan violence. Cash businesses, serving mostly black clienteles, black-owned barbecue joints were often self-sufficient. For racist whites, those independent businesses were social and economic threats. Dreamland Barbecue in the Jerusalem Heights neighborhood of Tuscaloosa, Alabama, was the object of a 1956 cross burning in which Klansmen torched the clapboard building where John Bishop had begun cooking earlier that same year.

When Bishop rebuilt, he laid his own bricks. Following the shift that many pitmasters made after moving from the country to the city, he switched from larger cuts like whole hogs to smaller cuts like ribs. Both modern adaptations were survival tacks. Bricks ensured that the restaurant couldn't be torched easily again. Ribs cooked faster, which meant less labor and a quicker turn on a dollar.

Like Bill Monroe, who popularized bluegrass music, Charlie Vergos, founder of the Rendezvous barbecue restaurant in Memphis, codified an American craft. When barbecue obsessives talked about dry ribs, they talked about the style that Vergos, grandson of a Greek immigrant, created when he first rubbed pork with a variation on a Greek seasoning mix, spiked with a Cajun spice mix that included cayenne. By 1955, he charcoal-grilled those ribs, which he basted with vinegar and sprinkled with what has come to be known as dry rub.

His crew cooked in a pit room built around a retrofitted coal chute. (In some family stories, that chute was an elevator shaft.) In later years, Vergos expanded what was a modest tavern into a subterranean barbecue palace, decorated with tchotchkes, neon beer signs, and signed celebrity glossies. As the city's reputation for barbecue grew, driven by publicity surrounding the annual World Championship Barbecue Cooking Contest, Memphis became a place of pilgrimage for barbecue fetishists and Rendezvous became a beachhead for their explorations.

Vergos said that his use of a vinegar baste for those ribs echoed the prevalence of lemon in the cooking of Greece. But he recognized that black Southerners deserved the credit for the dish. As rural blacks moved to cities, the barbecue they cooked changed. Just as Big Daddy Bishop of

Tuscaloosa discovered, ribs cooked far more quickly than whole hog and were easy to portion for sandwiches.

Barbecue was born of black cooks, Vergos said late in life. "They made it. And we took it and we made more money out of it than they did." In his restaurant, black men, wearing starched white shirts and tightly drawn black bow ties, made the experience, too. It was a formula from the Old South, repacked for the New South. But the rules had been altered. Unlike Booker Wright, black Rendezvous waiters earned broad respect.

An astute businessman, Vergos was good at leveraging relationships. Holiday Inn founder Kemmons Wilson was a Rendezvous fan who took visiting business associates there, beginning in the 1960s. When franchise owners arrived for training, Wilson fed them Rendezvous ribs, and they returned home with stories of the restaurant in the alley, staffed by wisecracking waiters, serving sausage and cheese appetizer plates, mugs of cold Michelob, and racks of spice-blanketed ribs. In 1985, Federal Express, founded in Memphis by Fred Smith, took those ribs national after Vergos bought a small advertisement in *The Wall Street Journal*, offering overnight shipment of ribs ordered via the toll-free number 1-800-Hogs-Fly. Like the Federal Express planes that convened nightly in Memphis, then jetted off for all points on the world map, Vergos's business took off. And so did the American love affair with Memphis ribs. By 1988, eight restaurants in town shipped overnight.

Twenty years later, Thomas Keller, the most decorated American chef of his generation, told his biographer that Federal Express had probably done more than any other business to change what Americans ate in fine dining restaurants. The effect on vernacular food proved strong, too, making the foods of the folk available to any and all. America no longer had to travel to eat. As Federal Express, along with Louisville-based United Parcel Service, made overnight deliveries, food traveled to America.

These companies reordered American ideas about value and exclusivity. Owing to Federal Express and Rendezvous, the most envy-inducing foods came from the Louisiana butcher shop that packed sausages in dry ice, the South Carolina diner that ladled she-crab soup into milk cartons, or the Tennessee barbecue pit, run by Greek descendants who benefited daily from accumulated black expertise and the entrepreneurial visions of native sons.

B y the time barbecue entered its early-twenty-first-century renaissance, the old ways had proved too time and labor intensive for some restaurants. At Harold's, near the Atlanta Federal Penitentiary, the Hembree family switched to flip-top electric pits. "We're cooking thirty hams a day," Billy Branyon, grandson of founder Harold Hembree, told me in a tone that sounded defiant. Downstate at Old Clinton Bar-B-Que, north of Macon, Georgia, the Coulter family ripped out the dogleg-shaped flue pit and installed a gas-fired and wood-fueled Southern Pride convection box manufactured in Illinois.

Many of the demigods had died off or retired. Maurice Bessinger, who had once led the National Association for the Advancement of White People, was in his dotage by the time barbecue got its due. L. J. Moore of New Bern, North Carolina, who bulldozed his business in 1967 instead of integrating his dining room, was dead. So was Ollie Mc-Clung, who had fought the integration of his Birmingham barbecue restaurant all the way to the U.S. Supreme Court. Old bigotries had been reduced to smolder.

If the popularity of barbecue as a cultural product and means of expression spiked in the 2000s, so did the profile of pitmasters. "I am Myron Mixon from Unadilla, Georgia, and I am the baddest barbecuing bastard there has ever been," declared the man with the foul mouth, smoldering cigars, and tendency to blast the AC-DC song "Back in Black" as a prelude to entering a room.

Mixon, who made his name on the barbecue competition circuit, emerged as a reality television star in 2009. He looked like a comic book supervillain for the heritage-not-hate set. Wreathed in a shawl of hickory smoke, he said things like, "What I do best is beat everybody else's ass." But Mixon was just one sinner among many at a moment when the vocation became vogue and television shows that depicted lives in the pits became Learning Channel standards.

Barbecue restaurant owners had once challenged their children to take alternate career paths. The work of a pitmaster was grimy, they said. It's thankless, they warned. Barbecue restaurants are joints where devotees go slumming, they chided. But a change came. Pitmasters climbed the same ladder-from-the-basement that chefs ascended a generation back. The men and women who stoked the fires, stuffed the sausages, flipped the hogs, and pitchforked the briskets became folk heroes. Laborers, who had earned their reputations amid the cinder swirl of pit houses, began to step into the light of day. Flashbulbs popped. Disciples flocked.

Barbecue emerged as a national folk food, worthy of excellence among practitioners and connoisseurship among consumers. Following the path blazed by Blue Smoke, white tablecloth chefs opened barbecue cafés where they explored and exploited authenticity. A new generation of restaurateurs reevaluated the labor and knowledge of pitmasters. At Smoke in Dallas, pecan wood–smoked pork sandwiches came with blue cheese slaw. At Hi-Lo in San Francisco, the definition of barbecue proved expansive enough to include a riff on pho, the Vietnamese soup, bobbed with hunks of smoked brisket.

To develop these new barbecue restaurants, chefs fanned across the South. Austin, from which a good eater could plot a two-day ten-joint pilgrimage through the Texas Hill Country, became a research center. So did the Triangle of North Carolina. From there, explorers traveled west to eat Piedmont shoulder trays in Lexington, and east to the onetime

tobacco market town of Wilson, where supplicants took seats at the feet
of Ed Mitchell.

I n the early years of the twenty-first century, Ed Mitchell of Wilson was
America's favorite pitmaster. In 2002, *The New York Times* profiled him
on the front page. The next year, he became a recurring headliner at the
Big Apple Barbecue Block Party. For outlanders in search of authentic
North Carolina barbecue, Mitchell was the go-to guy. When Zinger-
man's Roadhouse in Ann Arbor, Michigan, added hickory-roasted barbecue to their menu, they brought in Mitchell for a consult. When
Michael Pollan went south to research the science and technique behind
live fire cookery, he came looking for Mitchell.

Mitchell had earned college degrees in sociology and public administration and built a career with Ford before returning home. In Wilson,
where he cooked whole hogs for his mother to sell by the sandwich at
the family store, Mitchell honed a repertoire of techniques, learning to
bank his pits with charcoal and, in a twist on tradition, season his hickory wood with vinegar. Mitchell was new to the business, but he was not
new to barbecue, a traditional plantation feast on the state's eastern
fringe, cooked by blacks and eaten by both blacks and whites during fall
tobacco harvests. "I would stay up late with the old men when they
cooked," he said of his youth. "As the evening grew long, I took on more
of the responsibility, until sometime in the middle of the night, they usually fell out. It was my pig from then on."

Like most pitmasters of his generation, Mitchell cooked industrial-
grade hogs raised in confinement facilities. They were cheap to buy and
easy to source. But in 2003, he cooked a pastured pig, fed a diet of sweet
potato culls and peanut hulls by scientists at North Carolina A&T State
University in Greensboro, the historically black college whose students
had, just a generation earlier, driven the sit-in movement. Mitchell said

the pork tasted like what his grandfather ate, before North Carolina farmers went industrial. He was hooked.

To meet the coming demand for these idealized hogs, Mitchell recruited farmers who banned growth hormones and antibiotics and fed their Berkshires and Durocs local crops. The potential was great. "We look at this as our Gatorade," Danny Gatling, director of development for A&T, told me, referring to the financial boon that the University of Florida realized from the development of the first sports drink. In a state recently befouled by massive hog waste lagoon spills, small-scale farming with a relatively small environmental impact was a moral as well as environmental imperative. It mattered, too, that Mitchell was a black man, working with black farmers, cooking the way his black forebears had.

Mitchell planned a chain of Pitmaster Barbecue Markets, where he would smoke and sell pasture-raised hogs. He worked to convert his roadside restaurant to a teaching facility and customer service training academy. He presented investors with plans for a chain of Pitmaster Barbecue Restaurant and Lounges, much like the ones Louis Osteen had conceived, with pig-picking bars as focal points.

But Mitchell was too early to the market. The boom that he drove by force of personality wouldn't begin in earnest for another five years. By 2005, he was locked in battle with his bank over a loan foreclosure. Soon after, Mitchell pleaded guilty to tax evasion. Supporters argued that Mitchell, a black man enjoying success in a business that had long been controlled by whites, was the victim of age-old prejudices and selective prosecution. Other pitmasters showed more sustained success.

As Ed Mitchell fell, Rodney Scott rose. His family business, Scott's Bar-B-Q and Variety and Retail Services, perched at the corner of Cow Head Road and Hemingway Highway, beneath a flashing crossroad light on the outskirts of Hemingway, South Carolina, was a twenty-first-century vision of what an early-twentieth-century barbecue joint should look like. The main building was tin roofed. Dogs ranged the yard. Junked shopping carts, stacked with sweet potatoes, jammed the parking lot. On wooden church pews under the front eave, locals knee-balanced foam clamshells of pulled pork and crisped skins.

In the pit house, two concrete banks, burnished ebony by wood smoke and ash, smoldered. Deep in the bowels of those pits, oak and hickory embers hissed and flared. Rodney Scott's family approach to slow-smoking whole hogs over hardwood coals appeared vestigial. That was part of the appeal. Like the grits Glenn Roberts ground upstate, Scott's promised a taste of the past in the present. "They don't have to chase Granddaddy's flavor," Scott told me in 2009, as he worked a long-handled mop to drench a pig in vinegar and pepper sauce. "We got it for them."

It helped that Scott, who cooked his first pig when he was just eleven, was telegenic and knew how to keep the press spellbound. When he talked about sourcing wood, Scott used the same language that the food cognoscenti employed. The family traded labor and chain saw expertise for oak, hickory, and, occasionally, pecan. When a tree fell from a storm, Scott arrived with a chain saw in hand, a barbecue first responder. "I pick my own, right out of the woods," he said, sounding like the chefs then crowding into the barbecue market. By the time Sam Jones opened his barbecue restaurant in Greenville, Rodney Scott had begun planning his second location in Charleston.

Aaron Franklin came by his barbecue credentials honestly in Bryan, Texas, where his parents ran a barbecue stand. When he and his wife, Stacy, opened their first Austin spot in a converted travel trailer, Franklin took a different path to excellence. Owing to his previous work at a coffee shop, he stoked their sauce with espresso. Making the best of the materials they had on hand, Franklin, a skilled metalworker, cut a hole in the side of the trailer for the pit. Those 2009 developments screamed newfangled. But his commitment to tradition shone through when Franklin opened a brick-and-mortar location in East Austin, outfitted with barrel-shaped smokers that looked like supersized backyard pits.

By seven on Saturday mornings, clutches of acolytes stood on line at the new Franklin Barbecue, where he post-oak-smoked salt-and-pepper-rubbed briskets until the bark was coal-black and the core burst with jus. By eleven, when Aaron Franklin accepted his first orders, the line typically bulged to a couple hundred people, and a lawn chair rental service company arrived to rent perches. When Franklin handed over the first paper plate of the day, heaped with meat, beans, and slaw, throaty cheers rippled down the line and across the parking lot, the sort of outbursts more commonly associated with arrivals of potentates.

That same spring, Texas historian Joe Nick Patoski stood before a foodways conference crowd and declared that the old question—What happens when barbecue dies? What happens when the last pitmaster steps out of the smoke?—was no longer relevant. The contemporary barbecue question, he said, was "How much higher can you go? How much more can you elevate this?" Across the nation, old-guard and nouveau pitmasters answered that query. And many of the strongest answers came from Austin, where Miguel Vidal dished mesquite brisket on handmade tortillas at Valentina's Tex-Mex BBQ and Tom Micklethwait ran a trailer that won a citywide reputation for smoked lamb chorizo links.

In May of 2015, Patoski got a clear handle on the heights. Based on the strength of his work, and the beauty of those briskets, the James Beard Foundation named Aaron Franklin Best Chef Southwest. This was the first time a pitmaster had won a chef award in the twenty-year history of the organization. A cultural bookend to Robert Stehling's win for Best Chef South in 2008, the coronation signaled that barbecue, with its tangled and troubled racial history, was worthy of celebration. The moment telegraphed that pitmasters, long dismissed as mere muscle, were icons of American culture, worthy of deference.

I n the 2010s, barbecue became a modern business, distinguished by its connection to a deep past. When Nick Pihakis, a white man of Greek descent, founded the Birmingham-based Jim 'N Nick's Bar-B-Q restaurant chain in 1985, he hired Phillip Adrey, a Lebanese man who had once worked the pits at Ollie's Bar-B-Q, the infamous Birmingham restaurant that had fought desegregation all the way to the U.S. Supreme Court. Over three decades, the chain expanded to more than thirty locations, stretching across the South and as far west as Colorado. Along the way, Jim 'N Nick's embraced a sensibility that included beef brisket sandwiches, hot fried chicken, and pimento cheese–capped hamburgers. As Pihakis colonized Walmart parking lots and built restaurants in outparcels, he rolled out a no-freezer approach to fast-casual dining that set national standards for everyday quality.

As the industry matured, Pihakis emerged as a confidant and fixer, who advised second-generation pitmasters how to make the difficult leap to third-generation owner. He stepped in with bridge funding for operators who needed to refurbish after a pit fire or build a second restaurant. When Sam's Bar-B-Q in Humboldt, Tennessee, burned in 2013, Pihakis flew in a contractor from Denver to engineer the rebuild. After Cozy Corner in Memphis went up in flames in 2015, Pihakis arrived with a check and advice on how to deal with the insurance company. When the pit house at Scott's Bar-B-Q in Hemingway, South Carolina, burned in the fall of 2013, Pihakis rallied his friends in the Fatback Collective to help Rodney Scott rebuild.

The next wave of pitmasters emerged in the 2010s. Urban and educated, they were students of the history who spoke of their forebears in hushed tones and mapped sauce dispersals like cartographers. In the manner of the East Coast college students who helped reinvigorate the careers of bluesmen like Mississippi Fred McDowell during the folk revival of the 1960s, they traveled south to study with the masters. Instead of gathering at a juke to hear a guitar player hammer out "Shake 'Em On Down," they ducked into smoke-roiled pit houses to learn truths from Ed Mitchell and his elders.

When Arrogant Swine, a graffiti-tagged roadhouse on a potholed street often lined with dump trucks, opened on the industrial fringe of Bushwick in Brooklyn, New York, in 2014, Tyson Ho installed picnic tables in the blacktop parking lot behind a chain-link fence. Alongside a cook shed made from a shipping container, he set a burn barrel, based on one he saw behind the pit house at Jackie Hite's Bar-B-Q in Leesville, South Carolina. Inside, he hung state flags from both Carolinas and built a bar of pine planks charred black using the Japanese technique *shou sugi ban*.

Along with more traditional menu items like pork shoulder with Lexington-style dip and pork spareribs glazed with mustard sauce, he served chicken wings smoked over oak and glazed with a caramel sauce. "They are a thought experiment," Ho told me. "Hypothetically, it's three in the morn. What do those Degar people from the central highlands of Vietnam cook?" he asked, referring to the immigrant pitmasters he met on a visit to Stamey's in Greensboro, North Carolina.

Ho gave up a career in finance, doing high-yield debt research, for a life in the pits. Among thirty-somethings in the 2010s, that story sounded familiar. But his motivations didn't. "This is the oldest style of American cooking," he said, after we drank a tumbler of whiskey and gazed at his burn barrel. Ho, who resented being called an Asian American, staked his unhyphenated identity on barbecue. "Before America was even a country, some dude was already digging a hole and throwing on logs and a pig. Whether that person came over on the *Mayflower* or that person came over in chains, I share that history with them every time I light my fire."

B y 2015, more Americans were plumbing culinary history, taking first steps toward reconciling their past with their present. And they began their explorations with barbecue, the most primal American food. Many came looking for something ancient. Instead, barbecue revealed itself to be an ongoing process, not a product fixed in one time or place.

The landscape Americans explored was changed. Barbecue restaurants had once been thought bulwarks of tradition, where cooks preserved old techniques and old social patterns. By 2015, they were dynamic institutions that reflected new immigrants, new mores, and new finances. Across the region, pitmasters did right by their forebears, and consumers gained a better appreciation of the marriage of smoke, time, meat, and sauce. Beyond the region, America embraced barbecue as a national folk food and came to regard barbecue pitmasters as modern-day folk heroes.

Rodney Scott showcased the new relevancy of old ways. Sam Jones proved that barbecue was worthy of high dollar investment and entrepreneurial drive. And Tyson Ho made a case for the democratic principles embedded in that style of cooking. Listening to Ho talk about how to construct a proper burn barrel and how to define authenticity, I recognized that he would not be the last of his kind. And I noted that the culinary traditions codified and nurtured down South were in able hands up North.

Future Tenses

2010s Forward

Members of the Coalition of Immokalee Workers protested
outside a grocery store in Athens, Georgia.

Political Reckonings

These are definitely cotton field rabbits," Michael Twitty said as he sliced into a haunch on a spring day in 2015, freeing the thigh and leg from the skinned carcass. At his feet, a log fire burned. Before him stood a white-columned home, built by Hugh Craft, a Holly Springs, Mississippi, plantation owner who worked his fields with nine slaves. Across the way, four white anthropology students from the University of Mississippi in nearby Oxford troweled into the red clay at the base of an adjacent cookhouse, sifting for bones, shards of china, remainders of the day when black women cooked in that cabin for their families and white families, too. Inside the cookhouse, a sign propped on an easel documented the story of Callie Gray, who was eighty when she recalled, "Everything was cooked over the fireplace in them days. . . . On week days the niggers all ate at great long tables in the big kitchen, all three meals."

A black man with a bright spirit who has revived and interpreted African American foodways, Twitty was cooking a meal of rabbit, collard greens, and coal-roasted sweet potatoes as part of the Behind the Big House Tour, staged annually during the Holly Springs Home and Heritage Tour. A couple blocks away, Joseph McGill, founder of the Slave Dwelling Project, sweated through his wool Union-blue uniform, shading the sun from his face with a navy blue kepi cap, fielding questions from schoolchildren who wanted to talk about ghosts and battlefield mayhem. McGill steered the children toward imagining what life was like for the enslaved, telling them, "I wear my Civil War reenactor uniform to remind me of what the African American Union soldiers were fighting to get rid of."

Twitty stirred the fire with an iron poker, shifting the trivet back and forth so that the cast iron pot kept a constant temperature. He wheedled and harangued. He charmed and challenged. "My name is Mr. Twitty, and I come from Maryland and I cook like our ancestors cooked," he told a group of schoolchildren that was mostly black, but included two wide-eyed Mexican boys and three skinny white boys who kept inching too close to the fire and then fleeing the cinders that swirled in the morning breeze. "They knew how to make something from nothing and we need to know how to do that today." Twitty's choice of pronouns was purposeful. By speaking of *our* ancestors, he claimed the South for blacks past and present. And he claimed it for the Mexican kids who had more recently arrived in Mississippi.

Before that spring day was over, several hundred schoolchildren from the majority-black public middle school and a few from the private academy coursed through the outdoor history exhibit Twitty had jerry-rigged with the aid of the homeowner, Chelius H. Carter, a white architectural historian. When he wasn't fetching water for Twitty or sitting on an upturned flower pot and scrubbing clean a collection of rust-encrusted cast iron pans, Carter said things like, "The real prize here is that cabin. Houses like mine were the McMansions of the late nineteenth century, unsustainable in the post–Thirteenth Amendment economy." And "The idea that the enslaved narrative has not been included in the stories we tell about this place is a sort of cultural genocide."

These comments buoyed Twitty's spirits. As he toured the South over the two previous years on what he called a Southern Discomfort Tour, re-creating plantation feasts and teaching audiences about the roles that skilled black cooks played in the antebellum South, he had begun to hear from people like Carter who were genuinely curious about the ways that slavery and racism imprinted on Southern foodways. Black and white alike, they wondered what might be done to reckon with that legacy. Twitty played the role of father confessor, listening to their stories and setting a welcome table where reconciliation as well as rabbit was on the menu.

Later that summer, after Dylann Roof, who wrapped himself in the faded symbols of the Old South, gunned down nine black worshippers in a Charleston, South Carolina, church, America fitfully reacquainted itself with its Civil War past and with long unsettled discussions about why the war was fought and how it should best be remembered. In light of that horrific act, McGill and Twitty did not appear anachronistic. Instead, in the months to come, Americans regarded them as modern interlocutors, equipped to ask tough questions, game to connect past and present Souths.

Paula Deen had, in her way, made these conversations possible. A deposition taken in 2013 for a court case revealed that the Food Network star, born in Albany, Georgia, and deified in nearby Savannah, had used the word *nigger* in her kitchen. In the wake of that revelation, the woman who convinced America that a burger patty sandwiched between two glazed doughnuts was au courant, the cook who did for butter what Emeril had done for pork, fell from grace like an ill-mixed hushpuppy settling on the bottom of a fry kettle.

Headlines blared "CELEBRITY CHEF ADMITS TO RACIAL SLURS." And "PAULA DEEN'S GUILT-FREE ADMISSION OF USING N-WORD." Within a couple days, rancor drove reprisal. The Food Network cut her show. Smithfield, the biggest of the Big Pork conglomerates, terminated her endorsement deal. The problem was more than the slur. Many of the dishes that Deen celebrated and her fans lionized, from fried chicken to stewed okra to red rice, had been perfected and popularized by black cooks. If Deen used the word *nigger* in her kitchen, then she didn't respect the black cooks who worked there.

Forced to reckon with their relationship, Dora Charles, who had worked with Deen for more than twenty years and whom Deen once called her "soul sister," left The Lady and Sons, Deen's Savannah restaurant. As Deen backpedaled, Charles, who said that she had witnessed racism and had been underpaid and underappreciated, retreated to her double-wide trailer, where she wrote a cookbook that reclaimed the recipes her family had cooked for whites.

When that book was published in 2015, Charles, whose people had been sharecroppers and before that slaves, dismissed the mythology that drew many to Savannah in search of columned homes where fine linens draped tables and fried chicken came piled high on silver platters. "My great-grandmother was probably in the kitchen at some of those feasts, and she may have known a bit about how to prepare them," Charles explained, "but that old planter's table really is gone with the wind."

That nagging mythology was at the heart of the Deen problem: America believed it had flushed Deen and her ilk from the system. But an honest look at Southern food revealed new layers of complexity and old wounds that had yet to scab and heal. A week after Deen became a new symbol of old intolerance, Michael Twitty published an open letter to the television star.

"So it's been a tough week for you," he wrote, sounding world-weary. "I know something about tough weeks being a beginning food writer and lowly culinary historian." An autodidact who had read deeply on food history and was in the midst of tracing his family history from the days of enslavement back to Africa, Twitty didn't scold her. Instead, he pledged to teach Deen why so many people were so upset by her comments. His tone was conciliatory. Twitty asked the sort of questions

that John Egerton had long encouraged. He helped Southerners understand why Deen, whom many had written off as a caricature, mattered
to a national audience.

Deen had soared while exploiting stereotypes about Southern food
and manners. She plummeted as those cornpone myths came home to
roost on the Spanish moss–tangled verandas of Savannah. Deen was not
reconciled. She had not been redeemed. Deen embodied a troubled
South, a place where bigotry still thrived and racism rutted among the
magnolias. She confirmed the long-held suspicions of food world watchers and writers.

When we sat down for dinner at Lusco's in 2014 to talk about Booker
Wright and his legacy, television personality Anthony Bourdain told me
with a sneer that his pompano "tasted like racism." That same taint
clung to Deen. As she flailed, America recognized that it had never really
trusted the South or its people. That ill will propelled Deen's fall.

Twitty offered an alternate view. The problem, he said, was not
Deen. Instead, the Deen affair revealed patterns of exclusion in which
privileged whites spoke, often recklessly, for the region while people of
color were muzzled or muted. "I am probably more angry about the
cloud of smoke this fiasco has created for other issues surrounding race
and Southern food," he wrote. At a time when the South appeared to be
in renaissance, when fried chicken cooks and barbecue pitmasters garnered more press and respect than ever before, Twitty argued that black
people did not get their due, saying, "We are surrounded by culinary injustice where some Southerners take credit for things that enslaved Africans and their descendants played key roles in innovating." Barbecue, he
argued, might go the way of the banjo, an African instrument that most
people now associate with bluegrass music plucked by whites: "That
tragedy, rooted in the unwillingness to give African American barbecue
masters and other cooks an equal chance at the platform, is far more
galling than you saying 'nigger,' in childhood ignorance or emotional
rage or social whimsy."

Twitty's message spread quickly. With each tweet, with each Facebook "like," as each e-mail forward reached an in-box, momentum built. Academics, who had previously steered clear, assisted with plantation cookhouse reenactments. White chefs volunteered to peel his sweet potatoes. Speaking offers poured in from organizations like MAD, the Denmark-based congress of chefs. Michael Twitty became a media darling, a spokesperson for the American culinary id. His empathetic response won the day. And it won him an audience, attuned to honest stories about Southern food and eager to learn of the lives and labor on which that cultural capital had been built.

The Deen affair offered a new way to apprehend old problems that still festered in the modern South, troubling its people, defining its future. At their core, those problems were historical. And they were rooted on farms as much as they were in kitchens. The want for cheap field labor drove the eighteenth- and nineteenth-century spread of slavery from the rice fields of the Lowcountry to the cane fields of Louisiana and beyond. If small-scale agriculture was an American ideal, large-scale agriculture, which is to say plantation agriculture, was an original sin of the American South.

To fuel that growth, black men and women had labored without pay and under duress. Ever since the enslaved won freedom, the South has begun fumbling awkwardly toward a new labor system. During the 1950s and 1960s, many of its laborers went hungry. In the Deep South, plantations mechanized and white owners deemed fieldworkers expendable. Along the northern rim, the demise of industrial jobs and the rise of consumer culture drove an undereducated workforce deeper into poverty. At its core the key civil rights movement goal was the freedom to earn a living and feed a family, not just stuff a ballot box or claim a lunch counter seat.

By the 2010s, a new generation of laborers, a new underclass, chafed under intolerable working conditions in chicken houses and hog barns and on killing floors. They were new immigrants, from just across the border in Mexico and down the peninsula in Central America. These laborers were not chattel like the men and women who drove the Southern labor force throughout much of the nineteenth century. But they were just as vulnerable, and their children were often just as ill fed. If the Southern culinary renaissance was going to prove a true rebirth for the region, the region would have to reckon with their stories.

D uring the last quarter of the twentieth century, food got better for those who paid a premium. Advocates for animal welfare won some battles. Sensualists won others. Sunshine-yellow-yolked eggs, harvested from hens that pecked feed and weeds in a barnyard, came on the market. Grocers stocked natural beef from cows that were not injected with growth hormones. Heirloom pork, harvested from pigs that grazed on pastures, sold well at farmers' markets and in the stores of upscale grocers like Austin, Texas–based Whole Foods. While marketers used the term *heirloom* to describe these animals, many Southerners recognized them as nothing more and nothing less than the livestock their grandparents raised.

A new generation of Americans, attuned to the negative impacts of industrial farming on the environment and people, demanded these new choices. Even as this demonstrably better food came on the market, comparatively little progress was made on the human resource side. Animals got treated somewhat better. But the humans who raised them in virtual gulags and disassembled them on agricultural factory floors saw little in the way of labor relief or wage increases.

The thorniest problems in American agriculture remained mostly unaddressed. And they came into starkest relief in western Arkansas, where the chicken industry vertically integrated operations; in central Florida where, as late as 2010, virtual slave labor helped harvest winter tomatoes; and in eastern North Carolina, where Big Pork adopted the strategies that Big Chicken perfected in Arkansas. Born of the South, these tactics robbed agricultural workers of health and welfare. The net effect, Wendell Berry of Kentucky said, was "ecological vandalism."

The industrialization of chicken production began in the 1920s on the Delmarva Peninsula, south of Dover, Delaware, when farm woman Cecile Steele ordered brooder chicks for a yard flock but received ten times the chicks she needed. The story, like the scene, was sweet and simple. Instead of returning the excess, Steele built a small version of what America came to call a chicken house, fed the birds out to slaughter weight, and sold them for the contemporary equivalent of five dollars a pound. Two generations later, inspired by that windfall, truck farming of tomatoes and other crops had dwindled, and white frame chicken houses mushroomed on the landscape, first near the Atlantic shore, later across the hill country of Georgia and in the almost mountains of Arkansas.

Chicken farming blossomed where large plantation spreads were uncommon. In northwestern Arkansas, the move from birds raised to supplement family income and slaughtered to yield whole chickens reached its greatest efficiency. Chicken barns metastasized to accommodate tens of hundreds and then tens of thousands of birds. And men and women worked fast-paced disassembly lines, breaking down chickens into easily packaged legs and backs and thighs.

When Steele first raised birds, it took around four months to reach a slaughter weight of a little over two pounds. By the 1990s, growers produced chickens of twice the weight in half the time. Through genetic selection and new feeds, growers reinvented chickens. They were no longer gangly birds, haloed with feathers. They were livestock machines with oversized breasts, quick to convert feed to flesh, ideal for portioning into enhanced chicken products.

In the 1970s, the average American ate almost forty pounds of chicken annually. By 2015, Americans ate about twice as much. To meet the demand they created, the American broiler industry consolidated to gain efficiencies. Pilgrim's, Tyson, Sanderson Farms, and Perdue controlled the national chicken market in the 2010s. And three of those companies headquartered in the South.

During the decades before World War II, the South had made the national reputation for cast iron–fried chicken. Southerners rewrote that narrative during the 1970s rise of fast food. In the Tyson era, Southern entrepreneurs transformed chicken once again. This was not the skillet-fried chicken of Southern lore. These were not bone-in drumsticks and thighs, coated in batter and cooked in deep oil, either. These were tenders, cut into strips from oversized breasts. These were patties, pieced together from skin and back meat.

To supply McDonald's and other accounts, Tyson, based in northwest Arkansas, did more than reinvent the forms in which Americans consumed chicken. Tyson engineered systems that controlled the production of chicken "from semen to cellophane." Previous generations had purchased chicken by the bird. Tyson sold this new fried chicken by the part, and, increasingly, by forms that did not exist in nature. These were postmodern, postanatomical croquettes. Made from minced and slurried meat, mixed with stabilizers, salted, and breaded, McNuggets, which McDonald's commissioned from Tyson in 1979, drove the growth of the chicken industry.

Twenty years after it began, the industrialization of fried chicken was complete. Americans had off-loaded every step in the process. Even the frying took place in a plant, followed quickly by a conveyor belt run through a blast freezer. As the labor shifted from barnyards to chicken barns, and from home kitchens to factories, fried chicken exacted a greater human price.

Work on the disassembly lines, where workers gutted and carved birds into parts, led to repetitive motion ailments. As the pace of labor increased, new immigrants, who often lacked the language skills to complain about conditions, replaced native black and white laborers who could afford to find other work. The cycle was brutal. Americans destroyed their bodies by eating unhealthy foods, processed and manipulated beyond recognition. Immigrants, who ran the machines that processed the birds, destroyed their bodies, too, working machines that cut them into pieces just as they cut chickens into parts.

Promised returns that would lift them from paycheck-to-paycheck cycles, diversified farmers converted to raise chicken as a mono crop. Many chafed under the labor contracts that Tyson and its competition required. Provided a furnish of chicks and feed, farmers often failed to earn a profit at settlement. Just a generation after Southerners had fled sharecropping cotton, their grandsons and granddaughters began sharecropping chickens and pigs. Under contract arrangements, which transferred the risk to the farmers, they became serfs who served at the pleasure of corporate lords.

Beginning in the mid-1980s, Big Pig also leveraged the perceived healthiness of chicken, when it began marketing leaner hybrid varieties of pork as the "other white meat." Like chickens, farmers prized pigs for their efficient conversion of feed to flesh. Pigs became mammalian versions of chickens, data points in an industrial agriculture exposition. Female pigs became machines, receiving feed inputs and dropping litter outputs. Eighty percent of the industrial sows in the United States spent their entire adult life in metal cages.

When I visited pitmaster Ed Mitchell back in 2003, we took a tour of a confinement facility out on the North Carolina coastal plain, jammed with writhing pink pigs. Compared to five-thousand-head factory farm gulags, it was a small-time operation. He still exited with tears in his eyes, though it was unclear whether Mitchell cried from the high stench of hog urine or the realization that, by dint of his chosen career, he bore a burden of change.

Mitchell didn't tour a disassembly line that day. If he had, the pitmaster might have seen a largely Hispanic workforce, confined in a way that was comparable to the pigs. In this new livestock operation, the pigs couldn't move in their crates. And the humans who disassembled them after they died often couldn't freely leave the line to go to the bathroom. Bound by codes of silence and gag rules, with limited to little chance of landing jobs outside the system, the workers suffered alongside the pigs.

Coupled with the reports from Florida that described tomato picking operations as slave camps, these stories reminded Americans that our food system was broken. And, as had been the case in the 1950s and 1960s, when civil rights and voting rights were at stake, America confronted its worst self in the South. In response, Southerners developed and drove solutions to some of these problems. Though the problems of industrial livestock farmers appeared intractable, one of the best answers to the plight of farmworkers rose out of the Florida tomato fields in the early twenty-first century.

The men and women moved swiftly through the fields around Immokalee, Florida, on a winter day, picking green globes that blushed pink in the noonday sun, their gloves stained by a sticky black goo known as tomato tar. With loaded buckets, Mexican and Central American immigrants, their mouths shielded from pesticides with bandannas, sprinted toward the hopper, carrying buckets of tomatoes above their heads, jackknifing them up and over and into the truck. The workers were brown, the foremen white, the sun unrelenting. Living and working conditions for seasonal pickers on industrial-scale farms were often squalid. Pay based on pounds picked did not account for true hours worked. Rape among the furrows and in the back of supervisor pickup trucks was common. These scenes recalled the images captured by Edward R. Murrow for the 1960 documentary *Harvest of Shame*. The true shame was that the year was 2010.

Senate hearings, convened to air grievances and set paths forward, included testimony that compared the plight of farmworkers to that of slaves. As late at 2008, U.S. Attorney Douglas Molloy of Fort Myers called the tomato fields of south-central Florida "ground zero for modern-day slavery." When Americans ate winter tomatoes, purchased at large grocers or from fast-food chains, they ate fruit picked by slaves. That was not an assumption, Molloy told journalist Barry Estabrook. It was a reality of American life. In the early 2000s, federal officials prosecuted twelve cases of forced or trafficked labor in Florida fields.

The Coalition of Immokalee Workers (CIW), a worker-led human rights organization, didn't set up a parallel system, in which consumers paid more for tomatoes raised under better conditions, and workers got paid honestly for that work. That was the common tack at farmers' markets that sold to middle-class consumers. It served the consumers who were willing to pay premiums. To a lesser degree, it also served the workers. Instead, the CIW agitated to change the whole system through what it called a Campaign for Fair Food.

The goal appeared minor: Get retailers to pay one penny more per pound for tomatoes. But for a worker in a Florida tomato field, who picked a ton of tomatoes each day, that translated as a boost from $50 a day to $70. The idea was to leverage the buying power of the largest food retailers and restaurant chains to improve the lives of the farmworkers who pick Florida's $600 million annual fresh tomato crop. The CIW translated radical ideas into practical plans. Fifty years after Murrow first introduced America to the men and women who worked the Florida fields, the CIW offered a way forward.

As grocers and food chains grew into larger and larger companies, they wielded unprecedented purchasing power. To satisfy shareholders, the CIW recognized that these corporations pushed suppliers to deliver goods at lower costs. Farmworkers, the weakest links in the supply chain, absorbed that downward pressure. "In other words, your local grocery store makes farmworkers poor," Greg Asbed, cofounder of the CIW, said. He argued that food industry giants were culpable because they benefited from "pricing policies that drive farmworker poverty and exploitation."

A Taco Bell boycott came first. CIW-led marches followed. In 2004, hundreds of college students banded together to "Boot the Bell" from campuses. Many went on hunger strikes. More than twenty colleges kicked Taco Bell off campus, laying the groundwork for a 2005 decision by Yum! Brands, the Louisville, Kentucky–based parent of Taco Bell (and KFC) to adopt CIW's penny-a-pound protocols. Two years later, McDonald's followed. In 2008, after a headline-grabbing battle that included charges of spying by Burger King, the Florida-based fast-food giant assented, too.

The one-cent increase for the workers meant that, for every thirty-two-pound bucket picked, the men and women who harvested tomatoes bound for Burger King earned seventy-seven cents, up from forty-five cents. The CIW estimated that yearly wages for workers went from a miserly $10,000 to around $17,000.

In 2014, Walmart signed on with the CIW. A solution proposed by a Southern organization, designed to fix an American labor problem, received the ultimate validation from the world's largest retailer, a Southern company. By 2015, largely through the efforts of the CIW, slavery was again a historical reference point, not a current reality, and 90 percent of Florida tomatoes were harvested under equitable terms.

By the middle years of the 2010s, conversations over identity and responsibility began to shift again to public spaces. As Southern-inspired restaurants opened across the nation, a regional phenomenon went national. Some restaurants, like Big Jones in Chicago, went the traditionalist route, serving Virginia fried chicken, inspired by an Edna Lewis recipe, and Louisiana boudin rouge, enriched with pig blood and speckled with fatback. Others became showcases for redemption narratives. By 2015, there was no better showcase for redemption than The

Grey, a Savannah restaurant set in a once segregated bus station, just a seven-minute walk from Paula Deen's flagship restaurant. When admirers tried to make too much of her story, Mashama Bailey rejected civil rights movement comparisons.

Bailey said she was a chef running a restaurant, not an activist storming the barricades. But the comparisons came easy. The business she opened in late 2014 with business partner John O. Morisano boasted a lunch counter, built in 1938, at its center. For much of the time that lunch counter served Greyhound patrons, Bailey would not have been welcome to a seat.

Mashama Bailey is black. That's not the most important thing to know about her. An accomplished chef, she made her reputation at the New York City restaurant Prune, where Gabrielle Hamilton honed an idiosyncratic style that inspired a generation of female chefs. Recruited by Morisano to open The Grey, Bailey was not a stranger to the state. One of her grandmothers was born in Forsyth, just south of Atlanta. And Bailey herself had spent summers in Savannah.

When she accepted a partnership offer from Morisano, Bailey recognized the resonance in the narrative and the power in commanding a space where her grandmother would not have been able to eat a simple club sandwich. Their customers recognized the everyday justice communicated by a renovation in which the white powder room became a lounge, the colored waiting rooms became server stations, and the U-shaped lunch counter became an honestly democratic place, where all gathered to slurp trays of Harris Neck oysters, harvested from local waters, and spoon bowls of Sapelo Island clams, served atop dumpling clouds.

Before John Berendt memorialized the city's eccentricities in *Midnight in the Garden of Good and Evil*; before Lady Chablis, the drag queen at the heart of that story, wrote her own book, *Hiding My Candy*, Savannah was already a mythical Southern city. And food was already central to the storytelling.

Boardinghouse dining was an early draw. In the middle years of the twentieth century, Sema Wilkes took over a railroad boardinghouse near Pulaski Square. After eating in the basement dining room, travelers returned home with stories of a groaning board of snap beans, zipper peas, and collard greens, fresh from local gardens, red rice stoked with stewed tomatoes, and country fried steak pounded tender with a Coca-Cola bottle. At her tables, tourists reached for towel-wrapped baskets of buttermilk biscuits and formed impressions of Savannah as a place where black women cooks served at the pleasure of white matrons.

By the time Bailey settled into Savannah, a second wave of tourists, drawn by Paula Deen's cornpone television persona, had rethought the city as an oversized Cracker Barrel store, serving casseroles bound by cans of cream of mushroom soup. The Grey, with its ash-roasted sweet potatoes and roasted chicken with country captain, was a needed correction, a welcoming dinner companion to the midday lunches at Mrs. Wilkes's, where the renovated lunch counter served as a communal table for a renovated South.

As Southern culture and cuisine gentrified over the previous generation, white chefs became the primary interpreters of Southern cooking. There were exceptions like Darryl Evans, who rose to fame in Atlanta in the 1980s. And a new generation of immigrant cooks would, by the 2010s, change the idea of what it meant to be a person of color in a Southern kitchen. But those exceptions proved a rule. And the rule was that, even though the South's reputation for great cookery was built on the backs of black cooks, black chefs didn't lead most kitchens in the South.

To do her good work in the kitchen, Bailey drew on the resources of SAAFON, the Southeastern African American Farmers Organic Network. In that pairing, Bailey rethought the economic system that supported the restaurant, from the farms where eggplants grew to the waters where oystermen worked the pluff. SAAFON, which claimed Joseph Fields of Johns Island, South Carolina, as a member, helped black farmers capture some of the revenue stream from the rapidly expanding organic market. The organization was in it for the long game. And that game was helping black farmers earn enough money to prosper and retain their land.

In The Grey, those farmers found an exhibitor comparable to Husk in Charleston, a place where the possibilities of black agriculture and the excellence of black cooking could win a national audience. Bailey and Morisano saw the prospects clearly. When servers approached tables, they invited diners to explore the "Jim Crow–era building." They talked about the spicy roasted eggplant as "West African inspired." And they talked about Savannah as a "port city that draws many people, from many places." In the cooking and the telling, The Grey emerged as a restaurant fulcrum of a newer South, long on the horizon, now seemingly in reach.

S ixty years after Georgia Gilmore's kitchen became an activist clubhouse, the South was a human rights battleground again. As Michael Twitty corresponded with Paula Deen about the legacies of slavery and racism, America eavesdropped on a conversation that seemed Southern but revealed American fault lines. Issues of attribution and ownership, along with matters of cultural debts and legacies, captured the attentions of the food-obsessed who shopped for heirloom pork at farmers' markets.

Old questions about agriculture and its victims gained new traction in the hog barns of North Carolina and the chicken houses of Arkansas. Faced with stories of modern-day slave labor, the Coalition of Immokalee Workers set national standards for agricultural labor. In less than twenty years, the tomato fields of Florida went from being the most abusive places for American farmworkers to earn a living to one of the most progressive places to walk a furrow. The pace of change recalled Mississippi after the civil rights movement, when the state went from less than 7 percent registered black voters in 1961 to the highest number of black elected officials in any state by 1987.

As restaurants became central to social life, chefs emerged as interpreters of culture and dining rooms became backdrops for new Southern pageants. A generation before, neo-Confederates had set fabulist Old South scenes in Atlanta restaurants. By the 2010s, Mashama Bailey, a black chef, claimed downstate Savannah as her own. Her work, which reclaimed segregated spaces for integrated dining, was purposeful and resonant. The only thing it lacked was the taint of racism that Anthony Bourdain tasted while traveling the Mississippi Delta.

Houston rapper Chingo Bling argued, through songs about food and labor, that Mexican immigrants were here to stay.

Nuevo Sud

Laureled with collard leaves, okra spears, and corn ears, posters distributed around Louisville, Kentucky, in the spring of 2015 promised a "Live Cooking Show About Southern Identities" at Actors Theatre. When Charleston writers and television personalities Matt Lee and Ted Lee stepped to the stage on the night of June 19, chef Edward Lee of 610 Magnolia joined them. A New York City native of Korean ancestry who arrived in Louisville for Derby Week in 2002, he served as the local host. Born in New York City, the Lee brothers, who moved to Charleston, South Carolina, when they were boys, were white, like much of the audience. Each manned a stove outfitted with cast iron skillets and pots. Fronting Ted Lee's station was a stack of spiral-bound community cookbooks that included *Charleston Receipts* from South Carolina and *The New Fairyland Cooking Magic* from Lookout Mountain, Georgia.

Waiters coursed through the crowd, passing bourbon cocktails and fried pork rinds topped with pimento cheese. As the audience settled in, boiled peanut vapors wafted from an oversized kettle, stationed at the center of the room. Southerners traditionally boil peanuts with salt and not much else. The Lee collective served three different styles: a star anise translation from Vietnam, a pink peppercorn version inspired by Brazil, and chamomile peanuts flavored with that native American plant. When the lights came up, Ted Lee did a dramatic reading of a shrimp and deviled egg casserole recipe from the *Fairyland* book. And Matt Lee pointed out that, although they are cooked in many places, peanuts are native to current-day Bolivia. On cue, Edward Lee demonstrated a succotash dish of Native American origins and declared that Southern food was "the original fusion cuisine."

The men shared a belief in the region, a love of Nancy Newsom's Kentucky country hams, and a preference for Matt Jamie's Louisville-made soy sauce, aged in bourbon barrels. But none could claim a Southern grandmother. None told stories of ancestors whom Craig Claiborne or Bill Neal or Edna Lewis would have recognized as neighbors. Like many Southerners in the 2010s, the Lees were relatively new arrivals, actively engaged in the reinvention of the region, the expansion of ideas about their home, and the accommodation of new peoples.

At a time when public storytelling gigs *This American Life* and *The Moth* were vogue, the Lees bet that a performance focused on Southern identities would draw a crowd. The South was changing rapidly, and they believed the kitchen was the place to apprehend the revolution. They understood that cooking and eating and sharing food was a passkey to a newer South. Parochial Southerners of earlier generations, focused on black and white and North and South binaries, had referred to men like them as carpetbaggers, who arrived from elsewhere to profit from the region. By 2015, when the Lees stood to speak for the South, three hundred people paid $45 each to hear what they had to say about the place they called home.

What this newfangled kitchen family attempted didn't sound bold when compared with Henry Grady on the hustings in 1886 in New York City or John Egerton talking fried chicken and the welcome table ideal in Birmingham on the fiftieth anniversary of the 16th Street Baptist

Church bombing. In a region where the South Asian population sky-rocketed by nearly 70 percent between 2000 and 2010, the inclusion of Edward Lee in this band of brothers was eventual.

Claims to a Southern identity came easy for Edward Lee. Grits reminded him of congee. Chowchow recalled kimchi from his grandmother's kitchen. When he moved to Kentucky, buttermilk became his miso. Bourbon, aged in charred oak, reminded him of kalbi, grilled over hardwood. By 2015, when he opened a new restaurant in Maryland, the menu at Succotash included collards tossed with kimchi and fried oyster po-boys speckled with trout roe. "Something is simmering wildly throughout the American South," Edward Lee explained. "Every time I look around I see bold new expressions of Southern cuisine waving a proud flag. And this expression of food has captured people's attention, because it is the story not only of Southern cuisine, but also of America's identity."

As the Magnolia Curtain fell and the federal government loosened immigrant quotas for Asians, new peoples made their homes in the South, drawn by jobs in construction and agriculture. In 1970 the region contained the smallest proportion of foreign-born population in the nation. After 1990, the South welcomed more foreign immigrants than any other region of the country, a development that drove backlash nativist legislation in Alabama and Georgia, and, more positively, small-town bodegas and tortillerias in Tennessee and North Carolina and just about everywhere else.

Demographics told the story by 2015. From Arkansas, arcing down into the plantation belt of Mississippi and sweeping upward into the Carolinas, minority populations spiked. Arkansas, Georgia, North Carolina, and Tennessee led the nation in births to Hispanic mothers. Once a broad swath of farmland dotted by cities, the South became a cluster of urban hubs. Dallas, Austin, Houston, Atlanta, Charlotte, Orlando, and

Tampa were new magnets for migrations. (After two waves of out-migration that began in the 1910s, blacks had returned to the South. In the previous decade, Atlanta attracted nearly half a million new black residents.)

Foreign investment, drawn by low land costs, cheap energy, right-to-work labor laws, and tax abatements and incentives, yielded manufacturing jobs at Japanese, Korean, and German automobile assembly plants. Toyota opened a Georgetown, Kentucky, plant in 1988. In succeeding decades, BMW built an assembly plant near Greenville, South Carolina, and made its North American headquarters there. Alabama landed the Korean firm Hyundai and the German luxury standard-bearer Mercedes.

Foreign peoples transformed cities in the orbit of those plants. Overnight-flight sushi could be had in upstate South Carolina. So could okra yakitori, grilled over binchotan charcoal. In the eastern suburbs of Montgomery, Alabama, along roadways lined with car lots and Chick-fil-As, Koreans ran bowling alleys and barbecue restaurants and built Presbyterian churches. Billboards for downstate casinos advertised the "Ultimate Asian Gaming Experience" to Vietnamese slots players. And a French-inspired Korean bakery employed chefs who wore fluted white toques and turned out delicate quiches and fruit-gorged puff pastries. Instead of rolling biscuits and stuffing them with sausage, they baked croissants stuffed with hot dogs and morning buns filled with white sweet potato paste.

These new immigrants arrived to find a region that, viewed through the lens of food, appeared more historically diverse than suspected. Chinese immigrants had first arrived in Louisiana after the Civil War. Recruited to work sugarcane plantations, many washed clothes and cooked meals instead. By 1892, three Chinese restaurants operated in New Orleans. Musicians, prostitutes, and Chinese restaurateurs worked side by side in 1920s Chinatown and Storyville. Fusion came naturally. Chinese-owned restaurants served fried pork chops and cheap noodle bowls. "I used to hear the Negroes bragging about their Lead Beans and Lice!" said Louis Armstrong, who grew up in a neighborhood that abutted Chinatown, and who signed his letters "Red Beans and Ricely Yours, Louis." Leah Chase, the New Orleans chef, once told me that migrants from China to New Orleans shared a common palate with Creoles of Color. "We both like sweet and hot dishes. And we both eat rice with just about every meal."

Upriver, Mexican migrants arrived in the Mississippi Delta by the late years of the nineteenth century. Recruited to work bumper cotton harvests, they stayed to peddle husk-wrapped cylinders of pork and corn from pushcarts. What began as field meals for Mexican American laborers became street merchandise for African American vendors who sold tamales, often simmered in lard buckets over canned heat fires, to river town customers. "We were eating them before I ever recall seeing a Mexican," novelist and historian Shelby Foote, a native of the Delta town of Greenville, told me. "We were eating them all through the 1920s. In fact, I was eating hot tamales long before I had ever heard of a hushpuppy."

Ya ka mein, a dish of convoluted Asian origins, proved popular in Southern port cities by the early years of the twentieth century. Baltimore corner stores sold cups of yat gaw mein bobbing with hunks of pigs' feet. Chinese takeaways in the Tidewater cities of Hampton, Norfolk, and Newport News, Virginia, appended menus of cabbage-threaded egg rolls and pork fried rice with a dish called yock-a-mein. Tidewater cooks served yock at house parties, spooning the broth into white cardboard pails. Black churches sold boxes of chicken or pork yock, embossed with red pagodas and Chinese characters, to fund Christmas presents for children, gift baskets for elderly parishioners, and beauty packs for nursing home–bound women. In composition, taste, texture, and narrative, these dishes were Asian American, African American, and yes, Southern.

Arab immigrants to Jacksonville, Florida, opened groceries in mostly African American neighborhoods, where they sold sandwiches of lunch meat, stuffed into homemade pita bread, smeared with Italian salad dressing. As the sandwiches grew popular in the 1960s, so did the colloquial name, camel rider. Initially a pejorative, the term gained currency with Arabic makers and black and white consumers. Served with a side of tabbouleh and a cherry limeade, riders became the iconic Jacksonville lunch. At the Sheik, a local chain, sandwiches of scrambled eggs and patty sausage, tucked in pita and served with cups of grits, became drive-through breakfast standards.

Doused with hot sauce, eaten at a counter or in a car, these polyglot dishes showcased how port cities, coursing with peoples from all lands and latitudes, have informed the Southern experiment. By the early years of the twenty-first century, as new waves of immigrants made their homes in the South, these creolized dishes became such a part of the fabric that their underlying ethnicity was obscured. They were, as a well-meaning friend said to me, Southern dishes with funny names.

A new kind of hybridized South emerged in the twenty-first century. Chinese groceries in Jackson, Mississippi, stocked Louisiana-grown rice, marketed to Asian shoppers under the Jazzmen label, an elision of the term *jasmine rice*. Plastered with images of Louis Armstrong, the bags depicted the jazz great smiling broadly and blowing his horn. At strip mall charcuterie shops in Houston, Vietnamese artisans perfumed lunch meats with fish sauce and steamed bologna rolls in banana leaves. In Atlanta, Viet Cajun restaurants boiled crawfish in lemongrass broth and pressed sugarcane juice to order through wall-mounted rollers.

Truck stops on lonely Alabama interstate stretches marketed pork rinds as chicharones. Hunched in plyboard booths, drivers poured Louisiana-made Tabasco sauce into plastic bags of salted skins. At Kountry Xpress, a Punjabi-owned truck stop and gas station on I-40 near Fort Smith, Arkansas, Sudesh Sharma sold pizza sticks and samosas, which clerks handed over the counter in the same white Homestyle Fried Chicken bags they used to package legs and thighs. A sign by the register advertised minnow, cricket, and crawfish baits, packaged by a company named Worminators. The café at the rear advertised a driver's thali of a foam clamshell heaped with tandoori chicken, dal, naan, and tamarind chutney.

In 2014, Biscuitville, the North Carolina fast-food chain, announced that Alfonsa Martinez, a woman of Hispanic descent, had won their annual company bake-off. The knowledge as well as the food translated. Devotion to Bojangles' drive-through biscuits was so strong among Mexican construction workers in that state that customers on both sides of the language divide referred to the chain restaurants as Bo-jan-geles, converting the *j* to an *h* sound in imitation of typical Spanish pronunciation.

White tablecloth chefs also borrowed talent and ideas from immigrants. An early menu for Minero, which Sean Brock opened in Charleston, South Carolina, in 2014, included benne salsa and Carolina Gold rice tamales with the texture of congee. When Aarón Sánchez joined John Besh to open Johnny Sanchez in New Orleans in 2014, they served masa-fried Louisiana oysters with mirliton slaw. At Snackbar, an Oxford brasserie a mile from my house, Vishwesh Bhatt, a native of Gujarat, India, made okra chaat into a local standby. Tossed with fried pods and roasted peanuts, mixed with tomato, shallots, and cilantro, the dish came dusted with masala spices.

Southern food has never been static. Like all expressions of culture, from music to literature, foodways have been fluid reflections of time and place. Marriages of old ideas and new ethnicity defined a new creolized cuisine. By the 2010s, second-generation blendings of cultures proved essential in the making of the newest New South, in which expertise in tortilla making mattered as much as biscuit baking, and Indian chefs set the standard for fried okra.

A s the South urbanized, these creolizations intensified. Between 1990 and 2000, six of the nation's ten fastest-growing metropolitan areas were in the South. Atlanta drew many of those new immigrants. Buford Highway, the multicultural corridor that spiraled north from the strip mall suburbs to the mega-mall exurbs, was a magnet. A five-lane gauntlet of nail salons, foot massage parlors, dim sum houses, squat apartment complexes, and drive-through taquerias, that stretch of roadway, like much of the suburban South, was once populated by whites escaping blacks.

Suburbs, which strip malls served as longitudinal town squares, had been exclusive spaces where middle-class folk distanced themselves from the poor, where they codified sameness and deified ranch homes with attached garages. In the latter years of the twentieth century, as urban life became popular again, and as outer-ring country club suburbs with golf course amenities developed, that first ring of 1960s suburbs atrophied. Malls closed. So did fast-food restaurants and photo developer drive-throughs in parking lot outparcels.

Colonized by new immigrants, salad bowl suburbs emerged as modern Pangaeas where Korea abutted Pakistan, and Mexico and Bosnia were neighbors. In the suburbs of Charlotte and Jacksonville, in the exurbs of Atlanta and Richmond, on the fringes of Houston and Little Rock, immigrant businesspeople redeveloped those strip malls. During the late twentieth and early twenty-first centuries, they refashioned white flight spaces into models of entrepreneurial dynamism.

When the Long John Silver location on South Boulevard in Charlotte closed, the Choi family opened China Wing, a Korean restaurant. Beneath that same blue roof, they served Chinese American egg foo yong and Korean American burgers capped with kimchi. When the Pizza Hut

on Buford Highway in Atlanta shuttered, Cho Sun Ok, a Korean barbecue restaurant, replaced it. Charcoal braziers replaced pizza ovens. And
soju replaced Mountain Dew as the drink of choice. In Houston, Guate-
malans worked Hong Kong–style dim sum kitchens, and Cambodian
immigrants bought up the mom-and-pop doughnut shops. After survey-
ing their competition, they reinvented menus to include Czech-inspired
kolaches stuffed with Cajun-style boudin.

*A*s money and people poured into Houston in the 2010s, that Gulf
Coast megalopolis proved the most baroque and instructive example of what the South was rapidly becoming. An octopus of second-story
toll roads, twelve-lane loopty-loops, and double-decker strip malls, Houston appeared a dizzying place, the largest unzoned city in the world.
Strip joints and strip malls bracketed craftsman bungalows. Mexican
torta stackers shared strip mall berths with Korean burrito rollers. During
the first two decades of the twenty-first century, a new creole cuisine
emerged on the Gulf of Mexico, reflective of the various peoples who
called this postmodern port city home.

At Pondicheri, a swish Indian bakery, Anita Jaisinghani served breakfast regulars stone-ground yellow grits crumbled with peanuts and
tossed with cilantro. Omelets arrived with house-made paneer and mustard greens. Rolled in roti, breakfast taco riffs came with cilantro chutney. By the second decade of the twenty-first century, those dishes no
longer played like fusions of Southern, Mexican, and Indian ingredients.
Instead, they tasted like honest reflections of the cooks in the kitchen
and the diners on the other side of the counter.

"There's no one to tell us what's right and what's wrong," Alba
Huerta, a second-generation Mexican American, told me when we sat
down at the Houston coffee shop Blacksmith. Over a breakfast of Vietnamese hanger steak and eggs with chicken liver pâté–smeared French
bread, she spoke of her intent to stock a new sort of bar. "I'm working

with tepache right now," Huerta, owner of the Southern-themed bar Julep, said of the liqueur fermented in Mexico from various grains and fruits from barley to pineapple. "To explore the American South, you need to know the Mexican South, too."

Next door, at the restaurant Underbelly, Chris Shepherd forged a restaurant that reflected the city's status as a new creole capital for the region. Born in Oklahoma, Shepherd fell for Houston like only an immigrant could. He saw the place with bright and open eyes. And he telegraphed that devotion with a photo collage, mounted in the hall that connected the front door with the airy dining room. When visitors arrived, Shepherd swept his slab of a hand across fifty color-saturated photos, each tagged with a Houston zip code. Like a tour guide, Shepherd steered his customers to El Hidalguense for Saturday goat roasts, Long Sing for weekday char siu pork, Mala Sichuan for mapo tofu, and Vieng Thai for yum nhean.

At Underbelly, Shepherd stirred a textbook chicken fricassee, lifted from the recipe files of an east Texas grandmother. And he served it in a cast iron skillet atop butter-soaked biscuits. Shepherd stewed goat with Korean chili paste, served with tubular noodles from a Chinatown storefront factory. He fried rounds of cornmeal-coated okra, doused them in Vietnamese fish sauce, and garnished them with peanuts. Shepherd declared that those dishes belonged on the same menu, that they comprised a narrative of his adopted city. They spoke, he said, for the South he claimed as his own.

After breakfast with Huerta, Hugo Ortega drove me to his favorite lunch spot. I expected a down-market version of Caracol, his upscale Mexican seafood bistro. What I got was a story of three failed boyhood attempts to cross the border at Laredo followed by lunch at Himalaya, a Pakistani canteen run by Kaiser Lashkari. We ate hunter beef, which Lashkari served with mustard and naan and what he called Pakistani pastrami. We drank mango lassi from a coffee mug that could have been borrowed from a Waffle House. We ate steak tikka, a dish from the Bihar region of India, seasoned with chili powder, cumin, garlic, and other spices that suggested a Tex-Mex masala. "Food doesn't need a passport," Ortega told me as I marveled at the easy marriages of cultures. "Just like I didn't need a passport when I crossed with the coyote."

Back in the twentieth century, when ideas about workaday Southern food codified, many of the region's best cooks were members of the underclass. They were black men from Alabama who built fish markets around their ability to work trotlines. They were white women from Kentucky who worked corner cafés in mill towns, frying chicken in deep baskets instead of shallow skillets. They were lifelong students of elemental cookery, which they elevated to craft, sometimes to art.

By the 2010s, many traditional mom-and-pop restaurants were in retreat. While barbecue restaurants enjoyed a renaissance, meat-and-threes, catfish houses, and beans-and-cornbread diners faded. Some sacrificed quality for efficiency, relying on cheats like prebreaded pork chops, boxes of mashed-potato flakes, and cans of mulched turnip greens. Others moved to serve-yourself steam table buffets, where smoke dissipated from pork shoulder barbecue and fried catfish surrendered its crunch. Others still, acknowledging the workload shouldered by successful restaurateurs, closed their doors, rather than watch their children and grandchildren claim their stations on the duckboards and stand to face the stove.

In their stead, this new generation of immigrant cooks emerged. They were Asian. They were Latino. They ran corner stores and peddled carnitas out of the back. They fried fish filets to order, sandwiched them between white bread slices, and returned change from five-dollar bills. They were countervailing influences in an American South defined by black and white cooks, by barbecue joints and fried chicken shacks. Instead of interlopers, these newer immigrant restaurateurs were natural inheritors of working-class food traditions.

Fabulists, whose affections for the South were informed by xeno-phobic tendencies and neo-Confederate sympathies, howled over those developments. They voted to dismantle the federal food aid programs, denying sustenance to new immigrants while citing Reagan-era welfare queen statistics. They hatched plans to close the borders to the next gen-eration of American dream aspirants. They feared for the "Southern way of life," then stammered when asked to define it. As new immi-grants arrived, the South did not lose its identity. Instead, the region gained new peoples, new spices, new techniques, and new dishes. These evolutionary changes foretold an inclusive and delicious future for the American South.

W hen the Southern Foodways Alliance began its work in 1999, the focus was biracial. To declare our intent, I chose to illustrate our first brochure with a WPA-era Marion Post Walcott photograph of chil-dren, standing on an earthen berm with cantaloupes and watermelons in their arms. A close look at the photo revealed a white girl who hugged her melon just as tightly as the black girl alongside. My idea was to show that, no matter what stereotypes might hold, a love of melons knew no racial bounds. In a broader way, the message was that the love of South-ern food, and the expert knowledge of its preparation, was color-blind. Whites and blacks alike cracked open green melons to reveal red hearts. Southerners rich and poor took turns spitting seeds to see who could carry the longest distance.

Racism and its burdens was my primary concern when I began thinking and writing about food. Inspired by the work of John Egerton, the SFA told stories that we hoped black and white Southerners would recognize as ennobling. Debates in that era were sometimes fractious. At an early symposium, a shouting match erupted after an author who had just published a fried chicken cookbook made a case for the European origins of that dish. At a time when the South seemed to be finally paying down some of its debts to African American cooks, that idea inflamed.

Early gatherings sometimes slipped into essentialist conversations about regional identity. During the fourth symposium, focused on the foodways of Appalachia, author Rick Bragg delivered a hilarious talk that made sport of bagels in favor of biscuits. The audience howled as Bragg drew the line in the sand between us Southerners and those Yankees. But by the second decade of the 2000s, the SFA, like the South itself, had broadened its reach and recognized blacks and whites weren't the only Southerners who employed food to tell stories of their people.

In 2011, I watched Pedro Herrera of Houston step to the stage at a rock and rap club in Los Angeles, wearing a golden pendant that depicted a Mexican man, woman, and chicken running across the border. Performing as Chingo Bling, Herrera had built his initial audience at flea markets, before moving on to low-rider car shows, mom-and-pop record stores, and bodegas. He called that informal network of venues the Taco Circuit, a reference to the Chitlin Circuit that African American musicians played before clubs and theaters integrated. Like the Lees, who followed four years later, he grappled with identity, using food as metaphor.

On his debut album, *The Tamale Kingpin*, released in 2004 on his own Big Chile label, he sang "Masa and da Flour," a send-up of "Money and the Power" by Scarface. On his major label debut, *They Can't Deport Us All*, he rapped about the underground economy in which immigrants earned rent money by rolling tamales: "Making paper stacks / making paper stacks / slinging masa like crack." Hererra wanted to excise the stereotypes. "We're lawn people. Or we're lazy Mexicans," he told me. Instead, Herrera said Mexican immigrants were hustlers.

That hustle was American, he said. "And so are those tamale ladies who work the parking lots at Walmart, who keep their kids in the backseat of their cars, next to the coolers of tamales they made this morning, and whisper—tamales, tamales, tamales—as you walk by. Some of those ladies move big product," he said, slipping into a lingo more often associated with drug dealers, reminding me of the stereotypes that imprint on white conversations about brown and black people.

When chef Bill Smith, who followed Bill Neal at Crook's Corner, cooked the welcome meal for the 2014 SFA symposium in Oxford, he worked with a Mexican kitchen staff, most of whom immigrated from the town of Celaya in the state of Guanajuato. On the menu that night were mint juleps made with mint sorbet and Rebel Yell bourbon, shrimp salsa served with soda crackers, and pork shanks, braised until the meat fell lazily from the bones.

Mixed with drippings from country hams baked in Coca-Cola, the tamales he served were not part of the lexicon of the cooks who rolled them. Chingo Bling wouldn't have recognized them, either. Instead, they reflected a future-tense South still in the making, a place that will be as Mexican as West African, as Korean as Irish, and will lose none of its essential identity in the process.

Shared Palates:
An Afterword

T he South still suffers from profound problems. Seemingly intractable ones. Two generations ago, poor Southerners starved for food.
Today, a working-class diet of industrial foods renders their heirs
obese and diseased. Our public schools, now fitfully integrated, are inad-
equately funded, which means that when we score jobs, many of us arrive with lesser educations and receive inadequate pay for the good work
we do. Racism remains a vexing problem. Just six generations removed
from Appomattox, we don't talk honestly and openly about slavery and
its legacies, including the privileges that whiteness affords.

What Southerners have in common, in addition to an arguable
shared ear for music, is a definite shared palate, honed over four centuries of cooking out of the same larder, if not always eating at the same
table. Food serves the region as a unifying symbol of the creolized culture we have forged, making explicit connections between the breads
made from corn that Native Americans call pone and the breads made
from corn that Mexican Americans call tortillas, bonding Louisiana Cajuns of French descent who boil crawfish in water spiked with Tabasco

mash and Vietnamese Texans on the Gulf Coast who boil crawfish in pots that bob with lemongrass.

In this modern South, the likkers at the bottoms of those vessels sustain many peoples. And they remind Americans of the vitality that drives regional foodways. In this second decade of the twenty-first century, American culture, both good and ill, looks a lot like Southern culture. From religion, to music, to politics, notions born here have gone national. Today, Southern foods are not imperiled. They do not require preservation. Instead, they are vanguard.

Today, as the region evolves, so do its foods. Culture, as historian Lawrence Levine reminds us, is not a product fixed in time. It's a vigorous and ongoing process.

I was born in 1962, in the midst of the Civil War centennial. My son became a teenager as the nation marked the fiftieth anniversary of the Civil Rights Act of 1964. Jess and I talk often about our region, about its tragic history and bright future. We talk less about the Civil War and more about the civil rights movement. It's easy to talk with Jess about that war, about how the good guys won, freeing blacks and whites from a social choke hold.

Discussing the Civil War is more entangling, more confounding. But we try. When Jess was nine, we took a tour of the Civil War battlefield at Vicksburg, Mississippi. On a searing summer day, we tramped from monument to monument, gamboling over rammed-earth balustrades, weaving down lawns that could have doubled for country club fairways, crossing sweeps of land once strewn with gut-shot rebels and bayoneted Yanks. Jess and I didn't talk much. Instead, we sweated through our T-shirts, stared at white marble horses and soaring obelisks, and wondered why we took that June tour on foot.

As we approached the interpretive center, a park ranger looked up to ask if we had questions. Jess lingered. When I was out of earshot, he asked the ranger something. As he listened, Jess nodded intently. A few minutes later, he met me at the gift shop cash register with one of those stumpy kepi caps that soldiers wore during the Civil War. I knew the form. When I was a boy, my father bought me one at the Cyclorama, the Grant Park art installation that depicted the 1864 Battle of Atlanta. But there was a difference. The hat my father bought me was butternut gray. As a twenty-first-century Southerner who knows that the white South fought the Civil War to preserve slavery, Jess made the only purchase he could. He bought a blue bill.

The South of today demands more than divisive polarities. More than good guys and bad guys. More than blue and gray. Natasha Trethewey, elected our nation's poet laureate in 2012, works that puzzle in her head. Born in Mississippi to a black mother and a white father, she's a Southerner. Our collective past defines her, but she is not limited by that past. When Trethewey claims the region for herself, she claims it for all. "There are other Souths beyond the white Confederate South," she says.

Her South didn't lose the Civil War. Neither did Jess's. "Who can lay claim to the South?" she asks. "I don't want to take it away from anyone. I just want them to recognize that it's mine, too." I hear kindred refrains in the lyrics of Patterson Hood, the Alabama-born singer for the Drive-By Truckers. He, too, embraces the contradictions, which he refers to as the "duality of the Southern Thing." Instead of glibly celebrating our attributes or damning our neighbors and kin for historical failings, Hood has said that Southerners who are proud of the glory should have the courage to stare down the shame. That rings true when considering the great sweep of history. And it rings clarion when studying the history of time spent in fields, before stoves, and at tables.

My boy Jess is a Southerner of the Hood and Trethewey schools. His brogue is molasses. His hunger for roasted pork is bottomless. His taste in Civil War headgear trends toward the guys who fought to end slavery.

And his politics, now in gestation, span gay rights and animal rights. Those beliefs mark him as a newer sort of Southerner, no less grounded, no less complex, but perhaps less burdened by our two wars.

The South was once a place that did not brook intrusion. Now it's the region with the highest immigration rates. When I was a boy in 1970s Georgia, a barbecue sandwich and a Brunswick stew with soda crackers was my go-to meal. Jess prefers tacos al pastor, hold the cilantro, and cheese dip with fryer-hot tortilla chips. In his South, Punjabi truck stop owners in Arkansas fry okra for turban-wearing reefer jockeys. And Korean bakers in Alabama turn out sweet potato–gorged breakfast pastries.

His South is changing. For the better, mostly. In fits and starts, yes. New peoples and new foods and new stories are making their marks on the region. In those exchanges, much is gained. What was once a region of black and white, locked in a struggle for power, has become a society of many hues and many hometowns. His generation now weaves new narratives about what it means to be Southern, about what it takes to claim this place as their own. Given time to reconcile the mistakes my generation made with the beauty we forged amid adversity, his generation might challenge the region of our birth to own up to its promise.

THANKS

Ginny Smith Younce of Penguin Press bought this book two days after she returned from her first maternity leave, closing the deal fifty years to the day after President Johnson signed the Civil Rights Act of 1964 into law. When writers gather, it's common to begin conversations by saying, "Editors don't edit anymore." Those writers have not met the gimlet-eyed Mrs. Younce.

When publishers talk to me about my agent, David Black, they invariably say, "You are well represented." Embedded in that remark is recognition that David is a keen advocate. The next thing they say is, "He's also a sweetheart." Both are true.

As *The Potlikker Papers* moved from manuscript to book, Annie Badman, Kate Griggs, Sarah Hutson, and Matt Boyd at Penguin Press, along with publisher Scott Moyers and president Ann Godoff, devoted themselves to its success. So did copy editor Michael Burke, who showed a deft touch. Thank you, good people.

Before I began this project, I went back to school yet again to earn an MFA. My mentors at Goucher College, especially Jacob Levenson, were generous teachers. Valerie Boyd and Moni Basu, with whom I now teach in the low-residency Narrative Nonfiction MFA Program at the University of Georgia's Grady College of Journalism and Mass Communication, lead by example. I'm grateful to them for welcoming me to the fold.

Beginning in 1998, I learned this craft while writing for the *Oxford American*. First Marc Smirnoff, later Roger Hodge, and now Eliza Borné have afforded me the freedom and feedback and pages to tell complicated stories about the American South. Before beloved *Gourmet* magazine folded, Jane Daniels Lear and Ruth Reichl backed my telling of Southern stories. At *The New York Times*, Nick Fox and Pete Wells gave me license to deploy the skills I developed in the South to make sense of the nation in my "United Tastes" column. More recently, Dave Mezz and David DiBenedetto at *Garden & Gun* have invested deeply in my writing and perspective. I always get great feedback from the column and the features I write for that magazine.

A slew of friends and colleagues aided my research. A few of the kindest: Ellen Meacham shared insights on Robert F. Kennedy and his poverty tour. Alice Randall, who shared my enthusiasm for the Mahalia Jackson story, also shared her research. Marcie Ferris, author of the definitive book *The Edible South*, led by sterling example. Cliff Graubart turned over his carport, stacked with Nathalie Dupree's archive. Robb Walsh introduced me to the wonders of Houston.

Beth Macy went spelunking for potlikker references. Jan Longone and J. J. Jacobson at the Janice Bluestein Longone Culinary Archive at the University of Michigan went digging for records of the first Symposium on American Cuisine. Scott Barretta talked me through Greenwood geography. Davia Nelson and Nikki Silva of the Kitchen Sisters shared transcripts of their Georgia Gilmore interviews in Montgomery. Yvette Johnson schooled me on her grandfather, Booker Wright. Sara Roahen and Hanna Raskin read my musings on the restaurant renaissance. Moreton Neal and Kate Medley offered input on Bill Neal and his legacy. Nathalie Dupree recalled Paul Prudhomme. Members of the Southern Foodways Alliance, from here to Hahira, made possible the work of documenting, studying, and exploring the diverse food cultures of the changing American South.

Brian Kelley came through with clutch housing. Holed up in the

Warehouse District, I proved to myself that I could do more in New Orleans than drink and revel. Katie King scoured archives for Georgia Gilmore information, fact-checked me, and sourced photos. Amelia Brock, who also researched and fact-checked, was a graduate student in Southern studies when this project began. By the time it was completed, she, like Katie, had earned her degree and proved a trusted colleague.

Carly Grace Akers, whom I first knew as a waitress at Ajax Diner in Oxford, stepped in to apply her MLS degree and wrangle the endnotes. And my mother-in-law, Marleah Hobbs, bought me a hand-held pen scanner for Christmas. With that tool, I scanned everything I read into Evernote. Thanks for the digital assist, Marley.

Melissa Booth Hall and Sara Camp Arnold Milam, colleagues at the Southern Foodways Alliance, read drafts and offered generous insights. The whole darn office played a part. When I bunkered in to write, they took the reins of the SFA and ran the place like they own it. (They do.) Charles Reagan Wilson, who taught me in graduate school, stepped back in to read and comment on the final manuscript. Despite the efforts of all these good readers, any faults of fact, perception, or interpretation in this book are mine.

My wife, Blair Hobbs, is the best reader and thinker I know. Thanks to our cocktail conversations at Snackbar, this book is far smarter. Our son, Jess Edge, who turned fifteen about the time I submitted the final manuscript, gives me hope for this place we call home.

Notes

Foreword

x   **"otherwise dysfunctional societies"** John Egerton, "No Grits, No Glory: The Endurance of Southern Food," *Oxford American*, Spring 2005.

x   **"life in the region"** John Egerton, *Southern Food: At Home, on the Road, in History* (New York: Knopf, 1987), 4.

Potlikker: An Introduction

2   **"an agricultural act"** John T. Edge, "The Prophet," *Gourmet*, February 2008.

3   **"without being white"** Peter Applebome, *Dixie Rising: How the South Is Shaping American Values, Politics, and Culture* (New York: Times Books, 1996), 339.

5   **The debate was on** Julian LaRose Harris Papers, Stuart A. Rose Manuscript, Archives, and Rare Book Library, Emory University, Atlanta, GA.

6   **"upper and lower teeth"** John T. Edge, "The State of the Broth," *Oxford American*, March–April 2014.

6   **"facing cornpone and potlikker"** This quote and the other potlikker quotes that follow are from John T. Edge, "The Potlikker Papers: An Explication and Rumination on the Potlikker and Cornpone Debate of 1931 with Illustrative Asides" (master's thesis, University of Mississippi, 2002).

6   **Governor and the Dishwasher** John T. Edge, "The Little Man Will Tickle You to Death," *Oxford American*, Fall 2001.

6   **adopt a macrobiotic diet** UPI, "Maddox Gets Good News: No Sign of AIDS," *Los Angeles Times*, August 29, 1985.

7   **"greens kept me going"** Richard Wright, *Black Boy* (New York: Harper and Brothers, 1945), 161.

8   **"rejoin the Union"** Tom Matthews, "The Southern Mystique," *Newsweek*, July 19, 1976.

Chapter 1: Kitchen Tables

15   **"bleakness of nagging despair"** Lamont H. Yeakey, "The Montgomery, Alabama Bus Boycott, 1955–1956" (PhD diss., Columbia University, 1979), 667.

16   **the basement annex** Denise L. Berkhalter, "Just Cause," *The Crisis*, November–December 2005.

16   **fried chicken sandwiches** Vernon Jarrett, "'Club from Nowhere' Paid Way of Boycott," *Chicago Tribune*, December 4, 1975.

16   **"Here, let me give"** Joe Azbell, "At Holt Street Baptist Church," *Montgomery Advertiser*, December 7, 1954.

16   **walk around back** Montgomery Bus Boycott Transcripts, 1956, Alabama Attorney General's Office, Alabama Department of Archives and History, Montgomery, AL, microfilm SG24838, reel 17.

16   **"you could be a better person"** John T. Edge, "The Welcome Table," *Oxford American*, January–February 2000.

17   **"how to raise money"** Jarrett, "'Club from Nowhere' Paid Way of Boycott."

18   **"It came from nowhere"** Author interview with Betty Gilmore, Montgomery, AL, November 1999.

18   **"right will always win out"** Preston and Bonita Valien Papers, box 4, Amistad Research Center, Tulane University, New Orleans, LA. (Note that dialect has been recast.)

18   **"pretty enough to beat a nigger"** Yeakey, "The Montgomery, Alabama Bus Boycott, 1955–1956," 227–28.

18   **"we are not dogs or cats"** Valien Papers, box 4, Amistad Research Center.

18   **baked and sold cakes and pies** Davis W. Houck and David E. Dixon, *Women and the Civil Rights Movement* (Jackson: University Press of Mississippi, 2009), 64–65.

19   **lies didn't pay well** Letter from Inez Ricks, April 21, 1958, box 94, folder 5, Martin Luther King Jr. Collection, Howard Gotlieb Archival Research Center, Boston University, Boston, MA.

19   **"We rather walk"** Henry Hampton and Steve Fayer, *Voices of Freedom: An Oral History of the Civil Rights Movement* (New York: Random House, 2011), 29.

19   **throw her to the floor** Montgomery Bus Boycott Transcripts, microfilm SG24838, reel 17.

20   **"meanest, nastiest" people in the world** Evelyn Cunningham, "Dull Moments Were Few at Pastor King's Trial," *Pittsburgh Courier*, March 31, 1956; "Bus Boycott Spontaneous, King Says," *Chicago Defender*, March 31, 1956.

20   **in Montgomery County** Jamie York interview of Mark Gilmore, November 28, 2004, for the *Kitchen Sisters* radio series, collection of Davia Nelson and Nikki Silva.

20   **to prevent the races from mixing** Yeakey, "The Montgomery, Alabama Bus Boycott, 1955–1956," 28.

20   **mess after mess of collards** Author interview with Mark Gilmore, Montgomery, AL, November 1999.

21   **"worked for yourself"** Ibid.

21   **"we knew we had won"** Frank Sikora, *The Judge: The Life and Opinions of Alabama's Frank M. Johnson, Jr.* (Montgomery, AL: NewSouth Books, 2007), 53.

21   **their own black families** Rebecca Sharpless, *Cooking in Other Women's Kitchens: Domestic Workers in the South, 1865–1960* (Chapel Hill: University of North Carolina Press, 2010), xiv.

22   **bus boycott auto pool** Jarrett, "'Club from Nowhere' Paid Way of Boycott."

22   **whipped him with it** Author interview with Mark Gilmore, Montgomery, AL, November 1999.

22 **"she might cut you"** Author interview with Thomas Jordan, Montgomery, AL, November 1999.

22 **"down by Georgia's to eat"** Author interview with Mark Gilmore, Montgomery, AL, November 1999.

23 **"like you want"** Edge, "The Welcome Table."

23 **She called him "Guvs"** Author interview with Mark Gilmore, Montgomery, AL, November 1999.

23 **Gilmore's kitchen for pork chops** Sam Harper, "Civil Rights Advocate Dies at 70," *Montgomery Advertiser*, March 13, 1990.

24 **twelve-seat oak trestle table** Details of the house and kitchen were collected during author visit to the Gilmore house in November 1999.

24 **fried chicken and peach cobbler** Roster of guests and foods established through photographs and recollections of Mark Gilmore, author interview, November 1999.

25 **"write it in the books of law"** *Public Papers of the Presidents of the United States: Lyndon B. Johnson, 1963–64*, volume I, entry 11 (Washington, DC: Government Printing Office, 1965), 8–10.

25 **"already bad hot"** Emma Brown, "Rene Verdon, White House Chef for the Kennedys, Dies at 86," *Washington Post*, February 3, 2011.

26 **to suit his listeners** Lee White, "The Wind at His Back: LBJ, Zephyr Wright, and Civil Rights," in Thomas W. Cowger and Sherwin Markman, *Lyndon Johnson Remembered: An Intimate Portrait of a Presidency* (Lanham, MD: Rowman & Littlefield, 2003), 141.

26 **"country I want"** Transcript, Robert S. McNamara Oral History, Special Interview I, March 26, 1993, by Robbert Dallek, Lyndon Baines Johnson Presidential Library, Austin, TX.

27 **"not going to do it again"** "Legends in the Law: Leonard H. Marks" interview, *Bar Report*, District of Columbia Bar, June–July 2000.

27 **"having a dog along"** Todd S. Purdum, *An Idea Whose Time Has Come: Two Presidents, Two Parties, and the Battle for the Civil Rights Act of 1964* (New York: Henry Holt, 2014), 159.

27 **"That's wrong"** Robert A. Caro, *The Years of Lyndon Johnson: Master of the Senate* (New York: Vintage, 2003), 888–90.

27 **"change it by law"** Nick Kotz, *Judgment Days: Lyndon Baines Johnson, Martin Luther King Jr., and the Laws That Changed America* (New York: Mariner Books, 2005), 63.

28 **on her drive home** Robert A. Caro, *The Years of Lyndon Johnson: The Passage of Power* (New York: Vintage, 2012), 489.

28 **"kind of a country I want"** White, "The Wind at His Back," 141.

28 **"more than anybody else"** "Legends in the Law: Leonard H. Marks" interview.

Chapter 2: Restaurant Theaters

31 **"But what does he think"** "Mississippi: A Self Portrait," directed by Frank DeFelitta, posted by NBC News Archives on YouTube.

33 **"like they belonged to you"** Author interview with cotton planter, Greenwood, MS, March 1997.

33 **"BLACK POWER"** Gene Roberts, "Mississippi Reduces Police Protection for Marchers," *New York Times*, June 17, 1966.

33 **March Against Fear** Staff, "The Nation: Friends and Foes of the Marchers," *New York Times*, June 19, 1966.

34 **"We want Black Power"** Adam Goudsouzian, *Down to the Crossroads: Civil Rights, Black Power, and the Meredith March Against Fear* (New York: Farrar, Straus and Giroux, 2014), 143.

35 **"go through that again"** Author interview with patron, Greenwood, MS, March 1997.

35 **"iceberg of Mississippi politics"** William Henry Chafe, *The Unfinished Journey: America Since World War II* (New York: Oxford University Press, 2003), 166.

36 **that same year** Goudsouzian, *Down to the Crossroads*, 139.

36 **plotted violent resistance** Howard Zinn, *SNCC: The New Abolitionists* (Boston: South End Press, 1964), 147–48.

37 **hunkered in Silver Moon booths** Mary Stanton, *From Selma to Sorrow: The Life and Death of Viola Liuzzo* (Athens: University of Georgia Press, 2000), 47.

37 **blew out the back of his head** Michael Newton, *The FBI and the KKK: A Critical History* (Jefferson, NC: McFarland, 2005), 112.

37 **Blanche's husband, Herbert Guest** John T. Edge, "The Gathering Place," *Oxford American*, January–February 2003.

38 **"trouble in Athens"** John C. McAvoy, "Interview of Former Special Agent of the FBI Jack B. Simpson (1942–1978)," Society of Former Special Agents of the FBI, July 9, 2008, 11.

38 **that summer to investigate** Zach Mitcham, "On Race and Justice: A Look Back at the Murder of Lemuel Penn," *Madison Journal Today*, July 24, 2014.

38 **opposite black activists** McAvoy, "Interview of Former Special Agent of the FBI Jack B. Simpson (1942–1978)," 6.

38 **back door of an apartment** Associated Press, "In Georgia Slaying, Klansmen Arrested," *Nashua Telegraph*, August 7, 1964.

38 **black girl in the lip** Newton, *The FBI and the KKK*, 112.

39 **"killing a nigger with his car"** Ibid.

39 **rethink her business options** UPI, "Accused Penn Slayer Held for Pep Pills Sale," *Afro American*, April 23, 1966.

40 **agitated for service as early as 1957** Jesse Paddock, *Counter Histories: Durham*, southernfoodways.org, 2014.

41 **returned the next day** Wesley C. Hogan, *Many Minds, One Heart: SNCC's Dream for a New America* (Chapel Hill: University of North Carolina Press, 2013), 27.

41 **University of North Carolina joined** Howell Raines, *My Soul Is Rested: Movement Days in the Deep South Remembered* (New York: G. P. Putnam's Sons, 1977), 80.

41 **downtown department stores** Lynne Olson, *Freedom's Daughters: The Unsung Heroines of the Civil Rights Movement from 1830 to 1970* (New York: Scribner, 2001), 147.

41 **"Don't block entrances"** Harvard Sitkoff, *The Struggle for Black Equality* (New York: Hill and Wang, 2008), 67.

41 **"in front of the eyes"** Zinn, *SNCC: The New Abolitionists*, 24.

41 **"in every aspect of life"** Ella Baker, "Bigger Than a Hamburger," *Southern Patriot*, May 1960.

41 **system they believed corrupt** Olson, *Freedom's Daughters*, 147.

41 **spread through the movement** Winfred Cross, "Members of Friendship Nine Recall Historic Sit-In Arrests," *Sumter Daily Item*, February 1, 1986.

42 **theology at Benedict College** "S.C. Student Severely Stabbed During Sit-In," *Jet*, March 16, 1961.

42 **from an oak tree** *The Student Protest Movement: A Recapitulation*, Southern Regional Council Special Report, September 29, 1961, Atlanta, GA, crmvet.org/info/6109_src_sitins.pdf.

42 **over the heads of activists** Angela Jill Cooley, *To Live and Dine in Dixie: The Evolution of Urban Food Culture in the Jim Crow South* (Athens: University of Georgia Press), 122.

42 **slices of apple pie** Trip Burns, "Real Violence: 50 Years Ago at Woolworth," *Jackson Free Press*, May 23, 2013.

42 **"hogs to move"** Joseph Mosnier, "The Demise of an 'Extraordinary Criminal Procedure,'" *Journal of Supreme Court History* 2 (1996): 142–43.

43 **stood together and ate together** Marcie Ferris, *The Edible South: The Power of Food and the Making of an American Region* (Chapel Hill: University of North Carolina Press, 2014), 344.

43 **"Eat with niggers"** Virginia Foster Durr, *Outside the Magic Circle: The Autobiography of Virginia Foster Durr* (Tuscaloosa: University of Alabama Press, 1985), 122.

43 **"taking these white folks"** Staff, "The Nation: Civil Rights," *Time*, July 17, 1964.

43 **"to break the law"** Peter Millones, "Negroes in South Test Rights Act; Resistance Light," *New York Times*, July 4, 1964.

44 **closed the swimming pool** Civil Rights Act of 1964 Compliance Meetings, May–July 1964, Burke Marshall Papers, John F. Kennedy Library and Museum, Boston, MA.

44 **sexual predators at worst** Durr, *Outside the Magic Circle*, 276.

44 **"cup of coffee"** UPI, "Negro Is Killed in Fight in Café," *Birmingham Post-Herald*, October 30, 1964.

44 **his Pickrick Cafeteria** Peter Millones, "The U.S. Under the Civil Rights Act: Despite Some Bitter Resistance, Compliance Is Generally Good," *New York Times*, July 4, 1964.

44 **"I say not"** Associated Press, "Lester Maddox Shuts Cafeteria," *New York Times*, February 8, 1965.

44 **Robert E. Lee Hotel in Jackson** Compliance Meetings, May–July 1964, Marshall Papers.

44 **one nickel** Ibid.

45 **brought suit in 1964** Associated Press, "Diner Files Plea over Price List," *Cumberland Evening Times*, September 24, 1964.

45 **"believed in segregation"** Flyer, undated, in author's collection.

45 **"pull off our pickets"** James Tanner, "New Race Troubles: Negroes Ready Another Wave of Demonstrations Against Bias in South," *Wall Street Journal*, February 5, 1964.

45 **window service only** Jason Sokol, *There Goes My Everything* (New York: Knopf, 2006), 141.

46 **"GIVEN TO THE KKK"** UPI, "Sign Supporting Klan at Eatery Brings Suit," *Afro American*, January 24, 1970.

46 **to force its removal** Ibid. True redemption did not come until later, after Ayers closed, when the Solid Rock Holiness Church, a black congregation, began worshipping in that same space.

46 **Shady Nook café** "From 1932, a Reminder on Mississippi Main Street," *New York Times*, June 1, 1981.

Chapter 3: Poor Power

49 **told the world in 1967** U.S. Congress, *Examining the War on Poverty: Hearings Before the United States Congress Subcommittee on Employment, Manpower, and Poverty of the Committee on Labor and Public Welfare*, Part 2, 90th Cong., 1st sess. (1967), 22.

49 **chopping cotton for three dollars a day** Staff, "Lady Mayor of Mayersville," *Ebony*, December 1977, 54.

49   **close of the prosperous 1950s** Annelise Orleck, introduction to *The War on Poverty: A New Grassroots History 1964–1980*, eds. Annelise Orleck and Lisa Gaye Hazirjian (Athens: University of Georgia Press, 2011), 5.

49   **black Americans lived in poverty** Ibid.

50   **next battle to join** John Skipper, *Showdown at the 1964 Democratic Convention: Lyndon Johnson, Mississippi and Civil Rights* (Jefferson, NC: McFarland, 2012), 77.

50   **welfare rolls bulged** *Examining the War on Poverty*, 8.

50   **exacerbated problems** Robert Sherrill, "It Isn't True That Nobody Starves in America," *New York Times*, June 4, 1967.

50   **Delta farmworkers** *Examining the War on Poverty*, 19.

50   **eight thousand food stamp users in 1968** "Memorandum, Concerned Citizens for Hunger and Poverty," March 7, 1969, Fannie Lou Hamer Papers, box 10, Amistad Research Center, Tulane University.

51   **"just to feed their children"** *Examining the War on Poverty*, 22.

51   **surplus commodities** Sherrill, "It Isn't True That Nobody Starves in America."

51   **black child answered** Curtis Wilkie, "Robert Kennedy Meets Hunger," *Clarksdale Press Register*, April 12, 1967.

51   **cornbread across the floor** Wilkie, "Robert Kennedy Meets Hunger."

51   **crawled with rats and roaches** Nick Kotz, *Let Them Eat Promises: The Politics of Hunger in America* (New York: Prentice Hall, 1969), 1–2.

52   **"country like this allow this"** Harvey Levenstein, *Paradox of Plenty: A Social History of Eating in Modern America* (New York: Oxford University Press, 1993), 144.

52   **"Do something for your country"** Jean Stein and George Plimpton, *American Journey: The Times of Robert Kennedy* (Harcourt Brace Jovanovich, 1970), 279–80.

52   **umbilical knot** Sherrill, "It Isn't True That Nobody Starves in America."

53   **Charleston in 1968** Fritz Hollings, *The Case Against Hunger: A Demand for a National Policy* (New York: Cowles Book Company, 1970), 5.

53   **served thirty-eight families** Ibid.

53   **coughed up worms** Hollings, *The Case Against Hunger*, 63.

53   **leaving their land idle** Ibid.

54   **"developed a drone society"** Ibid.

54   **"I WORK"** Kotz, *Let Them Eat Promises*, 220.

54   **"not willing to work"** Hollings, *The Case Against Hunger*, 63.

54   **lived in Inez, Kentucky** Orleck, introduction to *The War on Poverty*, 2.

54   **"face of a young child"** Garth Pauley, *LBJ's American Promise: The 1965 Voting Rights Address* (College Station: Texas A&M University Press, 2007), 1–12.

55   **had failed whites as well as blacks** John Cheves, "The Face of Poverty Never Escaped His Moment of Fame," *Lexington Herald-Leader*, November 16, 2013.

55   **"plenty in this nation"** Orleck, introduction to *The War on Poverty*, 9.

55   **teeth for his wife and himself** Cheves, "The Face of Poverty Never Escaped His Moment of Fame."

55   **poorest county in the nation** Amy Nathan Wright, "Civil Rights 'Unfinished Business': Poverty, Race, and the 1968 Poor People's Campaign" (PhD diss., University of Texas at Austin, 2007), 291.

56   **museum of poverty** Calvin Trillin, "U.S. Journal: Resurrection City," *New Yorker*, June 15, 1968.

56 **"principles of liberty and justice"** Associated Press, "500 Begin 'Poor March' After Rally in Memphis," *Memphis Press-Scimitar*, May 2, 1968.

56 **"The march has begun"** Ibid.

56 **important as the destination** Wright, "Civil Rights 'Unfinished Business,'" 139–40.

56 **marked with slogans** Roland L. Freeman, *The Mule Train: A Journey of Hope Remembered* (Nashville, TN: Rutledge Hill Press, 1998), 41, 49.

57 **tour of Marks with Abernathy** Ibid.

57 **They were starving** Clyde Woods, *Development Arrested: The Blues and Plantation Power in the Mississippi Delta* (London: Verso, 1998), 185.

57 **startled by a car horn** Freeman, *The Mule Train*, 51.

57 **runneled between tents** Trillin, "U.S. Journal: Resurrection City."

57 **base of the Washington Monument** Mark Engler, "Dr. Martin Luther King's Economics: Through Jobs, Freedom," *The Nation*, February 2010.

58 **"disorganized, and powerless"** Trillin, "U.S. Journal: Resurrection City."

58 **discounted school meals** Wright, "Civil Rights 'Unfinished Business,'" 451.

58 **"I'd hate to live in a bad one"** Fannie Lou Hamer, *The Speeches of Fannie Lou Hamer: To Tell It Like It Is*, eds. Maegan Parker Brooks and Davis Houck (Jackson: University Press of Mississippi, 2011), 80.

58 **where she was born and raised** Maegan Parker Brooks, *A Voice That Could Stir an Army: Fannie Lou Hamer and the Rhetoric of the Black Freedom Movement* (Jackson: University Press of Mississippi, 2014), 158.

58 **"dying ones a chance to live"** Letter to Leslie J. Dunbar, November 16, 1971, Fannie Lou Hamer Papers, box 10, Amistad Research Center, Tulane University.

58 **destroying black families** Paule Marshall, "Hunger Has No Colour Line," *Vogue*, June 1970.

59 **"die forgotten"** Chris Myers Asch, *The Senator and the Sharecropper: The Freedom Struggles of James O. Eastland and Fannie Lou Hamer* (New York: New Press, 2008), 256.

59 **burned their meeting place to the ground** Correspondence, Franklin Graham, chairman, National Sharecroppers Fund, March 16, 1968, Fannie Lou Hamer Papers, box 10, Amistad Research Center, Tulane University.

59 **"pursuit of dead niggers"** James Cobb, *The South and America Since World War II* (New York: Oxford University Press, 2011), 5.

60 **owner's foot** Asch, *The Senator and the Sharecropper*, 66.

60 **farmland by 1971** Marshall, "Hunger Has No Colour Line," 191.

60 **she called self-helpers** Franklynn Peterson, "Pig Banks Reap Dividends," *Dallas Morning News*, January 31, 1973.

60 **"never go hungry again"** Chana Kai Lee, *For Freedom's Sake: The Life of Fannie Lou Hamer* (Urbana: University of Illinois Press), 1–23.

60 **crop her grandmother picked** November 1971 Freedom Farm Corporation Report, Fannie Lou Hamer Papers, box 4, folder 2, Archives and Special Collections, J. D. Williams Library, University of Mississippi, Oxford, MS.

60 **Freedom Farm struggled** Ibid.

60 **half a million African Americans** Pete Daniel, *Dispossession: Discrimination Against African American Farmers in the Age of Civil Rights* (Chapel Hill: University of North Carolina Press, 2013), 6.

61 **Hamer had gone hungry** Marshall, "Hunger Has No Colour Line," 191.

61   **two cows and three mules** Earnest Bracey, *Fannie Lou Hamer: The Life of a Civil Rights Icon* (Jefferson, NC: McFarland, 2011), 33.

61   **juke runner, and a bootlegger** Asch, *The Senator and the Sharecropper*, 52.

61   **rape by a white man** Ibid.

61   **to protect her children** Ibid.

61   **cooked them like turnip greens** Marshall, "Hunger Has No Colour Line."

61   **rooted in childhood hunger** Lee, *For Freedom's Sake*, 143.

61   **stave off malnutrition** Ibid.

62   **"Some socks rolled up"** Kay Mills, *This Little Light of Mine: The Life of Fannie Lou Hamer* (New York: Penguin Books, 1993), 302.

62   **solution to poverty and hunger** Lee, *For Freedom's Sake*, 10–11.

62   **the Oink Oink project, was bold** November 1971 Freedom Farm Corporation Report, Hamer Papers, University of Mississippi.

62   **piglets as dividends** Dorothy Height, *Open Wide the Freedom Gates* (New York: Public Affairs, 2003), 188.

62   **without store-bought pork** Letter from Inez Jackson to Dorothy Height, September 1972, Fannie Lou Hamer Papers, box 10, Amistad Research Center, Tulane University.

62   **$1,000 a year or less** Peterson, "Pig Banks Reap Dividends."

62   **"you got a good meal"** Brooks, *A Voice That Could Stir an Army*, 199.

62   **"tell you what to say or do"** *Journal of Community Action* 1 (Washington, DC: Center for Responsive Governance, 1981).

62   **build homes by 1972** November 1971 Freedom Farm Corporation Report, Hamer Papers, box 4, folder 4, University of Mississippi.

63   **"as it was outside"** Ibid.

63   **plumbing company in Moorhead** July 1973 Freedom Farm Corporation Report, Hamer Papers, box 4, folder 4, University of Mississippi.

64   **"so fat they shine"** Kotz, *Let Them Eat Promises*, 38.

64   **far-flung towns** H. Jack Geiger Oral History Interview, Conducted March 16, 2013, by John Dittmer in New York City, U.S. Civil Rights History Project, Library of Congress, loc. gov/item/afc2010039_crhp0076, transcript page 68.

64   **"keep it going"** Jack Geiger, in *Out in the Rural: A Health Center in Mississippi*, video produced by Judy Schader Rogers, Community Health Action 1969–1970, vimeo. com/6659667, posted by Prabhjot Singh, 2010.

64   **"Los Angeles freeways"** Senate Select Committe on Nutrition and Human Needs, *Promises to Keep: Housing Need and Federal Failure in Rural America* (Washington, DC: U.S. Government Printing Office, 1971), 2.

64   **prescriptions for food** Laurie B. Green, "Saving Babies in Memphis: The Politics of Race, Health, and Hunger During the War on Poverty," in *The War on Poverty*, 148.

65   **filled at local grocery stores** David Bornstein, "Treating the Cause, Not the Illness," *New York Times,* July 28, 2011.

65   **"therapy for malnutrition was food"** Jack Geiger, Calderone Prize Lecture, Columbia University, November 10, 2014, mailman.columbia.edu/public-health-now/news/message-public-health-jack-geiger.

65   **"They belong to us"** Marshall, "Hunger Has No Colour Line."

66   **"going to make it"** Ibid.

66   **"America owes us a debt"** Ibid.

Chapter 4: Black Power

69   **moviegoers crowded into the Booker T.** Scott Baretta, "Farish Street Blues: Rebuilding a 'Music Town,'" *Jackson Free Press*, February 26, 2004.

70   **"nothing but a turd"** Melvin Van Peebles, *Sweet Sweetback's Baadasssss Song* (New York: Cinemation Industries, 1971).

70   **"Dunbar food"** Ishmael Reed, *Flight to Canada: A Novel* (New York: Scribner, 1976), 91–92.

70   **"Soul people"** Helen Mendes, "Introduction," *The African Heritage Cookbook* (New York: Macmillan, 1971), 11–17.

70   **band of brothers and sisters** Ibid.

71   **"now as a sacrament"** Gene Baro, "Soul Food," *Vogue*, March 1970.

71   **"prattling about Soul Food"** Eldridge Cleaver, *Soul on Ice* (New York: Dell, 1968), 29.

71   **"four hundred years of oppression"** Vertamae Grosvenor, *Vibration Cooking, or, The Travel Notes of a Geechee Girl* (Garden City, NY: Doubleday, 1970), 175.

72   **community activism, they argued** Jennifer Jensen Wallach, "How to Eat to Live: Black Nationalism and the Post-1964 Turn," *Study the South*, July 2, 2014.

72   **"diabetes, and infectious diseases"** Therman E. Evans, "On the Health of Black Americans," *Ebony*, March 1977.

72   **"real vulgarity"** Althea Smith, "A Farewell to Chitterlings: Vegetarianism Is on the Rise Among Diet Conscious Blacks," *Ebony*, September 1974.

72   **"for a celery stalk"** Ibid.

72   **"white man's kitchens"** Elijah Muhammad, *How to Eat to Live: Book One* (Atlanta: Messenger Elijah Muhammad Propagation Society, 1967), 14–15.

73   **"30–40 million black people in America"** "Economic Program, the Three Year Economic Savings Program: Financing Ourselves Toward Independence," Nation of Islam.

73   **"operate in northern cities"** Hollings, *The Case Against Hunger*, 178.

73   **Cuban hatchery** John T. Edge, "Feeding Body and Soul," *Gourmet*, October 2003.

74   **"but not for you"** Muhammad, *How to Eat to Live: Book One*, 4.

75   **baked until custardy** Mike Sula, "Bean Pie, My Brother?" *Chicago Reader*, November 18, 2013.

75   **only six million acres** Lora Smith, "It Came from the Bottom Up: Understanding the Federation of Black Cooperatives," *Gravy* 53 (Fall 2014).

76   **no less destructive** Daniel, *Dispossession*, 1–25.

76   **bought goods at reduced prices** William F. Holmes, "Colored Farmer Alliance," *Handbook of Texas Online*, Texas Historical Association.

77   **white-owned store** Steven L. Piott, *American Reformers, 1870–1920: Progressives in Word and Deed* (Lanham, MD: Rowman & Littlefield, 2006), 59–61.

77   **"no justice for them here"** Marta Effinger-Crichlow, *Staging Migrations Toward an American West: From Ida B. Wells to Rhodessa Jones* (Boulder: University Press of Colorado, 2014), 19–20.

77   **go-between for small black businesses** "Black Markets Loan Fund to Stimulate Relationship Between the Martin Luther King Co-ops and Credit Unions," 1969, Hamer Papers, box 3, folder 14, University of Mississippi.

77   **mostly black farmers** Federation of Southern Cooperatives Land Assistance Fund, *25th Annual Report*, federationsoutherncoop.com, 1992.

77 **600,000 African Americans left their farms** Daniel, *Dispossession*, 6.

77 **"freedom, justice, and equality"** Malcolm X, "Message to Grass Roots," King Solomon Baptist Church, Detroit, MI, November 10, 1963.

77 **brownies, fruitcakes, and pralines** Staff, "Southern Co-op Is on Way," *Pittsburgh Courier*, October 12, 1968.

77 **recalled cotton bales** Sam Tarletan, "Fruitcake Factory Has Successful First Year," *Lake Charles American-Press*, November 7, 1965.

78 **"serve while the odor is strong"** Staff, "The Quiet Revolution of a Parish Priest," *Ebony*, May 1968.

78 **Fannie Lou Hamer's Pig Bank** Kentucky Mountains Feeder Pig Cooperative to Charles Prejean, October 15, 1970, box 18, 52, Federation of Southern Cooperative Papers, Amistad Research Center, Tulane University.

78 **how other co-ops worked** National Committee in Support of Community Based Organizations, *Sumter County Blues: The Ordeal of the Federation of Southern Cooperatives*, by Thomas N. Babel (Washington, DC: Center for Community Change, 1982), 6.

78 **vegetables in its first year** Fay Bennett, Report to the Board of the National Sharecroppers Fund, *The Condition of Farm Workers and Small Farmers in 1967*, Fannie Lou Hamer Collection, box 10, Amistad Research Center, Tulane University.

78 **peas and cucumbers** National Committee in Support of Community Based Organizations, *Sumter County Blues*, 6.

78 **stepped to the podium** Federation of Southern Cooperatives Land Assistance Fund, 25th Annual Report, federationsoutherncoop.com, 1992.

79 **claimed they were Communists** Daniel, *Dispossession*, 263.

79 **sign off on a grant** Kate Pickert, "When Shirley Sherrod Was First Wronged by the USDA," *Time*, July 23, 2010.

79 **racism reared its horned head** Tina Antolini, "Fighting for the Promised Land: A Story of Farming and Racism," *Gravy* podcast, December 31, 2015.

79 **"over his dead body"** Daniel, *Dispossession*, 263.

79 **"Get big or get out"** Michael Carlson, "Earl Butz: US Politician Brought Down by Racist Remark," *The Guardian*, February 4, 2008.

79 **"adapt or die"** Associated Press, "U.S. Agriculture Secretary Ousted over Racist Joke," *Los Angeles Times*, February 3, 2008.

79 **"fencerow to fencerow"** Ibid.

79 **"warm place to shit"** John Dean, "Rituals of the Herd," *Rolling Stone*, October 1976.

79 **soybeans to aquaculture** Clayton Beamer to Board Members, Freedom Farm Corporation, September 26, 1974, Fannie Lou Hamer Papers, box 10, folder 14, Amistad Research Center, Tulane University.

80 **"confused with a dollar bill"** Ibid.

80 **"back in the Black community"** Staff, "Black Atlanta Church Buys $100,000 Restaurant," *Jet*, December 14, 1972.

80 **Vaughan ate stuffed crabs** Lolis Eric Elie, "A New Orleans Original," *Gourmet*, February 2000.

80 **eat lemon ice-box pie** Leah Chase, interview by Sara Roahen and John Pope, Southern Gumbo Trail, June 6, 2014, archived at southernfoodways.org.

81 **"value on themselves or on their work"** Ibid.

81 **"black American's reality"** Houston Baker, *Black Literature in America* (New York: McGraw-Hill, 1971), 17.

81 **"Black element"** Nathaniel Burton and Rudy Lombard, *Creole Feast: 15 Master Chefs of New Orleans Reveal Their Secrets* (New York: Random House, 1978), xv.
81 **"Black hand in the pot"** Ibid.
82 **roped on the heat** Ibid., 16.
82 **instead of the customary ten** Ibid., 27–29.
82 **"they're Blacks"** Ibid., 53.
82 **renaissance of the late twentieth century** Author conversation with Barry Estabrook, Oxford, MS, February 2015.
83 **"perfect maid"** Staff, "'Perfect Maid' Dies at 101," *Gainesville Sun*, November 28, 2015.
83 **"strictly to myself"** Idella Parker, *Idella: Marjorie Rawlings' "Perfect Maid"* (Gainesville: University Press of Florida, 1992), ix, 69.
83 **"justice and peace"** Bobby Seale, interview by Blackside, "Eyes on the Prize II Interviews," November 4, 1988, Henry Hampton Collection, Washington University Libraries, Film and Media Archive, St. Louis, MO.
84 **"Bobby-que"** Bobby Seale, *Barbeque'N with Bobby: Righteous, Down-Home Barbeque Recipes by Bobby Seale* (San Francisco: Ten Speed Press, 1988).

Chapter 5: Landed Hippies

87 **"people that can work"** Stephen Gaskin, *The Caravan* (New York: Doubleday, 1972), unnumbered, final page.
88 **took the Family Dog stage** Rachel Lee Rubin, *Well Met: Renaissance Faires and the American Counterculture* (New York: NYU Press, 2014), 134.
88 **San Francisco State Experimental College** Jim Ricci, "Dream Dies on the Farm: Idealists of a Commune Decide to Grow Up for the Kids' Sake," *Chicago Tribune*, October 3, 1986.
88 **astrology and ecology** Douglas Martin, "Stephen Gaskin, Hippie Who Founded an Enduring Commune, Dies at 79," *New York Times*, July 3, 2014.
88 **"easier to be God than to see God"** Steve Chawkins, "Stephen Gaskin Dies at 79; Founder of The Farm Commune," *Los Angeles Times*, July 5, 2014.
89 **surreal Christian morality** Melvyn Stiriss, *Voluntary Peasants Labor of Love* (Warwick, NY: New Beat Books, 2014), Kindle edition.
89 **"kingdom here and now"** "Many Religious Communes of Young People Are Under the Sway of Compelling Leaders," *New York Times*, December 14, 1969.
89 **topped one thousand** "The Plowboy Interview: Stephen Gaskin and The Farm," *Mother Earth News*, May–June 1977.
90 **rural homesteaders** Carter Taylor Seaton, *Hippie Homesteaders: Arts, Crafts, Music, and Living on the Land in West Virginia* (Morgantown: West Virginia University Press, 2014), 25.
90 **"mental nudist colony"** John Coate, "Life on the Bus and Farm: An Informal Recollection," *Whole Earth Review*, Fall 1988.
90 **"avenues of commerce and of thought"** William G. Frost, "Our Contemporary Ancestors in the Southern Mountains," *Atlantic Monthly*, March 1899.
91 **more than 200,000 people** Seaton, *Hippie Homesteaders*, 25.
91 **migrations in the nation's history** Ibid.
91 **North Carolina Piedmont** James T. Sears, *Rebels, Rubyfruit, and Rhinestone: Queering Space in the Stonewall South* (New Brunswick, NJ: Rutgers University Press, 2001), 94.
92 **organic farming was the focus** Brock Thompson, *The Un-Natural State: Arkansas and the Queer South* (Fayetteville: University of Arkansas Press, 2010), 143.

92   "back from the patriarchy" Ibid.

92   Temperance Hall, Tennessee Sears, *Rebels, Rubyfruit, and Rhinestone*, 144.

92   "land-killing economy" Wendell Berry and Norman Wirzba, *The Art of the Common-place: The Agrarian Essays of Wendell Berry* (Washington, DC: Counterpoint, 2002), 210.

92   "between the spirit and tools" Chad Wriglesworth, *Distant Neighbors: The Selected Letters of Wendell Berry and Gary Snyder* (Berkeley, CA: Counterpoint, 2014), 28.

92   caravan across the nation Robert Faggen, "Ken Kesey, The Art of Fiction No. 136," *Paris Review* 130 (Spring 1994).

93   beginning in October 1970 Kevin Mercer, "The Farm: A Hippie Commune as a Countercultural Diaspora" (honors thesis, University of Central Florida, 2012), 36.

93   Astral Continental Congress Tim Hodgdon, *Manhood in the Age of Aquarius: Masculinity in Two Countercultural Communities, 1965–83* (New York: Columbia University Press, 2007), 123.

93   hold hands, trip, and smoke Gaskin, *The Caravan*, 164.

93   "anybody else's business" Timothy Miller, *The Hippies and American Values* (Knoxville: University of Tennessee Press, 1991), 30.

93   "THE MONKEYS ARE COMING" Staff, "The Monkeys Are Coming," *Columbia Daily Herald*, May 15, 1971.

93   rise from pastureland Mercer, "The Farm: A Hippie Commune as a Countercultural Diaspora," 39.

94   "your spiritual teacher" Stiriss, *Voluntary Peasants Labor of Love*.

94   mere fraternal organization Michael Lewis, "Kommemorating the Ku Klux Klan," *Sociological Quarterly* 40, no.1 (1999-01-01), 139–58.

94   recognized as a model Bob Smietana, "Tenn. Amish Community's Growth Follows National Trend," *The Tennessean*, October 10, 2012.

95   duty and service David Stoll, "Caravan of the Disenchanted Molds a New, Communal Life," *Michigan Daily*, September 22, 1974.

95   sold their brushes Kevin Kelly, "Why We Left the Farm," *Whole Earth Review* 49 (Winter 1985).

95   sold their tools Elizabeth Prugl, "'Technicolor Amish': History and World View of the Farm, a Communal Society in Tennessee" (master's thesis, Vanderbilt University, 1983), 23.

95   "as any had need" Rupert Fike, *Voices from the Farm: Adventures in Community Living* (Summertown, TN: The Book Publishing Company, 1998), viii.

95   Abortion was forbidden James Robison, "A Million-Dollar, Holes-in-the-Knees Society," *Chicago Tribune Magazine*, October 2, 1977.

95   birth control, until 1978 Louis Kern, "Pronatalism, Midwifery, and Synergistic Marriage: Spiritual Enlightenment and Sexual Ideology on The Farm (Tennessee)," in *Women in Spiritual and Communitarian Societies in the United States*, ed. Louis J. Kern, Wendy Chmiclewski, Marlyn Klee-Hartzell (Syracuse, NY: Syracuse University Press, 1993).

95   "better vibrations than pig stickings" Louise Hagler, *The Farm Vegetarian Cookbook* (Summertown, TN: The Book Publishing Company, 1975), 2.

96   adopted Summertown principles "The Farm in Summertown: A Historical Timeline," *The Tennessean*, July 4, 2014.

96   finance her flight Ethel Simpson, "Crescent Dragonwagon," encyclopediaofarkansas.net.

96 attracting lesbian farmers Thompson, *The Un-Natural State*, 147.

96 "shall be of every person" Crescent Dragonwagon, *The Commune Cookbook* (New York: Simon & Schuster, 1972), 186.

96 drive the new arrivals out Douglas Stevenson, *Out to Change the World: The Evolution of the Farm Community* (Summertown, TN: The Book Publishing Company, 2014).

97 "leg to a tree and try some" Fike, *Voices from the Farm*, 7.

97 Farmies were now landed Michael I. Niman, "Out to Save the World: Life at the Farm," *High Times*, February 1995.

97 boil sorghum Michael I. Niman, *People of the Rainbow: A Nomadic Utopia* (Knoxville: University of Tennessee Press, 1997), 181.

97 north of Summertown Howard H. Quint, "Julius A. Wayland, Pioneer Socialist Propagandist," *Mississippi Valley Historical Review* 35 (March 1949): 591–92.

98 more than thirty homes Bill Carey, "The Ruskin Cooperative Association," *The Tennessee Magazine*, May 2012.

98 "Because they were hungry" Al Gore, "Church Group Swaps Views with Gaskin's," *The Tennessean*, March 13, 1972. (Yes, that Al Gore.)

98 "we think you can" "Farm Report," *The Tennessean*, November 29, 1971.

99 "we ain't been rejected" Stephen Gaskin, *Hey Beatnik!: This Is the Farm Book* (Summertown, TN: The Book Publishing Company, 1974), unpaginated.

99 bricks for a holiness church Ibid.

99 through the gate each year Douglas Stevenson, *The Farm Then and Now: A Model for Sustainable Living* (Gabriola Island, Canada: New Society Publishers, 2014), 141–42.

99 matches and toilet paper Fike, *Voices from the Farm*, 65.

99 passive solar technology Robert Gilman and Diane Gilman, "The Farm, Twenty Years Later: An Interview with Albert Bates," *In Context: A Quarterly of Humane Sustainable Culture* 29 (Summer 1991).

100 build a Kmart Niman, "Out to Save the World: Life at the Farm."

100 solar food dehydrator Mercer, "The Farm: A Hippie Commune as a Countercultural Diaspora," 62.

100 marriage of six Edward B. Fiske, "Marijuana Part of Religion at Commune in Tennessee," *New York Times*, February 17, 1973.

100 dining tent next door Fike, *Voices from the Farm*, 35.

100 oven-fried gluten Hagler, *The Farm Vegetarian Cookbook*, 57.

100 Nuclear Regulatory Commission Prugl, "'Technicolor Amish,'" 60.

100 "cahoots all over the country" Gaskin, *Hey Beatnik!*

101 "take over the government's function" Ibid.

101 turned over to forest rangers Jim Windolf, "Sex, Drugs, and Soybeans," *Vanity Fair*, April 5, 2007.

101 wheat berries and not much else Fike, *Voices from the Farm*, 79.

101 came down with hepatitis Gaskin, *Hey Beatnik!*

101 flutes in the style of Pan Niman, "Out to Save the World: Life at the Farm."

101 Belgian mares and a plow Gilman and Gilman, "The Farm, Twenty Years Later."

101 "we can feed ourselves" Gaskin, *Hey Beatnik!*

102 sweet potatoes and watermelons Ibid.

102 they planted acres Stevenson, *The Farm Then and Now*, 37.

102 midst of a harvest Gilman and Gilman, "The Farm, Twenty Years Later."

102 syrup as well as their books Gaskin, *Hey Beatnik!*

102 **tempeh spore business** Stevenson, *The Farm Then and Now*, 47.

103 **feed hungry people in the decades ahead** William Shurtleff and Akiko Aoyagi, "History of Soybeans and Soyfoods, 1100 B.C. to the 1980s," soyinfocenter.com.

103 **for babies and children** Ibid.

103 **stuff soysage, and toast soyola** Ibid.

103 **Madison Foods by 1918** Ibid.

103 **Treatment Room in Nashville** Ibid.

103 **over a gas burner** Gaskin, *Hey Beatnik!*

103 **extracted soy milk** Ibid.

103 **rendered into tofu** Fike, *Voices from the Farm.*

103 **Ice Bean** Niman, "Out to Save the World: Life at the Farm."

103 **two carob-coated honey wafers** Shurtleff and Aoyagi, "History of Soybeans and Soyfoods."

104 **she prepared souse meat** John L. Puckett, *Foxfire Revisited: A Twenty-Year Experiment in Progressive Education* (Urbana: University of Illinois Press, 1989), 29.

104 **"I sure do"** Eliot Wigginton, *The Foxfire Book* (New York: Doubleday, 1972), 29.

104 **more than two million copies** Puckett, *Foxfire Revisited*, 33.

104 **mill was sold in 1957** Clifford M. Kuhn, *Contesting the New South Order: The 1914–1915 Strike at Atlanta's Fulton Mills* (Chapel Hill: University of North Carolina Press, 2001), 231.

105 **"James Agee and Oscar Lewis"** Puckett, *Foxfire Revisited*, 33.

105 **new farm communes slowed** Warren J. Belasco, *Appetite for Change: How the Counterculture Took on the Food Industry* (Ithaca, NY: Cornell University Press, 1993), 83.

106 **"maximum number of workers"** Twelve Southerners, *I'll Take My Stand: The South and the Agrarian Tradition* (Baton Rouge: Louisiana State University Press, 1930), 13.

Chapter 6: Faster Food

110 **"That's a bunch of shit"** Ira Simmons, "A Mac with the Colonel," in *Junk Food*, ed. Charles Rubin et al. (New York: Dell, 1980), 85–87.

110 **wallpaper paste and sludge** Josh Ozersky, *Colonel Sanders and the American Dream* (Austin: University of Texas Press, 2012), 90.

110 **"With a straw?"** Bill Carey, *Fortunes, Fiddles and Fried Chicken: A Nashville Business History* (Franklin, TN: Hillsboro Press, 2000), 245.

111 **he didn't appear happy** Josh Ozersky, "KFC's Colonel Sanders: He Was Real, Not Just an Icon," *Time*, September 5, 2010.

112 **Colonel's chicken to their menu** Ibid.

112 **"talk to the guests"** Ozersky, *Colonel Sanders and the American Dream*, 35.

112 **tight around their necks** Carey, *Fortunes, Fiddles and Fried Chicken*, 244–45.

112 **McDonald's arches** Ibid.

112 **pop culture phenomenon** Ibid.

112 **franchises in Mexico** William Whitworth, "Kentucky-Fried," *New Yorker*, February 14, 1970.

113 **Burlington, North Carolina** Emily Wallace, "It Was There for Work: Pimento Cheese in the Carolina Piedmont" (master's thesis, University of North Carolina, 2010), 5, 20–29.

113 **adopted in the post–World War II years** Warren J. Belasco, *Appetite for Change: How the Counterculture Took on the Food Industry 1966–1988* (New York: Pantheon, 1990).

114 **drive-in service across the nation** Daniel Vaughn, "The History of the Pig Stands," *Texas Monthly*, February 18, 2015.

114 **restaurants in suburban malls** Darren Grem, "The Marketplace Missions of S. Truett Cathy and Chick-fil-A," in *Sunbelt Rising: The Politics of Place, Space, and Religion*, ed. Michelle Nickerson and Darren Dochuck (Philadelphia: University of Pennsylvania Press, 2011), 295–97.

115 **Hand Squashed Biscuits** Jerry Clower, "My Mama Made Biscuits," *Clower Power* (MCA Records, 1973).

115 **par-baked quick breads** John T. Edge, "But Surely They're Homemade?," *New York Times*, April 14, 2009.

116 **open in smaller markets** Jerry Bledsoe, "The Story of Hardee's," *Our State*, May 27, 2011.

117 **"We like the biscuits at Hardee's better"** John T. Edge, "Our Daily Bread," *Oxford American*, May 2000.

118 **came with a compelling backstory** Amy Smith, "Original History: The Schlotzsky's History Begins with a Really Big Sandwich," *Austin Chronicle*, October 8, 2004.

118 **boats from Central America** Justin A. Nystrom, "Italian New Orleans and the Business of Food in the Immigrant City: There's More to the Muffuletta Than Meets the Eye," in *The Larder: Food Studies Methods from the American South*, ed. John T. Edge, Elizabeth S. D. Engelhardt, and Ted Ownby (Athens: University of Georgia Press, 2013), 128–54.

119 **plumbing supply house** Patricia Sharpe, "New Deli," *Texas Monthly*, February 1997.

119 **salable to the masses as music** "The Life of a Sandwich: Schlotzsky's from Sandwich to Bankruptcy," *Austin Chronicle*, October 8, 2004.

120 **"Nearly made Dow Jones go back to farming"** John T. Edge, "Stand by Your Pan," *Oxford American*, Summer 1998.

120 **relying on welfare** "Al Copeland Dies in Munich, Germany," *Times-Picayune*, March 28, 2008.

120 **"I don't want it"** Douglas Martin, "Al Copeland, a Restaurateur Known for Spice and Speed, Dies at 64," *New York Times*, March 25, 2008.

120 **"I can beat these guys"** David Chandler, "Now That His Chicken Business Is Booming, Al Copeland Wants to Muscle In on Cajun Cuisine," *People*, October 15, 1984.

120 **he couldn't afford one** Martin, "Al Copeland, a Restaurateur Known for Spice and Speed, Dies at 64."

120 **taking spectacular chances** Mary Foster, "Al Copeland, 64; Founder of Popeyes Chicken Chain," *Washington Post*, March 25, 2008.

121 **"tempting as the French Quarter itself"** Advertisement, *Paris News* (Paris, TX), December 10, 1978.

121 **"Spicy fried chicken"** Chandler, "Now That His Chicken Business Is Booming."

121 **"Louisiana's homegrown Liberace"** Martin, "Al Copeland, a Restaurateur Known for Spice and Speed, Dies at 64."

121 **more than $3 million** Whitworth, "Kentucky-Fried."

122 **"all my friends and neighbors"** John Haile, "Chicken Chain Plan Complete," *Nashville Tennessean*, June 18, 1967.

122 **buck-ninety-five price tag** Carey, *Fortunes, Fiddles and Fried Chicken*, 249.

122 **forty were in operation** Ibid.

122 **another fried chicken enterprise** Laurraine Goreau, *Just Mahalia, Baby: The Mahalia Jackson Story* (New York: Pelican, 1975), 485.

122 **"any time we want"** Carey, *Fortunes, Fiddles and Fried Chicken*, 253.

122   **modern culture and commerce** Angela Jill Cooley, *To Live and Dine in Dixie: The Evolution of Urban Food Culture in the Jim Crow South* (Athens: University of Georgia Press), 87–102.

123   **The grand opening was a bonus** Staff, "Mahalia Jackson Starts Fried Chicken Business," *Afro American*, September 10, 1968.

123   **"benefit the entire community"** Ibid.

123   **"Declaration of Negro Economic Independence"** Ibid.

123   **"partnership, not plantationship"** Ibid.

124   **"tell 'em 'bout the dream"** Todd S. Purdum, *An Idea Whose Time Has Come: Two Presidents, Two Parties, and the Battle for the Civil Rights Act of 1964* (New York: Henry Holt, 2014), 110.

124   **work as a cook and washerwoman** Alden Whitman, "Mahalia Jackson, Gospel Singer, and a Civil Rights Symbol, Dies," *New York Times*, January 28, 1972.

124   **"we mean to be a black business"** Humphrey White, "Mahalia Jackson's Chicken Product of Black Capitalism," *Post Tribune*, August 30, 1969.

125   **"Negro ownership of businesses"** Ibid.

125   **dressed with soul sauce** Newspaper unnamed. Vertical file, "Mahalia Jackson" Special Collections, University of Memphis.

126   **"You've got to be in"** R. J. Smith, *The One: The Life and Music of James Brown* (Garden City, NY: Avery, 2012), 225.

126   **"people who want to go into the business"** Ibid.

127   **"uncritical emulation of the North"** John Egerton, *The Americanization of Dixie, the Southernization of America* (New York: Harper's Magazine Press, 1974), 13.

127   **"must be the South still"** Twelve Southerners, *I'll Take My Stand*, 359.

Chapter 7: Carter Country

129   **"SPREAD SOME AROUND TODAY"** Richard Reeves, *Convention* (New York: Harcourt Brace Jovanovich, 1977), 177.

129   **"That's right"** B. Drummond Ayres Jr., "Democratic Unity Reflects Changes in the South," *New York Times*, July 16, 1976.

129   **"I'm proud of you"** Reeves, *Convention*, 177.

130   **"We ain't *trash* no more"** Larry King, "We Ain't Trash No More," *Esquire*, November 1, 1976.

130   **"speckled trout with them"** Roy Blount Jr., *Crackers* (New York: Knopf, 1980), 22.

131   **volunteer in India** Wolfgang Saxon, "Ruth Carter Stapleton Dies; Evangelist and Faith Healer," *New York Times*, September 27, 1983.

131   **runner peanuts shipped their way** Steven Rattner, "Peanuts: From Carver to Carter," *New York Times*, August 24, 1976.

131   **"in about a half hour"** Bernard Weintraub, "Southerners Feeling New Influence in the Capital," *New York Times*, January 19, 1977.

132   **"they're not hermaphrodites"** Ibid.

132   **"than did its predecessor"** Edwin De Leon, "The New South: What It Is Doing and What It Wants," *Putnam's Magazine*, April 1870.

133   **"Howdy folks, what'll it be"** Art Harris, "Atlanta's Aunt Fanny's Cabin a Caricature of the Old South," *Sarasota Herald Tribune*, December 10, 1982.

133 DIXIELAND **blinked beneath** Cortlandt F. Luce Jr., "Johnny Reb's Dixie Land Restaurant," November 1960, VIS 114.33.01, Photographs, Kenan Research Center, Atlanta History Center, Atlanta.

134 **"Good Old Days"** "Mammy's Shanty," Business Files, Kenan Research Center, Atlanta History Center, Atlanta.

134 **there for a meal** Eric Harrison, "Ray's Ill Health Gives Urgency to King Assassination Doubts," *Los Angeles Times,* January 7, 1997.

135 **"bourbon mixed with Coca-Cola"** Roy Reed, "Migration Mixes a New Southern Blend," *New York Times,* February 11, 1976.

135 **He figured right** Bruce J. Schulman, *The Seventies: The Great Shift in American Culture, Society, and Politics* (Cambridge, MA: Da Capo Press, 2002), 37.

135 **his wife, Pat Nixon** James Reston, "How Nixon Took Atlanta," *New York Times,* October 15, 1972.

135 **except for Georgia** Jacob Levenson, "Divining Dixie: Is It Another Country? Or a Place to Stow National Problems? A Yankee Journalist Gets Lost and Found in the South," *Columbia Journalism Review* 42.6 (March–April 2004).

135 **Great Migration** James N. Gregory, *The Southern Diaspora: How the Great Migrations of Black and White Southerners Transformed America* (Chapel Hill: University of North Carolina Press, 2006), 16.

136 **by 40 percent** Schulman, *The Seventies,* 109.

136 **"new roads and new factories"** Lerone Bennett Jr., "Old Illusions and New Souths: Second Reconstruction Gives New Meaning to the Failures and Promises of the Past," *Ebony,* August 1971.

136 **Confederate dead of Clarke County** Carl Arrington, Chet Flippo, and Eric Levin, "Is Rock Dead?," *People,* January 17, 1983.

137 **"since the interstate was built"** Jane Stern and Michael Stern, *Two for the Road: Our Love Affair with American Food* (New York: Houghton Mifflin, 2006), 9–11.

137 **ham, biscuits, and Coca-Cola** Marian Burros, "Real American Food on the Menu," *Springfield Union,* March 22, 1987.

138 **"where it is served"** Marian Burros, "Couple Hit the Road to Capture the Flavor of the Country," *Greensboro News & Record,* April 1, 1987.

138 **"retarded once in a while"** Bryan Miller, "Momma's Food Coming Around for a Second Helping," *State Journal-Register,* October 24, 1984.

138 **against a garbage mound** Stern and Stern, *Two for the Road,* 134.

139 **"fueled up to California and back"** Jane Stern and Michael Stern, *Roadfood and Goodfood* (New York: Knopf, 1986), viii.

139 **"what to eat when we got there"** Ibid.

139 **"have been eating for 200 years"** Janet Beighle French, "As American as . . . Apple Pie? Truffle Pizza? Pros Are Split," *Plain Dealer,* January 14, 1987.

139 **their discoveries** Correspondence, box 4, folder 9, John Egerton Collection, Archives and Special Collections, J. D. Williams Library, University of Mississippi, Oxford, MS.

140 **"two aldermen on the city council"** Anne Taubeneck, "Third Helpings," *Chicago Sun-Times,* May 25, 1983.

140 **Arthur Bryant's** Calvin Trillin, "No! One of the World's Foremost Authorities on Ribs, Cheeseburgers, French Fries and Frosty Malts Takes a Gourmet Tour of Kansas City," *Playboy,* April 1972.

141 **"take advantage of the percentages"** Calvin Trillin, *American Fried* (New York: Vintage Books, 2009), 113.

141 **"where the imagines comes in"** Justin Wilson, foreword to *The Justin Wilson Cookbook* (Denham Springs, LA: Justin Wilson, Inc., 1965), unpaginated.

141 **"like eggnog at Chris'mus' time"** Justin Wilson, *Justin Wilson Looking Back: A Cajun Cookbook* (Gretna, LA: Pelican, 1997), 197.

142 **Cajun doggerel** Shane K. Bernard, *The Cajuns: Americanization of a People* (Jackson: University Press of Mississippi, 2004), 126.

142 **language and culture in positive ways** Ibid.

142 **"gravy on them prunes"** Wilson, foreword to *The Justin Wilson Cookbook*.

143 **his home number** Tom Sancton, *Song for My Fathers* (New York: Other Press, 2010), 164–66.

143 **slumming style of the Sterns** Stella Pitts, "Buster Holmes: Returnin' the Favor," *Times-Picayune*, April 13, 1979.

143 **red beans burbled** Ibid.

144 **"who doesn't speak with an accent"** Charles Reagan Wilson, "Carter Era," in Charles Reagan Wilson, ed., *The New Encyclopedia of Southern Culture: Volume 4: Myth, Manners, and Memory* (Chapel Hill: University of North Carolina Press, 2006), 203.

Chapter 8: Black Pastorals

147 **for $950** Edna Lewis, *The Taste of Country Cooking* (New York: Knopf, 1976), xix.

147 **found a century before** Francis Lam, "Edna Lewis and the Black Roots of American Cooking," *New York Times Magazine*, October 28, 2015.

147 **classroom in his own house** Neely Barnwell Dykshorn, "Edna of Freetown," *Virginia Living*, October 2006.

147 **tended cattle and pigs** Molly O'Neill, "'To Eat a Church Supper Is to Want to Cry 'Amen,'" *New York Times*, August 15, 1990. (O'Neill's reporting was the source for much of this opening scene.)

149 **fried chicken, coffee, and fried pies** Psyche Williams-Forson, *Building Houses Out of Chicken Legs* (Chapel Hill: University of North Carolina Press, 2006), 32.

149 **"built houses out of chicken legs"** Ibid.

149 **ideal for frying** Lam, "Edna Lewis and the Black Roots of American Cooking."

150 **"we would pick it too"** John T. Edge, *A Gracious Plenty* (New York: G. P. Putnam's Sons, 1999), 70.

150 **"whole Southern meal"** Ibid.

151 **hauled from South Carolina** Barbara Costikyan, "Hey Good Cooking," *New York*, March 2, 1987.

151 **African queen** Michael Twitty, "Edna Lewis," in *Icons of American Cooking*, ed. Elizabeth Demers and Victor Geraci (Santa Barbara, CA: ABC-CLIO, 2011), 159.

151 **grandmother of everyone's dreams** Molly O'Neill, "Holiday Havens," *New York Times*, December 7, 1990.

151 **"sounds become faint and weak"** Edna Lewis, *In Pursuit of Flavor* (New York: Knopf, 1988), 289.

151 **"whoever was sick"** Lam, "Edna Lewis and the Black Roots of American Cooking."

151 **mother of purity** Paul Levy, "Edna Lewis," *Independent*, April 1, 2009.

151 **"ritual of the table"** Alice Waters, foreword, in Edna Lewis, *The Taste of Country Cooking 30th Anniversary Edition* (New York: Knopf, 2006), xiii.

152 **cook at the Brazilian embassy** Twitty, "Edna Lewis," 158–59.

152 **window dresser** Ibid.

152 **Marilyn Monroe** Richard Sax, *Classic Home Desserts: A Treasury of Heirloom and Contemporary Recipes* (New York: Houghton Mifflin Harcourt, 2010), 168–69.

152 **reelection of Franklin D. Roosevelt** Christiane Lauterbach, "The Odd Couple of Southern Cooking," *Atlanta* 41 (November 2001).

152 **agitating for equality** Twitty, "Edna Lewis," 159.

153 **cooking for a white family** Marian Burros, "An Innovator in Café Décor and in Food," *New York Times*, March 10, 1982.

153 **for fashion shoots** Ibid.

153 **"good flavors of the past"** Eric Asimov and Kim Severson, "Edna Lewis, 89, Dies; Wrote Cookbooks That Revived Refined Southern Cuisine," *New York Times*, February 14, 2006.

153 **"how we can go wrong"** Burros, "An Innovator in Café Décor and in Food."

153 **"fruits of their labors"** Lewis, introduction to *The Taste of Country Cooking 30th Anniversary Edition*, xxi.

153 **"food is really great"** Neely Barnwell Dykshorn, "Edna of Freetown," *Virginia Living*, October 2006.

153 **Lewis did not serve** Twitty, "Edna Lewis," 161.

154 **seed in a wind** Clementine Paddleford, "New Discovery in Restaurants," *New York Herald Tribune*, March 24, 1951.

154 **which she found limiting** Denise Gee, "The Gospel of Great Southern Food," *Southern Living*, June 1996.

154 **"Food is so good out here"** Phil Audibert, *In the Season: The Edna Lewis Story*, DVD (Audibert Photo, 1984).

154 **with her husband in New Jersey** Mary Rourke, "Edna Lewis, 89; Chef Drew on Family's History in Reviving Southern Cuisine," *Los Angeles Times*, February 14, 2006.

154 **foods of her youth** Carol Haddix, "Edna Lewis Southern Star Sparkles with Kitchen Simplicity," *Chicago Tribune*, April 23, 1987.

155 **first black undertaker in the state** Anna Stewart, "The Dardens Also Researched Their Past—and Got Tastier Profits Than Alex Haley," *People*, April 23, 1973.

155 **to research their book** Bernadine Morris, "Cooking Adds Some Spice to Her Life as Model," *New York Times*, July 4, 1973.

155 **in family lunch pails** Stewart, "The Dardens Also Researched Their Past."

155 **her tipsy cake recipe** Ibid.

155 **across the region** Ibid.

155 **"associated with all foods"** Vertamae Grosvenor, *Vibration Cooking: or, The Travel Notes of a Geechee Girl* (New York: Doubleday, 1970), xv.

156 **"wasn't anything but field food"** Nancy Finch, "'A Taste of Southern Cooking' Recipes Shared: Cooking Expert Is a Virginian," *Richmond Times Dispatch*, August 31, 1981.

156 **"something good to eat"** Robin Teater, "From Humble Southern Cook to the Rage of New York," *State Journal-Register*, July 6, 1983.

156 **"ghosts of our past"** Judith Jones, *The Tenth Muse: My Life in Food* (New York: Knopf, 2007), 92.

156 **Jones edited and Knopf published** Ibid.

156 **"perhaps a colt"** Lewis, *The Taste of Country Cooking 30th Anniversary Edition*, 2–3.

157 *Key Lime Pie* Sara Franklin, "Judith and Edna," *Gravy* 50 (December 2013).

157 **"on the railroads"** Nora Kerr, "When Chefs Celebrate; Salute to a Southern Master Chef," *New York Times*, November 1, 1992.

158 **benne seed biscuits** Ibid.

158 **"makes us who we are"** Edna Lewis, "What Is Southern," *Gourmet*, January 2008.

158 **stewed butter beans** Don O'Briant, "Harry's Honing a Taste for Dixie," *Atlanta Journal-Constitution*, September 21, 1993.

158 **Revival and Preservation of Southern Food** Gee, "The Gospel of Great Southern Food."

158 **together in suburban Atlanta** Carol Anderson, "Southern Cooking," *Free Lance–Star*, September 8, 1993.

158 **"salad with cilantro and snow peas"** Kerr, "When Chefs Celebrate."

159 **cooking seasonally, she said** Kate Sekules, "A Southern Thanksgiving," *Food & Wine*, November 1998.

Chapter 9: Kingmaker and Kings

163 **Gardiner's Bay** James Villas, *Between Bites* (Hoboken, NJ: Wiley, 2002), 151.

164 **"children and dogs"** Jane Snider, "Willie Morris: I Am Essentially a Small-Town Boy," *LI Interviewer*, July 2, 1978.

164 **high school football triumphs** Georgeanna Milam Chapman, "Craig Claiborne: A Southern-Made Man" (master's thesis, University of Mississippi, 2008), 13.

164 **declined to attend the funeral** Thomas McNamee, *The Man Who Changed the Way We Eat* (New York: Free Press, 2012), 149.

164 **"outside Sunflower County"** Chapman, "Craig Claiborne: A Southern-Made Man," 13.

164 **catfish ponds** Craig Claiborne, "Catfish, Long a Southern Delicacy, Branches Out," *New York Times*, November 11, 1981.

165 **hushpuppies and tartar sauce** Ibid.

165 **"next to your grandmother and grandfather"** Scott P. Anderson, "Craig Claiborne: An Elegant Epicure Talks About His Recipe for Success," *The Advocate*, January 6, 1983.

165 **in nearby Indianola** Chapman, "Craig Claiborne: A Southern-Made Man," 16.

166 **responsibility for the family finances** Craig Claiborne, *A Feast Made for Laughter* (New York: Doubleday, 1982), 18.

166 **"Kathleen's food was so good"** Beulah Karney, "The Best Cook in Town," *Liberty Magazine*, May 1948.

166 **at their skirt hems** Claiborne, *A Feast Made for Laughter*, 29.

166 **"snow-white chenille"** Ibid.

166 **"would be outstanding"** Ibid, 31.

166 **to steam couscous** Ibid, 65.

166 **banquet service** Ibid, 94–101.

167 **ascent to the *Times*** McNamee, *The Man Who Changed the Way We Eat*, 41.

167 **amplifying his drawl** Ibid., 52–58.

167 **pledged KA fraternity** Ibid.

167 **rice noodle soup** Craig Claiborne, "In Saigon, Delectable Food amid the War," *New York Times*, December 9, 1974.

167 **"politicians in Washington"** Chapman, "Craig Claiborne: A Southern-Made Man," 71.

168 **"French to be food"** David Newton, "Claiborne Stalked Revolution in Cooking," *Greensboro News & Record*, March 28–29, 1984.

168 **black-eyed peas vinaigrette** Craig Claiborne, "A Culinary Star Rises in the Lone Star State," *New York Times*, August 6, 1986.

168 **Marjorie Kinnan Rawlings** Craig Claiborne, "Kitchen Library Return of a Southern Classic," *New York Times*, May 21, 1980.

168 **"I grew up in one"** Craig Claiborne, "Eating High on the Hog in True Savannah Style," *New York Times*, April 9, 1980.

168 **"bastardized French"** Craig Claiborne, *Craig Claiborne's Southern Cooking*, 20th anniversary edition (Athens: University of Georgia Press, 2007), xxiv.

168 **Tex-Mex, and barbecue** Newton, "Claiborne Stalked Revolution in Cooking."

169 **"I'll lend it to you"** Bryan Miller, "Craig Claiborne, 79, Times Food Editor and Critic, Is Dead," *New York Times*, January 24, 2000.

169 **mouth of Edna Lewis** Paul Prudhomme, *Chef Paul Prudhomme's Louisiana Kitchen* (New York: William Morrow, 1984), 14–15.

169 **"completely different"** Ibid.

170 **Gulf of Mexico redfish stock** Rick Bragg, "New Orleans Is Singing the Redfish Blues," *New York Times*, May 16, 2001.

170 **"they sulk like children"** Craig Claiborne, "French Chef, New Orleans Style," *New York Times*, April 22, 1981.

170 **"motorboat pilot"** Peggy Mann, "Cajun Country," *Travel*, October 1957.

170 **clenched around a red crawfish** Shane K. Bernard, *The Cajuns: Americanization of a People* (Jackson: University of Mississippi Press, 2003), 86.

170 **"celebration of unshaven masculinity"** Joan Weintraub, "Milwaukee Firewater," *Milwaukee Journal*, December 14, 1988.

170 **founded in 1880** Brett Anderson, "Paul Prudhomme: An Oral History Chronicles His Role in Revolutionizing New Orleans Cuisine," *Times-Picayune*, June 12, 2005.

171 **harvest spring greens** Paul Prudhomme, Oral History Interview, southernfoodways.org, 2011.

171 **crabmeat and corn bisque** Tom Fitzmorris, *Hungry Town: A Culinary History of New Orleans* (New York: Stewart, Tabori & Chang, 2010), 46.

171 **Opelousas felt comfortable** Anderson, "Paul Prudhomme: An Oral History Chronicles His Role."

171 **sold the drinks as Cajun martinis** Fitzmorris, *Hungry Town*, 48.

171 **deep-fried crawfish tails** William Grimes, "Paul Prudhomme, Chef Who Put Cajun Cooking on National Stage, Dies at 75," *New York Times*, October 8, 2015.

172 **that Prudhomme dyed green** Anderson, "Paul Prudhomme: An Oral History."

172 **their cabins collapsed** Though it was referred to often in press reports as crème anglaise, Nathalie Dupree assured me that Prudhomme said it was Breyer's ice cream.

172 **"Pavarotti of American chefs"** Benjamin Davison, "When We Blackened Everything: Paul Prudhomme, the Cajun Food Fad, and the Quest for Authenticity, 1979–1989" (paper presented at Southern Foodways Alliance Graduate Student Symposium, September 11, 2015).

172 **"Guru of Gumbo"** Peggy Brawley, "Chef Paul Prudhomme, the Guru of Gumbo, Puts the Flames Under a New Fad for Cajun Cookin'," *People*, April 29, 1985.

172 **"let-the-good-times-roll cooking"** Molly O'Neill, "Jambalaya Passion Feeds Lengthy Lines on Broadway," *New York Times*, August 17, 1989.

172 **"whops up on something else"** Brawley, "Chef Paul Prudhomme, the Guru of Gumbo."

172 **"genius of massive girth, Paul Prudhomme"** Craig Claiborne and Pierre Franey, "Regional Cooking; Southern Cuisines," *New York Times*, May 6, 1984.

172 **"born in the United States"** Craig Claiborne, "French Chef, New Orleans Style," *New York Times*, April 22, 1981.

173 **chicken feed, cornmeal, and grits** Ibid.

173 **chicken-sausage gumbo** Ibid.

173 **redfish for the masses** Craig Claiborne, "All-American Menus for the Economic Summit," *New York Times*, May 18, 1983.

173 **shuttered nightclub** Pablo Lucchesi, "Celebrity Chef Paul Prudhomme Dies; Popularized Cajun Cooking," *San Francisco Chronicle*, October 8, 2015.

173 **too scarce and expensive** Marian Burros, "New Orleans Chef Takes On New York," *New York Times*, July 24, 1985.

173 **"under control"** Paul Prudhomme, *Chef Paul Prudhomme's Louisiana Kitchen* (New York: William Morrow, 1984), 28–29.

174 **"gut food"** Brawley, "Chef Paul Prudhomme, the Guru of Gumbo."

174 **Cajun Louisiana Kitchen** Hugh Mulligan, "Cajun Culture, Cuisine: The World Invades the Bayous," *Los Angeles Times*, April 16, 1989.

174 **seasoning mix into the dough** Davison, "When We Blackened Everything."

174 **pitmasters including Wayne Monk** Sara Engram, "Some South for Your Mouth: How Corn Bread Cuisine Became Haute," *Duke Magazine*, March 31, 2005.

175 **young chef cooked** Craig Claiborne, "For a Carolina Chef, Helpings of History," *New York Times*, July 10, 1985.

175 **"Crook's Corner in Chapel Hill"** Craig Claiborne, "Sophistication Spices Southern Food," *New York Times*, June 26, 1985.

175 **"monuments and architecture"** Claiborne, "For a Carolina Chef, Helpings of History."

175 **"Argenteuil asparagus"** William F. Neal, *Bill Neal's Southern Cooking* (Chapel Hill: University of North Carolina Press, 1985), 2.

175 **his wife, Moreton Neal** Claiborne, "For a Carolina Chef, Helpings of History."

176 **trout almandine at Galatoire's** Kate Medley and Jesse Paddock, "They Came for Shrimp and Grits," southernfoodways.org, 2015.

176 **line cook** Moreton Neal, *Remembering Bill Neal: Favorite Recipes from a Life in Cooking* (Chapel Hill: University of North Carolina Press, 2014), 75.

176 **"customs, and culture were foreign"** Neal, *Bill Neal's Southern Cooking*, 2.

176 **dishwashing job** R. W. Apple Jr., "Bliss from the South: A Chef's Grand Legacy," *New York Times*, July 23, 2003.

176 **mix drinks** Medley and Paddock, interview of Gene Hamer for *They Came for Shrimp and Grits*, collection of author.

176 **definition of the region** Rhonda Hubbard, "Local Chef a Master at Southern Cooking," *Daily Tar Heel*, April 15, 1986.

176 **"you get Southern cooking"** Ibid.

177 **"Battery on this day alone"** Nancy Harmon Jenkins, "For Liberty's 100th, Fireworks from 12 Top Chefs," *New York Times*, June 25, 1986.

177 **gestating Southern bohemia** Brett Anderson, "Bill Smith Turns Up the Volume," *Gravy* podcast, April 24, 2015.

177 **South Carolina Historical Society** Pat Caudill, "Southern Cooking Has Risen Again," *Fayetteville Observer*, February 5, 1986.

177 **bobbing in the broth** Claiborne, "For a Carolina Chef, Helpings of History."

178 **fancy meat loaf** Patricia Sharpe, "And They Said, 'Let There Be Cilantro,'" *Texas Monthly*, August 2014.

178 **"I've accomplished a great deal"** Claiborne, "A Culinary Star Rises in the Lone Star State."

178 **"restaurateurs and trend-setters"** Mimi Sheraton, "Summer's Bounty Inspires Young Chefs," *Time*, August 25, 1985, 58.

179 **ten thousand plates each year** Neal, *Bill Neal's Southern Cooking*, 89.

179 **"we would all eat them"** John T. Edge, "The Ballad of Bill Neal," *Food Arts*, June 2002.

179 **writhing carcasses** Marilyn Spencer, "History on a Plate," *News and Observer*, May 9, 1990.

179 **voice of a girl** Bland Simpson, "Bill Neal Had a Special Way with People, Food, and the South," *Greensboro News & Record*, December 10, 1991.

179 **"active Southern heritage"** Ibid.

Chapter 10: Generation Grits

183 **"what we are and carry on"** Paul Prudhomme, "Cajun Cooking: An Authentic American Cuisine" (First Symposium on American Cuisine, Louisville, KY, March 7–9, 1982), tape 7, Janice Bluestein Longone Culinary Archive, Special Collections Library, University of Michigan, Ann Arbor.

184 **foie gras, truffles, and walnut oil** Leslie Brenner, *American Appetite: The Coming of Age of a Cuisine* (New York: Avon Books, 1999), 202.

184 **"than our own"** Marian Burros, "American Cuisine: Purists Versus Innovators," *New York Times*, April 20, 1983.

184 **whitefish, perch, and trout** Lawrence Forgione, "Creating a Restaurant for the American Menu" (First Symposium on American Cuisine, Hyatt Regency Hotel, Louisville, KY, March 7–9, 1982), tape 2, Janice Bluestein Longone Culinary Archive, Special Collections Library, University of Michigan, Ann Arbor.

184 **chipotle mayo, followed** Sharpe, "And They Said 'Let There Be Cilantro.'"

185 **"like they test cuisines"** "The Year of the Yuppie," Special Report, *Newsweek*, December 31, 1984.

185 **"most convenient, efficient way"** Raymond Sokolov, *Fading Feast: A Compendium of Disappearing American Regional Foods* (New York: Farrar, Straus and Giroux, 1981), 8.

185 **known as boudin rouge** Ibid.

185 **"History has taken its inexorable toll"** Ibid.

186 **"Our cuisine"** Sharpe, "And They Said 'Let There Be Cilantro.'"

186 **native crop pecans** Jane Black, "The Chef Who Makes Perfect Happen," *Washington Post*, April 9, 2008.

186 **Vidalia onion jam** Louis Osteen Papers, Southern Food and Beverage Museum, New Orleans, LA.

186 **proliferated in that port city** Elizabeth Terry and Alexis Terry, *Savannah Seasons: Food and Stories from Elizabeth on 37th* (New York: Doubleday, 1996), xiv.

186 **defend it from bastardization** Sidney Mintz, *Tasting Food, Tasting Freedom: Excursions into Eating, Culture, and the Past* (Boston: Beacon Press, 1996).

187 **"IT'S THE ONLY ONE ALIVE"** Andrew P. Haley, *Turning the Tables: Restaurants and the Rise of the Middle Class 1880–1920* (Chapel Hill: University of North Carolina Press, 2011), 206–7.

187 fried oysters, stewed oysters, and frogs Mark Twain, *The Writings of Mark Twain: A Tramp Abroad*, Vol. 2 (New York: P. F. Collier & Son, 1907), 239–40.

187 "snowy white as on the plantation" Mary E. Parmelee, "Practical Housekeeping: February," *Table Talk*, February 1905.

188 "M. F. K. Fisher's mouth water" Brenner, *American Appetite*, 131.

188 "Californian tonight" Joyce Goldstein, *Inside the California Food Revolution* (Berkeley: University of California Press, 2014), 3.

188 to prove him wrong Mimi Sheraton, "Eat American! Summer's Bounty Inspires Young Chefs," *Time*, August 26, 1985.

189 They didn't know how to tip John T. Edge, "Going Deeper with Red Dog," *Oxford American*, March 2015.

189 "first Alabama strawberries" Frank Stitt, *Frank Stitt's Southern Table* (New York: Artisan, 2004), 100.

189 pall over the region James W. Loewen, *Sundown Towns: A Hidden Dimension of American Racism* (New York: Touchstone, 2005), 244.

190 "COOKED IN DE PIT" Herman Moore, *Eating Out in Alabama* (Birmingham, AL: Title Publishers, 1985), 68–69.

190 "going down South" Allan Gilbert Jr., "Satch Heads South Via Alaska," *Northwest Arkansas Times*, September 1, 1965.

191 "the way we think of Creole cooking" Gene Bourg, "Emeril's: Long May It Live," *Times-Picayune*, August 10, 1990.

192 hot sauces from Vietnam Susan Spicer and Paula Disbrowe, *Crescent City Cooking: Unforgettable Recipes from Susan Spicer's New Orleans* (New York: Knopf, 2009), 166–67.

193 "but it's now polenta" Rhonda Graham and Pamela Brown, "Black Chefs Rise to the Top," *Aberdeen Daily News*, October 7, 1990.

193 but closed quickly Staff, "Black Atlanta Church Buys $100,000 Restaurant," *Jet*, December 14, 1972.

193 Georgia caviar John Kessler, "Where Are All the Black Chefs?," *Oxford American*, Spring 2010.

194 white rocking chairs Jim Auchmutey, "The New South: 96 Southerners to Watch," special insert, *Atlanta Journal-Constitution*, March 24, 1996.

194 "spiritual general" of the new Charleston chefs Bryan Miller, "Choice Tables: A Modern Southern Cuisine in Charleston," *New York Times*, December 17, 1995.

194 "praline candy" John Mariani, "Goin' South for Sup," *Esquire*, May 2001.

195 "never went down so easily" Jim Auchmutey, "Louis Osteen: Coming Home to Southern Cooking," Olympic section, *Atlanta Journal-Constitution*, March 24, 1996.

195 "Southern seaport" Linda Ciampa, "Low-country Cooking Gets High Praise in Charleston," CNN, July 15, 1996.

196 Cajun tasso Eve Ziebart, "Southern Swank: Shrimp 'n' Grits," *Washington Post*, October 16, 1998.

196 Creole inspired instead of Cajun Pam Belluck, "Can Chicago Rewrite the Soul Food Gospel?," *New York Times*, July 21, 1999.

196 Montreal Steak seasoning Staff, "Veal Stock Is Secret to Flavorful Grits-and-Shrimp Dish," *Louisville Courier-Journal*, September 7, 1999.

196 "cultural strip mining" Lou Seibert Pappas, *New American Chefs and Their Recipes* (San Francisco: 101 Productions, 1984), 123.

196 made less than $20,000 Cobb, *The South and America Since World War II*, 18.

Chapter 11: Cooking School

200 **carried forward old ones** Dudley Clendinen, "Southern Cooks Look Back to Roots and Adapt Cuisine," *New York Times*, January 8, 1986.

200 **restaurant in Majorca, Spain** Ann Byrne Phillips, "Nathalie!," *Atlanta Constitution*, August 26, 1982.

200 **hometown of her second husband** Nathalie Dupree Oral History Interview, interviewed by Blake Swihart, International Association of Culinary Professionals, June 10, 2005, Schlesinger Library, Harvard University, Cambridge, MA.

200 **window of her Vega** Author interview of Nathalie Dupree, Charleston, SC, January 2016.

201 **sweetbreads with brown butter** Lisa Hughes, "What's a French Restaurant Like You Doing in Covington?," *Covington News*, May 16, 1974.

201 **rear of an antiques store** Dupree Oral History Interview, International Association of Culinary Professionals.

201 **and heirloom silverware** Author interview of Nathalie Dupree, January 2016.

201 **found Rich's Cooking School** Judy Powers, "Cooking and Dining Represent Intimacy, Says Nathalie Dupree," *Atlanta Gazette*, November 1978.

202 **drip that never came** Virginia Willis, "What a Dame!," *Charleston Magazine*, December 2011.

202 *Gone with the Wind* Tony Cooper, "Mrs. Talmadge Opens Home, Caters for 'Magnolia Suppers,'" *Atlanta Journal-Constitution*, November 2, 1979.

202 **Assley Wilkes** Margalit Fox, "Betty Talmadge, Ex-Wife of Georgia Senator, Dies at 81," *New York Times*, May 12, 2005.

202 **dish she learned in London** Phillips, "Nathalie!"

202 **"smelled like baby's diapers"** Ibid.

202 **Dupree hosted her** Dupree Oral History Interview, International Association of Culinary Professionals.

203 **"good old Southern food"** Anne Byrne, "Feed Julia Child Southern Style When She Comes Back, Ya Heah?," *Atlanta Constitution*, October 23, 1978.

203 **possibilities resident in Southern food** Marilyn Spencer, "In Kitchen, South Shall Rise Again," *Raleigh News and Observer*, October 9, 1986.

203 **"technique worth learning"** Clendinen, "Southern Cooks Look Back to Roots and Adapt Cuisine."

203 **"slaves who were our cooks"** Nathalie Dupree, *New Southern Cooking* (New York: Knopf, 1986), xiv.

204 **"get some of what you want"** Undated typewritten notes, Nathalie Dupree Papers, pending institutional deposit.

204 *Nathalie Dupree* "Ga. TV Will Feature Food Expert Dupree," *Statesboro Georgia Herald*, December 24, 1985.

204 **skittered across the set** Spencer, "In Kitchen, South Shall Rise Again."

204 *Today* **show cooking segment** Michael Neil, "Southern Comfort," *People*, September 28, 1998.

205 **"you can cut down on the pepper"** Louise Whiting, "Grandma's Way," *Albany Herald*, January 12, 1986.

205 **medical intrusions** Michelle Cohen Marill, "Nathalie's World," *Atlanta Magazine*, December 1991.

205 **opposition to her stance** Marill, "Nathalie's World."

206 **Cuisinart label** Judy Rose Sherrod, "Gourmet Party: Cordon Bleu Graduate Gives Demonstration," *Atlanta Journal*, August 6, 1975.

206 **black-eyed peas** Dupree Oral History Interview, International Association of Culinary Professionals.

206 *The Frugal Gourmet* Doug Cress, "The Sweet Taste of Success," *Atlanta Journal-Constitution*, May 25, 1994.

206 **"I'm too regional"** Ibid.

206 **"at her corner store"** Sarah Dunbar, "Nathalie Dupree," *Buckhead Atlanta*, October 12, 1979.

206 **"underwear in a suitcase"** Norman Arey and Martha Woodham, "Cook Travels 'Lite' on Trip to TV Show," *Atlanta Journal-Constitution*, January 2, 1991.

207 **it was unwise to sully** Ronni Lundy, "The Tao of Cornbread," in *Savory Memories*, ed. Linda Elisabeth Beattie (Lexington: University Press of Kentucky, 1998), 63–69.

207 **"cruel and flat-out wrong"** Ellen Sweets, "The Creole Connection," *Daily Advocate*, May 31, 2000.

207 **somewhere in France** Sandra M. Gilbert, *The Culinary Imagination: From Myth to Modernity* (New York: Norton, 2014), 145.

208 **she baked him a stack cake** Dylan Mullins, "Interview with Ronni Lundy," *Appalachian Heritage Blog*, April 8, 2015.

209 **"good Southern living ideas and qualities"** James C. Cobb, *Away Down South: A History of Southern Identity* (New York: Oxford University Press, 2005), 223.

209 **"traffic jams, noise, and tension"** Tracy Lauder, "The Southern Living Solution: How the Progressive Farmer Launched a Magazine and a Legacy," *Alabama Review*, July 2007.

210 **measured by advertising revenue** Ibid.

210 **"one front yard at a time"** Ibid.

210 **New South in new terms** Ibid.

210 **"mental and physical assets"** James Cobb, "'We Ain't White Trash No More': Southern Whites and the Reconstruction of Southern Identity," in *The Southern State of Mind*, ed. Jan Nordby Gretlund (Columbia: University of South Carolina Press, 1999), 135.

211 **"an unhappy congestion of ideas"** "Principles and Scope of the Magazine," *Uncle Remus's Magazine*, June 1907, Kenan Research Center, Atlanta History Center, Atlanta.

Chapter 12: Artisanal Pantry

215 **"the aromas fluoresce"** Author interview with Glenn Roberts, Columbia, SC, August 1999.

216 **almost-lost heirloom corn** Kay Rentschler, "A Grits Revival with the Flavor of the Old South," *New York Times*, March 24, 2004.

216 **milling in earnest** Ibid.

216 **before he ground it** Ibid.

217 **"buttered kitty litter"** Glenn Roberts, "Life Story: Gone Grits Crazy," presented at 2001 Southern Foodways Symposium, collection of the author.

219 **Italian sausage** Elizabeth Terry, *Savannah Seasons: Food and Stories from Elizabeth on 37th* (New York: Doubleday, 1996), 79.

220 **yellow grits for his soufflé** Frank Stitt, *Frank Stitt's Southern Table* (New York: Artisan, 2004), 22.

220 Jamison Farm of Pennsylvania Ibid.

220 fabled moonshiner Campbell Robertson, "Yesterday's Moonshiner, Today's Micro-distiller," *New York Times*, February 20, 2012.

221 "their situation and their character" William Goodell Frost, "Our Contemporary Ancestors in the Mountain South," *Atlantic Monthly*, March 1899.

222 whiskey sales doubled Clay Risen, "How Dreams and Money Didn't Mix at a Texas Distillery," *New York Times*, December 27, 2014.

223 "Drink of the Devil" John Raby, "Hatfields, McCoys Make Moonshine Legally," *Louisville Courier-Journal*, January 31, 2015.

223 made white whiskey or moonshine Estimates courtesy of Bill Owens, American Distilling Institute.

224 "POPCORN SAID FUCK YOU" Mark Essig, "[Pop]Corn from a Jar," *Gravy* 56 (Summer 2015).

224 flipping the nation the bird Mark Spivak, *Moonshine Nation: The Art of Creating Cornbread in a Bottle* (Guilford, CT: Lyons Press, 2014), 210.

224 Sutton was arrested Author conversation with Sean Brock, Palmetto Bluff, SC, November 23, 2013.

225 "that's why we went to the moonshine" Kate Springer, "Moon Pie Moonshine Makes for a Tasty and Winning Combination," *WDRB Louisville News*, April 12, 2015.

225 Tidewater region of Virginia Author interview with Sam Edwards, June 25, 2013.

226 salt-cured hams to England Ibid.

226 suspended from pinewood racks Logan Ward, "New Frontier of Country Hams," *Garden & Gun*, December 2010.

227 "purebred Tennessee hillbilly" John T. Edge, "His Ham Stands Alone," *Gourmet*, October 2006.

228 "Just long hours and patience" Ibid.

228 "for the rest of your life" David Chang and Peter Meehan, *Momofuku* (New York: Clarkson Potter, 2009), 79.

229 "the bum knows it and you know it" Andy Warhol, *The Philosophy of Andy Warhol* (New York: Harcourt Brace Jovanovich, 1975), 100–101.

229 called those absolutes into question Mark Pendergrast, *For God, Country, and Coca-Cola* (New York: Basic Books, 2000), 337, 504.

230 early adopters Associated Press, "A Taste of Nostalgia," *Los Angeles Times*, November 15, 2004.

232 hours instead of years Cass Herrington, "South Carolina Distiller Promises to Make Kentucky Liquor Quicker," *The Salt*, NPR, May 17, 2015.

Chapter 13: Restaurant Renaissance

235 "It was awful" Burkhard Bilger, "True Grits," *New Yorker*, October 21, 2011.

235 The stuff was, he said, garbage John Warner, "Education Is Not Like Eating at the Olive Garden," *Inside Higher Education*, July 20, 2014.

236 "tasted like nothing" Ibid.

237 "rice to Carolina and grew it" Sean Brock, *Heritage* (New York: Artisan, 2014), 15.

238 "I want to fix that" John T. Edge, "Southern to the Bone," *Garden & Gun*, October 2010.

238 demons that drove George Wallace Patterson Hood, "The South's Heritage Is So Much More Than a Flag," *New York Times*, July 9, 2015.

239 "Glorification of American Cookery" Andrew P. Haley, *Turning the Tables: The Aris-*

tocratic Restaurant and the Rise of the American Middle Class, 1880–1920 (Chapel Hill: University of North Carolina Press, 2011), 209.

239 **"why we know about it"** Paul Prudhomme, "Cajun Cooking: An Authentic American Cuisine," First Symposium on American Cuisine, Louisville, KY, March 7–9, 1982, tape 7, Janice Bluestein Longone Culinary Archive, Special Collections Library, University of Michigan, Ann Arbor.

240 **gâteau glacé au rhum** Hanna Raskin, "Interracial Feast Returns 19th-Century Chef Nat Fuller's Legacy to Prominence," *Charleston Post and Courier*, April 22, 2015.

240 **mid-twentieth-century gentry** Theresa Taylor, "The Late Lucille Grant Knew How to Keep It Fresh and Delicious," *Charleston Post and Courier*, March 4, 2012.

240 **from their book, *Charleston Receipts*** Beth Ann Crier, "A Way with Weird: Ten Speed Press Founder Phil Wood Has Made a Small Fortune Publishing Books No One Could Imagine in Print," *Los Angeles Times*, December 8, 1988.

240 **within sight of Fort Sumter** Jack Hitt, "Southern Fried Baked Alaska," *Gravy* podcast, December 17, 2015.

241 **crowned with apples and bananas** Author interview with Robert Stehling, Charleston, SC, November 2015.

242 **did not suit his graceful cooking** John T. Edge, "Civic Pride," *Gourmet*, January 2008.

242 **collapsed church spires** "Remembering Hugo 25 Years Later," *Charleston Magazine*, September 2014.

242 **more than 50 percent** David Slade and Adam Parker, "Who Lives on the Peninsula?," *Charleston Post and Courier*, October 18, 2014.

242 **first time in sixty years** Ibid.

243 **only ones to gain notice** R. W. Apple Jr., "A Southern Star Rises in the Lowcountry," *New York Times*, March 15, 2006.

243 **fine dining palaces** Ibid.

243 **black Charleston frolicked before integration** John T. Edge, *Southern Belly: A Food Lover's Companion* (New York: Algonquin Books, 2007), 224.

243 **"close to the sun itself"** Sam Sifton, "A Southern Chef Doesn't Stray Far," *New York Times*, February 8, 2011.

245 **ponzu sauce and adzuki beans** John Mariani, "Goin' South for Sup."

245 **"got out of hand"** Susan Houston, "The Flavor of the South," *Raleigh News and Observer*, November 11, 1998.

246 **lunches at Dooky Chase** Brett Anderson, "How Katrina Changed Eating in New Orleans," *New Yorker*, August 28, 2015.

246 **leavings of yesterday's rice pot** Kim Severson, "'Faerie Folk' Strike Back with Fritters," *New York Times*, December 6, 2006.

246 **lavished attention on the humble po-boy** John T. Edge, "Saving New Orleans Culture, One Sandwich at a Time," *New York Times*, November 10, 2009.

248 **parking lot canteens** Lolis Eric Elie, "A Letter from New Orleans," *Gourmet*, February 2006.

248 **truly hungry** Leslie Eaton and Cameron McWhirter, "An Unfinished Riff: New Orleans's Uneven Revival in Decade After Katrina," *Wall Street Journal*, August 26, 2015.

248 **poured into the city** Kim Severson, "From Disaster, a Chef Forges an Empire," *New York Times*, October 31, 2007.

248 **lemongrass, basil, and mint** Judy Walker, "John Besh's Shrimp Creole," *Times-Picayune*, March 31, 2011.

248   **old-guard Liedenheimer** Rien Fertel, "Vietnola," *Local Palate*, September 22, 2014.

248   **neighbors to the west** Mimi Read, "Real Cajun Food, from Swamp to City," *New York Times*, January 20, 2009.

249   **shuckers and waiters had lived** Adam Nossiter, "In New Orleans, Ex-Tenants Fight for Projects," *New York Times*, December 26, 2006.

249   **lived in the same city** Louisiana State University study in Abby Phillip, "White People in New Orleans Say They're Better Off. Black People Don't," *Washington Post*, August 24, 2015.

249   **American cultural richness** John T. Edge, "Mutt City," *Oxford American*, September 2012.

250   **21 percent fewer residents** Kim Severson, "The New Orleans Restaurant Bounce, After Katrina," *New York Times*, August 4, 2015.

251   **New Orleans population in 2015** Anderson, "How Katrina Changed Eating in New Orleans."

251   **Faux Marigny** Rien Fertel, "Our Bourbon Street, or: How I Learned to Stop Worrying & Love the Hand Grenade," *Gravy* podcast, April 24, 2015.

251   **Friday lunch menu** Elie, "A Letter from New Orleans."

Chapter 14: Pits and Pitmasters

255   **opened in 1947** Sam Jones, Oral History Interview, southernfoodways.org, 2011.

255   **U.S. Capitol rotunda** Author interview with Sam Jones, May 2016.

256   **tasted in the backs of their throats** John T. Edge, "A Bold Move in Barbecue," *Garden & Gun*, February 2016.

256   **his burger chain** Staff, "Hamburger Chain Founder Lost Controlling Share in Poker Game," *Los Angeles Times*, June 25, 2008.

257   **"fall of Western civilization"** Edward Felsenthal, "Memphis Barbecue Is Going Uptown; Some Sing the Blues," *Wall Street Journal*, August 31, 1991.

258   **Pollan told his followers** Michael Pollan, *In Defense of Food: An Eater's Manifesto* (New York: Penguin Press, 2008), 148.

258   **showcase of regional food culture** John Fasman, "Fire in the Hole: Barbecue Navigates the Twin Perils of Mass Appeal and Nostalgia," *The Economist*, December 16, 2010.

258   **famous bohunk sausage** Rob Walsh, *Legends of Texas Barbecue Cookbook: Recipes and Recollections from the Pitmasters* (San Francisco: Chronicle Books, 2012), 182.

258   **portrait along the dining room wall** Lolis Eric Elie, *Smokestack Lightning: Adventures in the Heart of Barbecue Country* (New York: Farrar, Straus and Giroux, 1996), 199.

259   **"rather than a New York restaurant"** Fasman, "Fire in the Hole."

259   **barbecue restaurants operated in New York City** Chris Shott, "How Barbecue Has Become New York City's Most Addictive Smoking Habit," *Food Republic*, July 22, 2014.

259   **forty-eight hours** Alex Witchel, "Magic in Smoke (No Mirrors)," *New York Times*, November 1, 2012.

260   **Grand Strand in Myrtle Beach, South Carolina** Staff, "House of Barbecue for All People," *Myrtle Beach Chronicle*, February 21, 2007.

261   **smaller cuts like ribs** Author interview with Roscoe Hall, grandson of John Bishop, February 23, 2014.

261   **elevator shaft** William Robbins, "Memphis Journal: Where Barbecue Lovers Go Simply Hog Wild," *New York Times*, January 11, 1988.

262 **"more money out of it than they did"** David Bransten, *Smokestack Lightning: A Day in the Life of Barbecue* (Bay Package Productions, 2001).

262 **good at leveraging relationships** John T. Edge, "Charlie Vergos, Memphis Barbecue King, Dies," *New York Times*, March 30, 2010.

262 **eight restaurants in town shipped overnight** Tom Eblen, "High-Flying Memphis Ribs Just a Call Away," *Chicago Tribune*, May 26, 1988.

262 **change what Americans ate in fine dining restaurants** Michael Ruhlman, *The Reach of a Chef* (New York: Viking, 2006), 166.

263 **tone that sounded defiant** John T. Edge, "Barbecue: Old Ways, Modern Technology," *Atlanta Journal-Constitution*, May 16, 2006.

263 **"baddest barbecuing bastard there has ever been"** Myron Mixon, *Smokin' with Myron Mixon: Recipes Made Simple, from the Winningest Man in Barbecue* (New York: Ballantine, 2011), xiii.

264 **"beat everybody else's ass"** Ibid., xvi.

265 **came looking for Mitchell** Michael Pollan, *Cooked: A Natural History of Transformation* (New York: Penguin Press, 2013), 69–87.

265 **"It was my pig from then on"** John T. Edge, "Redesigning the Pig," *Gourmet*, July 2005.

266 **pleaded guilty to tax evasion** "Restaurant Owner Gets Jail Time," *Fayetteville Observer*, February 27, 2006.

267 **"We got it for them"** John T. Edge, "Pig, Smoke, Pit: This Food Is Seriously Slow," *New York Times*, June 9, 2009.

268 **"How much more can you elevate this"** John T. Edge, "Holy Smokes! The New Golden Age of Barbecue," *Parade*, March 10, 2014.

270 **"every time I light my fire"** John T. Edge, "Keepers of the Flame," *Garden & Gun*, June–July 2015.

Chapter 15: Political Reckonings

275 **"cotton field rabbits"** Author interview with Michael Twitty, Holly Springs, MS, April 2015.

276 **"soldiers were fighting to get rid of"** Stratton Lawrence, "Overnight Historian," *Charleston Magazine*, July 2013.

278 **her family had cooked for whites** Kim Severson, "Paula Deen's Cook Tells of Slights, Steeped in History," *New York Times*, July 24, 2013.

278 **"gone with the wind"** Dora Charles, *A Real Southern Cook: In Her Savannah Kitchen* (New York: Houghton Mifflin Harcourt, 2015), 27.

278 **"lowly culinary historian"** Michael Twitty, "An Open Letter to Paula Deen," *Afroculinaria*, June 25, 2013.

281 **Austin, Texas–based Whole Foods** James E. McWilliams, *Just Food: Where Locavores Get It Wrong and How We Can Truly Eat Responsibly* (New York: Little, Brown, 2009).

282 **"ecological vandalism"** Wendell Berry, foreword, in Ken Midriff, *The Meat You Eat: How Corporate Farming Has Endangered America's Food Supply* (New York: St. Martin's Press, 2004), ix.

282 **five dollars a pound** William H. Williams, *Delmarva's Chicken Industry: 75 Years of Progress* (Georgetown, DE: Delmarva Poultry Industry, 1998), 13.

283 **drove the growth of the chicken industry** Craig Cavallo, "From Southern Tradition to Mechanical Marvel: How Fried Chicken Lost Its Bones," *Serious Eats*, July 16, 2015.

284 **just as they cut chickens into parts** Steve Siffler, *Chicken: The Dangerous Transformation of America's Favorite Food* (New Haven, CT: Yale University Press, 2005), 111–35.

284 **pleasure of corporate lords** Oxfam America, "Lives on the Line: The Human Cost of Cheap Chicken" (Washington, DC: Policy and Advocacy Office, 2015).

284 **"other white meat"** David Sax, "Bacon: Why America's Favorite Food Mania Happened," *Businessweek*, October 6, 2014.

284 **adult life in metal cages** Barry Estabrook, *Pig Tales: An Omnivore's Quest for Sustainable Meat* (New York: Norton, 2015), 97.

285 **to go to the bathroom** Oxfam America, "Lives on the Line," 7.

286 **to that of slaves** Barry Estabrook, *Tomatoland: How Modern Industrial Agriculture Destroyed Our Most Alluring Fruit* (Kansas City, MO: Andrews McMeel Publishing, 2012), 132.

286 **trafficked labor in Florida fields** Tracie McMillan, "Labor Gains," *Modern Farmer*, Winter 2015–16.

286 **$50 a day to $70** Estabrook, *Tomatoland*, 34.

287 **"farmworker poverty and exploitation"** Greg Asbed and Lucas Benitez, "Field Notes on Food Justice: Why Your Local Grocery Store Makes Farmworkers Poor," *Huffington Post*, May 22, 2012.

287 **fast-food giant assented, too** McMillan, "Labor Gains," 34.

287 **up from forty-five cents** Andrew Martin, "Burger King Grants Raise to Pickers," *New York Times*, May 24, 2008.

287 **around $17,000** Amy Bennet Williams, "CIW Debuts Fair Food Label Nationwide," *Fort Myers News-Press*, October 24, 2014.

287 **harvested under equitable terms** Steven Greenhouse, "In Florida Tomato Fields, a Penny Buys Progress," *New York Times*, April 24, 2014.

287 **speckled with fatback** Paul Fehribach, *The Big Jones Cookbook: Recipes for Savoring the Heritage of Regional Southern Cooking* (Chicago: University of Chicago Press, 2015).

288 **summers in Savannah** Allison Glock, "Mashama Bailey's Home Cooking," *Garden & Gun*, December–January 2016.

289 **oystermen worked the pluff** Jeff Gordiner, "At the Grey in Savannah, History Takes Another Turn," *New York Times*, July 27, 2015.

291 **highest number of black elected officials in any state by 1987** Staff, "South Leads in Black Officeholders," *Southern Changes 9.5*, 1987.

Chapter 16: Nuevo Sud

294 **"the original fusion cuisine"** Stage notes, collection of the author, courtesy Edward Lee, Matt Lee, and Ted Lee.

294 **accommodation of new peoples** Charles R. Wilson, "Exploring the South's Creole Identity: Life Writing from the U.S. South in the Obama Era," in *Obama and Transnational American Studies*, ed. Alfred Hornug (Heidelberg, Germany: Winter Verlag, 2016).

295 **band of brothers was eventual** Elizabeth M. Hoeffel, Sonya Rastogi, Myoung Ouk Kim, and Masan Shahid, "The Asian Population: 2010," 2010 Census Briefs, March 2012, C2010BR-11, U.S. Department of Commerce, Economics and Statistics Administration, U.S. Census Bureau, Washington, DC.

295 **grilled over hardwood** Edward Lee, "What I Cooks Is Who I Am," in *Cornbread Nation 7: The Best of Southern Food Writing*, ed. Francis Lam (Athens: University of Georgia Press, 2014), 32.

295 **"America's identity"** Edward Lee, *Smoke and Pickles: Recipes and Stories from a New Southern Kitchen* (New York: Clarkson Potter, 2012), x.

295 **just about everywhere else** Wanda Rushing, "Growth and Diversity in the Urban South," in *The New Encyclopedia of Southern Cultures, Volume 15: Urbanization,* ed. Wanda Rushing (Chapel Hill: University of North Carolina Press, 2010), 6.

295 **births to Hispanic mothers** Tracy Thompson, "Dixie Is Dead," *Bitter Southerner,* March 29, 2015.

296 **new black residents** Karen Pooley, "Segregation's New Geography: The Atlanta Metro Region, Race, and the Declining Prospects for Upward Mobility," *Southern Spaces,* April 15, 2015.

297 **"Red Beans and Ricely Yours, Louis"** Richard Campanella, "Chinatown New Orleans," *Louisiana Cultural Vistas* 18.3 (Fall 2007), 54–57.

297 **to river town customers** "Introduction," The Hot Tamale Trail, oral history project, archived at southernfoodways.org.

297 **"heard of a hushpuppy"** Edge, *A Gracious Plenty,* 164.

297 **hunks of pigs' feet** Laura Vozzella, "Pigs' Feet Fusion," *Baltimore Sun,* March 4, 2010.

298 **drive-through breakfast standards** John T. Edge, "A Taste of Jacksonville, Stuffed into a Pita," *New York Times,* July 12, 2012.

298 **wall-mounted rollers** John T. Edge, "Vietnamese Immigrants Carry On a Cajun Food Tradition," *New York Times,* April 27, 2010.

299 **company bake-off** Will Doran, "Biscuitville Worker Earns Grand Champion Maker," *Washington Times,* July 14, 2014.

300 **fastest-growing metropolitan areas were in the South** William H. Frey, "Population Growth in Metro American Since 1980," Metropolitan Policy Program at Brookings Institution, Washington, DC, March 2012.

300 **Mexico and Bosnia were neighbors** Tom Hanchett, "A Salad Bowl City: The Food Geography of Charlotte, North Carolina," in John T. Edge, Elizabeth Engelhardt, and Ted Ownby, eds., *The Larder: Food Studies Methods from the American South* (Athens: University of Georgia Press, 2013).

300 **capped with kimchi** Tom Hanchett, "In South Charlotte, Korean Delicacies in Unlikely Wrapper," *Charlotte Observer,* January 1, 2015.

302 **"Mexican South, too"** John T. Edge, "How Houston Is Redefining American Cooking," *Departures,* July 2013.

306 **conversations about brown and black people** John T. Edge, "Rapping About Tamales and Deportation," *New York Times,* May 24, 2011.

306 **Celaya in the state of Guanajuato** Bill Smith, "Pancho at the Flor de Celaya," in *Cornbread Nation 6,* ed. Brett Anderson (Athens: University of Georgia Press, 2012), 288–90.

306 **identity in the process** In 2017, when the SFA celebrates its twentieth anniversary, the focus of the annual symposium will be El Sur Latino.

Shared Palates: An Afterword

309 **He bought a blue bill** John T. Edge, "My Civil War," *Oxford American,* September 2014.

309 **"recognize that it's mine, too"** Cobb, *The South and America Since World War II,* 266.

309 **stare down the shame** Patterson Hood, "The New(er) South," *Bitter Southerner,* August 20, 2013.

Deeper Reading:
A Selective Bibliography

After a roster of general readings about the South and foodways, a chronological list of section-specific recommendations follows, tracking the progress of this book from "Freedom Struggles" to "Future Tenses." Though my research library was far larger and, in some cases, much denser, the subset of books and articles I suggest below are pleasures to read.

The South

Applebome, Peter. *Dixie Rising: How the South Is Shaping American Values, Politics, and Culture.* New York: Times Books, 1996.

Cobb, James C. *The South and America Since World War II.* New York: Oxford University Press, 2011.

———. *Away Down South: A History of Southern Identity.* New York: Oxford University Press, 2005.

Edge, John T. "My Civil War." *Oxford American,* September–October 2014.

Edge, John T., et al. *Cornbread Nation: The Best of Southern Food Writing,* volumes 4–7. Athens: University of Georgia Press, 2008–2014.

Egerton, John. *The Americanization of Dixie, the Southernization of America.* New York: Harper's Magazine Press, 1974.

Levine, Lawrence W. *Black Culture and Black Consciousness: Afro-American Folk Thought from Slavery to Freedom.* New York: Oxford University Press, 1978.

Thompson, Tracy. *The New Mind of the South.* New York: Simon & Schuster, 2013.

Wilson, Charles, et al. *New Encyclopedia of Southern Culture*, volumes 1–24. Chapel Hill: University of North Carolina Press, 2006–2013.

Woodward, C. Vann. *The Strange Career of Jim Crow*. New York: Oxford University Press, 1955.

Foodways

Edge, John T., Elizabeth Engelhardt, and Ted Ownby, eds. *The Larder: Food Studies Methods from the American South*. Athens: University of Georgia Press, 2013.

Egerton, John. *Southern Food: At Home, on the Road, in History*. New York: Knopf, 1987.

Ferris, Marcie. *The Edible South: The Power of Food and the Making of an American Region*. Chapel Hill: University of North Carolina Press, 2014.

Harris, Jessica. *High on the Hog: A Culinary Journey from Africa to America*. New York: Bloomsbury, 2011.

Kamp, David. *The United States of Arugula: How We Became a Gourmet Nation*. New York: Broadway Books, 2006.

Levenstein, Harvey. *Paradox of Plenty: A Social History of Eating in Modern America*. New York: Oxford University Press, 1993.

Mintz, Sidney. *Tasting Food, Tasting Freedom: Excursions into Eating, Culture, and the Past*. Boston: Beacon Press, 1996.

Tipton-Martin, Toni. *The Jemima Code: Two Centuries of African American Cookbooks*. Austin: University of Texas Press, 2015.

Freedom Struggles

Asch, Chris Myers. *The Senator and the Sharecropper: The Freedom Struggles of James O. Eastland and Fannie Lou Hamer*. New York: New Press, 2008.

Brooks, Maegan Parker. *A Voice That Could Stir an Army: Fannie Lou Hamer and the Rhetoric of the Black Freedom Movement*. Jackson: University Press of Mississippi, 2014.

Brooks, Maegan Parker, and Davis Houck, eds. *The Speeches of Fannie Lou Hamer: To Tell It Like It Is*. Jackson: University Press of Mississippi, 2011.

Caro, Robert A. *The Years of Lyndon Johnson: The Passage of Power*. New York: Vintage, 2012.

Cooley, Angela Jill. *To Live and Dine in Dixie: The Evolution of Urban Food Culture in the Jim Crow South*. Athens: University of Georgia Press, 2015.

Daniel, Pete. *Dispossession: Discrimination Against African American Farmers in the Age of Civil Rights*. Chapel Hill: University of North Carolina Press, 2013.

Freeman, Roland L. *The Mule Train: A Journey of Hope Remembered*. Nashville: Rutledge Hill Press, 1998.

Grosvenor, Vertamae. *Vibration Cooking, or, The Travel Notes of a Geechee Girl*. Athens: University of Georgia Press, revised edition, 2011.

Johnson, Yvette. *The Song and the Silence*. New York: Atria, 2017.

Kotz, Nick. *Let Them Eat Promises: The Politics of Hunger in America*. New York: Prentice Hall, 1969.

Lee, Chana Kai. *For Freedom's Sake: The Life of Fannie Lou Hamer*. Urbana: University of Illinois Press, 1999.

Orleck, Annelise, and Lisa Gaye Hazirjian, eds. *The War on Poverty: A New Grassroots History 1964–1980*. Athens: University of Georgia Press, 2011.

Randall, Alice, "Glori-fried and Glori-fied: Mahalia Jackson's Chicken." *Gravy*, December 2015.

Sharpless, Rebecca. *Cooking in Other Women's Kitchens: Domestic Workers in the South, 1865–1960*. Chapel Hill: University of North Carolina Press, 2010.

Sokol, Jason. *There Goes My Everything: White Southerners in the Age of Civil Rights, 1945–1975*. New York: Knopf, 2006.

Wallach, Jennifer Jensen. "How to Eat to Live: Black Nationalism and the Post-1964 Turn." *Study the South*, July 2, 2014.

Yeakey, Lamont H. "The Montgomery, Alabama Bus Boycott, 1955–1956." PhD diss., Columbia University, 1979.

Rise of the Folk

Belasco, Warren J. *Appetite for Change: How the Counterculture Took on the Food Industry 1966–1988*. Ithaca, NY: Cornell University Press, 1996.

Bernard, Shane K. *The Cajuns: Americanization of a People*. Jackson: University Press of Mississippi, 2004.

Berry, Wendell, and Norman Wirzba. *The Art of the Commonplace: The Agrarian Essays of Wendell Berry*. Washington, DC: Counterpoint, 2002.

Blount, Roy, Jr. *Crackers*. New York: Knopf, 1980.

Carey, Bill. *Fortunes, Fiddles and Fried Chicken: A Nashville Business History*. Franklin, TN: Hillsboro Press, 2000.

Darden, Norma Jean, and Carol Darden. *Spoonbread and Strawberry Wine: Recipes and Reminiscences of a Family*. New York: Doubleday, 1978.

Gaskin, Stephen. *The Caravan*. New York: Doubleday, 1972.

———. *Hey Beatnik!: This Is the Farm Book*. Summertown, TN: The Book Publishing Company, 1974.

Lam, Francis. "Edna Lewis and the Black Roots of American Cooking." *New York Times Magazine*, October 28, 2015.

Lewis, Edna. *The Taste of Country Cooking 30th Anniversary Edition*. New York: Knopf, 2006.

Mercer, Kevin. "The Farm: A Hippie Commune as a Countercultural Diaspora." Honors thesis, University of Central Florida, 2012.

Miller, Timothy. *The Hippies and American Values*. Knoxville: University of Tennessee Press, 1991.

Ozersky, Josh. *Colonel Sanders and the American Dream*. Austin: University of Texas Press, 2012.

Prugl, Elizabeth. "'Technicolor Amish': History and World View of the Farm, a Communal Society in Tennessee." Master's thesis, Vanderbilt University, 1983.

Puckett, John L. *Foxfire Revisited: A Twenty-Year Experiment in Progressive Education.* Urbana: University of Illinois Press, 1989.

Rubin, Charles J., et al. *Junk Food.* New York: Dell, 1980.

Sancton, Tom. *Song for My Fathers.* New York: Other Press, 2010.

Schulman, Bruce J. *The Seventies: The Great Shift in American Culture, Society, and Politics.* Cambridge, MA: Da Capo Press, 2002.

Stern, Jane, and Michael Stern. *Roadfood and Goodfood.* New York: Knopf, 1986.

Wallace, Emily. "It Was There for Work: Pimento Cheese in the Carolina Piedmont." Master's thesis, University of North Carolina, 2010.

Wigginton, Eliot. *The Foxfire Book.* New York: Doubleday, 1972.

Williams-Forson, Psyche. *Building Houses Out of Chicken Legs.* Chapel Hill: University of North Carolina Press, 2006.

Wilson, Justin. *The Justin Wilson Cookbook.* Denham Springs, LA: Justin Wilson, Inc., 1965.

Gentrification

Brenner, Leslie. *American Appetite: The Coming of Age of a Cuisine.* New York: Avon Books, 1999.

Chapman, Georgeanna Milam. "Craig Claiborne: A Southern-Made Man." Master's thesis, University of Mississippi, 2008.

Claiborne, Craig. *A Feast Made for Laughter.* New York: Doubleday, 1982.

Dupree, Nathalie. *New Southern Cooking.* New York: Knopf, 1986.

Lundy, Ronni. *Shuck Beans, Stack Cakes, and Honest Fried Chicken: The Heart and Soul of Southern Country Kitchens.* New York: Atlantic Monthly Press, 1991.

McNamee, Thomas. *The Man Who Changed the Way We Eat.* New York: Free Press, 2012.

Neal, Moreton. *Remembering Bill Neal: Favorite Recipes from a Life in Cooking.* Chapel Hill: University of North Carolina Press, 2004.

Neal, William F. *Bill Neal's Southern Cooking.* Chapel Hill: University of North Carolina Press, 1985.

Osteen, Louis. *Louis Osteen's Charleston Cuisine: Recipes from a Lowcountry Chef.* Chapel Hill, NC: Algonquin, 1999.

Prudhomme, Paul. *Chef Paul Prudhomme's Louisiana Kitchen.* New York: William Morrow, 1984.

Sokolov, Raymond. *Fading Feast: A Compendium of Disappearing American Regional Foods.* New York: Farrar, Straus and Giroux, 1981.

Stitt, Frank. *Frank Stitt's Southern Table.* New York: Artisan, 2004.

New Respect

Anderson, Brett. "How Katrina Changed Eating in New Orleans." *New Yorker*, August 28, 2015.

Brock, Sean. *Heritage.* New York: Artisan, 2014.

Edge, John T. "Redesigning the Pig." *Gourmet*, July 2005.

Elie, Lolis Eric. "A Letter from New Orleans." *Gourmet*, February 2006.

———. *Smokestack Lightning: Adventures in the Heart of Barbecue Country*. New York: Farrar, Straus and Giroux, 1996.

Fertel, Rien. *The One True Barbecue: Fire, Smoke, and the Pitmasters Who Cook the Whole Hog*. New York: Touchstone, 2016.

Gratz, Roberta Brandes. *We're Still Here Ya Bastards: How the People of New Orleans Rebuilt Their City*. New York: Nation Books, 2015.

Mitenbuler, Reid. *Bourbon Empire: The Past and Future of America's Whiskey*. New York: Viking, 2015.

Pendergrast, Mark. *For God, Country, and Coca-Cola*. New York: Basic Books, 2000.

Pollan, Michael. *Cooked: A Natural History of Transformation*. New York: Penguin Press, 2013.

Reed, John Shelton, and Dale Volberg Reed. *Holy Smoke: The Big Book of North Carolina Barbecue*. Chapel Hill: University of North Carolina Press, 2008.

Roahen, Sara. *Gumbo Tales: Finding My Place at the New Orleans Table*. New York: Norton, 2008.

Severson, Kim. "The New Orleans Restaurant Bounce, After Katrina." *New York Times*, August 4, 2015.

Spivak, Mark. *Moonshine Nation: The Art of Creating Cornbread in a Bottle*. Guilford, CT: Lyons Press, 2014.

Walsh, Robb. *Legends of Texas Barbecue Cookbook: Recipes and Recollections from the Pitmasters*. San Francisco: Chronicle Books, 2012.

Future Tenses

Charles, Dora. *A Real Southern Cook: In Her Savannah Kitchen*. New York: Houghton Mifflin Harcourt, 2015.

Edge, John T. "Taking Masa to Heart." *New York Times*, May 25, 2011.

Estabrook, Barry. *Pig Tales: An Omnivore's Quest for Sustainable Meat*. New York: Norton, 2015.

———. *Tomatoland: How Modern Industrial Agriculture Destroyed Our Most Alluring Fruit*. Kansas City, MO: Andrews McMeel Publishing, 2012.

Glock, Allison. "Mashama Bailey's Home Cooking." *Garden & Gun*, December 2015.

Greenhouse, Steven. "In Florida Tomato Fields, a Penny Buys Progress." *New York Times*, April 24, 2014.

Lee, Edward. *Smoke and Pickles: Recipes and Stories from a New Southern Kitchen*. New York: Artisan, 2013.

Lee, Matt, and Ted Lee. *The Lee Bros. Southern Cookbook: Stories and Recipes for Southerners and Would-be Southerners*. New York: Norton, 2006.

Leonard, Christian. *The Meat Racket: The Secret Takeover of America's Food Business*. New York: Simon & Schuster, 2014.

McWilliams, James E. *Just Food: Where Locavores Get It Wrong and How We Can Truly Eat Responsibly*. New York: Little, Brown, 2009.

Rawal, Sanjay, director. *Food Chains: The Revolution in America's Fields*. 2014.

Siffler, Steve. *Chicken: The Dangerous Transformation of America's Favorite Food*. New Haven, CT: Yale University Press, 2005.

Smith, Bill. "Pancho at the Flor de Celaya." In *Cornbread Nation 6*, edited by Brett Anderson. Athens: University of Georgia Press, 2012.

INDEX

INDEX

World Economic Summit, 173
world wars, 6, 113, 151, 166, 219, 283
Wright, Booker, 31–36, 46–47, 262, 279
Wright, Marian, 50–51, 56, 58, 75
Wright, Mose, 19
Wright, Sammy, 25, 27
Wright, Zephyr, 25–29, 236
writers, 3, 9, 144, 148, 150, 153, 177, 179, 186, 202, 221

critics, 191
food, 151, 162–69, 174–75, 189, 197, 203, 207–8, 279
on regional food, 7, 9, 185, 187

Young, Andrew, 201
Young, Stark, 127

Zolotow, Ellen, 96

PHOTOGRAPH CREDITS

Introduction

Photographer Vernon Matthews, reprinted with permission of the Preservation and Special Collections Department, University Libraries, University of Memphis.

Chapter 1

Copyright James H. Peppler, reproduced with permission of the photographer.

Chapter 2

Copyright Fred Blackwell, reproduced with permission of the photographer.

Chapter 3

Copyright Al Clayon, reproduced with permission of the photographer's family.

Chapter 4

Photograph by Stephen Shames, reproduced with permission of Polaris Images.

Chapter 5

Reprinted with permission of the Associated Press, copyright the Associated Press.

Chapter 6

Image of Colonel Sanders, Kentucky Fried Chicken, and related trademarks courtesy of KFC Corporation. All rights reserved.

Chapter 7

Copyright Owen Franken, reproduced with permission of the photographer.

Chapter 8

Copyright John T. Hill, reproduced with permission of the photographer.

Chapter 9

Photograph by Arthur Schlatz, reproduced with the permission of The LIFE Images Collection, Getty Images.

Chapter 10

Photograph by Charles E. Walton IV, courtesy of Pardis Stitt.

Chapter 11

Photograph courtesy of Nathalie Dupree.

Chapter 12

Photograph by Kay Rentschler for Anson Mills, copyright Anson Mills 2015.

Chapter 13

Photograph copyright Terry Manier, reproduced with permission of the photographer.

Chapter 14

Photograph copyright Peter Frank Edwards, reproduced with permission of the photographer.

Chapter 15

Photograph copyright A J Reynolds for the *Athens Banner-Herald,* reproduced with permission of the photographer.

Chapter 16

Photographer and designer, SHEMP, reproduced with permission of Pedro Herrera.